ETHICAL RATIONALISM AND THE LAW

What role does reason play in determining what, if anything, is morally right? What role does morality play in law? Perhaps the most controversial answer to these fundamental questions is that reason supports a supreme principle of both morality and legality. The contributors to this book cast a fresh critical eye over the coherence of modern approaches to ethical rationalism within law and reflect on the intellectual history on which it builds. The contributors then take the debate beyond the traditional concerns of legal theory into areas such as the relationship between morality and international law, and the impact of ethically controversial medical and technological innovations on legal understanding.

Ethical Rationalism and the Law

Edited by
Patrick Capps and Shaun D Pattinson

•HART•
OXFORD • LONDON • NEW YORK • NEW DELHI • SYDNEY

HART PUBLISHING
Bloomsbury Publishing Plc
Kemp House, Chawley Park, Cumnor Hill, Oxford, OX2 9PH, UK

HART PUBLISHING, the Hart/Stag logo, BLOOMSBURY and the Diana logo are trademarks of Bloomsbury Publishing Plc

First published in hardback, 2017
Paperback edition, 2019

A catalogue record for this book is available from the British Library.

Library of Congress Cataloging-in-Publication Data

Names: Capps, Patrick, editor. | Pattinson, Shaun D., editor.

Title: Ethical rationalism and the law / edited by Patrick Capps and Shaun D. Pattinson.

Description: Oxford [UK] ; Portland, Oregon : Hart Publishing, 2017. | Includes bibliographical (hardback) | ISBN 9781509909995 (Epub)

Identifiers: LCCN 2016045786 (print) | LCCN 2016046050 (ebook) | ISBN 9781849467865 (hardback : alk. paper) | ISBN 9781509909995 (Epub)

Subjects: LCSH: Law and ethics. | Law—Moral and ethical aspects. | Ethical relativism. | Gewirth, Alan.

Classification: LCC K247.6 .E79 2017 (print) | LCC K247.6 (ebook) | DDC 174/.3—dc23

LC record available at https://lccn.loc.gov/2016045786

ISBN: HB: 978-1-84946-786-5
PB: 978-1-50992-980-1
ePDF: 978-1-50991-000-7
ePub: 978-1-50990-999-5

Typeset by Compuscript Ltd, Shannon

CONTENTS

1

The Past, Present and Future of Ethical Rationalism

PATRICK CAPPS AND SHAUN D PATTINSON

I. Introduction

What role does reason play in determining what, if anything, is morally right? What role does morality play in law? Perhaps the most controversial answer to these fundamental questions is that reason supports a supreme principle of both morality and legality. According to this view, reason can determine what is morally right (ethical rationalism) and requires us to identify what is legal by reference to what is morally right (legal idealism).

The strong form of ethical rationalism, attributable to Immanuel Kant and Alan Gewirth, attracts particular scepticism. This holds that reason can determine what is morally right (contrary to the moral relativist) *and* show the irrationality of the amoralist who denies that we have any moral obligations at all. Such a view has been the source of both deep inspiration and provocation for moral philosophers, yet discussion of how it might inform law has been neglected when considered against the extensive discussions of other approaches within legal philosophy. There are exceptions. Kant's legal theory was presented in his *Doctrine of Right*, which forms the first part of *The Metaphysics of Morals*, in 1797.[1] Moreover, in *Law as a Moral Judgment* (hereafter *LMJ*),[2] Deryck Beyleveld and Roger Brownsword defend an influential version of strong ethical rationalism and legal

[1] We refer to Kant's works as found in the Academy edition of the *Gesammelte Schriften*, and cite the volume and page number in square brackets. Translations are to I Kant, *Groundwork of the Metaphysic of Morals* (HJ Paton tr, *The Moral Law*, Hutchinson, 1972) [vol 4 in the Academy edition]; I Kant, *Critique of the Power of Judgment* (P Guyer and E Matthews tr, CUP, 2002) [vol 5 and, for 2nd edn, vol 20]; *The Metaphysics of Morals* (M Gregor tr, CUP, 1996) [vol 6]; and *Logic* (JM Young tr, *The Cambridge Edition of the Works of Immanuel Kant*, CUP, 1992, 527–88) [vol 9].

[2] D Beyleveld and R Brownsword, *Law as a Moral Judgment* (Sweet & Maxwell, 1986, reprinted by Sheffield Academic Press, 1994).

idealism, which Stanley Paulson suggests is 'something akin to Kantian natural law theory'.[3] Given continuing interest in Kant's legal and moral philosophy, and as we reach the 30th anniversary of *LMJ*, we consider it appropriate to reflect on the influence and plausibility of ethical rationalism, and examine the insights it provides into the most pressing problems presented by contemporary legal philosophy and globalised society. That is the task of this collection.

II. The Strong Ethical Rationalism of Kant and Gewirth

Care must be taken with labels. Although morality and ethics are labels used by different people to capture divergent concepts, we are using the terms interchangeably. For our purposes, moral (or ethical) requirements refer to action-guiding imperatives that are both other-regarding and categorical. They are *other-regarding* or impartial in the sense that they require one to act in the interests of others and treat those interests as equal to one's own. They are *categorical* in the sense that they override other demands and have force independent of one's desires or inclinations. Strong ethical rationalism is the claim that acceptance of categorical other-regarding imperatives is a strict requirement of agential self-understanding. In our view, Immanuel Kant made this claim for the Categorical Imperative (CI) and Alan Gewirth made this claim for the Principle of Generic Consistency (PGC).

Kant declared that the 'sole aim' of his *Groundwork of the Metaphysic of Morals* was 'to seek out and establish the supreme principle of morality'.[4] Kant is often interpreted as seeking to show that anyone who accepts the 'common idea' of morality is logically required to accept the CI.[5] Such an enterprise would involve defence of the CI *from* a moral point of view. It would seek to show only that agents who already accept that there are moral oughts must regard the CI as the supreme principle of those oughts. This is *weak ethical rationalism*. We, like many of the contributors of this book,[6] understand Kant to have attempted something much more ambitious. Part 3 of the *Groundwork* sought to show that any 'rational being with a will', whatever that being's views on morality, is rationally required to accept the CI. Kant sought to establish the CI 'as a necessary law for all rational beings' by showing that it is 'connected (entirely *a priori*) with the concept of the

[3] S Paulson, 'Review of *Law as a Moral Judgment*' (1994) 7 *Ratio Juris* 111.

[4] [4: 392].

[5] See, eg, RM Hare, *Moral Thinking: Its Levels, Method and Point* (Clarendon Press, 1981) 109, 162; D Gauthier, *Morals by Agreement* (Clarendon Press, 1986) 6–7; A Gewirth, 'Foreword' in D Beyleveld, *The Dialectical Necessity of Morality: An Analysis and Defense of Alan Gewirth's Argument to the Principle of Generic Consistency* (University of Chicago Press, 1991) viii.

[6] See especially the chapter by Beyleveld.

will of a rational being as such'.[7] This puts him firmly within the tradition we call strong ethical rationalism.

Gewirth adopts what he terms the 'dialectically necessary method'. His method is 'dialectical' in the sense it 'begins from assumptions, opinions, statements, or claims made by protagonists or interlocutors and then proceeds to examine what these logically imply'.[8] It is 'necessary' in the sense that all the steps of the argument follow logically from understanding premises that cannot be coherently denied within this perspective. According to Gewirth,

> Two kinds of beginning points and hence two kinds of dialectical methods may be distinguished. The dialectically contingent method begins from singular or general statements or judgments that reflect the variable beliefs, interests, or ideals of some person or group. The dialectically necessary method begins from statements or judgments that are necessarily attributable to every agent because they derive from the generic features that constitute the necessary structure of action.[9]

Thus, while a 'dialectically necessary' method operates within strong ethical rationalism, a 'dialectically contingent' method operates within weak ethical rationalism.

The protagonists and interlocutors of the dialectical method, indeed of all practical discourse, are agents. Only beings able to act for voluntarily chosen purposes—Gewirthian agents or Kantian rational beings with a will—are meaningful addressees of practical precepts. We therefore share Beyleveld's view that Kant in the third part of the *Groundwork* sought to show the CI to be dialectical necessity.[10] In other words, Kant and Gewirth share an epistemological strategy in relation to their moral philosophy. They both seek to demonstrate that the supreme moral principle is a maxim that I (that is, any agent) must accept in order for me to understand what it is for me to be an agent.

III. The Dialectically Necessary Argument for the PGC

Gewirth's moral epistemology is drawn on, by way of critique or application, by all contributors to this collection. We are among those convinced by his dialectically necessary argument, as restructured and defended by Deryck Beyleveld in *The Dialectical Necessity of Morality*.[11] The skeletal outline below

[7] [4: 426].

[8] A Gewirth, *Reason and Morality* (University of Chicago Press, 1978) 43.

[9] ibid, 43–44.

[10] See D Beyleveld, 'Gewirth and Kant on Justifying the Supreme Principle of Morality' in M Boylan (ed), *Gewirth: Critical Essays on Action, Rationality and Community* (Rowman and Littlefield, 1999) 97.

[11] D Beyleveld, *The Dialectical Necessity of Morality: An Analysis and Defense of Alan Gewirth's Argument to the Principle of Generic Consistency* (University of Chicago Press, 1991).

follows Beyleveld's division of the argument into three stages and his refinement of the relevant terminology.[12]

Stage I

In claiming to be an agent I must (by definition) accept that

(1) 'I act (or intend to act) for a purpose that I have freely chosen',

which entails

(2) 'My purpose is good'.

Since

(3) 'There are generic conditions of agency',

I must accept

(4) 'My having the generic conditions is good for my achieving my purpose *whatever* that purpose is', which is to say that 'My having the generic conditions is (categorically instrumentally) good'.

This entails

(5) 'I (categorically instrumentally) ought to pursue and defend my having the generic conditions', which is to say that 'Unless I am willing to accept generic damage to my capacity to act, I categorically ought to pursue and defend my possession of the generic conditions of agency'.

Stage II

This entails

(6) 'Other agents categorically ought not to interfere with my having the generic conditions *against my will*, and ought to aid me to secure them when I cannot do so by my own unaided efforts *if I so wish*',

which is to say,

(7) 'I have both negative and positive rights to have the generic conditions'. In short, 'I have the generic rights'.

[12] See D Beyleveld, 'The Principle of Generic Consistency as the Supreme Principle of Human Rights' (2012) 13 *Human Rights Review* 1. See also SD Pattinson, *Influencing Traits Before Birth* (Ashgate, 2002) ch 1 and SD Pattinson, *Medical Law and Ethics* 4th edn (Sweet & Maxwell, 2014) ch 16.

Stage III

This entails (as shown by the Argument from the Sufficiency of Agency)

(8) 'I have the generic rights *because* I am an agent'

which, by the logical principle of universalisability, entails

(9) 'Every agent has the generic rights *because* it is an agent'.

Thus,

(10) 'All agents have the generic rights'.

Thus, by the logical principle of universalisability,

(11) It is dialectically necessary *for every agent* to accept that *all* agents have the generic rights. This is the PGC.

A crucial step in this outline is the Argument from the Sufficiency of Agency (ASA), seminally presented by Gewirth on a single page of *Reason and Morality*.[13] The ASA takes the form of a *reductio ad absurdum*. It seeks to show that an agent who denies that it is dialectically necessary for her to claim that she has the generic rights *because* she is an agent, denies that it is dialectically necessary for her to claim that she has the generic rights. This is because denying that she has the generic rights for the sufficient reason that she is an agent requires that she assert that she has the generic right because she has a property that is not necessarily possessed by all agents. However, this implies that if she lacked this property she would not have the generic rights, which contradicts the previously established statement, made on the basis of her claim to be an agent, that she has the generic rights. Thus, denying (8) contradicts (7). It follows that it is dialectically necessary for an agent to claim that she has the generic rights *because* she is an agent.

In the final chapter of this book, Beyleveld presents yet further refinements to the dialectically necessary argument. He argues that it requires acceptance of only three propositions:

(a) The Principle of Hypothetical Imperatives (*PHI*) is dialectically necessary. That is, in order for me (that is, any agent) to understand what it is for me to be an agent, I must accept that: 'if I wish to pursue a chosen purpose and having X, or doing Y, is necessary to achieve that purpose, then I ought to pursue/defend having X, or doing Y, or give up pursuing that purpose'.
(b) There are generic conditions of agency.
(c) Dialectically necessary commitments are not merely *distributively universal*, but also *collectively universal*. This is explained in the summary of Beyleveld's chapter below.

[13] See Gewirth, n 8, 110.

Beyleveld has elsewhere devised dialectically contingent arguments for the PGC, whereby the PGC is shown to follow from contingent premises that happen to attract widespread support.[14] The most recent of these argues that the PGC follows from acceptance of Stage 1 of the dialectically necessary argument with the contingent assumption that others are worthy of equal concern and respect. This argument combines the least controversial stage of the dialectically necessary argument with an assumption made or implied by all human rights instruments and accepted by all theories committed to moral impartiality, including utilitarianism and all variants of weak moral rationalism.

IV. Applying the PGC

Gewirth's argument for the PGC incorporates or implies various dialectically necessary meta-principles for its application. The generic rights shown to be dialectically necessary are rights to whatever an agent needs to act or act successfully, regardless of that agent's specific purpose. These generic needs vary in degree.[15] To act at all, an agent has basic needs, such as her life. To act successfully, she has nonsubtractive needs to those things required for her to maintain her current level of purpose-fulfilment and additive needs to those things required to increase her current level of purpose-fulfilment. A hierarchy of generic need and harm can therefore be measured by what Gewirth originally referred to as the 'criterion of degrees of necessity for action' and then later, in response to a critic's quibbles about necessity not varying in degree, referred to as the 'criterion of degree of needfulness for action'.[16] Accordingly, *basic* generic rights take priority over *nonsubtractive* generic rights, which in turn take priority over *additive* generic rights.

The dialectically necessary argument requires agents to accept that all agents have both negative *and positive generic rights*. The positive rights are limited by two provisos.[17] First, since dialectically necessary rights-claims derive from the agent's categorically instrumental need for the generic conditions, and the assistance of another agent is not so needed where she can achieve her purposes without assistance, it follows that she only has positive generic rights where she is unable to secure her possession of the generic conditions by her own unaided effort. This may be referred to as the 'own unaided effort' proviso.[18] Secondly, since an agent

[14] See D Beyleveld, 'Legal Theory and Dialectically Contingent Justifications for the Principle of Generic Consistency' (1996) 9 *Ratio Juris* 15 and D Beyleveld, 'The Principle of Generic Consistency as the Supreme Principle of Human Rights' (2012) 13 *Human Rights Review* 1.

[15] See Gewirth, n 8, 53–63.

[16] See ibid, 53–58 and A Gewirth, *The Community of Rights* (Chicago University Press, 1996) 45–46.

[17] See Gewirth, n 8, 217–30.

[18] Pattinson, *Influencing Traits Before Birth*, n 12, 35.

must first recognise the dialectical necessity of her own generic rights before recognising the dialectical necessity of other agents' equal generic rights, she has a duty to aid other agents to secure their generic conditions only when doing so does not deprive her of equivalent possession of the generic conditions, as measured by the degree of needfulness for action. This may be referred to as the 'comparable cost' proviso.[19]

In *Reason and Morality*, Gewirth argues that the 'Principle of Proportionality' operates to grant proportional generic rights to various groups who are 'excluded from the class of prospective purposive agents', such as young children, the mentally deficient, fetuses and non-human animals.[20] Gewirth's reasoning on this has been criticised by some of those who are convinced by the dialectically necessary argument to the PGC.[21] As argued in a 2000 paper, the principle of proportionality cannot operate within the dialectically necessary argument to effect proportional generic rights for non-agents, because (a) the duties correlative to the generic rights are waivable by the rights-holder and only agents can meaningfully waive duties; (b) the subjects of the generic rights are also objects of corrective duties and only agents can meaningfully have duties to any degree, and (c) the Principle of Proportionality is a quantitative manipulator so can alter the quantity of a variable, but cannot, by itself, alter the quality of a variable.[22] It does not, however, follow that the groups identified by Gewirth as non-agents are excluded from the remit of dialectically necessary moral duties. Deryck Beyleveld, with one of us, has argued that Gewirth made a further mistake when he assumed that those who appear to be non-agents are non-agents.[23] The categorical nature of the PGC renders the Principle of Precaution dialectically necessary, so that (i) those who appear to be agents must be treated as agents with the generic rights and (ii) those who appear to be only partial agents must be granted duties of protection tracking their presumed (but not exercisable) generic rights. Only when there is a single-variable conflict between the duties owed to two such beings may the Principle of Proportionality be invoked to give effect to the Principle of Avoidance of More Probable Harm.[24]

In *LMJ*, Deryck Beyleveld and Roger Brownsword direct their minds to the implications of the dialectically necessary argument for legal theory. They argue that if we understand law as being concerned with the enterprise of subjecting

[19] ibid, 35.

[20] Gewirth, n 8, 121–24, 140–45.

[21] See J Hill, 'Are Marginal Agents "Our Recipients"?' in E Regis (ed), *Gewirth's Ethical Rationalism: Critical Essays with a Reply by Gewirth* (Chicago University Press, 1984) 180 and EB Pluhar, *Beyond Prejudice: The Moral Significance of Human and Nonhuman Animals* (Duke University Press, 1995) ch 5.

[22] D Beyleveld and SD Pattinson, 'Precautionary Reasoning as a Link to Moral Action' in M Boylan (ed), *Medical Ethics* (Prentice Hall, 2000) 39, 46–47.

[23] See ibid and D Beyleveld and SD Pattinson, 'Defending Moral Precaution as a Solution to the Problem of Other Minds: A Reply to Holm and Coggon' (2010) 23 *Ratio Juris* 258. See also Pattinson, *Influencing Traits Before Birth*, n 12, ch 2.

[24] See further the chapter by Pattinson in this collection.

human conduct to rules,[25] then it is dialectically necessary to regard the PGC as the supreme principle of legality. Thus, we must side with *legal idealism*, which claims a necessary conceptual connection between law and morality, over *legal positivism*, which holds that law may be conceptually identified independently of morality.

V. Further Thoughts on the Relationship Between Kant and Gewirth

Kant's claims about agency and the supreme principle of morality ('What should I do?') inform his, often incomplete, answers to his other questions of humanity ('What can I know?' 'What may I hope?' 'What is Man?').[26] Given the connections between Kant and Gewirth set out above, some ethical rationalists have sought to revisit Kant's questions of humanity from a Gewirthian perspective. Thus, there is now a lively debate within ethical rationalism on human history and futures, free will, aesthetics and theism. These questions are likely to frame future debates within ethical rationalism and significant early steps towards answering these questions are to be found in some of the contributions to this collection.[27]

As already mentioned, Stanley Paulson recognised long ago the connections between Kant's legal theory in *The Doctrine of Right* and the Gewirthian legal idealism offered by Beyleveld and Brownsword in *LMJ*.[28] However, beyond Paulson's work, the relationship between these two texts is not well discussed in the literature. We would suggest that this is partly because *The Doctrine of Right* is a very difficult text, even by Kant's standards, and also because Kant is sometimes seen as a legal positivist.[29] If this view of Kant is correct, it means that while Kant's and Gewirth's moral philosophies are similar for the reasons set out above, there is opposition between the legal theories found in *The Doctrine of Right* and *LMJ*. But while Kant's legal philosophy raises serious interpretative issues, it is far from settled that Kant is a legal positivist. For instance, Patrick Capps, in this collection, argues that conformity to the perfect duties and rights[30] that are implied by a

[25] See *LMJ*, 120, citing L Fuller, *The Morality of Law* (Yale University Press, 1969). For a summary and further discussion of this point, see Patrick Capps's chapter in this collection.

[26] [9: 25].

[27] See, eg, the chapters by Düring and Düwell, Westphal, Toddington and Beyleveld.

[28] See Paulson, n 3.

[29] See, eg, J Waldron, 'Kant's Legal Positivism' (1996) 109 *Harvard Law Review* 1535; and T Pögge, 'Is Kant's Rechtslehre Comprehensive?' (1997) 36 *Southern Journal of Philosophy* 161.

[30] Kant considered the CI to give rise to both perfect and imperfect duties: see HJ Paton, *The Categorical Imperative: A Study in Kant's Moral Philosophy* (Harper and Row, 1965) esp 171. He considered perfect duties to be categorical, whereas imperfect duties admit exceptions and permit moral discretion ('playroom … for free choice': [6: 390]). Examples of imperfect duties are charity, self-preservation, health and individual perfection. In contrast, the generic rights prescribed by the PGC are correlative to perfect duties only, in that they are owed unconditionally/categorically.

supreme principle of morality is a necessary condition for legal authority to arise in both *The Doctrine of Right* and *LMJ*.[31]

VI. Summary of Chapters

We have placed the chapters in this collection into two groups: 'Philosophical Reflections' and 'Reflections on the Law'. These categories are somewhat rough and ready, because all the chapters advance philosophical reflections on or in response to ethical rationalism and thereby in some sense speak to the title of this book. Some, however, focus more on analysing central aspects of strong ethical rationalism and others focus on the implications of strong ethical rationalism for aspects of positive law or legal theory generally.

Philosophical Reflections

Both Stuart Toddington and Kenneth Westphal examine how Beyleveld's reconstruction of Gewirth's argument for the PGC is connected to the moral philosophies developed by Kant and Hegel.

Stuart Toddington argues that while Gewirth's moral philosophy is generally associated with Kantian ethical rationalism, it also has much in common with the Hegelian concept of Recognition (*Anerkennung*).[32] For Hegel, actual freedom can occur only when the subjective claims to possession emerging from potential or 'abstract' freedom are recognised as valid by another 'free being'. Toddington's view is that potentially free-beings must indeed mutually recognise as valid the subjective rights claims to whatever is necessary to actualise or externalise one's 'abstract' potential for freedom, but this is because such claims are necessarily grounded dialectically and *monologically* from the standpoint of each individual agent. The account of dialectical necessity *prior* to the dialogue of mutual recognition is overlooked by Hegel because the very purpose of Hegel's ethical critique is to reject the allegedly individualist consequences of Kant's model of the isolated, self-validating monological subject. Toddington argues that Hegelians and Gewirthians arrive at an identical description of the purposive agent whereby the plight of actualisation can indeed be 'recognised', but for this term to operate in an ethically transformative way as the ground of mutual *duty*, more argument is required. In Gewirth, this supplement appears as the ASA (now re-articulated by

[31] See also KR Westphal, *How Hume and Kant Reconstruct Natural Law: Justifying Strict Objectivity without Debating Moral Realism* (Clarendon, 2016).

[32] In GWF Hegel, *Grundlinien der Philosophie des Rechts oder Naturrecht und Staatswissenschaft im Grundrisse* (Nicolai, 1821): GWF Hegel, *Hegel's Philosophy of Right* (TM Knox tr, Clarendon Press, 1978).

Beyleveld); in *The Philosophy of Right*, we see instead the headlong leap into the allegedly self-substantiating claims to property right. According to Toddington, the fact that forms of property right can be derived from an account of the mutual obligations arising from a Gewirthian analysis of the sufficiency of agency, and that this argument is entirely compatible with Hegel's account of 'Abstract Right', suggest that its incorporation can but strengthen the undoubtedly important notion of Recognition in Hegel.

Kenneth Westphal assesses Beyleveld's refinements of Gewirth's argument for the PGC. Following Gewirth's intentions, Westphal's first part casts the argument for the PGC as a defence of moral duties against rational egoist objections. The specific objection is: if I (any agent) take a rational egoist position, I would accept that I should be opposed to unwilling interference with my access to and use of the generic conditions of agency, in view of my unique purposes, though because I value my unique purposes, not because I recognise that I am an agent. The counterargument is Gewirth's ASA, variously reformulated by Beyleveld. As mentioned above, this argument purports to show that the basis of my ought-claim to the generic conditions of my agency is my understanding of myself as an agent, which is dialectically necessary for me. For Gewirth and Beyleveld this argument is critical if the self-referring ought claim made at Stage 2 of Gewirth's argument is to be universalisable at Stage 3. Westphal endorses Beyleveld's response to the rational egoist, but does not fully support Gewirth and Beyleveld's subsequent universalisation of the claims that I must make about the generic conditions of agency. Instead, he argues that justifying the PGC requires assertoric, rather than dialectical, argument. Westphal argues that I must accept that I can only exercise my agency if I have the generic conditions of agency, but this acceptance implies that I accept that my capacity to freely pursue my purposes can only be actualised in a social system in which other agents act in accordance with my generic conditions of agency. Further, I must likewise afford the same freedom to others: if this arises as a valid (and unavoidable) claim for me because I am agent, then 'no one can justify rationally … arrogat[ing] to him- or herself generic entitlements s/he denies to anyone else'. Hence, Westphal argues, such a social system is, assertorically, a precondition for possession and exercise of the generic rights. Deryck Beyleveld responds in the concluding chapter of this collection.

Dascha Düring and Marcus Düwell take up the challenge of revisiting Kant's questions of humanity from a Beyleveldian perspective. In the *Critique of the Power of Judgment*, Kant explores the possibility of harmonising practical reason (which requires agents to accept the moral law) and theoretical reason (which requires agents to accept the law of nature) as dimensions of (self)understanding that reason in first instance requires us to distinguish.[33] Beyleveld contends that the postulates that Kant connects *a priori* with the idea of the moral law (free will, God, immortality and the *summum bonum*) should be seen *not* as objects of faith,

[33] I Kant, *Critique of the Power of Judgment* (P Guyer and E Matthews tr, CUP, 2002).

but as objects of *rationally required hope*.[34] Düring and Düwell build on Beyleveld's ideas on the *summum bonum* (the idea of the highest good) as an object of hope and fear in the attempt to secularise Kant's speculations regarding the possible unity of reason. They endorse the view that hope and fear are to be understood in a way that does not reduce to belief or faith, 'but is rather characterised by a radical epistemic openness towards the possible future'. This leads them to concur with Beyleveld's conclusion that the capacity to hope and fear is a necessary precondition for the possibility of agential self-understanding as such. They proceed to develop the capacity for hope and fear in light of the faculty of *feeling* that Kant introduces as a distinct phenomenological sense in the *Critique of the Power of Judgment*.[35] This entails an understanding of hope and fear that considers them as *aesthetically structured* forms of experience and judgement. Düring and Düwell then develop this line of understanding to provide an alternative to the 'Standard Account' of hope, as involving desiring and estimating a probability.[36]

Michael Boylan begins with Beyleveld and Brownsword's analysis of consent in medical ethics and law.[37] He argues that Beyleveld and Brownsword's view is to be contrasted with the social contractarian tradition, because their view holds that legal obligation arises from conformity to the PGC, rather than from consent to the establishment of state institutions. Boylan compares his reconstruction of Beyleveld and Brownsword's view to contractarian moral and political philosophers such as Charles Beitz and John Rawls.[38] He argues that contractarian grounds for legal obligation can produce 'bad' outcomes, not against one's prudential valuation of well-being, but against moral principle. A better approach, Boylan contends, is one that grounds the fundamental justification of the law in morality, such as a 'naturalistic moral theory', which he considers to be epitomised by the PGC.

Reflections on the Law

The remaining chapters focus on the relevance of ethical rationalism to law, either in terms of interpreting positive law or legal theory more generally. The contributors thereby take the debate beyond the traditional concerns of legal theory into areas such as the relationship between morality and international law, and the impact of ethically controversial developments or practices on legal understanding.

[34] See D Beyleveld and P Ziche, 'Towards a Kantian Phenomenology of Hope' (2015) 18 *Ethical Theory and Moral Practice* 927, esp 929. See also D Beyleveld, 'Hope and Belief' in RJ Jenkins and E Sullivan (eds), *Philosophy of Mind* (Nova Science Publishers, 2012) 1.

[35] [20: 206].

[36] Associated with RS Downie 'Hope' (1963) 24(2) *Philosophy and Phenomenological Research* 248 and JP Day, 'Hope' (1969) 6(2) *American Philosophical Quarterly* 89.

[37] D Beyleveld and R Brownsword, *Consent in the Law* (Hart, 2007).

[38] C Beitz, *The Idea of Human Rights* (OUP, 2011) and J Rawls, *The Law of Peoples* (Harvard University Press, 2001).

Shaun Pattinson analyses two challenges to advance refusals of life-sustaining treatment. The first challenge is determining whether an advance refusal sufficiently represents the now incompetent patient's will on what should happen in the situation in which she now finds herself. The second challenge, which is the particular focus to Pattinson's chapter, is the 'personal identity objection' to giving effect to a now incompetent's patient's prior will. According to this objection, the process that renders the individual incompetent will often destroy the conditions necessary for continuity of personal identity and thereby remove the moral authority of the advance refusal.[39] Pattinson argues that English law's rejection of the personal identity objection is supported by the PGC, because the objection invokes and applies criteria for identifying personal identity that are not required to give effect to the generic rights of agents and requires more assumptions to accept than to reject.

Roger Brownsword, the co-author of *LMJ*, revisits its central claims by way of an analysis of the regulatory implications of 'technological management'. Technological management seeks to design or automate products, places or processes to preclude certain conduct or behaviour. A modern example is digital rights management, whereby restrictions are embedded in digital products to protect the provider's intellectual property rights. Technological challenging of behaviour in this way has a long history. Other examples include the use of high fences to keep out trespassers and the deduction of income tax at source to prevent employees from evading tax on their wages.[40] Technological management, Brownsword argues, is regulatory in the sense of seeking to channel behaviour, but it does this by means other than the imposition of rules on human conduct. Regulation of technological management remains an enterprise of practical reason and agency, and thus governed by the PGC as the supreme principle of practical reason, but additional challenges are raised beyond those considered in *LMJ*. Brownsword argues that revising our understanding of the 'regulatory environment' requires that we consider not only the effectiveness and efficiency benefits of technological management, but also the dangers it presents to the conditions for moral community and autonomy.

Thom Brooks and Diana Sankey engage in a sustained analysis of the ethical rationalist project in legal theory. Their first criticism is that ethical rationalism devalues important emotions that are vital to a proper understanding of the relationship between law and morality. The correct moral response to dilemmas faced by real human beings is, in part, shaped by their emotional responses as well as their abstract, rational concern for others as right-bearing agents. Their second criticism develops and illustrates their first. They argue that the purported

[39] See, eg, A Buchanan, 'Advance Directives and the Personal Identity Problem' (1988) 17 *Philosophy and Public Affairs* 277.

[40] Deduction at source has been a key feature of the British income tax system since 1803: http://old.tax.org.uk/showarticle.pl?id=1622.

devaluation of emotions at the heart of ethical rationalism raises concerns as a model for understanding properly the nature of sexual offences and the response of law to them. Inappropriately, they argue, there are, and have been, various important contrasts drawn between, on the one hand, rationality and autonomy, and, on the other, emotion in sexual offences law, especially in relation to the idea of consent in relation to the adjudication of the offence of rape. Beyleveld and Brownsword, they claim to show, advocate an abstract, subjectively insensitive and rationalist concept of consent that sidelines the complex relationship between emotions and decision-making within cultures. Deryck Beyleveld responds in the concluding chapter of this collection.

Benjamin Capps develops Deryck Beyleveld's 'co-operative model' of conflicts between privacy and medical interests into a more general model of the nature of public goods.[41] Capps accepts Beyleveld's argument for a broad conception of privacy, which requires us to accept a co-operative model to recognise that the values protected by medical research both conflict with, and are supported by, the values protected by privacy. Capps then expands Beyleveld's idea that public goods are co-operative rather than conflictual into a general discussion of public interests and the public good. He pits two such conceptions against each other: the 'commodity model' and the 'welfarist model'. The commodity model, based upon a libertarian conception of freedom and choice, considers public goods to be really only 'collective consumption goods'. The welfarist model holds that public goods secure universal access to rights to the generic conditions of agency. The difference between the two models is that while the commodity model does not treat the right to obtain the generic conditions of agency (in the Gewirthian sense) any differently from the right to obtain any other commodities, the welfarist model affords special moral status to the generic conditions of agency. This particular feature of the welfarist model of public goods makes it better suited to protecting rights under the PGC. He then worries that the commodification of areas of modern life (such as personal data) is much closer to the commodity model than the welfare model. Capps then argues that social arrangements such as markets, public-private partnerships, private ownership and the like should be organised along the lines of the welfare model. This reorientation towards the welfare model does not preclude social arrangements such as these just mentioned, but rather requires that they be directed towards particular ends: that is, the balancing of fundamental rights to the generic conditions of agency in a co-operative and not conflictual way, thus amplifying Beyleveld's specific claim about the relationship between privacy and other values in medical research.

[41] D Beyleveld, 'Conceptualising Privacy in Relation to Research Values' in SAM McLean (ed), *First Do No Harm* (Ashgate, 2006) 151; D Beyleveld, 'Data Protection and Genetics: Medical Research and the Public Good' (2007) 18 *King's Law Journal* 275. See also D Beyleveld and SD Pattinson, 'Moral Interests, Privacy and Medical Research' in M Boylan (ed), *International Public Health Policy and Ethics* (Springer, 2008) 45.

David Townend presents an analysis of the boundary between the individual and others by re-examining privacy and the idea of politeness. He explains that privacy is a 'contested concept', sub-divided by Allen into 'informational privacy', 'decisional privacy', 'physical privacy', and 'proprietary privacy'.[42] The difficulty, he argues, is that what individuals identify as their privacy rights vary according to their own self-defined boundaries with others and the particular situations in which they find themselves. Therefore, according to Townend, the problem of privacy is the problem of addressing competing rights. Drawing inspiration from an article written by Beyleveld and Brownsword on applying the PGC in a community of rights,[43] Townend advances the seventeenth- and eighteenth century philosophy and practice of 'politeness' as a vehicle for addressing the difficulties presented by the move from abstract rights-based theory to modern-day regulatory problems. He then applies his idea of politeness to the problem of generating a governance or regulatory environment for medical research using biobanks and genetic information.

The next two chapters consider the relationship between ethical rationalism and international law. Thomas Franck has argued that international law is now in a post-ontological era,[44] which allows international lawyers to move past the question posed by Bentham and Austin as to whether it is really law. While the chapters by Patrick Capps and Henrik Palmer Olsen implicitly take this 'post-ontological' position, both are alive to the practical difficulties presented by attempts to establish authority in a world divided into states with positive sovereignty. Both of these chapters reflect on how legal theory rooted in strong ethical rationalism can answer questions on how authority may emerge genuinely within this new legal field.

Patrick Capps uses the model of authority found in *The Doctrine of Right* and *LMJ* to consider the vast number of international or transnational regulatory bodies that have emerged in the last two decades, which are usually described as global administration. He begins with a discussion of Llewellyn's and Hale's realism, and Fuller's *eunomics*,[45] to establish that forms of global administration can be said to be coercive bodies whilst being disconnected from state institutions. Questions as to the authority of global administration to coerce then arise. He uses examples such as GLOBALG.A.P., the European Systemic Risk Board, and the Security Council Sanctions Committee, to consider how global administration may ground its authority. Capps argues that political authority emerges in global

[42] AL Allen, 'Genetic Privacy: Emerging Concepts and Values' in Rothstein (ed), *Genetic Secrets: Protecting Privacy and Confidentiality in the Genetic Era* (Yale University Press, 1997) 31, 33.

[43] D Beyleveld and R Brownsword, 'Principle, Proceduralism, and Precaution in a Community of Rights' (2006) 19(2) *Ratio Juris* 141.

[44] T Franck, *Fairness in International and Institutions* (OUP, 1995).

[45] See K Llewellyn, 'What Price Contract? An Essay in Perspective' (1931) 40 *Yale Law Journal* 704; R Hale, 'Our Equivocal Constitutional Guarantees' (1939) 39 *Columbia Law Review* 563' L Fuller, *The Morality of Law* (Yale University Press, 1963, revised edn, 1969).

administration to the extent that it establishes the most important goods, or is reflective of the will, of those that it governs. Rather than constituting the authority of global administration, state consent describes one way in which political power can be harnessed to establish authoritative forms of global administration. Capps then uses Richard Stewart's notion of 'disregard'[46] to explain why much global administration fails to be authoritative in its attempt to coerce.

Henrik Palmer Olsen poses a problem for *LMJ* that arises from his work at the iCourts project at the University of Copenhagen. The iCourts project has shown that, in contrast to domestic tribunals, international courts rely heavily upon the goodwill of the states comprising their various jurisdictions and are thus more sensitive to political pressure. If this is the case, it may be prudent in certain circumstances for international courts to accede to pressure, and garner goodwill, even if it means issuing sub-optimal judgments from the perspective of the PGC. The implications of a court not being politically prudent may mean that its judgments are disregarded or even that the court is closed down, as shown by his example of the Southern African Development Community Tribunal. But the history of the European Court of Human Rights and Court of Justice of the European Union has shown that over a longer term international courts can be less careful about showing deference to states as they themselves gather political capital. So the possibility arises that by playing the 'long game' international courts could be able to offer more legally defensible judgments. This is a problem presented by making good moral judgements in the individual case where this carries the risk of both (a) undermining the longer term ability of courts to sustain a morally defensible rule of law within its jurisdiction and (b) leaving the individual good moral judgements unenforced by domestic governments. Should political prudence dictate that a short-term denial of justice be the cost of establishing autonomous international courts in the longer term? It would seem that it should, and thus, Palmer Olsen concludes, there can be no clear separation between law and politics, just as there can be no clear separation between law and morality.

Concluding Chapter

Deryck Beyleveld is the principal defender of Gewirth's foundational argument for the PGC and has spent over 30 years analysing, defending, criticising, reconstructing and applying Gewirthian theory. An important part of this reconstruction and re-articulation emerges in response to Westphal's careful examination of the logical scope of dialectically necessary commitments. Westphal accepts that such commitments are 'distributively universal'—which is to say that if it is dialectically necessary for A to claim X for herself, then it must also be dialectically

[46] R Stewart, 'Remedying Disregard in Global Regulatory Governance: Accountability, Participation, and Responsiveness' (2014) 108 *American Journal of International Law* 211.

necessary for B to claim X for himself—but expresses reservations about their collective universality. In a compelling analysis and re-statement of the argument, Beyleveld demonstrates why it is dialectically necessary for A (any specific agent) to act in accord with the dialectically necessary commitments of *all* agents.

VII. Conclusion

This collection presents chapters that have been developed and refined over a lengthy period. From an early stage, the authors of specific chapters were paired up for cross-review and draft versions of their chapters more widely distributed for comment some months in advance of the project conference in Durham in October 2015. This collection has an accompanying website, on which readers will find complete PDFs of three books written by contributors of this volume: www.dur.ac.uk/cells/erl.

The first of these is the book presenting Deryck Beyleveld and Roger Brownsword's seminal defence of legal idealism as an implication of Gewirth's strong ethical rationalism and referred to by many contributors to this collection: *LMJ*. Readers will also find Stuart Toddington's *Social Action and Moral Judgment* and Shaun Pattinson's *Influencing Traits Before Birth*.[47]

All that remains is for us to thank those who have supported the production of this book, and helped organise the conference upon which it is based. The University of Bristol Law School and Durham CELLS (Centre for Ethics in Law and in the Life Sciences), housed in Durham Law School, provided funding for the conference. We would also like to record our appreciation for those who helped to organise the conference, especially Marion Tait. Finally, though, we would like to thank those who contributed to this volume and, more generally, those who have otherwise inspired us to step beyond contemporary fashions in moral and legal scholarship and take seriously the claims of strong ethical rationalism.

[47] S Toddington, *Rationality, Social Action and Moral Judgment* (Edinburgh UP, 1993) and Pattinson, *Influencing Traits Before Birth*, n 12.

2

How to Become a Successful Hegelian

STUART TODDINGTON*

I. Introduction

Gewirth's moral philosophy is almost automatically associated with a Kantian model of agent subjectivity, and, as is well known, Hegel held entirely antithetical views in this regard. Notably, Hegel rejected Kant's *monological* model of the self-sufficient, self-validating, transcendental subject, arguing that it led to a fruitless reliance upon a purely formal and infinitely interpretable Categorical Imperative. In its place, Hegel can be said to subscribe to a notion of mutually complementary subjectivity whereby individuals establish their freedom and worth in a process of ethical 'recognition' (*Anerkennung*). This can be called a *dialogical* model of the ethical subject and as such differs in every respect from the isolated, self-sufficient subject of Kantian philosophy that is forever alienated not only from 'other minds' but also from the *noumenal* reality of things-in-themselves. In opposition to the Kantian idea of the spontaneously active, fully formed, transcendental subject, the image of individual freedom as the by-product of a coming-together of *potentially* free wills is undoubtedly the substratum of Hegel's ethical and political thought.

The Hegelian account of subjectivity is a reaction to Kant: it is *purpose-built* from the outset to engineer a phenomenological solution to the practical and theoretical alienation imposed by Kant's transcendental philosophy. But if we set aside for a moment the historical sources of the tension between *monological* and *dialogical* accounts of subjectivity, there is an immediately plausible sense in which talk about a mutuality of agent recognition leading to an objective account of rights and duties should make us think of Alan Gewirth. My suggestion is that, abstracted from history and viewed purely as deontological strategies, there are striking symmetries between Hegel's theory of Recognition and Gewirth's argument to the PGC: both seek to transform *subjective* (and in a maximally general sense) 'prudential' claims necessarily arising from the abstract potential of prospective, purposive action, into *objectively* defensible *entitlements* to forbearance

* Professor of Jurisprudence, University of Huddersfield.

on the part of others. The thesis of similarity becomes more compelling when we acknowledge that, prior to Beyleveld's development of a more powerful formulation of the Gewirthian 'Argument From the Sufficiency of Agency',[1] Gewirthians were beginning to realise that their position was precarious. In seeking to establish at Stage II that, 'I have a right to the Generic Conditions of Agency', and in attempting to universalise the inference at Stage III such that, 'Because I am a PPA, PPAO has a right to the GCA', Gewirthians found themselves in much the same predicament as the 'abstract' Hegelian 'Personality' striving for 'Recognition' in the early stages of *The Philosophy of Right.*[2] In Hegel, the 'Natural Law' account of the primordial moment of rightful possession and, ultimately, property rights in general, bears a heavy burden in forging the general justification for mutual recognition. In one great cinematic leap of breath-taking power Hegel, in the first part of *The Philosophy of Right*, takes us from the most abstract metaphysical speculations on the conscious but 'contentless' potential of the will to the very moment at which it burst the bonds of finitude 'to claim the external world as its own'. But if we rewind and replay this action sequence frame by frame we can identify a deficiency in the Hegelian narrative of Recognition. I will suggest that this might be remedied by a more careful demonstration of the dialectical-necessary commitments that can be seen to accrue to the model of the practical subject as it evolves conceptually in Hegel's Idealism. A review of this evolution might not only allow the theory of mutual recognition to serve as a compelling illustration of the logic of Gewirth's argument to the PGC, but in turn provide us with a critique of the misplaced importance of the rôle of the *dialogical* subject in the determination of Right. In fact, if the seeds of Recognition can be shown to be immanent in the Hegelian phenomenology of the abstract personality, then we can be sure that only a *monological* concept of the ethical subject is able to achieve a moral synthesis without begging all the interesting questions.

II. Orthodox Reason: Monological and Dialogical

Gewirth, in *Reason and Morality*, begins from an ideal-typical model of 'the will' or agent subjectivity. In the presentation of his argument he refers to 'the agent', or schematically to the prospective, purposive agent or *PPA*. The model of agent rationality is underpinned by an orthodox (we might say 'Kantian' or even

[1] See A Gewirth, *Reason and Morality* (Chicago University Press, 1978); and D Beyleveld, 'Williams' False Dilemma: How to Give Categorically Binding Impartial Reasons to Real Agents' (2013) 10 *Journal of Moral Philosophy* 204.

[2] GWF Hegel, *Grundlinien der Philosophie des Rechts oder Naturrecht und Staatswissenschaft im Grundrisse* (Nicolai, 1821), cited by main sections (§). Translations and page numbers given to GWF Hegel, *Hegel's Philosophy of Right* (TM Knox tr, Clarendon Press, 1978).

'Cartesian') model of the knowing subject. That Gewirth refers to the 'dialectical necessity' of his method of establishing the argument to the PGC should not be seen as introducing some idiosyncratic or customised modification of orthodox reasoning; on the contrary, the idea of 'dialectical necessity' is *ultra* orthodox—it means simply that if one finds oneself in a position where one has to claim *P*, and (if *P* then *Q*) ; then one will be castigated in the most orthodoxly dreary manner imaginable (by recourse to the ritual invocation of the taboo against contradiction) if one quibbles over the acceptance of *Q*, or if one attempts to claim (*not* –*Q*). For orthodox and thus 'monological' dialecticians of a Gewirthian persuasion, the opprobrium becomes extreme when, in the light of a rational conception of agency seen as the decision to employ means in pursuit of ends voluntarily chosen, *P* represents the proposition that 'I am a prospective purposive agent', and *Q* signifies, 'I must value my freedom and well-being as generically necessary means to my purposes'. Thus, although there is no reason to object to the claim that the argument to the PGC rests upon a 'Kantian' account of rational subjectivity in so far as a Kantian account of reason subscribes to orthodox logical procedures, we should be aware of the depth of political and ethical sentiment that usually accompanies such an observation. When Reason or rational subjectivity is referred to disparagingly as 'Kantian', or as 'transcendental', this indicates that these words are to be taken as synonyms for *monological*. The *monological* subject receives negative criticism from some quarters because this Enlightenment construction thrusts itself upon us as spontaneously active, self-sufficient, fully formed, and the arbiter of its own judgements. It is this lofty, self-validating independence that sees it implicated in the most vehement objections to the legitimation strategies of Enlightenment Liberalism where it is denounced as the root of the dominant *attritional* model of individual rights, the denigrator of collective wisdom and the destroyer of community. Thus the *monological* subject in post-Liberal thinking is *persona non grata*. The reason why Hegel exerts so much contemporary influence in political philosophy is that he is without doubt the most comprehensively accomplished critic of monological reason and similarly the most compelling advocate of a *dialogical* alternative.

This being said there is, at least rhetorically, a plausible case for reconsidering our options in this regard. I say 'rhetorically' because, in describing *Reason* itself as imperiously infallible and inherently unsociable in the introductory account I provided above, a humble and generous person might be wary of accepting any ethico-political theory based upon it. This is because the attributes of monological self-sufficiency begin to sound unattractive if they are imputed to the individual *personality*. These unappealing first impressions are compounded epistemologically by the notorious difficulties that beset the attempt to synthesise 'other-regarding' or communal-ethical principles from the thin gruel of individual and instrumental practical reason. If, after all this bad press, we are then offered the promise of a powerful, radical solution in the form of the *dialogical* subject, it becomes clear to us why the 'Kantian' or the 'transcendental' subject has had a rough time of it. For a generous and sociable person might argue that if we are supposed to do what is rational, and to seek to justify authority and obligation in reason, then, if rationality springs from monological subjectivity, Reason can but infuse our institutions with an insular and 'unsociable' prudence. From here, if monological subjectivity can be shown to be merely a necessary—but not sufficient—ingredient of Reason, and Reason becomes actual and complete in a special form of *inter*-subjectivity that instantiates a mutually recognised respect for other-regarding freedoms, then it is not so much that we must strive for rational justifications for respectful community, it is rather that *establishing* community actualises Reason as the product of a unity of subjectivities. The Hegelian idea of 'recognition' appears to be the key to theorising this type of social transformation and we find much enthusiastic elaboration and application of this methodology behind the political critique that endorses it. Kojève[3] in the 1930s, and Honneth, in his *The Struggle for Recognition*,[4] offer influential accounts and reconstructions of the three main aspects of mutual recognition ('love', 'rights' and 'self-esteem') that emerge from both Hegel's early and more mature writings. We have also seen important reconsiderations of the origin and scope of the idea[5] as it appears in Rousseau, in Fichte, and the importance of the idea of 'recognition' as the basis of property right in the relationship between Hegel and Marx.[6] In a useful summary of these developments, Schmidt am Busch suggests that we are witnessing a 'renaissance' of the philosophy of recognition in accounts of moral and practical rationality, in social ontology, economic analysis, the politics of identity, and multicultural studies.[7] We should welcome this proliferation of interest in the problem of mutual recognition, but, as Chitty points out in his 'Recognition and

[3] See A Kojève, Introduction *to the Reading of Hegel: Lectures on the Phenomenology of Spirit* (J Nichols tr, Alan Bloom ed, R Queneau, assembler, Cornell University Press, 1969).

[4] A Honneth, *The Struggle for Recognition. The Moral Grammar of Social Conflicts* (Polity Press, 1995).

[5] Among them, notably, are: F Neuhouser, *Rousseau's Theodicy of Self-Love: Evil, Rationality, and the Drive for Recognition* (OUP, 2008); T Pinkard, *Hegel's Phenomenology. The Sociality of Reason* (CUP, 1994); R Pippin, *Hegel's Practical Philosophy: Rational Agency as Ethical Life* (CUP, 2009).

[6] See A Chitty, 'Recognition and Property in Hegel and the Early Marx' (2013) 16 *Ethical Theory and Moral Practice* 685.

[7] H-C Schmidt am Busch, 'Introduction to Recognition' (2013) 16 *Ethical Theory and Moral Practice* 679. Of this renaissance, he says:

> Within practical philosophy, a number of philosophers have claimed that 'being rational' is not a natural characteristic of human individuals, but rather a normative status that is ascribed to humans within the framework of a social practice of mutual recognition … In the area of social ontology, it has been argued that institutional facts (pertaining for instance to the economy or to politics) are to be analysed with the help of the category of 'acknowledgement' … Furthermore, moral and political philosophers have raised the question of which forms of social recognition are necessary for the formation of a stable individual 'identity', and what results this might have for how institutions ought to be structured in multicultural societies … Finally, Frankfurt School critical theorists have discussed the possibilities and difficulties of founding a critical theory of society in terms of recognition theory under the political and economic conditions of the twenty-first century. (ibid, 679)

Property in Hegel and the Early Marx',[8] the word and the concept lend themselves to ambiguity. The suggestion is that in charting the frequency of appearances of references to 'recognition' in the literature it is possible to wander far and wide and lose sight of what is asserted to be of genuine epistemological interest in the theory of recognition. To be clear: at the level of the *epistemology of the subject* Hegel's theory of recognition must explain how the *very act of* identification/recognition/acknowledgement by *one* subject of an assertion to an entitlement by *another subject*, such that consequences for action arising from the putative entitlement in question is mutually understood, can transform the *assertion* of entitlement into an *objectively valid right* to the entitlement. The model of political organisation *implied by a successful account* of this transformation would thus serve as the basis of a genuine critique of 'atomistic' liberal social relations. Such a project is envisioned in Alan Brudner's *Constitutional Goods.*[9] Brudner explains that the 'Unity of Reason' envisioned by Hegel is not merely a compromise, but a genuinely dialectical resolution of the contradiction between, on the one hand, an individualism that fosters an attritional consumerism and the decline of the public sphere, and on the other, an illiberal collectivism (what Brudner calls the *Ethos* community) that no longer subscribes to a genuine respect for what Brudner refers to as the 'liberal confidence' in the 'final worth' of the individual:[10]

> the individual agent possesses final worth … So that there is no *more* fundamental end to which it may be unilaterally subordinated, that it does so on its own, that is, as a separate individual, distinct from … other individuals as well as from the larger groups, society, or political associations of which it is a member; and that the individual's worth is inviolable, which means that everyone is under a duty to respect it by forbearing from attempts to subdue the individual's agency to his own ends or to some supposed superior end such as tribe, nation, society, or state. This set of propositions constitutes what I shall call the liberal confidence.[11]

This is the *claim* that is made by the 'atomistic' or 'self-supporting' (monological) subject and which seeks validation *dialogically* through the process of recognition. The monological subject, says Brudner, is indispensable to the completion of rational society, but 'deficient', because 'its *subjective* claim of absolute worth lacks

[8] See A Chitty, n 6, 685. H Ikäheimo and A Laitinen, 'Analysing Recognition: Identification, Acknowledgement and Recognitive Attitudes between Persons' in B Van den Rink and D Owen (eds), *Recognition and Power: Axel Honneth and the Tradition of Critical Social Theory* (CUP, 2007).

[9] A Brudner, *Constitutional Goods* (OUP, 2004).

[10] ibid, 31–33 for a brief synopsis of the general thesis and, in respect of the 'despotism' of *Ethos* see 302–06. Brudner attempts to show that Hegel's theory of recognition seeks an integration of the most coherent conceptions of liberty, equality and community that it is possible to frame. Brudner does not deny the existence or the vital importance of the 'self-supporting self' but tries to show that it is the basis of a rational conception of community and that only genuine community can offer the reflection of self-worth that it craves.

[11] ibid, 13.

the *object* that validates the claim'. In his reply to critics of *Constitutional Goods*, Brudner says:[12]

> Because the atomistic self's rational worth is inherently a mediated worth, it too is deficient to itself in its isolation, for its subjective claim of absolute worth lacks the object that validates the claim. So it yearns and it strives. In order to overcome its inner deficiency, the atomistic self enters into relationships of mutual recognition (private property, contract, the market, due process of law) through which its claim to worth is confirmed by another. These relationships, however, also confirm community or mutual recognition as the matrix of valid worth claims, and they do so now (unlike in the *ethos* community) out of the mouth of community's adversary—the self who claims to be self-supporting.

III. The Compatibility of the Monological and the Dialogical

The plausible politics of dialogical community rest upon the transformation of the 'atomistic' or monological subject into subjectivity seeking confirmation of its value within the process of recognition. But the 'transformation' is, I suggest, illusory. In the quotation above the sanctity of the final worth of the *transcendental* subject is preserved by equivocation: 'the atomistic self's rational worth is *inherently* a mediated worth'. This is simply another way of saying that the monological subject is *inherently* a dialogical subject. Thus in Brudner's account of how individual worth might be reconciled with, and confirmed by, law and community, ambiguity at the level of the epistemology of the subject still persists. But the ambiguity can be removed by giving the passage a straightforwardly *monological* reading. For the issue is one of justification, and the fundamental question is not whether my self-worth is recognised by another, or whether there exists another who might recognise it, it is whether or not it is the case that, as an isolated individual, I *have* self-worth; in other words, whether my *subjective assertion* that I possess self-worth might be demonstrated to be objectively valid. The demand for *objectivity* is thus never at issue: rather, it is Hegel's rejection of Kant's formal-transcendental imposition of what appears as an impossible task in this regard that fuels the strategy of a dialogical alternative to *attaining* objectivity. Hegel's philosophy of recognition is specifically designed to overcome Kant's introspection on the form and phenomenal limits of the process of knowing *per se*—not only the theoretical-empirical divide between subject and object, but also the practical-ethical divide between *subject and subject*. But this latter, along with a host of other problems associated with the notion of dialogical subjectivity, suggests that *either* the 'other' free being (agent) already possesses some power of

[12] A Brudner, 'A Reply to Critics of *Constitutional Goods*' (2009) 22(2) *Canadian Journal of Law and Jurisprudence* 237.

ethical *imprimatur* that is lacking in the agent who is the initial focus of recognition, *or* that something very special occurs *epistemologically* at the moment of *mutual* recognition. The upshot is that unless dialogical reason is understood as a critically testable hypothesis of *monological* reason, the account of the nature of this epistemological sacrament is the *general* problem of the theory of recognition.

The monological view must hold that, ideal-typically, an agent, as a thinking, practical subject, has within its own cognitive and reflective capabilities, not only the ability to recognise (from the point of view of one who has the present or prospective intention to employ means to ends voluntarily chosen), that some claims on other agents must necessarily be made, but also that the agent in question is able objectively to *self-validate* such claims. These claims, let us note, are not in any substantial sense different from the kind of claims that the dialogical subject or the dialogical philosopher would wish to make or defend, they are simply the kind of claims that would emerge as rational within an Hegelian process of recognition. In other words, in a monological epistemology of rights the conceptual model of a potential agent regarded as *a practical subject*—in Hegel, this means the potential for freedom existing in tension between 'personality' and the 'abstract freedom' of the 'content-less will'[13]—is already assumed to contain within itself the capacity to synthesise the criteria[14] that will determine what claims *ought to be mutually recognised* (that is, ought to be accepted as morally valid) between agents. In other words, a particular agent (*A*) does not depend upon the actual acceptance/agreement/'recognition' of another (*Ao*) (in the sense of receiving some arbitrary form of *imprimatur* as the justificatory *ground*) to *validate* a claim-right on the part of (*A*) to express their agency in the world, but rather *deduces it dialectically* from the practical perspective of the ideal-typical agent.

This amounts to the epistemological (not moral) claim that an agent can not only synthesise 'other-regarding' principles of action *monologically*, but can posit the dialogical context in which the principle is scrutinised *and* simulate a dialogical test upon it. In other words, a monological practical consciousness is held to be capable of adopting a *dialogical* perspective on action. It is worth noting that the logical device that Gewirth employs to universalise subjective, practical, self-regarding 'ought' judgements made monologically from the standpoint of the agent (and thus through universalisation transform them into *moral* or 'other-regarding' judgements) receives a technical label in the literature: 'the ASA', or 'the Argument from the Sufficiency of Agency'.[15] This is the ability to be able to abstract from one's personal biography as a *particular* agent and adopt a hypothetical viewpoint from the basis of the most general or 'ideal-typical' features

[13] Hegel, n 2, §§34 and 35.

[14] By 'synthesise the criteria' I mean that the ideal agent is assumed to be in possession of the reflective capacity to reason practically (in Kant) to a point where it can glean and apply a substantive principle. 'Criteria' is more accurate than 'maxim' or belief because the monological agent must be able to subject maxims themselves to some form of dialogical test.

[15] See A Gewirth, *Reason and Morality* (Chicago University Press, 1978) 109–10.

of action or being an agent in general. Thus if a monological account of what we can now safely refer to as 'mutual agent recognition' is to be established, it must be possible to show that agents do not distort, or equivocate upon, the logic of recognition when they shift from, on the one hand, their *unique, biographically contingent* agent-perspective, to, on the other, the perspective of the agent generally conceived—that is, the perspective that defines any such agent as a relevant *type* for the purpose of the analysis. This essential or universal conception of the practical being, ironically, is an archetypally Hegelian notion.

IV. Dialogical Subjectivity and Alienation in Hegel

The view that the monological operation as described above is not only impossible, but also functions as an ideological tool in the service of sectional interests, is responsible for the split between Kant and Hegel and is the source of the considerable antipathy to 'the knowing subject' in contemporary social and legal theory. The most prominent and repeated criticisms of Kant to be found in Hegel arise from his dissatisfaction with the limits imposed upon the theory of knowledge. This is not exclusively an epistemological concern: it must be attributed in part to Hegel's theological and spiritual dissatisfaction with the alienation of the modern mind, and to his hopes for the liberation and emancipation of humanity through their striving. Hegel's theory of knowledge is not a search for what can be known, it is a journey back from the Truth about Being that is gleaned by the human spirit, and his philosophy of history is a narrative that is daily constructed by a faith that the world is working towards the Unity of Reason: towards the overcoming of the spiritual and cognitive chasm of the subject/object divide. The transcendental philosophy denies this faith and *endorses* this alienation and separation as the pinnacle and limit of theoretical reason. This is the source of Hegel's most vehement denunciation of the ethical emptiness of Kant's practical philosophy. Specifically and notoriously, Hegel thinks that the doctrine of the Categorical Imperative is the ethical equivalent to the neutered theory of knowledge that turns our scientific enquiries in upon ourselves noting only the *form* in which our understanding might interpret what forever remains an hypothesis: the *noumenal* world beyond us. Hegel's motivation to reject not only Kant's systematic philosophy of the subject, but the entire interior or 'mentalist'[16] framework of phenomenology that preceded it, thus lies in the refusal to accept both the 'inward looking' constraints of a philosophy of nature based upon transcendental deductions of empirical experience, and a philosophy of right based upon transcendental deductions of *morality*.

[16] Habermas uses this term to refer to Cartesian and Kantian phenomenology as distinct from putatively 'de-transcendentalised' approaches. See J Habermas, 'From Kant to Hegel and Back Again' (1999) 7 *European Journal of Philosophy* 129, 134.

The limits set to our *phenomenal* experience by the transcendental method is a self-imposed alienation of the most total kind. Hegel's *dialectical* and *dialogical* ambition is to set aside these constraints and, as Habermas says, 'to free the essentially practical spontaneity of the transcendental subject from the prison of self-enclosed interiority of an ego narcissistically aware of its own operations'.[17]

We are thus urged to recast the subject/object relation as a form of striving in the praxis of history, language, work and creation. In this process, cognitive relationships between the self and the world, and the self and others expressed in belief, judgement and action constitute the external expression of our rational freedom. It is not the constant recourse to *internal* subjectivity that brings this emancipation to fruition, but the very act of the giving and taking of an agent's reasons for action, mediated by a shared ethical-institutional context. Kant's conception of ethical freedom, however, says Hegel, leads only to an 'empty formalism' and reduces the science of morals to 'the preaching of duty for duty's sake'.[18] But this being said, Hegel makes an important admission at a crucial juncture in *The Philosophy of Right* that appears at odds with his outright rejection of the Categorical Imperative. Cautioning us to avoid 'formalism' and to prepare for the transition from the introversion of 'morality' to the worldly extroversion of 'ethics', Hegel nevertheless concedes: 'thanks to Kant's philosophy … the pure unconditioned determination of the will as the root of duty, has won its firm foundation and starting point for the first time owing to the thought of its infinite autonomy'.[19]

V. Hegel and Kant: Looking Inward and Looking Outward

There is no doubt that for Kant, as much as Hegel, and however differently it might be *expressed*, the direction of philosophical progress from the formal and abstract concept of freedom points towards an external realisation of Reason in moral action. In Kant, our practical strivings are to be constantly referred to a validating principle of duty: the Categorical Imperative. But to say, as Hegel does, that this is a demand that our practical strivings are to be referred *inwardly* and thus in some sense *vacuously* to this supreme principle is a tendentious articulation. Hegel's aim, of course, is to promulgate a philosophy of praxis. 'Inward' reflection—at least metaphorically—suggests a less vital image than talk of venturing outward and appropriating, shaping and transforming the world. But we should not be swayed by this figure, because, as we have noted, there is, in a very straightforward sense, little difference in the respective *points of departure* between

[17] ibid.
[18] Hegel, n 2, §135.
[19] ibid.

Hegel and Kant in the philosophical determination of the concept of Right. Kant's resignation to the subject/object divide in the transcendental critique on the one hand, and on the other, the affirmation in Hegel of the primordial unity of Being as Reason itself, appears as a dramatic ontological and epistemological division, but whatever the primordial status of Being, and despite the respective differences in the prognosis for human subjectivity, *both* philosophies begin their critique from the *fact* of the fractured individual phenomenology of the subject/object divide. It is thus important to note that neither Kant's point of departure, nor his deduction of the universality of the will, attracts any objection from Hegel. Rather, it is an objection to Kant's *inward looking perspective* on the will—the obverse side of the same moral-practical coin—that, Hegel alleges, leads only to an 'empty formalism'.[20]

For all this we find that, in the *Philosophy Of Right,* Kant's 'inwardly focused, unconditioned moral consciousness' is rendered by Hegel in essentially identical terms as 'abstract universality'. This is the 'self-conscious' but otherwise 'contentless' will; a 'simple relation of itself to itself' which, Hegel tells us, is 'only a formal identity whose nature it is to exclude all content and specification',[21] but which nevertheless constitutes, for Hegel, a 'person'; and this personality conceived as 'abstract freedom' is *still a bearer of abstract rights and duties.* We are supposed to be soaring upwardly and outwardly away from the 'emptiness' of the Categorical Imperative but Hegel tells us that the active and, one assumes, *substantial* 'imperative' of abstract freedom is, 'Be a person and respect others as persons'.[22] The critical discussion writes itself from here on in, beginning with the inquiry, 'What are we to understand by reference to 'a person'?

Hegel explains the process of recognition by which the 'contentless' potential that is the nascent personality becomes an objectively free, substantive being. It begins, metaphysically, in the *Phenomenology*:

> [I]t is necessary that the two selves opposing each other should, in their existence [*Dasein*], in their being-for-another, posit themselves and recognize [*anerkennen*] themselves as what they are in themselves or according their concept, namely, not merely natural but rather free beings. Only in this does true freedom come about; since this consists in the identity of myself with the other, I am only truly free when the other is also free and recognised by me as free.[23]

It is later given elaborate economic, legal and political expression in *The Philosophy of Right* through what is, in itself, an account of the Natural Law of rightful possession in which *private property* is seen as the fundamental *embodiment* of the will.

[20] ibid.
[21] ibid.
[22] ibid, §36.
[23] GWF Hegel, *Encyclopaedia of the Philosophical Sciences*, Part 3, 'The Phenomenology of Mind'. Translation of this passage (ES §431A) by Andrew Chitty in Chitty, n 6, 685.

In this latter work, under the heading of *Transition from Property to Contract*, we find the following:[24]

> Existence as determinate being is in essence being for another … One aspect of property is that it is an existent as an external thing, and in this respect property exists for other external things and is connected with their necessity and contingency. But it is also an existent as an embodiment of the will, and from this point of view the 'other' for which it exists can only be the will of another person. This relation of will to will is the true and proper ground in which freedom is existent. The sphere of contract is made up of this mediation whereby I hold property not merely by means of the thing and my subjective will, but by means of another person's will as well and so hold it in virtue of participation in a common will.

This passage (which admittedly presupposes moral and legal concepts yet to be established foundationally or 'naturally') is perhaps the best illustration we have of Hegel's methodological strategy. It seeks to present the will as a self-conscious, practical potential: the potential is actualised in the act of possession and use and in the transformation of the external world; the primordial or natural right of actualisation is announced in this act of possession and this act embodies the will. Through the subjective appropriation of property, and through the *recognition* of this appropriation by another subject, *my* subjective claim becomes 'objectified': my appropriation, it appears, becomes validated in the moment of mutual willing. When, eventually, contract is institutionalised ethically and legally, I can thus articulate my (formerly natural, subjective) right to property by recourse to participation in, and submission to, the objective authority of a common will.

Working back from this point in Hegel to the first steps of the synthesis, the plausible logical structure of the methodology of recognition is revealed.[25] Notably, the first words uttered by Hegel in the chapter on 'Abstract Right' under the heading of 'Property' tell us that 'A person must translate his freedom into an external sphere in order to exist as Idea'.[26] This is *personality* conceived as 'abstract freedom', and in order to project abstract freedom *outward* into an external sphere, the bearer of this freedom—the 'person'—must somehow enter into a realm of objects that is 'not mind, not free, not personal, without rights'. A Person begins to overcome the subject/object divide by pursuing:

> as his substantive end the right of putting his will into any and every thing and thereby making it his, because it has no such end in itself and derives its destiny and soul from his will. This is the absolute right of appropriation which man has over all 'things'.[27]

In the act of appropriation, therefore, 'I am an object to myself in what I possess and thereby also for the first time an actual will, and this is the aspect which

[24] Hegel, n 2, §71.
[25] ibid, §45 and §48.
[26] ibid, §41.
[27] ibid, §44.

constitutes the category of *property*, the true and right factor in possession'. Hegel makes it clear that property is intrinsic to freedom: He says:

> If emphasis is placed on my needs, then the possession of property appears as a means to their satisfaction, but the true position is that, from the standpoint of freedom, property is the first embodiment of freedom and so is in itself a substantive end.[28]

At this point the Hegelian trajectory is more than reminiscent of the themes and logic of the Argument to the PGC; but we are heading towards a predictable question that ultimately must be answered by both accounts of agent rights: 'abstract freedom' is going to turn out to be the idea of a *potential* for purposive action; the person becomes incarnate as a physical practical being, the physical individual as agent thus becomes a link between purposive consciousness and nature or the world; purposive personality thus embodied must enter into the world and interact with it in a way that expresses the intention of continuing agency and this must involve a *display* of acquisition hinting at a subjective claim to exclusive use and so on. There is no doubt, then, that other similarly embodied persons (agents) are capable of 'recognising' the rights claims expressed in this kind of activity, and these are the indispensable first few steps towards a theory of mutual recognition, but much will turn on what, precisely, is held to be 'recognised'.

VI. Property is Not a Relation to a 'Thing'

The first problem we face is the prospect of a head-on collision with the most intractable aspects of the subject/object divide. The Hegelian account of the objectification of freedom through a shift from natural possession to contractual Property is a severe test of the notion of recognition in pure praxis. It seems that Hegel must show how a relationship between *a person and a thing* (as opposed to *legal or moral relations between persons*) can generate a right to exclusive possession. The theory of property is not, in itself, unusual. It is close to, if not identical to, that of Locke—perhaps the most familiar account of acquisition in the history of political philosophy. In this regard Locke and Hegel stand diametrically opposed to Kant in theorising the property relation, and reflection on this divergence of view might prove useful to our understanding of the issue. In considering the act of appropriation, Kant asks, 'Could this external rightful relation of my choice be a direct relation to a corporeal thing?' In suggesting that it could *not* he says:

> Someone who thinks that his right is a direct relation to things rather than to persons would have to think that since there corresponds to right on one side a duty on the other, an external thing always remained under obligation to the first possessor even though it has left his hands; that, because it is already under obligation to him, it rejects anyone else who pretends to be the possessor of it. So he would think of my right as if it were a

[28] ibid, §45.

> guardian spirit accompanying the thing, always pointing me out to whoever else wanted to take possession of it and protecting it against any incursions by them.[29]

He adds, however,

> It is therefore absurd to think of an obligation of a person to things or the reverse, even though it may be permissible, if need be, to make this rightful relation perceptible by picturing it and expressing it this way.

We should bear in mind this generous leeway for expression when considering our eventual interpretation of Hegel's suggestion, noted above, that, to realise my freedom it is necessary, rightful and possible for a 'person' to 'put [their] will into [a] thing'. But however generous we are with our reception of that proposition we have to remember that we urgently require an explanation of how property, in the sense of *a right of exclusive use*, is established. Because, as Hegel accepts:

> Since property is the *embodiment* of personality, my inward idea and will that something is to be mine is not enough to make it my property; to secure this end occupancy is requisite. The embodiment which my willing thereby attains involves its recognizability by others.[30]

Hegel's claim that 'I' can and must 'put my will into a thing' has a plausible precursor in Locke's theory of property. Locke's famous idea is that I can make a thing my own by appropriating it or altering it and thereby imbuing it with something *essential* to my practical being—that is, my capacity to labour.

> Whatsoever then he removes out of the state that nature hath provided, and left it in, he hath mixed his labour with, and joined to it something that is his own, and thereby makes it his property. It being by him removed from the common state nature hath placed it in, it hath by this labour something annexed to it, that excludes the common right of other men.[31]

Establishing an exclusive right over an object seems to be a one-stage process in Locke, but Hegel seems to reproduce it more carefully in two stages: possession and then recognition. Hegel says that I can make a thing recognisably mine in three ways: 'We take possession of the thing (*a*) by directly grasping it physically, (*b*) by forming it, and (*c*) by merely marking it as ours.'[32] And Hegel has

[29] I Kant, *The Metaphysics of Morals* (M Gregor tr, CUP, 1996) ([6: 261] in the Academy edition of the *Gesammelte Schriften*).

[30] Hegel, n 2, §51.

[31] J Locke, *Two Treatises on Government* (P Laslett tr, CUP, 1997) ch 5 of second treatise, 282–302.

[32] Of these three acts of appropriation he says:

> (*a*) To grasp the thing physically is the most complete of these modes, because then I am directly present in this possession, and therefore my will is recognisable in it. But at bottom this mode is only subjective, temporary, and seriously restricted in scope, as well as by the qualitative nature of the thing grasped. (§55) [However] (*b*) When I impose a form on something, the things determinate character as mine acquires an independent externality and ceases to be restricted to my presence here and now and to the direct presence of my awareness and will … etc' (Hegel, n 2, §54).

much to say about the subtle distinctions of display between these types of 'taking possession', but little or nothing about how or why *recognition* transforms the appropriation into a right to exclusive ownership.[33] There is no doubt that these seizing and controlling activities reveal one to be a *practical* being—an agent—and insofar as this can be seen as an attempt to objectify oneself as such, might plausibly result in one being recognised (identified) as such. But does 'recognising' a person in this sense entail more than simply identifying their activity as practical? That is, does my identification of their intentions as appropriating, manipulating, and marking out objects as 'their' property simultaneously dispose me or oblige me to act in accordance with what we *ordinarily understand* as the rights accruing to property owners, namely, that one ought not to interfere with another's possession or use of a thing? The answer to this must turn not only on (a), what it means to *recognise* others, but also (b), what it means to recognise others as *persons*.

VII. The Monological Sufficiency of Agency

Whatever is meant by the 'recognition of persons' in this regard, if it is to be successful in establishing the ground of the property relation, it must be expressed in terms of some substantively 'other-regarding' duty intrinsic to the notion of *person*. Without it, Hegel's alternative to Kant's allegedly 'empty' Categorical Imperative—that is, 'Be a person and respect others as persons' seems to fall victim to the same formalism that is alleged to characterise Kant's supreme principle. This injunction (which we find at §36 of *The Philosophy of Right*) points towards an account in which the conscious personality that strives to transform its 'abstract freedom' into external freedom knows that the actualisation of its potential as a free, purposive being—an agent—depends upon its access to, and control of, objects in the world. In expressing the intention to actualise this potential, abstract freedom must not only enter into the world and lay claim to parts of it, but must do so with the confidence that its 'other' has a symmetrical conception of its destiny. If we are to cut to the chase this means that a *potentially* free being must rationally *expect* recognition to take the form of reciprocal rights and duties. And if we recall the metaphysics of *Hegel's Phenomenology* this expectation arises from the *necessity* of potentially free beings to 'posit themselves and recognise [*anerkennen*] themselves as what they are *in themselves* or 'according their concept', namely, not merely natural, but 'free beings'. This is perhaps the closest that Hegelian terminology comes to referring to the *dialectical necessity* that 'free beings'—the Hegelian equivalent of unrequited PPAs—must necessarily accept as arising from the logical implications of their existence as such. It might also be what the contemporary (Beyleveldian) articulation of the interpretation of Gewirth's universalization step—the ASA—seeks to demonstrate.

[33] Hegel, n 2, §§53–56.

'Abstract Freedom' in Hegel is identical to the concept of a conscious capacity for agency, and because agency (the general and abstract capacity to act purposefully in full knowledge of the relationship between means and chosen ends) is always prospective, it must look towards a future of action and purpose not yet contemplated. This is viable only on the basis that any prospect of successful purpose fulfilment whatsoever requires access to an unspecified range of goods that might be regarded as a generic wherewithal for action. It is the crucial justification of the claim to rightful access to these 'generic conditions of agency' (GCA) that Gewirth sought to ground in the Argument from the Sufficiency of Agency. And if it is possible to render the narrative of Abstract Freedom's destiny that constitutes the methodology of the *Philosophy of Right* into the frame of a Gewirthian solution, then it is surely here, at this precise co-ordinate in Gewirth, that we will find a transferable logic that, if valid, would suffice to give us the rational conception of the Hegelian theory of recognition. The quickest way to test this is to consider whether the straightforward problems of the theory of recognition as it is presented in correspondingly strategic points in Hegel can be solved with Gewirthian resources. I suggest that sections 37, 38, and 39 of the *Philosophy of Right* serve our experimental purposes here. These vital sections in Hegel reveal a primordial moment in the anatomical evolution of a free being as an *as yet unreconciled tension* between, on the one hand, the 'particular will' as 'desire, need, impulse, casual whim and so forth', and, on the other, the 'character of freedom' that is to be imparted by 'personality'—from which thus far the will remains '*sundered*'. At this point Hegel says:

> As *immediate* individuality, a person in making decisions is related to a world of nature directly confronting him, and thus the personality of the will stands over against this world as something subjective. For personality, however, as inherently infinite and universal, the restriction of being only subjective is a contradiction and a nullity. Personality is that which struggles to lift itself above this restriction and to give itself reality, or in other words to claim that external world as its own.[34]

In the very next sentence Hegel plunges into the blunt assertions that the route to universality and objectivity for the personality is first to take possession of objects as property thereby distinguishing themselves from others in this action; to then relate to others as property owners, and finally, to consummate their identities as free beings in the act of transferring property from one to another with a common will and without detriment to the rights of either—that is, in contract. I want to suggest that rather, the particularity, the one-sided subjectivity, and what Hegel rightly laments as the immanent contradiction of *a will bereft of universal ethical personality* must eschew the question-begging device of property relations and take a metaphysical stand on what is *dialectically necessary* from the standpoint of the agent confronting the world as Hegel describes.

[34] ibid, §39.

What if at §40 of the *Philosophy of Right* we found not the rapid fire of: 'possession—property—exchange—contract—freedom', but rather a more sympathetic account of the plight of a would-be practical being? We begin with a finite, particular subject—full of doubt and contradiction—seeking to enter a world of purposive action among objects (some of which are other prospective agents). It finds itself confronting a world where, whatever its prospective purposes, it must seek to secure (or relinquish) an unspecifiable range of goods pertinent to circumstances that range from the avoidance of starvation to the zenith of self-actualisation. This 'wherewithal' of successful personhood might reasonably be referred to as comprising the generic conditions of action (GCA), and this terminology is surely preferable to references to 'possession', 'occupancy', or 'property' simply because of the unavoidably *distributive* issues raised by association with this language. And there is good reason to make this point, because in the lengthy addition to §39 of *The Philosophy of Right*[35] Hegel is emphatic that the implicit subjective rights claim for recognition involved in the struggle to externalise one's abstract freedom is *not* to be confused with an argument for equality of distribution of land or other available resources, or even, in this context, the (civil) right to subsistence.[36] Rather, we are concerned with an argument that seeks to show how *universally* mutual obligations arise from *unilateral* expressions of the will to act purposively in the world. In short, both Hegel (and Gewirth) must demonstrate that understanding oneself as a prospective purposive agent demands that one must lay claim to the GCA, and that in so doing discover the *essential* justification that underpins one's own, and all other agents', claims in this regard. In the remainder of this discussion I shall try to make a case for suggesting that where dialogical subjectivity is not interpreted literally or ontologically, but made amenable to dispassionate synthesis, §40 of *The Philosophy of Right* might well have incorporated the Beyleveldian elaboration on what Gewirth, in *Reason and Morality*, referred to as 'the Argument from the Sufficiency of Agency'.

VIII. Beyleveld's Account of the Argument from the Sufficiency of Agency

In its original incarnation, Gewirth's Argument from the Sufficiency of Agency offered a concise logical strategy of universalisation from what is conventionally

[35] ibid, §49.

[36] Hegel says, at this point, equality could be only the equality of abstract Persons as such, and therefore the whole field of possession, this terrain of inequality, falls outside it (ibid). Gewirth—in the original formulation of the 'Generic Features of Action' (GF) in terms of 'freedom and well-being', or in subsequent Beyleveldian formulations (GCA) are not to be read, then, as arguing primarily for a right to subsistence, nor as a right to property because of need, nor as an argument that all should receive equal shares—although rational policies related to issues of subsistence, need and egalitarian distribution might be edifyingly informed by the Principle of Generic Consistency.

referred to as Stage II of the classical Argument to the PGC. Stage II turns on the Stage I premise that the notion of voluntariness or 'unforced action' contained in the understanding of PPA's claim ('I do x for End E') necessarily implies a valuing of purposes (ends) on the part of PPA. This subjective but normatively unavoidable conferment of value on voluntarily chosen ends in turn implies either a proactive valuing of the particular *means* required to realise particular ends or the abandonment of the ends in question. In general terms, then, the capacity to act purposively presupposes access to an unspecifiably generic set of means: Gewirth's 'freedom and well-being' or access to GF (Generic Features of Agency) or what Beyleveld now refers to as the Generic Conditions of Agency (GCA). We understand by GCA the practical 'wherewithal' required for purposive action *per se*. Stage II thus holds that Stage I entails the dialectical necessity of a rights claim to GCA on the part of PPA. A PPA must claim rights to the GCA on pain of contradicting itself as a PPA. In other words, dialectically if not assertorically, PPA *validly* makes this claim to the GCA. Stage III universalises the claim made in Stage II by insisting that the dialectical ground of this rights claim to the GCA is—and must be—made for the *sufficient* reason that one is an agent. It is incoherent for any PPA not to make the claim, and it is incoherent for any PPA to make the claim on grounds less general than that of being a PPA. A swift and happy ending to the argument to the PGC would thus result in PPA acknowledging dialectically that (a) another PPA must necessarily claim rights to the (GCA); (b) that the other PPA does so validly, and (c), that (a) and (b) imply that PPA must acknowledge a reciprocal duty not to interfere with PPA's access to the GCA. This is a very powerful result, because if Stage III is dialectically necessary for PPA, then we can say that it is dialectically necessary for *all* PPAs to accept that {All PPAs validly claim rights to GCAs} and thus all PPAs accept the reciprocal duties thereby entailed. This would seem to be an elegant model of mutual recognition, but there have been important criticisms of its validity.

Whilst these criticisms have been directed at the universalisation stage of the argument to the PGC, it is not so much that the Argument from the Sufficiency of Agency is brought into question—the logical sufficiency of agency implicated in PPA's claim to the GCA is beyond dispute. Rather we have seen arguments from, among others, Chitty,[37] Korsgaard[38] and Williams[39] that reject the notion of a generic conception of agency *per se*, in that practical rationality (in respect of what can be logically extrapolated from the relationship between choices for action and the prudential presuppositions of those choices) is essentially a private—and non-transferable—matter for the real, biographical, individual agent in question. These powerful and plausible attacks on the Argument to the PGC

[37] A Chitty, 'Protagonist and Subject in Gewirth's Argument for Human Rights' (2008) *King's Law Journal* 191, 1–6.

[38] See, eg, C Korsgaard, *The Sources of Normativity* (CUP, 1996) and also Beyleveld, 'Korsgaard v Gewirth on Universalization: Why Gewirthians are Kantians and Kantians Ought to be Gewirthians' (2013) *Journal of Moral Philosophy* 1.

[39] B Williams, *Ethics and the Limits of Philosophy* (Fontana, 1985).

are all the more effective because they draw on intuitions and habits of thought with which we can easily identify. For example, Andrew Chitty—an accomplished critic of the normative lacuna to be found in Hegel—finds a similar deficiency in the Gewirthian attempt to ground the universal recognition between agents. His argument is that although one might necessarily be obliged to claim rights to the GCA (for such is required for one's current and prospective purposes) and that we might also recognise this as a common logic of prudence applicable to each particular agent, there is no necessary *prudential* requirement for *me*, in respect of *my* purposes, to acknowledge the binding obligation to respect the generic rights of others. This is because I do not (necessarily) need another agent's generic well-being for my purposes. In other words, the dialectical necessity of the rights claim is a private thing. Bernard Williams offers an objection in a similar vein: he too objects to the very idea of extrapolating ethical principle from the concept of agency.[40] His criticism of Ethical Rationalism in general is based upon the observation that we face the dilemma of introducing on the one hand, a general and abstract conception of the agent, that is, a literally non-existent, unreal entity of which only ethically empty generality can be extracted, or, on the other, referring to real, biographical particular agents, upon whom only contingent and particular observations can be made. In outlining Beyleveld's development of a set of dialectically necessary principles that underpin the new conception of the Argument From the Sufficiency of Agency, I will concentrate on this attempt to 'privatise' the concept of agency. These principles are important in themselves, but in the context of working towards a successful account of agent recognition, I want to suggest that Beyleveld's contribution is also a response to something that we have seen to be of profound concern to Hegel. In the era of rampant privatisation I have in mind what is at stake in failing to acknowledge the philosophical consequences of equating 'agency' with *a will bereft of universal ethical personality*. The Argument from the Sufficiency of Agency then, as Beyleveld states in his response to privatisers in general and Williams in particular, must respond to the following:

> [An agent] must either conceive of himself as bound *only* by the particular contingent properties that make him the individual agent that he is or conceive of himself as bound *only* by the properties that make him an agent like any other agent.[41]

The defence begins by reflection on what Beyleveld considers to be the false dilemma introduced by Williams. In what Beyleveld refers to as 'The Principle of Reflective Judgement' (PRJ), an agent must accept that although he or she can and often must think of themselves as finite, particular agents distinguished by certain powers and characteristics from other agents, 'I cannot think of myself as *a* particular agent unless I think of myself as *an* agent, as possessing the properties and characteristics that make me and any other agent … *agents*'.[42] There is a second

[40] ibid, ch 4.

[41] D Beyleveld, 'Williams' False Dilemma: How to Give Categorically Binding Impartial Reasons to Real Agents' (2013) 10 *Journal of Moral Philosophy* 204.

[42] ibid, 208.

clarificatory principle we should consider: the Principle of Hypothetical Imperatives (PHI). Where the PRJ is logically analytic independently of practical issues, the PHI underpins the move from valuing one's ends to valuing one's means: 'If doing X (or having Y) is necessary for me to pursue or achieve E then I *ought to* do X (or ought to act to ensure that I obtain or keep Y), or give up my pursuit of E'. Acknowledging the PHI in the light of the PRJ is not just an awareness of the fact that if one misses the 6.45 pm bus to town one misses the start of the movie, it is an awareness of a dialectically necessary principle applicable to *all* agents in that the failure to employ and abide by it is *a failure to understand what it means to be an agent*. In fact, this failure of understanding gives us, in straightforwardly bi-conditional terms, the definition of what is meant by 'dialectically necessary'. Thus the key to understanding the power of the Argument From the Sufficiency of Agency lies in moving from a superficially 'prudential' understanding of universalising what is logically required in instrumental terms by particular agents for the more or less viable pursuit of their range of particular and contingent purposes, to an awareness that knowing what is necessarily required of one's behaviour in this *finite* mode stems from the essential properties that one possesses *qua* agent. Beyleveld illustrates the true operation of the Argument from the Sufficiency of Agency in the drama of Albert and Brenda.[43] Albert and Brenda are *agents*, and for this same sufficient reason it is dialectically necessary for each of them to defend their GCAs from interference against their will. This does not, says Beyleveld, mean simply that Albert must consider Brenda's claim to non-interference to be of equal status to his own claim; things are far more interesting than that. Beyleveld says,[44]

> Albert must consider that it is simply by virtue of his possession of the generic properties that make him an agent that he is duty bound to … defend his possession of the GCA's from interference against his will … But this means that Albert is required to take the fact that he is an agent (the fact that he has these generic properties, 'possesses agency in his person') as laying down the rules for *his* behaviour in relation to his possession of the GCA's. Albert must, in other words, recognise agency in his person (not as an end in itself—as Kant has it), but as the legislative authority that delegates to his (contingent) will supreme authority over what *he* may or may not do in relation to the disposal of his person. Equally, it is dialectically necessary for Albert to recognise that Brenda is required to recognise agency in her person as the legislative authority that delegates to her (contingent) will supreme authority over what she may or may not do in relation to disposal of her person.

IX. Conclusion

I cannot see anything in this articulation of what *must* be meant by mutual recognition ('dialogical' or otherwise) that would be logically inconsistent with Hegel's

[43] ibid.
[44] ibid, 218.

conceptual model of the striving personality. This 'inward' exploration of the universality of the free will is Kantianism modified by the lucidity of Beyleveld's insight into the Gewirthian project. Gewirthians, as Beyleveld suggests, should be Kantians and *vice versa*. We have discussed at length the anti-transcendental motivations of Hegel, and it is no surprise that a philosophy of the subject that sets itself from the outset against the critical self-sufficiency of the isolated and individual ego will reject this introspective path. But this bold gesture is costly. A *dialogical* model of rational justification in ethics must 'build in' just enough rationality in the individual will to facilitate an understanding of the importance of inter-subjective accounts of normative universality, but yet contrive to deny it the power to comprehend the genuinely universal aspects of its own practical nature. In giving an account of the transition from the 'abstract freedom' of the will into actual practical freedom in the world, we see that the logic of the transition demands that we recognise ourselves and others as essentially practical beings. And it is not at the level of empirical recognition and practical action that we find, as Hegel says, the 'true and proper ground in which freedom is existent', but 'by the Idea of the real existence of free personality, "real" here meaning "present in the will alone"'.[45] Recognition, says Hegel, is a relationship at the level of 'mind objective'. For Hegel this must mean the fully developed concept of the relationship between free beings. Thus from an ontological conception of Reason as we find in Hegel, or from a Cartesian or Kantian model of subjectivity, it means exactly the same thing to say that mutual recognition is *essentially* presupposed in the exercise of 'free personality'. Recognisable 'free personality' is *agency*—in the simple sense of the external demonstration of a practical will in purposive action in, and upon, the world. It is purposive in the sense of self-conscious manipulation, appropriation and control of the material world, and it is 'voluntary' in the superficial sense of a self-conscious 'desire' or decision to move from an abstract *potential* for action, to a condition of *actual* purposive activity. Ideal typically, or 'at the level of mind objective', the Hegelian 'person' knows, in recognising that its essence and potential lies in its initially *contentless* freedom, 'free of all specification', that this substance is thus equally and identically present in all *others* displaying practical intent. To recognise this formal essence of oneself as present in others is to recognise that all such beings must strive through intervention in and appropriation of the world to give content to this form. To recognise in *oneself* the rational ground of the demand for forbearance intrinsic to this practical activity in the world is, as Beyleveld shows in his careful re-iteration of the principles underpinning the Argument from the Sufficiency of Agency, to understand the ground as identical in other free beings. To exist as such a being for *another* is to be assured in all certainty of the *mutual recognition* of the *validity* and necessity of the claims intrinsic to the actualisation of freedom.

[45] Hegel, n 2, §71.

3

Identifying and Justifying Moral Norms: Necessary Basics

KENNETH R WESTPHAL*

I. Introduction

Alan Gewirth and Deryck Beyleveld have assiduously developed a three-stage dialectical analysis to justify adherence to the basic moral principle they call the Principle of Generic Consistency (PGC). This principle requires each of us to act in accord with everyone's right to access to and use of sufficient portions of the generic conditions required for our effective, human rational agency. Stage I argues that the Principle of Hypothetical Imperatives (PHI, governing instrumental rationality) entails that each of us is committed to our own access to and use of sufficient portions of the generic conditions of our own effective agency. Stage II argues that the result of Stage I commits each of us to willing that no one else hinder or thwart our own access to and use of sufficient portions of the generic conditions of our own effective agency. Stage III argues that, because these rights are generic, pertaining to any human agent as such, *as* an active agent though regardless of any particular ends anyone may have, we are each thus committed to respecting others' rights to access to and use of sufficient portions of the generic conditions of effective human agency. (Other generic conditions may pertain to other forms of agency, and other or further conditions may pertain to less than fully competent persons, but these I set aside to focus upon basics.)

Beyleveld focuses upon any rational agent's self-understanding as an agent, lacking which no agent can coherently assert or deny any normative claims.

* Professor of Philosophy, Boğaziçi Üniversitesi (İstanbul). I am very grateful to the organisers of the conference 'Ethical Rationalism and the Law', now the editors of this volume, Patrick Capps and Shaun Pattinson, for their very kind invitation to participate, and to the vigorous and instructive discussions there, to Deryck Beyleveld for his comments on that occasion and in subsequent (intensive) correspondence, as also to Marcus Düwell, who kindly provided funding for my travel and accommodation. The present research was generously supported in part by the Boğaziçi Üniversitesi Research Fund (BAP; grant code: 9761).

The central strategic point of Beyleveld's analysis is that, *qua* rational agent, anyone has an interest in sufficient, unimpeded access to and use of the generic conditions of agency (GCA; plural: GCAs), and that, *qua* rational agent s/he is subject to the Principle of Hypothetical Imperatives, and so must, *qua* rational agent, use *and* claim to make *rightful* use of those GCAs. Such use and rights claims can only be justified by appeal to the facts that S/he *is* an *agent* and that these are claims to unimpeded access to and use of sufficient portions of *generic* conditions of human agency. Hence understanding oneself as a rational agent able and entitled to set one's own aims, act to achieve them and to make any such claims requires understanding that these very same points hold for every one of us. Accordingly S/he cannot consistently deny to any other agent these same access, use or claim rights.

These stages and the links between them have been debated and refined ever since Gewirth published *Reason and Morality*, especially by Deryck Beyleveld's *The Dialectical Necessity of Morality*.[1] Yet recently Beyleveld reports new appreciation of the character and strength of their dialectical method. Speaking of representative rational human agents 'Albert' and 'Brenda', Beyleveld observes:

> that the coupling of Stage I with a commitment to complete impartiality requires Albert to grant the generic rights to Brenda itself entails that Stage II of the dialectically necessary argument is valid. This has not hitherto been appreciated either by Gewirthians (including myself) or by Gewirth's critics.[2]

It is considerable testimony to Beyleveld's acuity that 25 years of intensive research on these fundamental issues regarding basic moral principles, their identification and their justification continue to afford new insights into and refinements of his account of the dialectical necessities of morality.

My aim is dual: to distinguish Beyleveld's analysis of the dialectical necessity which commits any agent to the Principle of Generic Consistency from a distinct strategy of seeking to respond to the rational egoist's sceptical challenge to morality on that egoist's own terms. This strategic aim formed Gewirth's point of departure, and continues to form the basis for persisting misunderstandings of Beyleveld's subtle reconstruction and refinement of Gewirth's original strategy. Second: to compare and contrast Beyleveld's and Kant's strategies for identifying and justifying our most basic moral obligations, both ethical and juridical. Accordingly, I revisit rational egoism (Sections II and III) to underscore some distinctive features of Beyleveld's analysis (Section IV). I then examine how important morally are our self-understanding and character, and how Beyleveld's new 'Principle of Reflective Judgement' (PRJ) can and ought to be further developed to justify moral principles (Section V). As Hegel recognised, this involves returning to and further developing Kant's natural law constructivism.

[1] A Gewirth, *Reason and Morality* (University of Chicago Press, 1978)—hereafter *RM*; D Beyleveld, *The Dialectical Necessity of Morality: An Analysis and Defense of Alan Gewirth's Argument to the Principle of Generic Consistency* (University of Chicago Press, 1991)—hereafter *DNM*.

[2] D Beyleveld, 'The Principle of Generic Consistency as the Supreme Principle of Human Rights' (2012) 13 *Human Rights Review* 1, 7.

II. What Rational Egoists Seek in a Moral Theory

Much Anglophone moral philosophy in the preceding century has been preoccupied by rational egoism, just as epistemology has been preoccupied by Cartesian scepticism. The generic aim of most contemporary forms of moral constructivism is to construct a tenable moral theory using nothing but non-moral resources: empirical facts and non-moral principles of reasoning.[3] In moral philosophy as in epistemology, it has been widely assumed that to justify a principle, claim or action requires justifying it *to* some person(s), *on the basis* of his, her or their antecedent commitments (of whatever preferred variety). In moral philosophy this internalist presumption has been reinforced by the attempt to link justifying reasons closely to behavioural motives, and to conform with the belief-desire model of human action common (it is widely supposed) to empirical social sciences, especially economics.

It may appear that Gewirth's *Reason and Morality* is committed to just this framework because, in developing and justifying the PGC, the criteria of rationality that Gewirth employs in drawing these inferences are confined to 'the canons of deductive and inductive logic, including among the latter its bases in particular sense perception'.[4]

However, Gewirth's account of the generic conditions of our human rational agency, and what these conditions require of us as instrumentally rational individuals, is significantly richer than first appears. Central to Gewirth's and to Beyleveld's view is the Principle of Hypothetical Imperatives, that to achieve any end requires using necessary, jointly sufficient resources. This principle belongs neither to deductive nor to inductive logic, nor is it an analytic truth about agency *per se*. It holds, however, for any form of agency which cannot create what it seeks *ex nihilo*. Accordingly, the Principle of Hypothetical Imperatives holds of human willing. This does not rule out the possibility of our being fantasts, but underscores that fantasies are mere fancies, and neither results nor sufficient bases of effective action—and that none of us can be pure fantasts for very long, because we must tend to our nutritional requirements.

This elementary observation underscores that our self-understanding is central to our agency, to morality and to our being moral agents. Such considerations have become more pronounced in Beyleveld's recent work, and rightly so—for reasons I shall try to highlight by contrasting Beyleveld's analysis of the dialectical necessities of morality to more familiar (anti-)egoistic issues and strategies. Revisiting concerns raised by such critics as Scheuermann, Williams and Bittner about

[3] M Timmons, 'Constructivism, Moral' in DM Borchert (ed), *The Encyclopedia of Philosophy* (2nd rev edn, Thompson-Gale, 2006) 2: 471–73.

[4] *RM* 22.

rational egoism helps illuminate what kind of self-understanding is central to moral philosophy, and why so.[5]

Rational egoism highlights the question, what, if anything, justifies linking individual self-regarding prudential considerations to any specifically *moral* considerations or obligations? This concerns links between Stages II and III of the Gewirth/Beyleveld analysis. Their critics acknowledge that, as a matter of instrumental rationality, each individual agent—let's call her or him Sam (Samantha or Samuel as you wish)—must be committed to all others not interfering with Sam's own access to and use of sufficient portions of the generic conditions of human agency to achieve Sam's own chosen ends. Their critics also acknowledge that, in view of (very) rough equality amongst members of our species, a personal policy of non-interference with others' actions—so far as our actions are or can be made mutually compatible—is prudent.

In sum, prudential reasoning alone suffices to justify—prudentially, instrumentally—this first-person principle of non-interference [Principle 1]:

> Principle 1: I … must be opposed to courses of action that would remove my basic freedom.[6]

In this context, 'remove' covers any cases of restricting, hindering, blocking, infringing, violating or impeding one's basic freedom, which itself requires access to and use of sufficient portions of the generic conditions of one's own very human agency. In this regard, Beyleveld acknowledges that, 'if we are to show that there is a categorically binding *impartial* principle, [then] the reason why Albert and Brenda'—and our representative third party Sam—'must accept' each person's opposition 'to courses of action that would remove' one's own 'basic freedom':

> must be the same reason … and not merely a parallel one, because the reason why Albert must accept [Principle 1] must necessarily be a reason for Brenda to act as [likewise] must the reason why Brenda must accept [Principle 1] necessarily be a reason for Albert to act.[7]

A problem appears to arise in Beyleveld's introductory summary of his response to this point. In this connection he introduces this Principle of Reflective Judgement (PRJ):

> PRJ: For me (Albert) to think of myself as *a* particular real (ie finite, embodied) agent, I must think of myself as having the particular powers and characteristics that distinguish me from any other real agents that make me *the* particular agent that I am; but, equally, I cannot think of myself as *the* particular agent I am without recognising that I am *a* particular agent, and I cannot think of myself as *a* particular

[5] J Scheuermann, 'Gewirth's Concept of Prudential Rights' (1987) 37 *Philosophical Quarterly* 291–304; B Williams, *Ethics and the Limits of Philosophy* (Fontana, 1985), ch 4; and R Bittner, *What Reason Demands* (CUP, 1989).

[6] D Beyleveld, 'Williams' False Dilemma: How to Give Categorically Binding Impartial Reasons to Real Agents' 10 (2013) *Journal of Moral Philosophy* 204, 206.

[7] ibid, 206.

> agent unless I think of myself as *an* agent, as possessing the properties and characteristics that make me and any other agent (eg Brenda) *agents*.[8]

Beyleveld reiterates that the generic conditions of agency and Principle 1 hold of any and all human agents, *as* the particular agents they are. Speaking of the Self-Regarding Obligations (SRO) holding of Albert and Brenda (indicated by 'A' and 'B' suffixes: SROA, SROB), Beyleveld previews his rejoinder to Williams, stating:

> what is binding on Albert as *an* agent is also binding on him as *the* particular agent that he is. But, because [Principle 1] is justified relative to Albert's possession of the generic properties that make him *an* agent, the parallel prescription, [Principle 1] … which Brenda must hold, is justified relative to her possession of the same properties. Consequently both SROA and SROB will be categorically binding on both Albert and Brenda as real agents, which means that Albert and Brenda are categorically bound to defend any agent's possession of the GCAs from interference against that agent's will, which renders Gewirth's PGC the supreme practical principle for real agents.[9]

Beyleveld's characterisation of his rejoinder may appear to equivocate about types and tokens. As a generic principle of instrumental rationality and as generic conditions of human agency, Principle 1 and the generic conditions of agency pertain equally to each and to any human agent. What concerns egoist, individualist and sceptical critics of Gewirthian and Kantian moral philosophy is that these generic principles and conditions only secure each individual's token-reason for each of their first-person cases. Nothing in the generic *type*-identity of the principles or conditions of instrumentally rational agency secures Sam's having a first-person reason for acting in consideration of anyone *else's* instrumental rationality, conditions (GCAs) or commitments. This is the opening bargaining position of game theory and of Gauthier's radical contractarianism.[10]

Can this rejoinder be rebutted? If so, how and how well? The refinement presented in Beyleveld's recent paper lies in more clearly articulating 'the interrelationship between the dialectically necessary and prudential (categorically instrumental) commitments of agents'.[11]

Granting that principles of instrumental rationality—centrally: the Principle of Hypothetical Imperatives (PHI)—commits each of us to having an interest in, and wanting, unimpeded access to and use of sufficient portions of the generic conditions for our own human agency, the following imperative—a 'self-regarding ought' (SRO)—is prudentially, instrumentally rationally justified to and for each finite human agent:

> Principle 2: I ought to oppose unwilled interference with my having the GCAs.[12]

[8] ibid, 208.
[9] ibid, 208–09.
[10] D Gauthier, *Morals by Agreement* (Clarendon, 1986); *Moral Dealing* (Cornell University Press, 1990); 'Political Contractarianism' (1997) 5 *Journal of Political Philosophy* 132.
[11] Beyleveld, 'Williams' False Dilemma', n 5, 209.
[12] ibid, 214.

This is Step (4) in Beyleveld's rejoinder to Williams. It is agreed that, for this reason, each of us has an instrumentally justified interest in all others' non-interference with our own activities, and that prudentially considered, it is generally most likely we can expect others to comply with our need for and interest in their non-interference only if we reciprocally refrain from interfering with their activities and counter-part need. The crux comes in trying to show that each of our obligations to refrain from interfering with others in these regards does not reduce to these entirely instrumental, prudential, individualistically first-person considerations which hold only distributively of and for each of us. How Beyleveld shows this requires distinguishing the 'dialectical necessities' central to his analysis from typical anti-egoist strategies.

III. Arguing from the Sufficiency of Agency: Terms and Tokens

In reply to Singer, Beyleveld allowed Gewirth to 'label these prescriptions in any way that he likes, provided that he explains what he means'.[13] That is too generous; incautious terminology courts confusion and fallacy, especially when such important issues are at stake as the relations between egoism, prudence, prescription and morality.[14] Accordingly, I dissent from Beyleveld's stated indifference regarding whether these prescriptions are 'moral' or 'prudential'.[15] Gewirth may 'mean' that Sam must hold that S/he is committed to others not interfering with her or his own sufficient access to and use of the generic conditions of agency, and Gewirth may 'mean' that Sam must be committed to the principle that 'others ought not to interfere with my own sufficient access to and use of the generic conditions of agency', but that is still at most a prudential 'ought', not a moral 'ought', and whether Sam must be so committed to *imputing* that prudential 'ought' to others does not, by itself, show that any others *are* so obligated to refrain, whether prudentially or morally. Beyleveld there states:

> According to Gewirth's argument, I must hold that you ought not to interfere with my generic needs against my will. If you ask me why you should comply, I will *offer* as justification that this is in my interests. *From my viewpoint as an agent*, it is entirely appropriate to express this as 'You have sufficient reason not to interfere with my generic needs', meaning 'From my point of view as an agent, my demand that you not interfere with my generic [needs] is a strictly justified demand'.[16]

[13] D Beyleveld, 'A Reply to Marcus G Singer on "Gewirth, Beyleveld and Dialectical Necessity"' (2002) 15 *Ratio Juris* 458, 463.

[14] *cf* O O'Neill, 'Kant: Rationality as Practical Reason' in AJ Mele and P Rawling (eds), *The Oxford Handbook of Rationality* (OUP, 1994); A Wood, 'Kant on Practical Reason' in M Timmons and S Baiasu (eds), *Kant on Practical Justification: Interpretive Essays* (OUP, 2013).

[15] Beyleveld 'Reply to Singer', n 13, 467.

[16] ibid, 465.

Here appears an issue about agent-relative reasons reflected in the type/token ambiguity noted above (Section II): that I have sufficient reason *for me* to claim you should do or omit some act is not *your* reason, even if you have sufficient reason regarding what I should do or omit in regard to you, regardless of whether these alleged prescriptions are understood to be moral or merely prudential, and regardless of whether these prescriptive commitments are warranted only by generic considerations of human agency (and so in this sense are 'categorical', though conditional upon our generic human form of agency, instantiated respectively in each of us). This same circumstance appears to recur in Beyleveld's reply to Chitty, in steps (7), (9); the inference from (5) and (6) to (7) appears to establish no more than a prudential prescription, and only to establish it first-person.[17]

The sceptical egoist reply is twofold: As an agent, each of us may have sufficient prudential and instrumental interests and reasons to assert or to claim access to and use of sufficient portions of the generic conditions of human agency, but formulating these reasons, assertions, claims or prescriptions in terms of 'rights' and 'duties' is merely a terminological achievement, but no justification of specifically *moral* rights or duties. Prudential prescription comes easy; specifically *moral* prescription must be earned. Furthermore, that each agent has these (so far merely nominal) 'rights' does not demonstrate that any agent has a *duty* to act according to anyone else's (putative) 'rights', even if these (putative) rights and duties are generically of the same kind for each agent. That the relevant conditions of agency are generic (by stipulation) ensures that each and any human agent has generically the same need for and interest in sufficient access to and use of those conditions (resources). However, nothing *in* the 'Argument from the Sufficiency of Agency' (ASA) at Stage II justifies the specifically *moral* status of those needs, interests or claims; expressly so.[18] What requires justification is the link between GCAs, the PHI and any specifically *moral* prescriptions holding of human agents generally (in Kant's terms, holding with collective, not distributive, generality), and of their specifically moral prescription as duties each individual agent owes to others. Here Russell's rebuke to Dedekind appears pertinent: presupposition has all the advantages over deduction that theft has over honest toil.[19]

Sceptical egoists may grant that being a finite semi-rational human agent involves my acting toward ends by using various means, that doing so effectively requires the PHI and that these two claims entail that each of us has an interest in securing sufficient access to and use of generic conditions of one's own agency. They may further grant that these three considerations suffice to warrant (justify) a self-regarding prescription that each of us ought to act so as to secure

[17] D Beyleveld and G Bos, 'The Foundational Role of the Principle of Instrumental Reason in Gewirth's Argument for the Principle of Generic Consistency: A Response to Andrew Chitty' (2009) 20 *Kings Law Journal* 1, 6.

[18] *DNM* 29, 30, 33, 36, 42.

[19] B Russell, *Introduction to Mathematical Philosophy* (George Allen & Unwin, 1919) 71.

and protect our own sufficient access to and use of the generic conditions of agency. (These points are formulated to accord with Beyleveld's presentation.)[20] Their question is: How, exactly, are 'rights' or 'duties'—as a specifically moral classification of prescription—to be justified on these grounds alone? The 'deliberator neutrality' of these considerations appears only to show that these same considerations hold distributively for each individual human agent.[21] There appears to be a type/token ambiguity in the Gewirthian reasoning. Precisely because, on that reasoning, each of us 'must judge that I have the generic'—not (moral) 'rights', but rather: needs and interests—'that are validated relative to my interests', shows nothing about what may or may not be *my* moral *duties* towards any other agent who, *qua* agent, falls under the same pattern of first-person, instrumental, entirely prudential reasoning. Exactly what reasons justify such claims as *rightful* or such prescriptions as *moral* remains to be specified, or so it appears from the egocentric amoral ('adeonticist') predicament.

IV. The Distinctively Dialectical Necessity of Moral Claims

Beyleveld argues that each of us has *two* reasons to comply with generic rights of all agents to unimpeded access to and use of sufficient portions of the generic conditions of our human agency. One reason lies in the merely prudential, instrumental reason detailed above (Sections II, III). Beyleveld aims to show that

> it is irrelevant that 'I necessarily want my basic freedom' does not universalise to 'I necessarily want your basic freedom'.[22]

The second reason is that it is 'dialectically necessary' for each of us to exercise such forbearance, which reason 'takes precedence' over the merely prudential reason. How so? In this regard Beyleveld identifies this conditional necessity:

> CIA (= 'I categorically instrumentally need to have the GCAs in order to achieve the purposes I choose to pursue') [.][23]

The necessity of this need is conditional, not upon any particular aim one chooses to pursue, nor upon the entire collection of such aims one chooses to pursue during one's lifetime. This need is necessary for each and any of us *qua* finite rational agent, in order to be at all *able* to choose ends, make claims (whether assertoric

[20] Beyleveld and Bos, n 17, 14.
[21] *cf* ibid, 15.
[22] Beyleveld 'Williams' False Dilemma', n 6, 217.
[23] ibid, 217.

or prescriptive, whether narrowly prudential or moral) or to act to achieve any end(s) whatever. Referring to the second principle quoted above (Section II), specifically:

> Principle 2: I ought to oppose unwilled interference with my having the GCAs,[24]

Beyleveld's key point appears to be this:

> [Principle 2] is derived from 'It is dialectically necessary for me to structure my practical reasoning in accordance with the [Principle of Hypothetical Imperatives, PHI]' coupled with CIA, which coupling provides the dialectically necessary PHI with a dialectically necessary substantive content.[25]

Specifying this 'dialectically necessary substantive content' requires some care.

Centrally, the 'dialectical necessity' for which Beyleveld argues avoids the issues noted about types and tokens because he does not seek to demonstrate anyone else's rights or obligations based upon one's own first-person needs, claims, rights or obligations. His analysis of the relevant 'dialectical necessity' is entirely first-person. Because his analysis of dialectical necessity focuses upon *generic* conditions of agency, it holds of all agents because it holds likewise for each. Accordingly, the 'dialectical necessities' at issue hold for each, any and every agent. Specifically, these dialectical necessities highlight what Sam must understand about her- or himself in order to understand her- or himself as *an* agent. To *act* at all requires understanding oneself to be an agent (however implicitly or inadequately). In order to understand her- or himself as *an* agent, Sam must understand that S/he is one particular agent, of whom the generic features and conditions of agency hold. To understand this requires *understanding* that the very same considerations regarding one's own agency likewise hold of any and all other agents. Because Beyleveld's analysis focuses upon *generic* conditions of agency, there can be no distinguishing feature(s) of any agent which make Sam morally exceptional in any regard which entitles Sam to liberties or rights, nor which impose upon Sam obligations or duties, which any other agents lack.

The *dialectical* necessities lie in avoiding contradictions between one's own attitudes, were one to claim liberties or rights one denies to others (or fails to recognise in their case), or to deny (or fail to recognise) one's own obligations or duties which one claims against others. The point of CIA (quoted at the start of this section) is that to *be* a human agent at all requires one to have access to and use of sufficient portions of the generic conditions of being a human agent, whatever these are. (Food, water, air and shelter count; factories, no.) To pursue any end whatever requires acting in accord with the principle of hypothetical

[24] ibid, 214.
[25] ibid, 217.

imperatives, where so acting—in any case, even the speech acts which make or deny any claim whatever (whether an assertion, a prudential prescription or a rights claim)—requires that we now have and use—and up to now have had and have used—sufficient portions of the generic conditions of human agency. This is a conditional necessity, regardless of any end or aim one may have (including any choice or act of suicide). This conditional necessity commits each of us, regardless of whether we acknowledge or claim it (either prudentially or morally), to having and exercising our access to and use of sufficient portions of the generic conditions of human agency. To understand (rather than mis-understand) ourselves *as* human agents requires understanding this conditional necessity. Understanding this conditional necessity requires understanding that it holds of oneself just as it does of any and every other human agent, simply because we each *are* human agents, who accordingly (in view of our limited, vulnerable finitude) each equally require access to and use of sufficient portions of the generic conditions of human agency.

In this regard, the attitudinal consistency important to Beyleveld's analysis is not only consistency amongst one's claims or avowals; such an explicit basis could be evaded by any egoist sufficiently sly to avoid various avowals or to avoid holding various morally relevant beliefs or attitudes. Attitudes relevant to Beyleveld's analysis of the 'dialectical necessity' of morality are exhibited by any goal-directed rational behaviour.

The key reason why Sam has the liberties, rights or obligations under consideration is that Sam is *an agent*; this is *the same* reason in each agent's first-person case (collectively: as the class 'agent' they each instantiate); it is not merely a parallel token-reason holding for each agent individually (distributively or disjunctively). In this regard, Beyleveld's analysis accords with Kant's attention to the distinction and the relations between distributive and collective forms of universality, especially in connection with basic rights and freedoms.[26] In this regard, Beyleveld's analysis also accords with an important, oft neglected feature of Kant's analysis of the 'categorical' character of these prescriptions: These prescriptions hold regardless of any particular wants or desires anyone may have, whether distributively or collectively; they hold insofar as one is a *finite* rational agent who can only achieve or attain ends by using means (including bodily comportment in space and time).

In this way, Beyleveld's analysis justifies a series of biconditional claims regarding agency and any agent's sufficient access to and use of generic conditions of agency (GCAs). In formulating these biconditionals, I use 'shall' and 'ought' to

[26] See I Kant, *Gesammmelte Schriften* [23: 320–24]; for discussion, see BJ Edwards, 'Disjunktiv- und Kollektiv-allgemeiner Besitz: Bemerkungen zu Kants Theorie der ursprünglichen Erwerbung' in B Tuschling and D Hünning, *Kants Metaphysik des Rechts* (Duncker & Humblot, 1998).

distinguish between prudential and moral prescriptions. I use 'require' and 'must' to indicate the necessity of the commitment to the specified claim as constitutive to understanding oneself as an agent who achieves ends by employing sufficient means (PHI). Each of these constitutive claims is necessary; none is sufficient, not even taken together. ('→' designates logical entailment; '≡' designates biconditionality: 'if and only if'; braces '{…}' indicate that these claims are 'dialectically necessary' for each agent; '*S*' designates any individual human agent.) Sam is committed to these claims by understanding her- or himself as *an agent*, where such self-understanding is manifest in acting in any instrumentally rational way. *Adequate* self-understanding would involve affirming these biconditionals.[27] I present these biconditionals graphically to make visible their structure; they include:

(1) {I am an agent → I require GCAs} ≡ {*S* is an agent → *S* requires GCAs}

(2) {I am an agent → PHI holds of me} ≡ {*S* is an agent → PHI holds of *S*}

(3) {I am an agent → others shall not interfere with my GCAs}
≡ {*S* is an agent → I shall not interfere with *S*'s GCAs}

(4) {I am an agent → I shall defend my GCAs against unpermitted interference by others}
≡ {*S* is an agent → *S* shall defend *S*'s GCAs against my unpermitted interference}

(5) {I am an agent → I ought to defend my GCAs against interference by others}
≡ {*S* is an agent → *S* ought to defend *S*'s GCAs against my interference}

(6) {I am an agent → others ought not to interfere with my GCAs}
≡ {*S* is an agent → I ought not to interfere with *S*'s GCAs}

(7) {I am an agent → I ought not to interfere with others' GCAs}
≡ {*S* is an agent → *S* ought not to interfere with my GCAs}

These biconditional claims are supported by Beyleveld's 'Argument for Dialectically Necessary Mutual Recognition'.[28]

This new argument presents an important consideration not yet mentioned: Our self-regarding imperatives are all based upon each of us regarding ourselves as 'the supreme authority over what [we ourselves] may or may not do in relation to disposal of [our own] person'.[29] This 'supreme authority' over one's own disposal

[27] I say 'involve'; affirming these biconditionals would not constitute adequate self-understanding.
[28] Beyleveld, 'Williams' False Dilemma', n 6, 218–19.
[29] ibid.

of one's own person is said to be a 'legislative authority' exercised by one's own will in one's own regard. This disposal involves one's disposal over one's access to and use of sufficient portions of the generic conditions of agency. These considerations afford three further biconditional claims:

(8) {I am an agent → I have supreme legislative authority over disposing of my own person}

≡ {*S* is an agent → *S* has supreme legislative authority over disposing of *S*'s own person}

(9) {I am an agent → others shall respect my supreme legislative authority over the disposition of my own person}

≡ {*S* is an agent → I shall respect *S*'s supreme legislative authority over the disposition of *S*'s own person}

(10) {I am an agent → others ought to respect my supreme legislative authority over the disposition of my own person}

≡ {*S* is an agent → I ought to respect *S*'s supreme legislative authority over the disposition of *S*'s own person}

The entire analysis turns on *generic* conditions of human agency, on one's access to and use of sufficient generic resources (GCAs) to *be* an agent, and on one's own effective conduct (in accord with PHI) in any instance whatever. Consequently, claims justified in the first-person case are *equally*, and equally *well* justified in Sam's (Albert's, Brenda's) case. Conversely no one can consistently maintain one's own claim, nor can one so much as *act* and so exploit these preconditions, whilst denying, neglecting or violating anyone else's counter-part claim.[30] One's token (first-person) reason *is* one reason holding of and for *all* finite human agents.

Beyleveld's dialectical analysis shows that anyone who claims a moral right to liberty from unpermitted or 'un-willed' interference with one's access to and use of suitable portions of the generic conditions of agency cannot consistently deny or violate a counterpart moral claim made by any other agent(s). However, moral sceptics and rational egoists will want to know whether, why or by what justification Sam can or does make any specifically *moral* claim, about what anyone else *ought* (not) to do, and they will want to know what (if anything) justifies anyone else so acting (or refraining). Alternatively, moral sceptics or rational egoists may rejoin that 'morality' is merely a nice name for enlightened self-interest; that nothing justifies formulating our claims as *moral* 'oughts' rather than as

[30] Beyleveld, 'Williams' False Dilemma', n 6, 218; *cf* D Beyleveld, 'The Principle of Generic Consistency as the Supreme Principle of Human Rights', n 2, 6–8.

enlightened, mutually regarding prudential 'shalls'; or put otherwise, that nothing justifies these as specifically *moral* claims rather than interest claims. To pose and address these sceptical concerns, in (1)–(10) I have distinguished prudential and moral considerations terminologically by distinguishing 'shall' and 'ought', reserving the latter for moral prescriptions. Drawing this distinction is important to determine whether or how Beyleveld's analysis meets the challenges posed by amoralists, egoists, radical individualists or adeonticists.

One point Beyleveld rightly stresses in this regard is that these claims (1–10) hold categorically of each and any human agent, regardless of any particular wants or desires Sam may have, conditional only upon Sam *being* an agent. In contrast, prudentialist reasoning about long-term enlightened self-interest issues only hypothetical imperatives, based upon anyone's *de facto* interest in or desire for long-term maximisation of individual utility, in the form of maximally satisfying one's various chosen ends. The moral status of principles (5)–(7) and (10), which I have formulated using 'ought' rather than 'shall', is due to these prescriptions being conditionally necessary for any and every human agent simply in virtue of Sam *being* a finite human agent. One's token (first-person) reason *is* one reason holding of and for *all* finite human agents. This is the first point concerning the moral status of the prescriptions identified and justified by Beyleveld's analysis.

V. Self-understanding, Moral Character and the Character of Morality

I understand Beyleveld's doubts about some aspects of Kant's views he finds implausible.[31] I am much more sanguine about Kant's views, because in several important regards Kant succeeded in formulating and justifying much more cogent (and sufficient) views than some on which he officially staked central features of his moral philosophy, and he succeeds in these regards without invoking transcendental idealism.[32] One oversight merits correction. Against Kant's analysis of freedom of the will in *Groundwork* §3, Beyleveld and Brownsword contend that 'a will would not cease to be an efficient cause of action just because it itself had an efficient cause'.[33] This neglects Kant's express point that a *will* acts in view of

[31] D Beyleveld and R Brownsword, *Human Dignity in Bioethics and Biolaw* (OUP, 2001) 100–05.

[32] KR Westphal, 'Norm Acquisition, Rational Judgment and Moral Particularism' 10 (2012) *Theory & Research in Education* 3; KR Westphal, *How Hume and Kant Reconstruct Natural Law: Justifying Strict Objectivity* without *Debating Moral Realism* (Clarendon, 2016); KR Westphal, 'How Kant Justifies Freedom of Agency *without* Transcendental Idealism' 24 (2016) *European Journal of Philosophy* (forthcoming).

[33] Beyleveld and Brownsword, n 31, 103.

principles, not in reaction to occasioning causes.[34] Kant's account of freedom of the will stands independently of his transcendental idealism.[35] I shall not detail Kant's views here, but instead highlight some other features of the 'dialectical' character of Beyleveld's reasoning, features which I think can be developed much more effectively.

Above (Section II) I noted Gewirth's aim to address rational egoists and moral sceptics persuaded they must work within the confines of empiricist resources of logic and sensory evidence. Those do not exhaust his resources; Beyleveld highlights issues of what is and what is not 'logically *impermissible*' for us as agents to espouse.[36] Regarding the relation between universal human rights and the principle of generic consistency, Beyleveld recently noted that it would be

> insincere to declare that Albert has a right to do something yet deny Albert a right to possess the means necessary for him to exercise that right.[37]

Another expression for such insincerity is hypocrisy. In a detailed, published remark on various forms of self-serving rationalisation, and those which count specifically as hypocrisy, Hegel noted that the once common charge of 'hypocrisy' had fallen into disuse.[38] It has long since vanished, perhaps altogether, after more than a century of egregious hypocrisy on the part of too many occupants of high (or mighty) office. Beyleveld rightly highlights the importance of sincerity and what ought still to be designated and honoured as moral integrity, embracing both ethics and justice. In this I join not only Beyleveld but also Kant and Hegel, both of whom recognised that moral principles—both of ethics and justice—exist and are effective only insofar as we understand them and act accordingly.[39]

[34] I Kant, *Groundwork of the Metaphysics of Morals* [4: 41].

[35] See KR Westphal, 'How Kant Justifies Freedom', n 32; for defence of Kant's analysis of freedom in *Groundwork* §3, see M Wolff, 'Warum der kategorische Imperativ nach Kants Ansicht gültig ist. Eine Beschreibung der Argumentationsstruktur im Dritten Abschnitt seiner *Grundlegung zur Metaphysik der Sitten*' in D Schönecker (ed), *Kants Begründung von Freiheit und Moral in Grundlegung III*". *Neue Interpretationen* (Mentis, 2015).

[36] *DNM* 48, 145.

[37] D Beyleveld, 'The Principle of Generic Consistency as the Supreme Principle of Human Rights', n 2, 7.

[38] GWF Hegel, *Grundlinien der Philosophie des Rechts oder Naturrecht und Staatswissenschaft im Grundrisse* (Nicolai, 1821) §140R¶e; *Elements of the Philosophy of Right* (A Wood (ed), HB Nisbet (tr), CUP, 1991).

[39] KR Westphal, 'Hegel' in J Skorupski (ed), *The Routledge Companion to Ethics* (Routledge, 2010) 168. I cannot omit noting that revisions on this paper were made as ISIS shocked the Occident by its triple terrorist attack in Paris. ISIS owes its very existence—and much of its armaments—to GW Bush's overweaning desire to be a wartime president. Precautionary reasoning is vital to morals, to justice and to politics—and justice, nationally and internationally, is vital to peace. These are not someone else's problems; these are *our* problems. We can only win the peace by investing personnel and materiel in securing sufficient access to and use of the generic conditions of agency for *everyone*, not just for our clan, faction, country or club. On precautionary reasoning, see D Beyleveld and R Brownsword, 'Principle, Proceduralism, and Precaution in a Community of Rights' 19 (2006) *Ratio Juris* 141; D Beyleveld and R Brownsword, 'Complex Technology, Complex Calculations: Uses and Abuses of Precautionary Reasoning in Law' in P Sollie and M Düwell (eds), *Evaluating New Technologies* (Springer, 2009); D Beyleveld and SD Pattinson, 'Defending Moral Precaution as a Solution to the Problem of Other Minds: A Reply to Holm and Coggon' 23 (2010) *Ratio Juris* 258.

What, exactly, is the character and the status of conclusions demonstrated to be 'dialectically necessary' by Beyleveld's analysis? How, exactly, are the attitudes and commitments established by such analysis related to Sam's actual moral responsibilities? Because Beyleveld's analysis explicates implications of any agent's acting in any instrumentally rational way, without appeal to an agent's avowals or reasons, that analysis is highly subjunctive and appears to turn on imputing commitments and consequent duties to that agent. Why not simply impute moral duties to the agent? Indeed, the dialectical analysis appears to turn on our *being* subject to imputation, simply insofar as we can and do *act* in any instrumentally rational way. This is why Kant is correct to stress that a *will* counts as rational insofar as it can act upon a *conception* of lawful regularity: a will can *act* on principles, not merely *react* to occasioning causes.[40] Kant's justification of usufruct need not dwell upon generic conditions of agency, by focusing instead upon our very human finitude: we can create nothing *ex nihilo*, but must act by using space, time and materials surrounding us. The only conditions under which we can use our surroundings *legitimately* is by recognising that in claiming use of anything we obligate ourselves to respect counterpart claims by all others, who are likewise governed by these same conditions of action, legitimacy and self-obligation.[41]

Here lies a further generic condition of human agency: What conditions enable us to understand and use any rational principles or sensory evidence? How can *we* human beings actualise our capacity to act upon principles (even empirical principles) and thus to *be* imputable agents? Only insofar as we are raised and educated by others, and (focusing now upon practical principles) only insofar as action-guiding principles are instituted, observed and maintained by the societies in which we live—so that those principles, including principles of evidence, can *be* used at all—are *any* of us at all able to understand and use any rational principles or sensory evidence whatever. Here is where Gewirthians should join Kant and Hegel by grasping the self-serving egoistic bull by the horns: Egoists, too, require others for their birth, nurture, education and for many of their typical, ordinary actions[42]—quite aside from their anti-social, sociopathic deceitful acts which exploit social practices and others' vulnerabilities.[43]

[40] I Kant, *Groundwork to the Metaphysics of Morals* [4: 412].

[41] KR Westphal, 'Do Kant's Principles Justify Property or Usufruct?' 5 (1997) *Jahrbuch für Recht und Ethik/Annual Review of Law and Ethics* 141; KR Westphal, *Hume and Kant Reconstruct Natural Law*, n 32, §§36–38.

[42] See B Herman, *Moral Literacy* (Harvard University Press, 2007) 130–53; KR Westphal, 'Norm Acquisition', n 32, KR Westphal, 'Hegel's Natural Law Constructivism: Progress in Principle and in Practice' in S Stein and T Brooks (eds), *Hegel's Political Philosophy: On the Normative Significance of Method and System* (OUP, 2016).

[43] Beyleveld denies that these conditions for nurture, education or (just below) the social and institutional preconditions of individual human agency and action belong to the generic conditions of agency. On this count I must request more precise specification of which conditions of agency are generic (but not others), and why so. Likewise, greater clarity and specificity about just what is, and what is not, 'internal' to any individual agent's first-person point of view—and exactly why so—would be most welcome, not least because egoists and moral empiricists only regard any agent's own aims and

The key to Kant's universalisation tests—as Hegel too argued—lies not in whether there are any incommensurable values, nor whether we—of all unholy beings!—may merit the incommensurable value Kant called the 'dignity'—not of human, but of *rational* nature. Kant's universalisation tests stand independently of such issues about values, motives, agents' beliefs or noumenal freedom. The key—both for theoretical and for practical philosophy—lies where Onora O'Neill identified it.[44] Due to our very finite rational powers and our mutual interdependence for our information and other material and conceptual resources, a key *conditio sine qua non* for the rational justification of any principle, judgement or claim in all non-formal domains (that is, outside pure axiomatics) is that sufficient justifying grounds for it *can* be addressed to *all* other concerned, that is, affected, parties. We are very dependent, very interdependent, fundamentally social creatures. What no one can justify rationally is to arrogate to him- or herself generic entitlements S/he denies to anyone else. Insofar as specific, differential entitlements can be justified, they can only be justified within social systems which conscientiously accredit those entitlements according to earned, demonstrated merit or competence.[45] Impartiality is justified, ultimately, by Kant's *conditio sine qua non* for rational justification in all non-formal domains.[46] This very same *conditio* is justified by Hegel's analysis of mutual recognition and its fundamental role in rational justification.[47]

Beyleveld's Principle of Reflective Judgement (PRJ; above, Section II) requires one further step. Each of us must indeed understand ourselves as the particular yet *human* agent S/he is, yet to understand ourselves adequately and to act with appropriate integrity, each of us must recognise that we each can only *be* a rational agent insofar as *we together* are rational agents. Impartiality, and also permissible (justifiable) cases of partiality, follow as close corollaries, as does Rousseau's *conditio sine qua non* of legitimate social institutions: recognising in theory and safeguarding in practice sufficient individual security and well-being so that each person can co-operate with others only voluntarily; that is, that no one be allowed the kind or extent of power or wealth by which S/he can unilaterally

motivational set as 'internal' to that agent's first-person point of view. With all due respect, it appears that some reasons for persisting disagreements or misunderstandings are expository. A further question in this regard is, if the 'dialectical' analysis is conducted first-person, why is any reference to anyone else's claims relevant? Why not seek to demonstrate first person that one's own claim directly entails one's own obligation to respect anyone else's counter-part claim?

[44] O O'Neill, *Constructions of Reason* (CUP, 1989) 81–125, 138–39; O O'Neill, 'Vindicating Reason' in P Guyer (ed), *The Cambridge Companion to Kant* (CUP, 1992).

[45] Or perhaps distribute them on a rotating basis by lots, as (eg) many ancient Greek polities did with public offices.

[46] See KR Westphal, 'Kant: Vernunftkritik, Konstruktivismus and Besitzrecht' in J-C Merle and ATG Trivisonno (eds), *Kant's Theory of Law* Beiheft 143 (2015) *Archiv für Rechts- und Sozialphilosophie*, 57; KR Westphal, *Hume and Kant Reconstruct Natural Law*, n 32.

[47] KR Westphal, 'Rational Justification and Mutual Recognition in Substantive Domains' 53.1 (2014) *Dialogue: Canadian Journal of Philosophy/Revue canadienne de philosophie*, 57–96.

command the choice and action of anyone else.[48] This is Kant's 'sole innate right' to freedom, which expressly includes independence from others' unilateral will.[49] This independence requirement is equally fundamental to Hegel's uncompromising (lower-case 'r') republicanism.[50] These basic features of our mutual interdependence and our consequent obligations have been occluded by a century of ideological nonsense.[51]

Gewirthians should look to Kant's greatest student, Hegel.[52] Kant's and Hegel's method for identifying and justifying basic moral principles I call 'Natural Law Constructivism'. It is demonstrative and assertoric, rather than 'dialectical' in Beyleveld's sense. Basic features of our very finite, mutually interdependent, semi-rational agency, together with Kant's *conditio sine qua non* for rational justification within all non-formal domains and his universalisation tests, suffice to identity fundamental moral duties and rights—both ethical and juridical, both perfect and imperfect—beginning with the crucial test case of usufruct. Natural Law Constructivism succeeds in these regards, without taking—and without needing to take—any stand on moral (ir)realism or human motivation. As for aligning motivation and character with moral requirements, that is a primary assignment of education, both formal and informal.[53] There I must leave matters for the present; I look forward to Deryck's rejoinder!

[48] KR Westphal, 'Natural Law, Social Contract and Moral Objectivity: Rousseau's Natural Law Constructivism' (2013) 4 *Jurisprudence* 48.

[49] I Kant, *Metaphysics of Morals* [6: 237].

[50] KR Westphal, 'Hegel's Natural Law Constructivism', n 42.

[51] KR Westphal, 'Substantive Philosophy, Infallibilism and the Critique of Metaphysics: Hegel and the Historicity of Philosophical Reason' in L Herzog (ed), *Hegel's Thought in Europe: Currents, Cross-Currents and Undercurrents* (Palgrave-Macmillan, 2013); KR Westphal, *Hume and Kant Reconstruct Natural Law*, n 32, §41.

[52] KR Westphal, 'Hegel', n 39.

[53] See T Green, *Voices: The Educational Formation of Conscience* (University of Notre Dame Press, 1999); R Curren, *Aristotle on the Necessity of Public Education* (Rowman & Littlefield, 2000), R Curren, 'Education as a Social Right in a Diverse Society' (2009) 6 *Journal of Philosophy of Education* 337; R Curren, *Education for Sustainable Development: A Philosophical Assessment* (PESGB Impact Series 2009, rpt Wiley Online Library, 2011), R Curren, 'Aristotle's Educational Politics and the Aristotelian Renaissance in Philosophy of Education' (2010) 36 *Oxford Review of Education* 543; KR Westphal, 'Norm Acquisition', n 32.

4

Hope, Agency, and Aesthetic Sensibility: A Response to Beyleveld's Account of Kantian Hope

DASCHA DÜRING* AND MARCUS DÜWELL**

Heralded by Ernst Bloch in 1954 and Karl Menninger in 1959, the past decades have known an increase in especially psychiatric and psychological research focusing on hope. 'Philosophy will have conscience of tomorrow, commitment to the future, knowledge of hope, or it will have no more knowledge', exclaimed Bloch in his attempt to give Minerva's owl wings to spread at daybreak.[1] 'We have a duty,' said Karl Menninger in his famous address, 'to speak up as scientists, not about a new rocket or a new fuel or a new bomb or a new gas, but about this ancient but rediscovered truth, the validity of Hope in human development'.[2]

Other than in the above-mentioned sciences, the question of hope in philosophy still generally seems to be regarded as a marginal issue. Deryck Beyleveld, inspired by Immanuel Kant, has taken quite the opposite stance: he has argued that hope—or more specifically, the capacity to hope and fear—forms a necessary *a priori* condition for the possibility of coherent (self-)understanding as such. In this chapter we aim to take up this claim and develop it further. After briefly introducing how the nature and role of hope are discussed in contemporary discourse, we turn to Beyleveld's understanding of hope and fear as primordially directed towards the *summum bonum*—towards the idea of the highest good. We endorse Beyleveld's suggestion that the challenge here is to think hope and fear in a way that can neither be reduced to *belief* nor to *faith*, but is rather characterised by a radical epistemic openness towards the possible future. We continue to develop this line of understanding hope and fear as *aesthetically structured*. Ultimately we attempt to make plausible that the openness characteristic to the aesthetic makes a form of practical self-understanding in the form of hope and fear accessible,

* Doctoral candidate, University of Utrecht.
** Professor of Philosophy, University of Utrecht.

[1] E Bloch, *The Principle of Hope* (MIT Press, 1986) 7.

[2] K Menninger, 'The Academic Lecture on Hope' (1959) 116 *American Journal of Psychiatry* 491.

which could function as an alternative to the assertiveness of, for example, a religious perspective or a teleological interpretation of history.

I. Introducing Hope

Studies in psychology and psychiatry have shown that hope plays an important role in practical self-understanding. 'Low-hope persons', people who experience themselves as little able to relate the past and present to imaginable futures in a positive motivational way, display decreased capacities for self-affirmation and/or agency. They are less psychologically resilient, show lesser recovery ratings in cases of illness (including cancer), and appear less able to commit themselves to pursuable ends as well as deriving the means adequate to achieving these ends.[3] High-hope people, on the other hand, are found to 'occasionally alter even those seeming absolute failure situations so as to attain the impossible'.[4] Empirical evidence thus suggests that hope, even hoping against hope, is no superfluous form of wishful thinking but rather an empowering capacity that is part and parcel of our self-understanding and the way we orient ourselves in the world. However, the difficulty with interpreting these findings and their practical significance (and perhaps with self-report data more generally) is that it is assumed that it is clear—to both researcher and test subject—what hope *is*. How, for example, is hope distinguished from faith, confidence and optimism on the one hand, and fear, pessimism, despair on the other? Is hope a more general mind-set or is it directed towards specific objects? Is hope a 'given' or does it involve a moment of choice?

In contemporary philosophy we find discussions on hope in different fields, notably a quite specific discussion on the *importance* of hope in climate change ethics and a more general discussion on the *nature* of hope that bears a direct relation to the above-mentioned studies in psychology and psychiatry. Climate change ethicists increasingly stress that hope should play a central role in how people relate to both the immediate and distant future, in order to at all open up

[3] CR Snyder, C Harris, JR Anderson et al, 'The will and the ways: development and validation of an individual-differences measure of hope' (1991) *Journal of Personality and Social psychology* 60; CR Snyder, *The Psychology of Hope: you can get there from here* (Free Press, 1994); RS Lazarus, 'Hope: an emotion and vital coping mechanism against despair' (1999) 66 *Social Research* 665; PR Magaletta, JM Oliver et al, 'The hope construct, will, and ways: their relative relations with self-efficacy, optimism, and general well-being' (1999) 55 *Journal of Clinical Psychology* 539; K Herth, 'Enhancing hope in people with a first recurrence of cancer' (2000) 32 *Journal of Advanced Nursing* 1431; CR Snyder, 'Hope theory: rainbows in the mind' (2002) 13 *Psychological Inquiry* 259; AD Ong, LM Edwards, CS Bergeman, 'Hope as a source of resilience in later adulthood' (2006) *Personality and Individual Differences* 41, 1263; S Bonney and T Stickley, 'Recovery of mental health: a review of the British Literature' (2008) 15 *Journal of Psychiatric and Mental Health Nursing* 140; B Schrank, M Hayward and G Stanghellini, 'Hope in Psychiatry' (2011) 17 *Advances in Psychiatric Treatment* 227.

[4] Snyder, 'Hope theory: rainbows in the mind', ibid, 251.

the space for people to act sustainably.[5] Under the assumption that there will be future generations, and thus human beings towards which present generations have responsibilities, hope is put forward as the attitude mediating the uncertainty that simultaneously surrounds such a concept of long-term responsibility. In order to act according to the obligation to respect prospective human beings in their rights to living a dignified life, current generations arguably need to *hope* that their actions will contribute to the possibility of future generations to realise this right—in the absence of the *knowledge* that these will. However, although there appears to be consensus on the relevance of hope in various contexts, the *nature* of hope is rarely discussed in this field.[6]

The more general philosophical discussion seems to understand hope primarily in line with the kind of concept that psychological research (implicitly) assumes. What is now sometimes called the 'orthodox definition' or 'Standard Account'[7] reconstructs hope as follows: Hope involves (1) desiring and (2) estimating a probability. In other words, 'A hopes that P' is true if and only if 'A wishes that P, and A thinks that P has some degree of probability, however small' is true.[8] It sees hope thus as a combination of a *desire* and the *belief* that it is to a more or lesser extent probable that this desire can be satisfied. Now we can imagine that such a kind of hope is responsive to, for example, Day's question 'When May I Hope that P?'[9] and those of Snyder's hope scale.[10] After all, at the very least common sense (if not philosophical analysis) tells us that we can more or less accurately indicate about ourselves whether or not we have certain beliefs and desires. And perhaps this is also the kind of hope that is most common in everyday life—when we say things such as 'Jack hopes that Jill caught her train yesterday' or 'I hope that I will get that job' we articulate hopes towards concrete and specific objects, of which it does not seem as far-fetched to assume that these may be measured by psychological self-report. However, the Standard Account has in the past two decades increasingly been criticised, not so much for its inaccuracy but rather for its incompleteness. The two aforementioned features arguably need to be complemented by, for instance, 'mental imaging'[11] as the conscious entertainment of the object of hope; by a 'justificatory rationale'[12] that integrates hopeful considerations into our

[5] *cf* SM Gardiner, *A Perfect Moral Storm: The Ethical Tragedy of Climate Change* (OUP, 2011); D Jamieson, *Reason in a Dark Time* (OUP, 2014); C Johnstone and J Macy, *Active Hope: how to face the mess we're in without going crazy* (New World Library, 2010); D Orr, 'Hope in Hard Times' (2004) 18(2) *Conservation in Context* 295–98, H Shue, *Climate Justice* (OUP, 2014); C Turner, *The Geography of Hope* (Random House Canada, 2010).

[6] NA Alexander-Naidoo, 'Climate courage and radical hope: how ought we to respond to the decreasing likelihood of effectively addressing climate change?' (2015) *Graduation Thesis Applied Ethics, Utrecht University.*

[7] Associated with RS Downie, 'Hope' (1963) 24(2) *Philosophy and Phenomenological Research* 248 and JP Day, 'Hope' (1969) 6(2) *American Philosophical Quarterly* 89.

[8] Day, ibid, 89.

[9] ibid, 93.

[10] Snyder et al, n 3.

[11] L Bovens, 'The value of hope' (1999) 59(3) *Philosophy and Phenomenological Research* 674.

[12] AM Martin, *How We hope: a moral psychology* (Princeton University Press, 2014) 35.

agential self-understanding; by 'the extra feature of acting as if a certain animating assumption held true';[13] by an 'external factor'[14] in the sense that hope presupposes a consciousness that its object cannot be brought about by the agent himself; and by rather an active engagement to bring the object of hope about.[15] There is probably a point to all of these addenda. Perhaps it would be possible to develop a unified account of the nature and characteristics of hope by simply stacking all of these on top of each other. But perhaps there is something else going on here.

Can all of our hopes be analysed as if these are directed to clear and distinct objects? Are all of them directed towards determinate ends that agents desire, and believe are possible to attain (or be brought about) in the future? That seems rather implausible. Some of our hopes, especially those projected into the more distant future, are indeterminate rather than clear in nature. My hope, for instance, that in the autumn of my life I will be able to look back with satisfaction, is not very distinct at all—I have no fixed idea what this should entail; it could encompass myriad different life-plans, and reflections and feelings about these. Such hope is perhaps more of an 'inkling' about a setting or situation than any concrete object or end. Indeed,

> Sometimes we hope. Not for anything concrete or determinate, or particular. Sometimes we just hope.[16]

We hope for 'things working out well' for people that are dear to us, or more generally for future generations, for instance, where it seems overly strong to even speak of a 'setting' and we should perhaps rather say 'scenario' or something of the like. Our hopes towards such settings or scenarios are hardly the kinds of things that can function as P in Day's question, or can be measured by psychological self-report. But at the same time it seems that especially these kinds of hopes articulate something that is fundamental to our practical self-understanding—to the way we conceive of our existence as beings with the capacity to reflect upon their own finitude. This is the kind of hope that Kant seemed to be after in asking 'What May I Hope?',[17] and according to Beyleveld it is this kind of hope that grounds 'the essence of being human'.[18] And we would suggest that this hope is of a different *kind* than the one that is nowadays predominantly discussed: it is a *general* rather than a specific hope,[19] which is directed towards a *conceptually indeterminable* rather than clear and distinct object.[20]

[13] P Pettit, 'Hope and its place in mind' (2004) 592(1) *The Annals of the American Academy of Political and Social Science* 165.

[14] A Meirav, 'The Nature of Hope' (2009) 22(2) *Ratio* 220.

[15] Orr, n 5, xix.

[16] D Webb, 'Modes of Hoping' (2007) 22(3) *History of the Human Sciences* 69.

[17] I Kant, *Critique of Pure Reason* (CUP, 1998) A805–06.

[18] D Beyleveld and P Ziche, 'Towards a Transcendental Phenomenology of Hope' (2015) 18(5) *Ethical Theory and Moral Practice* 941.

[19] S Kierkegaard, *Sickness unto Death*; 'Christian Discourses' in *The Essential Kierkegaard* (Princeton University Press, 2000); *cf* R Fremstedal, 'Kierkegaard on the Metaphysics of Hope' (2012) 53(1) *The Heythrop Journal* 51.

[20] This distinction bears similarities to the one that Webb makes between 'goal-oriented' and 'open-ended' hope, in the sense that we seem to be after the same kind of thing with regard to the latter.

II. Hope in Beyleveld's Kantianism

Beyleveld's approach to hope, as embedded in the broader framework of his philosophical position, aims to provide a *transcendental* argument for hope. That is, it aims to 'show that some … relation(s) must obtain in order for us to think at all, or hence to raise questions about whether any—or which such—relations obtain'.[21] More specifically, it aims to show that the capacity to hope (and fear) is an a *priori* requirement for agential self-understanding: that the capacity to hope and fear is a necessary condition for reason to be in unity with itself. Beyleveld, following Gewirth, calls his form of transcendental reasoning the method of *dialectical necessity*: the method of argument that (1) 'begins from [judgements] made by protagonists or interlocutors and then proceeds to examine what these logically imply'[22] and (2) does not start by examining opinions that subjects happen to hold or even those foundational of specific traditions, discourse, or practice,[23] but those explicating the necessary *a priori* conditions of the possibility of self-conscious thought and experience as such. And the capacity to hope and fear, so Beyleveld ultimately suggests, is one such necessary condition in taking up the slack where cognition and belief have reached their limits.

As mentioned, Beyleveld sees Kantian hope in the context of a fundamental *dialectic within reason*. Beyleveld and Ziche sketch the two poles of the dialectic as follows:

> pure reason in its practical application requires agents to accept the moral law, which requires them to consider that they have free will … At the same time, pure reason in its theoretical application requires agents to accept that every event has a cause (the law of nature).[24]

Now so far as their self-understanding is concerned, this implies that agents dialectically necessarily consider themselves under two aspects. To the extent that they understand themselves as having free will, they consider themselves as subjects with the capacity to 'give themselves the law':[25] as having the power to think for themselves, and to act accordingly. They can only deny that they are free at pain of self-contradiction: in thinking that they cannot legislate themselves in action and primordially in thinking, they simultaneously affirm that they *can*—in the act of thinking itself they performatively endorse that they are free in that they have to understand themselves as *doing* the thinking. However, since agents cannot understand themselves without including the recognition of being the particular agent that they are,[26] they cannot merely understand themselves as having

[21] K Westphal, 'Kant, Wittgenstein, and Transcendental Chaos' (2005) 28(4) *Philosophical Investigations* 310.

[22] A Gewirth, *Reason and Morality* (Chicago University Press, 1978) 43.

[23] Gewirth and Beyleveld would consider such an enterprise to be dialectically contingent.

[24] Beyleveld and Ziche, n 18, 928.

[25] I Kant, 'Critique of Practical Reason' in *Kant's Practical Philosophy* (CUP, 1996) 162, 5: 29.

[26] D Beyleveld, 'Williams' False Dilemma: how to give categorically binding impartial reasons to real agents' (2013) 19(2) *Journal of Moral Philosophy* 1.

the capacity to *think and act*—they also have to assume that they can *experience and be acted upon*. That is, it is presupposed that they have a 'phenomenological sense'[27] that they are individuated: that they are selves, as distinct from other objects, other selves, etc, where they *qua* selves are receptive in the sense that they have the capacity to experience.[28] They can only deny that they are particular selves at pains of self-contradiction: in thinking that they are not a particular self, they simultaneously affirm that they *are*—in the act of thinking as such they performatively endorse that they are particular selves in that they have to hold that it is *they themselves* that are doing the thinking. Thus, freedom and particularity do not contingently pertain to self-conscious thought and experience (in Kant's terms: judgement). Rather, in order for judgement to obtain at all, it is necessary that there is a particular self that considers him*self* as *doing* the judging—a self that considers himself as active and free in self-legislation as well as particular and receptive to experience.

Now, *qua* free and particular agents there are many things about which we have *beliefs*—things that we claim to cognise. We have various theoretical beliefs, for example, the belief that climate change poses huge and partly irreversible threats to the lives of future generations; that most people will not be inclined to act against their short-term interests; that some voters are susceptible to political arguments that play upon their fears, and that we ourselves only respond morally to situations wherein a direct harm is pictured. We also have various practical beliefs, for example, the belief that morality requires us to act sustainably; that in most situations it is better to be cautious when one does not know the outcome; that in some situations it is morally justified to take prudential considerations as action-guiding; and that acting in accordance with our own happiness is something that we evaluate as good. Holding and reflecting upon such beliefs is crucial to how we understand ourselves and how we interpret our world—as well as our own (possible) existence and role in that world. But sometimes such beliefs clash. There can be clashes between different theoretical beliefs, and between different practical beliefs—usually such clashes can be solved by higher-order reflection where the status of one belief is weighted against that of another, which can amount to developing a perspective wherein both can still obtain or to dismissing one belief in favour of another altogether. But the situation is more difficult when in such reflection we lack the knowledge we would need to solve such conflicts; for example, when we want to take into account the long-term consequences of

[27] Beyleveld and Ziche, n 18, 940.

[28] One example of such receptivity is, of course, agents' vulnerability to external determination, eg feeling pain when someone steps on your foot or getting angry when someone insults you. But receptivity is here understood in the much broader sense: it means having the capacity of self-conscious experience in general. This includes not merely experiences that are understood in terms of vulnerability and/or finitude, but also of being liked and loved, of being a being who likes and loves, who is suspicious of politicians, swoons at the singing of Jonas Kaufmann—it includes experiences of being a being who thinks and acts. The dimension of particularity refers to the sense of *self* that is irreducible to self-consciousness in general.

our actions, which we have no way of estimating. Such problems, on the Kantian viewpoint, are thought to point back to a deeper problem, namely one regarding the relation between the *a priori* assumptions of understanding oneself as active and free in self-legislation and as particular and receptive to experience as such. Or in terms that are most close to home: they point back to the problem how we can understand ourselves simultaneously as authors of our own lives and at least as co-authors of history, and as beings that are 'thrown'[29] and bound by an embodiment and world that is not of their choosing, and not theirs to make. The Kantian intuition is that such conflicts essentially derive from a tension between the assumptions of freedom and particularity, and that the problem—and its potential mediation—should thus also be seen in this light.

Such potential unity is, according to Beyleveld (and also Kant), not something that we can 'prove': freedom and (vulnerable) particularity are assumptions that we dialectically necessarily have to make, and as *a priori* necessities these go beyond what we can claim to cognise or believe to be true or false. We have to assume freedom and particularity in order for truth and error to come into the picture in the first place, but these themselves—as well as their possible unity—are not things about which we can have true (or false) beliefs.[30] That is, on the Kantian position it can never be proved that human beings 'are' free in a world that 'is' determined by natural law: such claims go beyond what can be supported by physical evidence or metaphysical arguments. We simply cannot know this. But that does not necessarily imply that conflicts as exemplified above are irresolvable. Indeed, accepting that freedom and particularity are beyond the limits of cognition implies neither that these are in contradiction nor that these are in unity. It merely indicates that we should not interpret the question of the possible unity as requiring an answer in terms of cognition and beliefs, but rather as whether it is at all possible for agents to *think or experience* such a unity—after all, 'if we cannot think [or experience] something, then the question whether we can know it cannot even arise'.[31]

It is here that the notion of the *summum bonum*, the highest good, finds its introduction in Kantian philosophy. The *summum bonum*, broadly understood, is part of a broader problem that Kant attempts to mediate: namely that of *unifying or synthesising* dimensions of practical (self-)understanding that reason requires us to distinguish. This includes the above-introduced question of whether a life according to the law of freedom can be possible in a world determined by the law of nature, but it also includes the unity of the moral and eudaimonistic perspective.[32]

[29] M Heidegger, *Sein und Zeit* (Max Niemeyer Verlag, 1972) 135.

[30] Note: this mutatis mutandis implies that also the Categorical Imperative, and Beyleveld's Gewirthian interpretation in the form of the Principle of Generic Consistency, is 'beyond good and evil'. It is a formal structure in thinking that *enables* truth and error in the domain of morality, but the principle itself is neither true nor false.

[31] W Waxman, *Kant's Anatomy of the Intelligent Mind* (OUP, 2014) 3.

[32] Kant's practical philosophy assumes that agents have a natural inclination to strive for happiness, and that agents are committed to follow this inclination. *cf* K Steigleder, *Kant's Moralphilosophie: die Selbstbezüglichkeit reiner praktischer Vernunft* (JB Metzler, 2003) 23–58. But the moral viewpoint

We cannot discuss in detail here why Kant formulates the considerations regarding the *summum bonum* in a way that compels him to make all kinds of assumptions about the existence of God and the immortality of the soul.[33] Suffice it to say that this raises all kinds of interpretative issues, and that one can at least wonder why Kant is so quick to introduce the religious perspective and does not consider another line of thinking about the *summum bonum*. At least from the viewpoint of systematic philosophy it would be important to examine other possibilities before assuming that only faith can render our (self)understanding coherent. And this, we suggest, is exactly what Beyleveld attempts to do when he suggests that the appropriate way to think the *summum bonum* is in terms of *hope and fear*.

Hope and fear, according to Beyleveld and Ziche, as epistemic attitudes are distinguished from any attitude of holding-true (*fürwahrhalten*):[34] these are rather characterised by a radical *epistemic openness*. That of course does not mean that there is no relation whatsoever between hope or fear and, for example, beliefs. Indeed, what we claim to cognise *limits* what we can claim to hope for or fear. When an agent judges that it is impossible that God exists, he cannot simultaneously hold to hope/fear that God exists (and the same holds for when he judges that it is certain that God exists). But *within* the realm that is left open by what we believe, reason allows agents to adopt a 'dubiety, a questioning, as against an affirmative stance'[35] towards something in thought and experience, which then appears as no more and no less than a *possibility*.[36] Such a possibility need not appear as a conceptually clear and distinct image. Indeed, when we consider the *summum bonum* as a possibility we perhaps rather have an inkling of 'a framework that *inherently* leaves open that/how it will be filled in'.[37] For hope or fear to obtain it is merely necessary for something to appear as possible—however indeterminate and unclear its representation in thought may be. But that is of course not sufficient: for an agent to be in a state of hope or fear, it is also needed that he *cares* about what he judges as possible. Hope and fear entail that the agent is not merely agnostic, but that it matters to him whether or not the possibility will be realised—

is independent of such eudaimonistic perspective: indeed, morality will in various instances require that we restrict our pursuit of happiness in order to respect the moral law. The *summum bonum* in this sense is understood as 'the state of affairs in which all receive their just desert in relation to moral virtue' (Beyleveld and Ziche, n 19, 927).

[33] But *cf* R Wimmer, *Kants kritische Religionsphilosophie* (de Gruyter, 1990).

[34] Beyleveld and Ziche n 18, 932–36. Importantly, for Beyleveld this also includes *faith* (*Glaube*): an epistemic attitude that is beyond proof but also reasons, however is still expressive of a form of *certainty*.

[35] Beyleveld and Ziche, n 18, 934.

[36] The notion of possibility here in play is different to *probability*. When we hold that something is probable, we *do not* adopt a questioning stance: we *affirm* that it is to a more or lesser extent likely that something will be the case. This can still be grasped in cognitive terms. Genuinely entertaining that something is possible in the above-described sense, arguably, is a different form of relating to a representation altogether: a stance that is strictly questioning, without progressing/relapsing to one that is assertive or affirmative. We come back to this below.

[37] Beyleveld and Ziche, n 18, 935, our italics.

while simultaneously accepting that this is something that he cannot know. And hope obviously expresses that the realisation of the possibility concerned would be evaluated as positive; the state of fear rather articulates that the agent judges it to be bad if the state of affairs would come about.

Now, when it comes to the *summum bonum*, the suggestion would be that reason does not merely 'allow' agents to hope and fear. The *summum bonum*, from a perspective that does not at the get-go assume a religious embedding, can be seen as a state of affairs in which a self-legislated existence can be realised in the world and wherein the particular agent can experience such an existence as significant, and in this quality the *summum bonum* holds a systematic place that is not a contingent element of worldviews that agents may have. As a notion that unifies crucial but different aspects of self-understanding, being able to relate to the *summum bonum* is rather a *necessary condition* for self-understanding to be coherent at all. And since agents cannot relate to the *summum bonum* as cognitive beings, but only in their quality of hoping and fearing beings, the latter form the keystone of agential self-understanding. Indeed, Beyleveld and Ziche claim that the 'essence of being human' resides in the capacity to hope and fear.[38] But hope and fear, even if they be two sides of the same coin, are of course different modes of relationality. When agents relate to the *summum bonum* in terms of fear, the lack of knowledge of the possibilities and limits regarding their own existence will appear as a *threat* to their sense of agency; when they relate to it via hope rather, they are given the epistemic tools to consider the lack of certainty as an *opportunity* upon which they can act. But at this stage, there are no compelling reasons for agents to identify themselves as hoping—over and against fearing—beings.

In the above we have followed Beyleveld in reconstructing hope and fear as attitudes that are characterised by irreducible epistemic openness: when agents hope or fear, this implies that they consider something merely as a *possibility that matters to them qua agents*, but of which they are radically uncertain that it will come about. We have suggested that in situations of such radical epistemic uncertainty, hope and fear are attitudes that enable coherent self-understanding. And since some such epistemic uncertainties—notably in the form of the *summum bonum*—are irreducible, the capacity to hope and fear is an *a priori* condition for self-understanding as such. It thus belongs to what we may call a 'transcendental phenomenology',[39] 'transcendental philosophy of mind',[40] '*a priori* psychology',[41] or *a priori* anthropology. However, hope and fear have a different phenomenological appearance: hope empowers agents' sense of agency, whereas fear rather undermines their possibilities of orienting themselves in the world as practical

[38] Beyleveld and Ziche, n 18, 941.

[39] ibid.

[40] R Makkreel, 'Imagination and temporality in Kant's theory of the sublime' (1984) 42 *Journal of Aesthetics and Art Criticism* 303.

[41] Waxman, n 32.

beings. But, at least at first sight, it seems impossible to give an additional reason why agents 'should' hope rather than fear.

Now, it is imaginable that this account of hope strikes many a reader as deeply disheartening (although this would constitute a brilliant trick of irony not foreign to the masters in the field: Schelling, Kierkegaard, and Nietzsche). And to an extent it is, in the sense that it does not (and cannot) prove that it is justified for agents to believe that they are free and that there is meaning to their existence, nor even that they have reasons to hope that this is the case rather than fear that it is not. And indeed, Kant himself seems reluctant to draw this conclusion so straightforwardly. There is at least ambivalence in his thought, where he on the one hand (the strand that Beyleveld and Ziche elaborately discuss) plays with the idea that hope needs to be supplemented by faith in order for hope to prevail as guideline for thinking and acting.[42] His intuition here seems to be that hope itself is too thin—because subjective—a basis for agents to consider their own existence 'as an assignment, rather than a given'.[43] Hope would have to be supplemented by an attitude of holding true (vis-à-vis God and immortality), in order for agents to rationally take the mere possibility of the summum bonum as a source of hope rather than fear. Possibility itself arguably is insufficient for agents to understand and orient themselves in the world in what Nietzsche would entitle a 'life-affirming' way.

But before concluding that contemporary practical philosophy is clueless because it eliminated faith in God from the equation, we should explore other epistemic options. And that requires us to further elaborate hope and fear as forms of judging. What does it imply for agents to consider something as a possibility that matters to them? Which capacities are involved in so judging? Are hope and fear strict mirror images, or are there differences between the two epistemic attitudes? In what follows we pursue another line in Kant's own thinking, which is worked out in the *Critique of the Power of Judgment* and more specifically in Kant's theory of aesthetic experience and judgement.

III. Aesthetic Perspectives on Hope

In the third Critique Kant gives three faculties or capacities pride of place, which played a marginal or at least subservient role in the *Critique of Pure Reason* and the *Critique of Practical Reason*: the faculty of feeling, the power to judge reflectively, and the imagination. The interplay between these faculties makes its 'purest'[44] appearance in aesthetic experience and judgement, but the form of this interplay

[42] Kant, 'Critique of Practical Reason' in *Kants Practical Philosophy* (MJ Gregor tr, CUP, 1996), 235, 5: 119ff.

[43] R Musil, *Der Mann ohne Eigenschaften* (Reinbek, Rowohlt, 1978) 16–17.

[44] I Kant, *Critique of the Power of Judgment* (P Guyer and E Matthews tr, CUP, 2002) 108, 5: 224.

is not restricted to the realm of the aesthetic alone. In what follows we reconstruct how these faculties can be taken to function aesthetically, and use this as a blueprint in reflecting upon the capacity to hope and fear.[45]

Kant introduces the faculty of feeling—or as he also says: 'feeling of pleasure and displeasure' and 'feeling of life' (*Lebensgefühl*)—as taking up the middle ground between the faculty of cognition and that of desire,[46] and contrary to the latter feeling is put forward as part of our 'proper self'.[47] For agents, unlike for purely rational beings, there is 'something that it's like'[48] to *be* them: a phenomenology that is *particular* to how the specific agent thinks about and experiences being a thinking and experiencing being. This is reconstructed as grounded in the faculty of feeling, which is thus portrayed as a *distinct phenomenological sense* grasping the particularity of agency. Kant reconstructs feeling as the sense or sensibility to be affected by the world in a way that cannot be conceptually determined in any clear and distinct sense. That is, we cannot determine about feelings that they are x as categorically distinguished from y—for example, anger as clearly distinguished from jealousy. Feelings are blurry and in flux, and agents cannot *qua* feeling beings make determinate and final judgements about what they are and are not. But simultaneously feelings are crucial to how we understand ourselves and our world, and how we orient ourselves therein: it would be impossible to see ourselves as practical beings if we did not presuppose that there is something that it's like to be us.

Now, *qua* feeling beings we relate to the world in a way that can neither be described in terms of cognition nor in terms of desire. To the extent that we relate to the world as feeling beings, we judge it neither for what it *is* nor for what we *desire* it to be—we relate to the world in how it *affects* us. This requires a different form of judgement altogether, one that Kant calls 'reflective' (*reflektierend*).[49] The power of reflective judgement is a form of judgement that is primordially an *explorative* way of reflection: when judging something reflectively we apprehend, question, and engage something in experience or representation for possible ways in which it *can* be considered. It is a form of interpretation that is essentially open-ended in that it does not aim for a specific, concrete, determinate answer: it rather aims to grasp different possibilities of perceiving something. That is, the power of judgement in

[45] It is important to note that this is not an exegetical endeavour. We rather take inspiration from Kant at various points, and develop our own Kant-inspired thoughts on aesthetics and hope. For a more elaborate account of how we understand the critical Kantian project, see D Düring and M Düwell, 'Towards a Kantian Theory of Judgment: the power of judgment in its practical and aesthetic employment' (2015) 18(5) *Ethical Theory and Moral Practice* 943.

[46] Kant, *Critique of the Power of Judgment*, n 46, 20: 206: 'We can trace all faculties of the human mind without exception, back to these three: the faculty of cognition, the feeling of pleasure and displeasure, and the faculty of desire.'

[47] I Kant, *Groundwork for the Metaphysics of Morals* (OUP, 2002) 4: 458.

[48] T Nagel, *Mortal Questions* (CUP, 1979) 165–81.

[49] Strictly speaking: as containing the *a priori* principle for this faculty. *cf* I Kant, *Critique of the Power of Judgment*, 93, 5: 208.

its reflective employment is essentially 'playful':[50] it is a form of interpreting for no other purpose than interpretation itself—or as Kant has it: it is a 'disinterested'[51] form of judgement. Now, we would suggest, when feeling beings judge the world in such a way, the reflective employment of the power of judgement specifically plays a crucial role. In orienting themselves in the world—in engaging the world in how it affects them, in what it's like to be the particular agent that they are in that world—agents need to be capable of adopting an explorative stance that is not directly restricted by theoretical or practical purposes, but in which they are free to simply develop different interpretative possibilities. If agents would not be open to adopting such a stance, they would not be capable of interpreting themselves as beings whose relation to the world of experience is at least to an extent *dynamic*—as beings who have to orient and re-orient themselves in an ever-changing world, and who themselves experience forms of character-development.

In this form of reflectively judging how the world affects us, says Kant, the imagination plays a crucial role—and a different one than it usually plays. The imagination mostly, and perhaps even always, plays a role in how we orient ourselves as agents. But in usual cases, the imagination is ancillary: it serves a purpose that is determined by the demands of cognitive or prudential considerations. In playful judgement, arguably, it does *not*. In exploring for exploring's sake, in open-ended reflection, the imagination is rather left to roam free: when we engage something in experience or representation merely under the rubric of how it *can* be considered, the imagination is restrained only by its own lawfulness. That is, it is not allowed only to picture an object under the constraints of it being cognisable or desirable, but it can bring an image to consciousness merely under the restriction that it is *imaginable*. This allows the imagination for instance to 'transfer'[52] the content and meaning of other images to the object of judgement—such as in symbolism or analogy. And, we would suggest, precisely in this quality the imagination plays a role in our self-interpretation as feeling beings. When we reflect upon how the world affects us, upon what it's like to be us, we develop different interpretative possibilities on the basis of the imagination in its free employment. We play with interpreting ourselves under different possibilities, where these possibilities are fleshed out by an imagination that does not merely transpose memories and judgements past or actual into the possible—but by an imagination that spontaneously and creatively designs new pathways that we can engage.

As said, Kant sees such a way of playful self-interpretation as exemplified in aesthetic experience and judgement. When we are listening to music, for example, or contemplating a landscape, although our reflection concerns an object in the external world, it concerns the quality that the object has *for us*. That is, our reflection is characterised by a form of relationality in the sense that we reflect upon

[50] ibid, 102, 5: 217.
[51] ibid, 90, 5: 205; 93, 208; 96, 211.
[52] ibid, 135, 5: 252.

how an object in experience *affects us*. This aesthetic form of reflection is inherently open-ended in that my form of aesthetic sensibility is 'useless' from the viewpoint of cognitive and prudential purposes: how I experience and think about my being affected by a musical piece or landscape has in no way a direct connection to how I see myself as a cognising or desiring being. And in that sense my imagination is free in bringing to consciousness all kinds of images and associations; in aesthetic experience the imagination can bring to consciousness memories of times lost, speculations of a time yet to come, and simply picture all kinds of feelings that cannot even in such a broad way be coherently grasped. Aesthetic reflection has its 'ground' in feeling,[53] and is in that sense irreducibly subjective. But that does not mean that it is merely a contingent factor in our self-interpretation. Indeed, precisely the *aesthetic distance* to our beliefs, our desires, gives us a special form of access to ourselves as feeling beings. It is a 'pure' form of relationality in which we inherently abstract from what we hold to be true and desire, wherein how we simply experience ourselves as we are is fore-grounded—and therewith also a space is opened up of relating to ourselves in an imaginative stance on what we, and what the world, *can be*—which is not constrained by what we think we are or what we desire to be, and what we think the world is or what we desire it to be. That is, aesthetic experience and judgement opens up a space for agents to relate to themselves and the world via a pure and affective '*sense of possibility*'.[54]

We would now propose to consider *hope and fear* in terms of a sense of possibility that is aesthetically structured. That would mean that hope and fear, judging something as a possibility that matters, (1) has its ground in feeling; (2) involves a reflective form of judgement; wherein (3) the imagination is restrained only by its own lawfulness (albeit *within* the limits of what is judged to be impossible/certain). This breaks in fundamental ways with how hope is understood under the above-mentioned 'Standard Account': hope would concern neither a judgement of probability nor desire—indeed, it importantly has a *distance* to both. Hope, but also fear, rather is an explorative and imaginative stance that is not restricted by probability assessments or by what we happen to desire. Precisely in the absence of such restrictions do the objects towards which hope is directed appear as important to us, as things that *matter* to us as the *particular* agents that we are *regarding* the world in which we live and our existence therein. Our hopes and fears are significant to us in a way that is irreducibly subjective, but that we do not hold to contingently pertain to us. We hold neither our hopes nor fears to express judgements that can be analysed and communicated in terms of probability assessments, nor do we consider them to belong to the craving-a-glass-of-wine genre. Our hopes and fears are subjective because they are grounded in feeling, but feeling transcends subjectivity in the trivial sense: feeling is subjective in a peculiar way, in a way that simultaneously explicates something about us as agents *and* about the

[53] ibid, 109, 5: 225.

[54] R Musil, *Der Mann ohne Eigenschaften*, 16–18.

world as it affects us. This relational, and as we have suggested *explorative and imaginative*, dimension is lost when construing hope in terms of probabilities and desires. While exactly this dimension, we would argue, is crucial to understanding why hopes and fears matter to us as agents. Our hopes and fears articulate how we imagine the world and ourselves in that world as it *can* be, where a crucial aspect of this possibility is that it is *we* who are imagining it. *Qua* hoping and fearing beings we can relate to the world in a way that explicitly recognises its inherently dynamic character, and not merely that: the playful or imaginative aspect of engaging the world as feeling beings allows us to transcend reflection on what has been or is actual. Via hoping and fearing we can develop *new* ways of thinking the world and our role therein, possibilities wherein agents can consider themselves as an integral *part* of the world as a whole—as opposed to a mere cog in the wheel of time. This is why we could think that hopes and fears matter to us: because these are expressive of a way of interpreting and orienting ourselves in the world in a way that assumes the possibility of an *open future*.

On this point, we could wonder whether there is not something dangerously arbitrary about hope and fear so construed. When hope and fear are seen as affective responses to products of one's own imagination, are hope and fear as a whole then not attitudes of drifting in sensation, imagination, possibility, that are essentially *egoistic* in nature? Could not conceiving of feeling as the keystone of agency make the agent into a type of Don Juan or Faust, the narcissist who is fundamentally bored with reality, and whose primary aim is to manipulate the boring into the interesting or beautiful?[55] Indeed, Kierkegaard goes on to reconstruct the egoism or narcissism inherent to the '*Verweile doch! Du bist so schön!*'[56]—the moment of aesthetic sublimation—as something that should be transcended in the 'open-hearted courage' of surrendering to God's mercy. Now, if Kierkegaard is right then we are back to where we started. But perhaps there are other possibilities open to us here; and perhaps this is also the point where we should stop thinking of hope and fear as mirror images in the strict sense.

If it is plausible to reconstruct hope and fear in aesthetic terms, then from the Kantian viewpoint these bear a relation to moral—or more broadly, social, other-regarding—dimensions of practical self-understanding. Advanced in the aesthetic part of the Third Critique Kant describes the capacity for aesthetic experience and judgement ('taste') as the '*sensus communis*', the communal sense,[57] and proceeds to claim:

> Humanity on the one hand means the universal feeling of participation [*Teilnehmungsgefühl*] and on the other the capacity for being able to communicate one's inmost self universally.[58]

[55] S Kierkegaard, 'Either/Or' in *The Essential Kierkegaard* (Princeton University Press, 2000) 38–83.
[56] 'Stay awhile, thou art so fair': JW Goethe, *Faust* (Reclam, 1971) ch 7.
[57] Kant, *Critique of the Power of Judgment*, 175, 5: 295.
[58] ibid, 120, 5: 536.

Our 'social sense' is here thought as grounded neither in our cognitive capacities nor in the faculty of desire: our social sense is suggested to lie in *feeling*, and in the capacity to *communicate* this feeling. This suggests that Kant holds that there is at least a social potential to feeling, which finds expression in the status he ascribes to articulations of these. When we communicate feelings in terms of reflective judgement, such as about experiencing some object as beautiful or some event as upsetting, we ascribe these judgements a special status that Kant calls '*Ansinnen*'.[59] There is a huge scholarly discussion on how precisely to understand this, but at the very least we can say that Kant thinks that *inherent* to the judgement expressing a feeling is the affirmation that it can be shared—that it is in its peculiar way universally communicable. This does not mean that when we judge that something is beautiful, we express an anticipation that others *will* agree; we express that they *can* agree. But simultaneously we do more than that. When we articulate a feeling in judgement, we do not make a judgement about the quality that an object has for me and 'subsequently' ascribe a normative universality to this judgement. The term '*Ansinnen*' rather indicates that if we analyse the experience that is expressed in a reflective judgement of feeling, 'we will acknowledge that one of its *essential* aspects is the claim we make upon others to share it with us'.[60] So the suggestion would be that there is a social or other-regarding dimension to the way we reflect upon, the way we imaginatively explore, what it is like to be us in the world of which we are part. And that there is also, at least to an extent, a social or other-regarding potential in our capacity to feel as such.[61]

But perhaps here it is no longer adequate to understand hope and fear as senses of possibility in the same way. Although both are explorative and imaginative attitudes towards what we judge to be an essentially open future, the way we relate to the feeling of hope seems crucially different to the way we relate to fear. In the moment that we affirm ourselves as hoping beings (explicitly or implicitly over and against fearing beings), we affirm ourselves as participants in a community that shares in a 'social imaginary'. When we, for instance, affirm that we hope that climate change does not undermine the possibility for future people to live a life with dignity, the feeling of hope and the way that we express it in judgement has the status of *Ansinnen*: inherent to hope as a sense of possibility is the imputation that others share it with us. That is, that others participate in the feeling that the lives of future people matter, and engage in imagining and exploring possible interpretations of the world and (current) agents' role therein that would allow for the possibility that future generations can live a dignified life. In the state of

[59] ibid 27, 20: 225; 102, 5: 217–18; 121, 5: 237; 161, 5: 281; 174, 5: 294.

[60] B Longuenesse, 'Kant's theory of Judgment, and judgments of taste: On Henry Allison's Kant's Theory of Taste' (2010) 46 *Inquiry* 151, our italics.

[61] We cannot elaborate on this here, but notwithstanding want to highlight that there are some striking similarities between the way we have sketched Kant's idea of *Ansinnen*, and how Beyleveld understands the Argument for the Sufficiency of Agency; *cf* D Beyleveld, *The Dialectical Necessity of Morality* (University of Chicago Press, 1991) 43–44. We thank Patrick Capps for pointing us to this.

hope, we call upon ourselves but equally upon others to share in imagining possible scenarios that fill in what we judge to be an open future—in light of what we feel to matter, and such that it gives us guidelines to think and act. In endorsing ourselves as fearing beings, on the other hand, we seem to do rather the opposite. We relate negatively to our imaginative and explorative capacities, and to the idea of an open future altogether; which may appear to us as stifling and an infringement upon our sense of agency. And at least part of this, we would suggest, has to do with the incapacity or unwillingness to engage with the social community. Perhaps the problem with the archetypes of Don Juan or Faust is not that they are 'strictly aesthetically' oriented—perhaps they are not aesthetes *at all.* Perhaps they are simply afraid. Afraid *because* they cannot share in a feeling of social participation, or afraid *that* they cannot share in a *sensus communis.* And perhaps the moment of 'open-hearted courage' does not require a leap of faith so much as the leap to participate in the social imaginary.

IV. Hope Revisited

This chapter has attempted to take up Beyleveld's reflections on Kantian hope and develop these further. We fully agreed with his claims that the capacity to hope and fear, attitudes characterised by a radical epistemic openness, is a necessary *a priori* condition for the possibility of coherent self-understanding. We have subsequently made different proposals to continue this line of thinking.

First of all, we developed a perspective on hope and fear from the Kantian viewpoint of the *summum bonum.* Herein we reconstructed hope and fear as not primordially concerned with concrete and determinate objects as in 'Jack hopes that Jill caught her train', but as a more *general* attitude towards an open future. We also picked up Beyleveld's claim that hope and fear should not be understood in terms of belief, nor in terms of faith: considering something as a possibility requires that agents adopt a questioning, explorative stance that is structurally *dissimilar* to the affirmative, assertive one that is appropriate to belief (including the belief that something is probable), but also appropriate to faith. As hoping and fearing beings, it is required of agents that they have the capacity to be affected by, to care about, things that appear in consciousness merely as *possibilities.*

Second, and in order to further explore the possibility of a practical philosophy that does not fall back on faith, we developed the capacity of hope and fear as a sense of possibility on the basis of Kant's ideas on aesthetic experience and judgement. We reconstructed aesthetic experience as an exemplary form of being affected by the world in a disinterested way, wherein agents are free to explore and imagine possible ways of interpreting themselves and the world beyond the constraints of theoretical or practical purposes. We have suggested to see hope and fear as aesthetically structured, where the openness characteristic to the aesthetic makes a form of practical self-understanding accessible that could function as an alternative to the assertiveness of, for example, a religious perspective or a teleological interpretation of history.

Third, we have considered hope and fear in the context of the social community. We have suggested that albeit hope and fear appear as two sides of the same coin *qua capacity*, these are no longer mirror images to the extent that we consider the psychology of *endorsing* oneself as a hoping or fearing being. We have suggested that affirming oneself as a hoping being implies identifying oneself as a participant in the social community, in taking part in—and perhaps also accepting responsibility for—exploring and imagining possible ways of giving colour to the open future. Endorsing oneself as a fearing being, on the other hand, we have put forward as the real locus of Kierkegaard's suspicion of egoism and narcissism; those who give in to their fears, rather than the aesthetes, are those who do not share in the feeling of social participation.

Many important questions remain, questions that are crucial to address from both the more abstract level of the philosophy of self-consciousness as well as the more concrete level of reflection on social-political institutions. What, for instance, should we exactly make of *uncertainty* in the context of hope? We have said that when a person hopes something, he can neither hold that it is impossible nor that it is necessary that this thing will be the case—but this still leaves many options open. What form of uncertainty is necessary for agents to be capable of affirmatively relating to the idea of an open future? How much (in)determinacy does the idea of an open future presuppose? These are questions that have a direct bearing on how we think about the role of hope as a possible mediating force in challenges such as climate change, as well as how we conceive appropriate institutional structures that enable and possibly even encourage agents to endorse themselves as hoping beings. And crucially this also presupposes that we gain clarity on the relationship between *hope and morality*. It is evident that to Kant the question of hope only comes into the picture from a viewpoint that already accepts the validity of the moral law, but what does that mean in practice? Does that, for instance, require that agents hope for (to an extent) specific things over and against others—are agents, for example, required to hope for 'progress in history'[62] rather than the 'end of history'?[63] What kind of requirement would this be; does it make sense to say that (under certain institutional conditions) agents have a 'duty to hope'?[64] And how would this work the other way around; if we accept that there is a link between hope and the *sensus communis*, does this suggest that hope is conducive to morality? If so, in what sense?

These are but examples, but if Beyleveld has been right in considering hope as a necessary *a priori* condition of agential self-understanding, then such questions should adopt a prominent place on the agenda for future research.

[62] I Kant, *Conflict of the Faculties* (Abaris Books, 1979) 141–69.
[63] F Fukuyama, *The End of History and the Last Man* (Hamilton, 1992).
[64] *cf* D Moellendorf, 'Hope as a Political Virtue' (2006) 35(3) *Philosophical Papers* 413.

5

Justification in Morality and the Law

MICHAEL BOYLAN*

Deryck Beyleveld and Roger Brownsword have set out two important senses of consent in the law. The first meaning I will refer to (for clarity) with a lower case 'c.' This meaning is primary for much of their book, *Consent in the Law.*[1] This understanding of consent refers to *permission* in a procedural context. In medical ethics a patient who is about to undergo a medical operation is presented with a document of informed consent. When the patient (under the proper circumstances of personally understanding the relevant risks and rewards)[2] signs the form, it is an authorising act that is between the patient, X, and his doctor, A. The logical realm of this event is token-oriented.[3] This means that the consensual relation between X and A has no causal bearing upon another patient Y and A: it is a particularised event proximately concerning X and A. The logical status of clinical informed consent is a permission that is particular.

But there is also a second sense of consent that we will characterise with a capital 'C'. Under this sense of Consent, we are talking about a more abstract mode of permission as a type notion of substantive rectitude. This latter sense of Consent is all about the underlying conditions of the very notion of Consent. When I worked in 1999–2001 with the Academy of Orthopedic Surgeons in the USA in creating their ethics manual this became a contentious issue. I first asked orthopaedic surgeons what they were actually doing in going through the process of discussing with their patients the details of their forthcoming operation in order to get consent (legally necessary in order to proceed with the operation) and then whether this procedure was adequate in a more fundamental sense of gaining Consent. I

* Professor of Philosophy, Marymount University.

[1] D Beyleveld and R Brownsword, *Consent in the Law* (Hart Publishing, 2007).

[2] Creating these conditions of patient autonomy as being the legitimating level for consent is an instance of Consent.

[3] Obviously it is against a type background condition (which is why Beyleveld and Brownsword set up their two fallacies of sufficiency and necessity). The type-token distinction is variously represented. My use of the distinction owes its source to P Grice, 'Utterer's Meaning and Intentions' (1969) 78 *Philosophical Review* 147 and WV Quine, *Quiddities: An Intermittently Philosophical Dictionary* (Harvard University Press, 1987).

found that most male orthopaedic surgeons I interviewed[4] spent between five and seven minutes asking their patients (often when the patients were already in the hospital ready for the operation and sometimes when they were already under preliminary anaesthesia) whether they consented to the operation![5] This sort of consent may technically fulfil the legal procedural consent, but it is inadequate to the underlying context of what is necessary to ensure some level of patient-autonomous participation.

What is missing is something grounding the entire endeavour, a first order meta-ethical principle.[6] This is the Consent that legitimates consent.[7] Beyleveld and Brownsword recognise this two-level dynamic when they set out their two fallacies: the fallacy of necessity (that falsely views consent as necessary for always bringing about a good outcome when it is not) and the fallacy of sufficiency (that falsely views consent as sufficient to always bringing about a good outcome when it is not).[8]

The role of Consent and consent in creating a foundation for the law is a central question in jurisprudence. Almost no one (save for vicious dictators) would assert that Consent/consent play *no* part in justifying particular laws and/or the legal system in general. However, it is an issue of some contention whether either consent or Consent is the *ultimate* justification. Deryck Beyleveld and Roger Brownsword contend that it is not. Rather, some other grounding is needed in order to solve certain foundational groundings of the law. This chapter will agree with Beyleveld and Brownsword and will defend them on this critical point against positivist contractarians whom I see as the primary objectors.

[4] It should be noted that this is rather anecdotal since I did not perform a scientific study based upon best practices of pollster procedures. However, I did talk to 50 or so randomly selected individuals who self-reported that their experience was mainstream.

[5] I noted that the informed consent process in my analysis sanctioned by the Academy of Orthopedic Surgeons in the United States of America was gender-linked. Female orthopaedic surgeons (often disproportionally 'hand' surgeons) gave on average 35 minutes of discussion before the informed consent form was signed and it was generally in their private medical surgery before the patient even went to the hospital.

[6] Most readers are familiar with second order metaethics in which language is about how language works (often self-referentially—as in Richard's paradox or Russell's paradox). Much of contemporary metaethics lives in this realm. Gewirth wrote an article on this: A Gewirth, 'Must one Play the Moral Language Game?' (1970) 7(2) *American Philosophical Quarterly* 107. Following Gewirth, there is a different sort of metaethics: first order metaethics. In this variety one stays at a single level and examines terms at that level only instead of engaging in a dual-level analysis that brings in dynamics that often obfuscate rather than clarify.

[7] Of course, these two senses of 'consent' are not analysed in Hart or in Austin. Hart assumes a sort of contractualism in his treatment of ethics in chs 8 and 9. However, his discussion there shows that he is unaware of the contemporary debate on this to be of any use in this chapter.

[8] Beyleveld and Brownsword examine these two fallacies in a variety of contexts that are beyond the scope of this essay; Beyleveld and Brownsword, n 1, 355–57.

I. Grounding the Law: Positivism/Contractarianism

Positivism

Near the beginning of Section 4 of *Consent in the Law*, Beyleveld and Brownsword say:

> Whether we are guided by Lon Fuller's pre-theoretical identification of law with the enterprise of subjecting human conduct to the governance of codes, or Karl Llewellyn's non-institutional law-jobs theory, or HLA Hart's institutional view … we get to pretty much the same place.[9]

It is true that once in the realm of procedures (in one sense) it does not matter how you get there—*if* you get there and can establish a rule of law.[10]

However, given judicial discretion (in practice) and the whole enterprise (in theory) it *does* matter how we justify things. The rest of this essay will focus on this problem. We will begin with the strongest objection to the moral grounding to law (also known as natural law): legal positivism grounded by contractarianism.

We will start our journey with a gloss on HLA Hart. For clarification in understanding this dynamic let us agree on a distinction between first- and second-order rules and meta-foundational rules.[11] A first-order rule is the rule-making function. It concerns the process of making rules in the society and the scope of the intended obligations. A second-order rule addresses shortcomings in first-order rules considered by themselves: uncertainty, static character, and inefficiency. By employing rule-remedies to these shortcomings second-order rules create a richer sense of a legal system. They answer the uncertainty defect with a rule of recognition. The static character is handled by rules of change. Finally, the inefficiency problem is addressed by rules of adjudication (and the creation of a court system).[12]

A meta-foundational rule concerns the higher order authority that the legislators or sovereign use to justify the rules that are set out.[13] This justification can be an abstract moral principle or an appeal to an historical community worldview with its attendant institutions and the procedures that can bring about rational

[9] ibid, 311.

[10] Unfortunately, the establishment of the *rule of law* in the world today is a rarity when measured against the population of the world; see M Boylan, *Natural Human Rights: A Theory* (CUP, 2014) esp Part 3.

[11] HLA Hart makes a similar distinction in *The Concept of Law* (OUP, 1961) 208–31, 255–57. I have changed the terms from primary and secondary rules to first- and second-order rules to try to alleviate confusion. Though there is some overlap in Hart's and my distinctions, I have modified his distinctions substantially for my own purposes.

[12] Here I am following Hart closely (ibid, ch 5).

[13] My understanding of foundational rules departs radically from Hart.

understanding and consensual acceptance of first- and second-order rules in the given domain (for example, the state of the world). Those who advocate a positivist understanding of law on the model of John Austin will take rules (such as those dealing with human rights) to be answered, in cases where the statute is ambiguous, first from British common law and, in cases in which that is still undetermined, to Britain's adopted parent, the Roman Empire.[14] Like Hegel, Austin holds that meta-foundational authority lies in history: precedent.

Whether one grounds law in morality or in the historical community (shared community worldview, authoritative texts, past legislative enactment, or judicial precedent), it is assumed that meta-foundational rules exhibit more authority than first order rules. This is because meta-foundational rules condition first order rules and not vice versa. Observance must be maintained via specified sanctions (including moral suasion administered socially).

With respect to first and second-order rules, in democracies the people, in principle, can change the rules through the political process. The way they do it sets out the statute itself and the way it is brought about which enhances rule recognition (the most important second-order rule). In autocracies the people, in principle, can change the law through violent or non-violent revolution. Rule recognition comes from putting people into jail or killing them.

For the most part (in democracies) popular movements ground their desires for first-order rule change in morality-based appeals. But this need not be the case. One might say that he wants a rule changed from advocating A to advocating B from a principle of personal self-interest or because it fits in with the group self-interest in some way construed. In either event, first-order rules are only changed on the basis of arguments from a meta-foundational rule vantage point.

One example of this can be found from the history of the United States of America. In the United States, the women's suffrage movement began in the middle of the nineteenth century. From 1832 onwards it did not really gain traction. It wasn't until the suffrage movement linked up with the abolitionist movement that sufficient political momentum made the Seneca Falls Convention in 1848 possible. Suffragists like Elizabeth Cady Stanton and Lucretia Mott teamed up with abolitionists such as William Lloyd Garrison and Frederick Douglass to try to energise a national movement.[15] They were unsuccessful. Other tactics were needed.[16] The movement sought another partner. Enter the prohibitionists. Together they won the day so that on 4 June 1919 the Senate followed the House (which had ratified the Constitutional Amendment a year earlier) and it went to the States, which

[14] J Austin, *Lectures on Jurisprudence*, R Campbell (ed), 5th edn (John Murray, 1885).

[15] Two accounts of this dynamic are: EC Dubois, *Feminism and Suffrage: The Emergence of an Independent Women's Movement in America 1848–1869* (Cornell University Press, 1999) and JH Baker, *Sisters: The Lives of America's Suffragists* (Hill and Wang, 2006).

[16] If the reader wants a feel for these sorts of tactics see the interactive book: KL Holihan, *Rightfully Ours: How Women Won the Vote* (Chicago Review Press, 2012).

promptly began ratifying the Amendment until Tennessee on 18 August 1920 put it over the top and it became law eight days later. Women won the right to vote in the United States on 26 August 1920. When my late mother was born (1917) women could not vote in the United States. The UK followed suit in 1928, Canada declared women to be people (and thus able to vote) in 1929, and at the time of writing this chapter women still cannot vote in Bhutan, Lebanon, Brunei, Saudi Arabia or the United Arab Emirates.

The essence of this story is that 51 per cent of the population (women in a biologically statistically normal sample space) were denied the right to vote by law. In order to alter this, the law had to be changed. In one sense (a strictly legal one based on the first-order rule model) women in the United States did not have the right to vote before 1920. But what about the meta-foundational moral sense? Did they always have a right to vote except that the society did not recognise this moral right? If meta-foundational rules are interpreted merely as the history of the shared community worldview, then the answer is, 'No!' Women did not possess a meta-foundational right to vote. This position is called the *emergent rights* position of human rights: particular human rights only exist when there is a society that recognises that right.[17]

However, I will contend that women have always had this right (via natural law). It was simply a right that was not recognised (a failure of second-order rules) by the given society. Such an omission is to any society's discredit.

Contractarianism and Consent

The second worldview behind the emergent hypothesis[18] follows from the first and asserts a contractarian view of rights (the cornerstone of how we begin to situate the law) and morality. John Rawls and Charles Beitz offer examples on how this sort of procedure works. Rawls' argument runs this way:[19]

1. [These conditions of—(a) there being a reasonable starting point for liberal societies to provide rightly based stability; (b) an advancement toward democratic peace; and (c) a social contract that ties together our considered political convictions and moral judgments—jointly would justify the argument for the law of peoples for liberal societies]—A[ssertion][20]
2. [A reasonable utopia should be the goal for the law of peoples]—A

[17] For a fine defence of this position see B Singer, *Operative Rights* (SUNY Press, 1993); and PG Lauren, *The Evolution of International Human Rights: Visions Seen* (University of Pennsylvania Press, 1998).

[18] The emergent hypothesis has no account about the *how* and *why* rules emerge other than vague references to some social history. At least this second anti-realist account, explicit contractarianism, seeks greater, formal explanatory power.

[19] J Rawls, *The Law of Peoples* (Harvard University Press, 2001).

[20] My reconstruction of logical arguments in this chapter follows the rules I set out in *Critical Inquiry: The Process of Argument* (Westview, 2010).

3. 'Reasonable' means that: (a) it relies on socially feasible pluralism, and (b) it recognises primary goods and basic liberties—F[act][21]
4. 'Utopia' means that: (a) the society is constitutional; (b) liberties are assigned a special priority; (c) all citizens are given at least minimal primary goods; (d) the principle of reciprocity is manifested—A[22]
5. A 'reasonable utopia' employs: (a) a political conception of justice; (b) political and social institutions; (c) a commitment to a consensus of compatible comprehensive doctrines; and (d) a reasonable amount of tolerance—A[23]
6. The law of peoples satisfies conditions mentioned in premises 3–5—A[24]
7. [The law of peoples satisfies the goal of a reasonable utopia]—2–6
8. Liberal peoples are (a) under a constitutional government, (b) united by common sympathy; and (c) have a dual moral nature (a sense of justice and a conception of the good)—A[25]
9. Liberal peoples consider themselves first as states and then internationally—A[26]
10. [The process of law-making internationally is analogous to that of law-making nationally]—A
11. National law-making requires an original position imposing five essential features: (a) the original position models the parties as representing citizens fairly; (b) it models them as rational; (c) it models them as selecting from among available principles of justice those to apply to the appropriate subject, in this case the basic structure; (d) the parties are modelled as making these selections for appropriate reasons; and (e) the parties select reasons related to the fundamental interests of citizens as reasonable and rational—A[27]
12. International law-making requires an original position imposing three additional points: (a) parties are situated symmetrically and thus fairly; (b) parties are rational and guided by fundamental interests of democratic society; and (c) subject to a veil of ignorance properly adjusted for international terms—A[28]
13. The process that liberal peoples engage in when making international law should contain the two original positions—8–12
14. The two original positions along with the character of liberal peoples imply the traditional principles of international justice: (a) Peoples are free and independent, and their freedom and independence are to be respected by other peoples; (b) Peoples are to observe treaties and undertakings; (c) Peoples are equal and are parties to the agreements that bind them; (d) Peoples are to

[21] ibid, 12–13.
[22] ibid, 14.
[23] ibid, 15–16.
[24] ibid, 14–16.
[25] ibid, 23–24.
[26] ibid, 26.
[27] ibid, 30–31.
[28] ibid, 32.

observe a duty of non-intervention; (e) Peoples have a right of self-defence but no right to instigate war for reasons other than self-defence; (f) Peoples are to honour human rights; (g) Peoples are to observe certain specified restrictions in the conduct of war; (h) Peoples have a duty to assist other peoples living under unfavourable conditions that prevent their having a just or decent political and social regime—A[29]

15. [The traditional principles of international justice are highly plausible and provide stability for the right reasons]—A
16. The second original position (a reasonable starting point) is highly plausible and provides stability for the right reasons—7, 8, 13, 14, 15
17. There are three sorts of international organisations: (a) trade; (b) bank lending; and (c) a quasi-legislative group (like the United Nations)—A[30]
18. The organisations cited in #17 provide stability for the right reasons (as opposed to the stability formed out of fear)—A[31]
19. To create real peace, societies have to disavow extending their territories and ruling over other nations and to accept the peace hypothesis: (a) all just democratic societies should accept their political institutions, their history, and their achievements: this acceptance makes their peace more secure; (b) to the extent that societies satisfy (a), they will be less likely to go to war except in self-defence—A[32]
20. One is inclined to accept the conditions of the principles in premise #19 if they possess the five features of a just society: (a) fair equality of opportunity; (b) a decent distribution of income and wealth; (c) society as an employer of last resort; (d) basic healthcare for all; (e) public financing of elections—A[33]
21. Liberal societies will be just and satisfied by fulfilling the conditions in #20—A[34]
22. Liberal societies advance democratic peace by meeting the conditions of a satisfied society—17–21[35]
23. Public reason requires reciprocal debate from the standpoint of being an 'as if' legislator—A[36]
24. [Debating from the standpoint of liberal people 'as if' they were legislators unites various sections of society]—A
25. The social contract understanding of the Law of Peoples coherently ties together our considered political convictions and moral judgments—8, 23–25[37]
26. The Law of Peoples is sound and justified for liberal peoples—1, 16, 22, 26[38]

[29] ibid, 37.
[30] ibid, 42.
[31] ibid, 43–44.
[32] ibid, 49.
[33] ibid, 50.
[34] ibid, 50–51.
[35] ibid, 50, 51–54.
[36] ibid, 56.
[37] ibid, 54–57.
[38] ibid, 58.

Under Rawls' theory applied internationally, decent societies that fall short of liberal societies should be tolerated, but benevolent absolutist societies and outlaw societies should be changed. The force of this argument follows from the second form of the original position along with public discourse.

Much has been said about the national or statist standpoint of Rawls' 1971 argument from *A Theory of Justice*. Documents such as *The Universal Declaration of Human Rights* or *The Helsinki Accord* have an international scope. Thus, if our purview in human rights discussion (as a way to understand the grounding of the law) were *only* about what we do within the contexts of nations, then it would seem that they would be inadequate to handle what the present age demands. For this reason, Rawls follows his earlier work (*A Theory of Justice* 1971) with one that has an international scope (*The Law of Peoples* 2001). Here, Rawls introduces criteria in order to achieve a reasonable utopia. These criteria are grounded in his conception of a liberal society. Only a liberal society can achieve this goal. The criteria listed in premises 19 and 20 set out these conditions that allow for a second original position to go forward. This original position is not the same as the original position of his earlier work because it has more exacting outcomes. Those arguments were set against the nationalist version. Objectors to *A Theory of Justice*'s original position focused upon: (a) the veil of ignorance since it makes such unreasonable expectations upon the parties involved that it fails in its avowed goal to illustrate pure human nature because no real persons can ever be situated in a veil of ignorance—it is a thought experiment about a possible world that is not and cannot be ours,[39] and (b) the mini-max view of rational decision theory[40] is flawed because it presents a skewed view of rationality that does not account for a wider view of individual preference assessment according to a multi-variable model that may (for example) include gambling.[41] These alleged shortcomings are only accentuated here when applied internationally.

Sen makes a similar point against Rawls when applied broadly.[42] He claims that Rawls' contractarian bias limits the desired contrast between Rawls' own theory and utilitarianism (thus excluding capability theory). When seen in the perspective of the agency approach to justifying human rights (as I depict capability theory), Sen and I are in agreement in our criticism of Rawls's contractarianism to justify the above argument.

[39] I have called such moves 'the thought experiment fallacy'. It occurs when one creates a possible world that is unlike our own in essential ways. Then the practitioner poses and solves a problem in that possible world and seeks to apply the conclusion to our own world. See M Boylan, *The Good, The True, and The Beautiful* (Bloomsbury, 2008) 211–13.

[40] 'Mini-max' refers to minimum risk and maximum reward. It is one of four common strategies in decision theory.

[41] Advocates of gambling generally set out that there is an *intrinsic* pay-off in trying for one's ideal profession (for example). Even if the recent PhD in philosophy from a top school cannot get a job and ends up selling insurance, it may have been worthwhile to have given it a shot: the gamble contains an intrinsic value. Outcomes analysis only (that are generally the part of game theory simulations) are not sufficient to describe worldview self-fulfilment.

[42] A Sen, *The Idea of Justice* (Harvard University Press, 2009) ch 2.

Another proponent of a different sort of contractarianism is Charles Beitz. Beitz's argument runs this way:[43]

1. Agreement theories conceptualise human rights as standards that are objects of agreement among members of different cultures whose moral and political values are dissimilar—F[44]
2. There are two main sorts of agreement theories: (a) common core, and (b) overlapping consensus—A[45]
3. Common core advocates exclude rights to democracy, religious toleration, legality for women, and free choice of a marriage partner because these protections are not found in every country—F[46]
4. Common core advocates also exclude rights that incur too heavy duties, such as physical and mental health—F[47]
5. Common core advocates frequently refer only to the major societies in the world (to the exclusion of others)—F[48]
6. Common core agreement theories are deficient—2–5/[49]
7. Overlapping agreement consensus comes from John Rawls—A/[50]
8. Human rights theories are supposed to be critical norms to judge or to revise national laws—A/[51]
9. If actual consensus is the standard, then the existence of a racist society might agree with genocide, but this is to get agreement and justification backwards—F/[52]
10. Actual consensus agreement theories should be rejected because they mix up agreement and justification—6–9/[53]
11. One way to rectify the problem in #10's problem is to put conditions upon deliberation that would be used in international agreement à la Bernard Williams[54] that a regime is legitimate if most people obey the law from a justified belief and not out of a fear of punishment—A/[55]
12. Abdullahi An-Na'im[56] sets out pragmatic grounds that support consensus theories (since without consensus there will not be compliance)—F/[57]

[43] C Beitz, *The Idea of Human Rights* (OUP, 2011) 73–95.
[44] ibid, 73.
[45] ibid, 74.
[46] ibid, 75.
[47] ibid.
[48] ibid.
[49] ibid.
[50] ibid, 76–77.
[51] ibid, 78.
[52] ibid.
[53] ibid.
[54] B Williams, 'Human Rights and Relativism' in *In the Beginning was the Deed* (Princeton University Press, 2006) 62–64.
[55] Beitz, n 43, 78–80.
[56] AA An-Na'im, 'Universality of Human Rights: An Islamic Perspective' in N Ando (ed), *Japan and International Law: Past, Present, and Future* (Kluwer Law International, 1999) 315.
[57] Beitz, n 43, 80–81.

13. The Helsinki Declaration is an example of a swap: USSR gets recognised boundaries for Eastern Europe and in return accepts the existence of certain human rights—F/[58]
14. An-Na'im's approach is to create a trade-off discussion of this (Helsinki) sort to spur moral development around the world (thus satisfying the objections to actual consensus)—10–13/[59]
15. The American Anthropological Association's Executive Board in 1947 was sceptical about the Universal Declaration of Human Rights concerning the issue of paternalism—F/[60]
16. Appeal to some common worldview assumptions can create a climate wherein actual agreement is replaced by progressive convergence—A/[61]
17. All agreement theories possess this dilemma: (a) human rights are supposed to provide reasons for action to members of every culture to which human rights apply, and yet (b) human rights as an international doctrine cannot be seen as actually shared among the world's main political/moral cultures; thus, it is not an object of agreement—A/[62]
18. Premise #17 implies that either human rights must be a small subset of possible rights (the ones agreed to) or give up agreement as a basis of rights—A/[63]
19. An alternative to #18 is to move away from actual agreement to possible emergent agreement that might evolve—15–18/[64]
20. This possible emergence is called progressive convergence—F/[65]
21. Progressive convergence is supported by Charles Taylor's 'unforced consensus,'[66] An-Na'im's 'evolutionary interpretation,'[67] and Joshua Cohen's 'justificatory minimalism'[68]—A/[69]
22. Progressive convergence relies on what is reachable from a particular worldview stance (for example, An-Na'im's progressive reform in Islam from passages in the Quran, p 92)—F/[70]

[58] ibid, 82.
[59] ibid, 82–83.
[60] ibid, 83–85.
[61] ibid, 86–88.
[62] ibid, 88.
[63] ibid.
[64] ibid.
[65] ibid.
[66] C Taylor, 'Conditions of an Unforced Consensus on Human Rights' in Joanne R Bauer and Daniel Bell (eds), *The East Asian Challenge for Human Rights* (CUP, 1999) 124–44.
[67] AA An-Na'im, *Toward an Islamic Reformation: Civil Liberties, Human Rights, and International Law* (Syracuse University Press, 1990) 179.
[68] J Cohen, 'Minimalism about Human Rights' (2004) 12 *Journal of Political Philosophy* 201, 202.
[69] Beitz, n 43, 88–89.
[70] ibid, 90.

23. This reachability can be enhanced by Bernard Williams' 'sound deliberative route'[71]—A/[72]
24. If human rights are reachable from a worldview, then action to enforce human rights in a society in which that worldview was widely accepted would not be objectionable—A/[73]
25. A doctrine of human rights should express a toleration appropriate to a wide range of moral and religious worldviews: this is another aspect of 'reachable from'—A/[74]
26. [Progressive convergence of worldviews is the best form of agreement theory]—1, 2, 6, 10, 19–25
27. Progressive convergence risks circularity unless we apply sympathetic imagination—A/[75]
28. Though progressive convergence via sympathetic imagination is the best agreement interpretation, it still falls short of the [utopian] goal that human rights should be recognisable as common concerns among all the world's cultures—26–27/[76]

Beitz's argument is forceful. It operates on a more concrete level than does Rawls'. The first part of the argument sets out the contrast between common core (using existing common values/interests to create compromises) and overlapping consensus (which leads to progressive convergence with the addition of boundary conditions and the sympathetic imagination). This is not too far removed from my own argument about the way everyone confronts novel normative theories.[77] I call my version *overlap and modification.* The direction is to how people can change their worldviews when confronted by an alternative that shares features of the former view. This is certainly a much more productive approach than the common core advocates who elicit either coinciding and amplification or dissonance and rejection.

Then there is the setting of the key issue in premise #10 about the difference between agreement and justification. I do agree that this is a central failing in contractarian theories.[78] However, Beitz believes that he can overcome this difficulty by presenting a version of contractarianism that he calls progressive convergence. What this really amounts to is a strategy for conflict negotiation in which the worldviews of the parties are taken into account as they search for common ground

[71] B Williams, 'Internal Reasons and the Obscurity of Blame' in *Making Sense of Humanity* (CUP, 1995) 35.

[72] Beitz, n 43, 90–91.

[73] ibid, 92–93.

[74] ibid, 93.

[75] ibid, 94–95.

[76] ibid, 95.

[77] M Boylan, *A Just Society* (Rowman and Littlefield, 2004) 11–12.

[78] M Boylan, *Basic Ethics* 2nd edn (Prentice Hall, 2009) 11–12, 36–37.

to agree on some common endpoint (say human rights, for example). It can be anything such as environmental protection, tariff treaties, fishing rights, etc. These are sound principles of negotiation, but they are not *distinctive* of human rights. A contrast can be made here to Robert Paul Churchill, who also puts forth a theory of rights negotiation but in the context of a naturalistically grounded justification scheme.[79] Churchill's stance is that there is a difference between negotiation among a diverse group with vested interests (cross-cultural negotiation) and one's own justification standpoint regarding human rights. I support Churchill here. We can accept something like progressive convergence as a negotiation strategy without buying into it as a mode of justification. My own preference for justification is set out in my book on human rights.[80] It depends upon an agency-based theory that sets out strict deontological conditions for what constitutes a necessary claim right. My approach shares some general strategies employed by Alan Gewirth in his Principle of Generic Consistency (PGC),[81] which is the approach that Beyleveld and Brownsword adopt. Our common approach is a naturalistic moral realism with outcomes that are strictly necessary.

What I find problematic about contractarian or agreement theories as justifications for human rights (or for morality that creates the context for Consent) is that they are so invested in asserting that people acting within some constraints (such as Rawls' notion of rationality within the two original positions or Beitz's belief in constructive dialogue that will lead to progressive convergence) will generate a normative conclusion that is sufficient to yield Consent. What is there about agreement that yields positive normativity? There are many agreements that are made that are strikingly immoral as Hegel and Marx have set out (the master-slave dialectic and the stages of alienation within industrial society).[82] What *agreement* produces is a voluntary pact between people or between institutions/countries. But agreements can be *bad* (as judged by the PGC, for example).[83] The 1939 Nazi-Soviet Non-Aggression Pact was an agreement that was voluntary—but the ends for which it was conceived were evil. There are countless other examples like this.[84] Of course that is not a problem for the PGC because it does not depend upon interpersonal agreement on whether some action or policy is moral or not.

[79] RP Churchill, *Human Rights and Global Diversity* (Prentice Hall, 2006) ch 3.

[80] Boylan, n 10, ch 6.

[81] M Boylan, '"On Pain of Contradiction": A Key Moment in Deductive Agency Arguments' in P Baum (ed), *Gewirthian Perspectives* (Routledge, forthcoming). In this chapter I compare the approaches of Gewirth and myself in the way we justify moral claims; *cf* Boylan, n 10, ch 6.

[82] On the master–slave dialectic from Hegel see GWF Hegel, *The Phenomenology of Mind* (JB Baillie tr, Allen and Unwin, 1931) 228–40 and on Marx see K Marx, 'The Economic and Philosophical Manuscripts' in Karl Marx, *Early Writings* (TB Bottomore tr, McGraw-Hill, 1963) 120–34, 147–57.

[83] I would include other agency-based morality/rights theories here as well, such as my own.

[84] In Boylan, n 78, 10–11, I cite the case of Wolf Sullowald, a former butcher who enters into a contract (consent) with an Austrian to be killed on an Internet site, butchered, and eaten. By all accounts the arrangement was agreeable to both sides—and there were witnesses. This is an extreme example of the defects in contractarianism as the foundation of ethical theory since it conflates consent with Consent. This conflation violates the PGC.

Instead, certain generic features of action are deduced from the structure of action itself. Actions are right or wrong independent of what various agents might feel or agree upon. This is how the PGC validates Consent over consent.

Those who hold contractarian theories often reply that the sorts of contracts that I am trotting forth are not *authentic* contracts. By 'authentic' they really mean that they are contrary to morality (which they surreptitiously bring in by the back door). Unless they mean anti-real, non-natural intuitionism, they are involved in begging the question. If they *do* mean anti-real, non-natural intuitionism, then they have seceded from the realm of inter-subjective discourse.[85] In this vacuum, only power is left. The power players engage in treaties with lesser states while they seek to exact terms favourable to their own advantage according to their shared community worldview.[86]

This may be descriptively correct on how much of human history has progressed, but it is hardly a defensible normative position. Might makes right (what I call *kraterism*) is really the absence of morality and *a fortiori* a proper groundwork for human rights. The world needs something better.

Critique of Contractarianism

Though consent is very important in private transactions, Consent is the major contender in the context of a broader understanding of the grounding of law. But what does such a move really mean? I contend that it is about a hypothetical move that reduces to a calculation about the interests of groups of agents in the society (and so becomes a ticket for utilitarian justifications).[87] At the heart of this sort of justification is the notion of *interest* (which is generally interpreted as well-being). My analysis of this sort of project follows Tim Scanlon.[88] Scanlon sets out three uses of well-being: (a) the basis of individual decision-making (first person); (b) the basis of a concerned benefactor's action (third person); and (c) the answer to the 'why should I be moral?' question.[89] Well-being (a) is experientially made known to us subjectively. Sense (b) is generally understood as 'fulfilling desire'.[90] However, mere *desire* is not sufficient for fulfilling rational choice.

But perhaps mere desire can be amended to *rational desire as grounding a preference for some good* and in this way be brought forward as a ground for well-being.[91] However, Scanlon asserts (and I agree) that the good is not dependent

[85] See my discussion of the dualism of realism and anti-realism in Boylan, n 10, ch 6.

[86] For a discussion of my understanding of personal and community worldview see Boylan, n 77, chs 2, 5, 6.

[87] I attack the utilitarian justification in Boylan, n 78, 107–09.

[88] TM Scanlon, *What We Owe to Each Other* (Harvard University Press, 1998).

[89] ibid, 108.

[90] ibid, 113.

[91] ibid, 116.

upon preference (informed desire) but the reasons that make it worthwhile.[92] Just because I have a rationally grounded preference for some good does not confer the realisation of that good to include my well-being. Again, Rawls's grass-blade counter comes to mind. I may have a rational desire to count the blades of grass (for personal, aesthetic or horticultural reasons) but these reasons do not confer the activity's being worthwhile. And only worthwhile rationally grounded preferences count as increasing my well-being. But in order to determine what is *worthwhile* I must import a separate moral principle derived from some other source than 'interest' or 'well-being' (otherwise one would be involved in a circular argument).[93] The only candidate that one could bring forward (based upon the text) is ethical intuitionism.

Many rational desires, such as scientific investigation or Aristotelian goodness-based friendships, are not directed toward increasing well-being. In the case of science one may be driven to discover some truth that can be personally and generally painful (such as the trajectory of an asteroid that will shortly collide with the earth killing millions of people). Further, one of the basic tenets of scientific inquiry is that it is disinterested. To take an interest and thus increase well-being takes the investigator away from the objective mental state that is the goal of researchers.[94] Similarly, this is the case with Aristotle's goodness-based friendships.[95] It follows from the way Aristotle sets up the three forms of friendship: utility-based, pleasure-based, and goodness-based, that the goodness-based cannot be for the sake of increasing well-being, nevertheless; Aristotle argues (and I agree) that the object (goodness) is the highest of the three forms of friendship.

Therefore, joining forces again with Scanlon, I would contend that though rational aims and well-being share some connections, the former does not determine the latter. Further, well-being, as such, is without limits. One can always imagine a higher state of well-being.[96] This creates a boundary problem for well-being. Morality is a science, which, by necessity, must have constrained boundaries.[97] Therefore, well-being is an inappropriate grounding for morality, and if well-being is synonymous with *interest*, then there can be no interest-based grounding for morality and *a fortiori* for the law.

Well-being can also make one selfish. This was the first sense of well-being mentioned above. If one goes through life concentrating on how one will increase one's own well-being, then the focus becomes upon the self only. This solipsistic disposition I have termed *the egg carton approach.*[98] Egg carton individuals live

[92] ibid, 119.

[93] This last twist of the argument moves away from Scanlon.

[94] See my essay, 'Ethical Limitations on Scientific Research' in S Giordano, J Coggon and M Cappato (eds), *Scientific Freedom* (Bloomsbury, 2012) 149–61.

[95] Aristotle, *Ethica Nicomachea* (I Bywater ed, OUP, 1894) 1156a 7–1156b 4; 1156b 31.

[96] *cf* Scanlon, n 88, 129.

[97] My definition of morality as the science of the right and wrong in human action (Boylan, n 78, 3) should be noted here. This reflects my ethical realism position; see Boylan, n 10, ch 7.

[98] Boylan, n 77, 115–16.

in geographical communities, but just like eggs in a carton, they aspire to touch no one. There is no sense of social community. Some proponents of individual human rights are like this. They concentrate upon the individual to the exclusion of the community. By side-stepping this perspective they become *free riders* who live for themselves and indulge themselves in a fantasy that they have achieved whatever they have *all by themselves with no help from anyone.* Since no one has helped them, why should they help anyone else? Becoming an egg carton free rider is a real risk in the well-being (aka interest) approach. Thus, Scanlon's first sense of well-being when applied to Raz is shown to be flawed when used as a general support of morality and human rights.[99]

In the second, third-person, sense of well-being the perspective shifts from the decision-maker to that of a good friend or parent.[100] These individuals (benefactors) have different reasons for why x should or should not do y. The well-being component may shift from what will directly benefit x (as selfishly understood) to what might make x flourish (were he to do y). This may also include wider contexts such as family, community, country et al. The benefactor is acting according to what she sees as X's well-being (and thus in his interest). But this can become dicey when classical cases of paternalism present themselves. Benefactor A (say a parent) may say to her son, X (who wants to be a playwright) that a career as a lawyer is steadier and a better use of his talents. Mother may try to use her influence and any strings she still has attached to X in order to dissuade him from Y (trying it out on Broadway) in order to do Z (becoming a corporate lawyer). Mother may be correct if one gauges success on being able to support oneself financially. From a statistical viewpoint *ceteris paribus* Mother may be right in her assessment that her son chose doing Z over Y. If X is really interested in his well-being (gauged by statistically probable outcomes), then he should choose Z over Y.

According to this analysis well-being, as such, is also inadequate to justify Consent as an underpinning of the law.[101]

II. Grounding the Law: Morality

The alternative to the positivist/contractarian account that uses Consent to give legitimacy to legal systems is to base the fundamental justification of the law upon something else, such as a naturalistic moral theory. Beyleveld and Brownsword are on board here. They promote Alan Gewirth's PGC. The PGC enjoins us to 'Act in

[99] See my discussion in Boylan, n 10, ch 5.
[100] Scanlon, n 88, 134.
[101] Of course many readers of this chapter will respond that Gewirth founded his basic rights upon freedom and well-being. This is why I created the Table of Embeddedness to give greater specification of just what goods can scientifically be attached to the possibility of action. For the argument on this see Boylan (2014), n 10, ch 6.

accord with the generic rights of your recipients as well as yourself'.[102] The PGC works as a deontological single principle of morality in the same logical axiomatic structure as Kant's first and second forms of the categorical imperative.[103] The functional value of the single principle strategy in moral theory is that it employs the logical structure of axiomatic geometry (the most mechanically defensible machine of inference) to the realm of human action.[104] This is what I call the *naturalisation process*. This process creates naturalistic criteria that ground morality and *a fortiori* the law and Consent.

Now there has been some debate on whether this enterprise entails that the so-called 'is-ought' problem has been solved. Alan Gewirth certainly thought so.[105] However, it has been my contention that the framework of the 'is-ought' problem harks back to Hume's mistaken conjecture that there are pure fact and pure value statements that are separated by a great divide.[106] Instead, many in contemporary philosophy of science hold that there is some residue of value in all factual statements and some residue of fact in all value statements.[107] Thus, in the spirit of Aristotle's *epi to polu*, we can modify the enterprise to one which characterises 'largely factual statements' and 'largely value statements'.[108] Accepting my ontological characterisation over Hume's will silence many of the critics of the PGC.

Examining the foundations of human action as a means of describing *human nature* is a naturalistic exercise of considerable importance. Gewirth's PGC and my own work on 'The Moral Status of Basic Goods', 'The Table of Embeddedness' and 'The Personal Worldview Imperative' aspire to a common goal of grounding human nature in purposive action toward some end that the agent considers to be good.[109] Others who focused upon human action as a general grounding for morality include Alan Donagan and Donald Davidson (who were together for a few years at the University of Chicago). Together the three would get into extended verbal exchanges on action theory at the University of Chicago's seminar

[102] A Gewirth, *Reason and Morality* (University of Chicago Press, 1978) 135.

[103] My connection between the theories of Kant, Gewirth, and Alan Donagan are set out in M Boylan, *Basic Ethics* 1st edn (Prentice Hall, 2000) ch 4.

[104] I discuss this in terms of formal logical inference in Boylan, n 77, ch 1. For a critical discussion of my account see JS Gordon (ed), *Morality and Justice: Reading Boylan's A Just Society* (Lexington Books, 2009).

[105] A Gewirth, 'The "Is-Ought" Problem Resolved' (1973–74) 47 Presidential Address, *Proceedings and Addresses of the American Philosophical Association* 34.

[106] D Hume, *An Enquiry Concerning Human Understanding* (E Steinberg ed, Hackett, 1977) 12.2–3.

[107] eg H Putnam, *The Collapse of the Fact/Value Dichotomy and other Essays* (Harvard University Press, 2004).

[108] Here I am following J Griffin, *On Human Rights* (OUP, 2008) 35–36.

[109] The first sentence of my book *A Just Society* reads: 'All people, by nature, desire to be good.' This means that the object of their action aspires to fulfilment of an outcome that they consider to be good (from the perspective of their own personal worldview—which may be excellent or corrupt (judged by the Personal Worldview Imperative: 'All people must develop a single comprehensive and internally coherent worldview that is good and that we strive to act out in our daily lives') (Boylan, n 77, 21). These all come together to support natural law in Boylan, n 10.

series.[110] These discussions affected each philosopher's consequent writings. What set Gewirth apart from the other theorists was his penchant for the *freedom* component of human action. This freedom was for the sake of the agent's well-being. By making the interaction dialectical, the alleged result would have a powerful effect on the other agents in society. The dynamics of this dialectical interaction were forcefully interpreted by Deryck Beyleveld in his powerful book *The Dialectical Necessity of Morality*.[111]

This tack moves us into the region of natural law. Now some people (particularly contemporary philosophers) are loath to accept theories of natural law because they believe that they are consistent with organised religion. And since contemporary philosophers in Europe, North America and Australia are (for the most part) atheists, this is a real problem for some advocates of natural law.

However, it should be noted that Beyleveld and Brownsword explicitly reject any relationship between faith in God and acceptance of the PGC.[112] They argue that both theism and atheism deny the PGC. Their argument is based on their reconstructions of arguments by Kant and Leibniz in the context of the PGC's dialectical necessity.[113] Gewirth said that he explicitly held a theory of natural law, but did *not* tie it to any belief in God. This stance was also present in our co-written article on Marsilius of Padua.[114] Thus, one need not be a theist to be a defender of natural law. Gewirth and those (like Beyleveld and Brownsword) who accept the PGC and its impact upon society are bound to natural law (via naturalistic morality) as the grounding for *legal* systems around the globe and throughout human history. This is similar to the strong claims made by another deontologist, Immanuel Kant.

However, some say that there is a problem with *Consent in the Law* because so few European, North American and Australian philosophers agree with the PGC.[115] It is my considered judgement that this is a bogus argument. Since when is Truth a popularity contest? If a philosopher can bring forth various points of contention that fit together into a larger argument and can defend them against attack, then that is all that is required. To those supposed detractors, I would say, 'Put up [your counter arguments] or shut up!'

[110] A Donagan, *The Theory of Morality* (University of Chicago Press, 1977) 41–42; 44–47; 55–56; 124–25; D Davidson, 'Psychology as Philosophy' (237) and 'Mental Events' (222) in *Essays on Actions and Events* (Clarendon Press, 1980).

[111] D Beyleveld, *The Dialectical Necessity of Morality* (University of Chicago Press, 1991).

[112] D Beyleveld and R Brownsword, *Human Dignity in Bioethics and Biolaw* (OUP, 2002) 134–41.

[113] They conclude that 'it is dialectically necessary for agents to aspire to radical agnosticism … [otherwise they] deny that there is a categorical imperative, and thus there are any moral duties or rights at all as conceived of in Gewirthian theory': ibid, 140–41.

[114] See M Boylan and A Gewirth, 'Marsilius of Padua' in DM Borchert (eds), *The Encyclopedia of Philosophy* 2nd edn (Macmillan, 2006).

[115] For examples of this argument see NC Manson, 'Consent in the Law' (2010) 27(2) *Journal of Applied Philosophy* 215; B Capps, 'Consent in the Law' (2008) 28(1) *Legal Studies* 149; W Lucy, 'Consent in the Law' (2009) 4(4) *International Journal of Law in Context* 419.

III. Conclusion

What this chapter has sought to do is to explore a central tenet of Beyleveld and Brownsword's book *Consent in the Law* by examining first consent as a personal permission within a procedural context and Consent as a substantive grounding that must be seen in the context of a single-principle naturalistic moral theory that is epitomised by the PGC. As such, I characterise it as a non-theistic instance of the natural law. I have also examined briefly a formal positivist grounding and a contractarian grounding (as possible objectors to Beyleveld and Brownsword) in order to show that these popular forms of Consent are not as strong as Beyleveld and Brownsword's natural law approach. As the presiding judge in the courtroom of truth, the verdict of this judge sides with Beyleveld and Brownsword. Case dismissed.

6

Advance Refusals and the Personal Identity Objection

SHAUN D PATTINSON*

I. Introduction

Imagine Anna who contemplates requiring future medical treatment or care, and wishes to make a decision to be applied when she is no longer competent. She wishes to ensure that, if specified circumstances occur, she will not be given life-sustaining treatment and will therefore be allowed to die. The moral and legal authority of such an *advance refusal* can clearly be no greater than the authority of a contemporaneous refusal.[1] It could, however, be less. In English law, an adult has an almost unlimited right to contemporaneously refuse treatment, even if life-sustaining.[2] And, under s 26(1) of the Mental Capacity Act 2005 (the 2005 Act), a 'valid' and 'applicable' advance refusal of treatment has the same legal force as a valid contemporaneous refusal. Thus, in theory at least, an advance refusal complying with certain procedural conditions is binding in English law.

Advance refusals—indeed any attempt to give effect to a patient's prior views and values—present two challenges. The *first challenge* is ensuring that an advance refusal sufficiently represents Anna's will on what should happen in the situation in which she later finds herself. The application of Anna's previous refusal presents practical difficulties beyond those presented by a contemporaneous refusal by a competent individual. The issue is that the scope and meaning of her wishes needs to be interpreted in a context with potentially unanticipated features without the

* Professor of Medical Law and Ethics, Durham University. I am grateful to Deryck Beyleveld, Roger Brownsword, Patrick Capps and Zoe Gounari for reading and commenting on an earlier draft of this chapter and for additional comments from the participants of the *Ethical Rationalism and the Law* conference in Durham, October 2015. The usual caveat applies.

[1] I have considered contemporaneous and advance requests elsewhere: SD Pattinson, 'Contemporaneous and Advance Requests: The Fight for Rights at the End of Life' in J Herring and J Wall (eds), *Landmark Cases in Medical Law* (Hart Publishing, 2015) 255–69.

[2] eg *Re T* [1993] Fam 95 and *Re B (Consent to Treatment: Capacity)* [2002] EWHC 429. In contrast, the courts have denied that there is a right to requested treatment, whether the request is contemporaneous or made in advance: see Pattinson, n 1.

ability to return to Anna for further discussion and consideration. The *second challenge* builds on Parfit's musings on personal identity[3] and will be referred to as the *personal identity objection*. According to this objection,

> the very process that renders the individual incompetent and brings the advance directive into play can—and indeed often does—destroy the conditions necessary for her personal identity and thereby undercuts entirely the moral authority of the directive.[4]

That is to say, some contend that the loss of ability to make contemporaneous treatment decisions will (at least sometimes) change Anna's identity, so that the individual to whom the advance refusal is to apply is no longer Anna.

This chapter will evaluate the response of English law to these two challenges by reference to the ethical rationalism of Gewirth, as expanded and applied by Beyleveld.[5] The focus will be on the second challenge, namely, the personal identity objection. Support will be offered for the implicit rejection of this objection by English law. It will be argued that the plausibility of the personal identity objection derives from the principle that life-sustaining treatment should not be removed at the whim of a third party, but (contrary to appearances) the objection does not fully engage this principle. It will also be argued that while at first sight it appears that the approach of English law to the first challenge suggests some normative inconsistency with its response to the second, in practice, this normative inconsistency is more apparent than real. That is, the response of English law to the challenge of ensuring that the advance refusal represents Anna's will is evolving and thereby becoming easier to reconcile with its rejection of the personal identity objection.

A preliminary terminological issue arises with regard to the use of 'competence' and 'capacity' in this chapter.[6] An individual will be described as *competent* when judged to possess sufficient cognitive-functional faculties to be able to make a decision with respect to a given situation. An individual will be said to have *capacity* when possessing the decision-making authority required for a legally valid decision. This distinction is useful because capacity need not track competence. In English law, for example, a child who is considered cognitively able to make a particular treatment decision (that is, competent) may be denied the legal authority (that is, capacity) to validly refuse treatment in the face of judicial or parental consent.[7] An attribution of competence (so defined) requires that the patient be

[3] D Parfit, *Reason and Persons* (Clarendon Press, 1984) esp 204–17.

[4] A Buchanan, 'Advance Directives and the Personal Identity Problem' (1988) 17 *Philosophy and Public Affairs* 277, 280. See also A Buchanan and D Brock, *Deciding for Others* (CUP, 1989) 155.

[5] See, eg, A Gewirth, *Reason and Morality* (University of Chicago Press, 1978); D Beyleveld, *The Dialectical Necessity of Morality: An Analysis and Defence of Alan Gewirth's Argument to the Principle of Generic Consistency* (University of Chicago Press, 1991); D Beyleveld and SD Pattinson, 'Precautionary Reasoning as a Link to Moral Action' in M Boylan (ed), *Medical Ethics* (Prentice-Hall, 2000) 39.

[6] See further SD Pattinson, *Medical Law and Ethics* 4th edn (Sweet & Maxwell, 2014) ch 5.

[7] eg *Re W (A Minor) (Medical Treatment: Court's Jurisdiction)* [1993] Fam 64, esp [84] and [86] and *An NHS Foundation Hospital v P* [2014] EWHC 1650, esp [12].

considered to have the cognitive ability to understand and able to exercise that ability in the context under consideration. Since competence is task specific, patients who apparently have the cognitive abilities to make a decision must be considered to lack competence if they apparently cannot exercise those abilities in relation to a specific task or decision. For example, a patient who is completely overcome with emotion every time she thinks about her cancer is (unless and until this is addressed) incompetent to make decisions concerning her cancer, even if considered cognitively able to make other decisions at an equivalent level of complexity.

II. The Personal Identity Objection

The personal identity objection has its origins in the view that psychological continuity with one's past self is a necessary condition for personal identity.[8] According to this view, continuity with previous memories, states and dispositions varies in degree and a sufficient degree of continuity is required for the retention of personal identity.[9] An individual who falls below the relevant threshold of continuity is severed from his or her past identity and, if alive, acquires a different identity.[10] Such is said to have occurred when an individual's memory retention and personality is considered to have changed profoundly. In such circumstances, it is supposed, giving effect to an advance refusal involves illegitimately applying one individual's will to a different individual.

There are two important points about the personal identity objection to which I will return below. *First*, to regard Anna in the past (Anna Then) as a different individual to Anna in the present (Anna Now) is to deprive Anna Then of various rights and responsibilities over her body in the future. *Secondly*, it requires a particular type of metaphysical story to be told about the two Annas. Anna Then must be considered to have either a continued existence disconnected from her physical body or to have ceased to exist. Similarly, the living body of Anna Now must be considered to be either connected to a different mind or an empty shell without a mind.[11]

Supporters of the personal identity objection differ with regard to its ambit. This chapter will examine and respond to the use of this objection by Dresser and

[8] J Locke, *An Essay Concerning Human Understanding* (R Wooldhouse ed, Penguin Classics, 1997) 302; Parfit, n 3, 204–09.

[9] See esp Buchanan, n 4, 280.

[10] See, eg, R Dresser, 'Dworkin on Dementia: Elegant Theory, Questionable Policy' (1995) 25 *Hastings Center Report* 32, 35 and Buchanan, n 4.

[11] This latter option is only consistent with the personal identity objection where a mind is not required for moral status, because otherwise there can be no objection to imposing Anna Then's views on Anna Now.

Buchanan. Dresser rejects the authority of advance refusals in favour of treating incompetent patients according to their 'present best interests' and invokes the personal identity objection as one of her reasons.[12] She cites Parfit to support her view that where Anna has 'undergone substantial psychological alteration', Anna Then's views lack moral authority with regard to the treatment of Anna Now.[13] In contrast, Buchanan holds that Anna Then's past views only become irrelevant if Anna Now, though incompetent, is a *person*.[14] He argues that imposing advance decisions on another *person* involves their subjugation (and is thereby analogous to slavery), whereas non-persons can legitimately be subject to the 'surviving interests' of the past person they used to be.[15] Buchanan's conditions for personhood are sufficiently similar to Gewirth's conditions for agency to enable them to be considered equivalent for the purposes of this chapter.[16] That is to say that, in this chapter, a person/agent is a being that is capable of acting for voluntarily chosen purposes.

Three Hypothetical Patients

To facilitate discussion of the personal identity objection, as invoked by Dresser and Buchanan, consider three hypothetical patients with key differences with regard to their current abilities: Bob, Cuc and Eve. All have made advance refusals of life-sustaining treatment to be applied in specified future circumstances, which now arise. At the time of making those refusals, all were adults considered to have acted both voluntarily and competently, and to have understood their medical prognosis and future medical situation. All three appear to have suffered significant (in some cases total) memory loss. Doctors consider administration of the care or treatment refused in the advance refusals to be necessary to keep the patients alive.

Bob: Antibiotics Refused in Advance of a Vegetative State

Following a stroke, Bob is judged to be in a vegetative state. His heart continues to beat, his brain-stem continues to function, he turns, he sleeps and he wakes, but is

[12] eg R Dresser, 'Life, Death, and Incompetent Patients: Conceptual Infirmities and Hidden Values in the Law' (1986) 28 *Arizona Law Review* 373, 374.

[13] R Dresser, 'Missing Persons: Legal Perceptions of Incompetent Patients' (1994) 46 *Rutgers Law Review* 609, 628 (n 49); Dresser, 'Life, Death, and Incompetent Patients: Conceptual Infirmities and Hidden Values in the Law', n 12, 380–81; Dresser, 'Dworkin on Dementia: Elegant Theory, Questionable Policy', n 10, 35.

[14] Buchanan, n 4, 284.

[15] See Buchanan, n 4, esp 281–82 and 287.

[16] Buchanan, n 4, 284 lists a number of popular criteria for personhood: (a) conceiving oneself as conscious over time, (b) the ability to appreciate reasons for or against acting and (c) the ability to engage in purposive sequences of actions.

considered irreversibly unconscious due to damage to his higher brain.[17] He had made an advance refusal of antibiotics to be applied if he enters a vegetative state. Bob now has an infection, which can be treated with antibiotics.

Dresser and Buchanan differ over Bob. Both would consider Bob Then and Bob Now to be different individuals. Buchanan cites a permanent vegetative state as an example of a condition that severs psychological continuity and therefore causes a loss of personal identity.[18] Dresser and Buchanan differ, however, because Buchanan's view is that Bob Now is a 'nonperson' and Bob Then has surviving interests that 'override whatever extremely limited obligations we may have to sustain the life of the surviving individual'.[19] Dresser is likely to agree that not providing antibiotics to Bob is defensible, but this would not be because Bob Then's advance refusal applies; rather it would be because antibiotics are simply not in Bob Now's interests. In short, Buchanan would apply Bob's advance refusal, whereas Dresser would consider it to lack authority on the basis of the personal identity objection.

Cuc: Antibiotics Refused in Advance of Severe Dementia

Cuc[20] is suffering from Alzheimer's disease. During the very early stages, she made an advance refusal of antibiotics and any other life-saving treatment. Her condition has deteriorated significantly and she now lives at home with the help of carers. She has apparent problems making new memories and those around her consider her old memories to be fading rapidly. Cuc talks to those around her and is considered able to make some simple day-to-day decisions. She regularly reads, though her place in the book seems to jump randomly from one day to the next, and paints, though she paints the same picture every day. Her carers consider her to be extremely happy and gaining great pleasure from her activities. Cuc now has a chest infection and requires antibiotics. Her doctors consider her to lack the competence required to make this decision.

Cuc is the type of patient for whom the personal identity objection is typically raised. Dresser and Buchanan consider apparently permanent memory loss capable of depriving a dementia patient of her past identity.[21] Their writings suggest that both would consider Cuc Now to lack sufficient psychological continuity with Cuc Then to be considered the same individual. Both would conclude that her

[17] See B Jennett, 'The Vegetative State' (2002) *73 Journal of Neurology Neurosurgery and Psychiatry* 355.

[18] Buchanan, n 4, 280–81.

[19] Buchanan, n 4, 287.

[20] Cuc is loosely based on Margo: see AD Firlik, 'Margo's Logo' (1991) 265 *Journal of the American Medical Association* 201 and R Dworkin, *Life Dominion: An Argument about Abortion and Euthanasia* (Harper Collins, 1993) ch 8.

[21] Consider, eg, Buchanan, n 4, 281.

advance refusal now lacks moral authority on account of the personal identity objection and would want her to be treated with antibiotics.

Buchanan only accepts the validity of the personal identity objection while Cuc remains a 'person' (that is, an agent). It seems that he would consider Cuc Now to be a person on the basis of her apparent ability to act for *some* voluntarily chosen purposes. Cuc's condition is, however, degenerative. Buchanan opines that there

> will be cases like that of a profoundly and permanently damaged demented individual with Alzheimer's dementia, where neurological damage has destroyed a person, and all that survives is a terminally ill nonperson with what we may call radically truncated interests.[22]

Thus, at some point in the future, Buchanan would hold that Cuc Then's advance refusal will gain authority on the basis that she will have neurologically deteriorated to the point of being a 'nonperson' to whom it would be legitimate to apply Cuc Then's 'surviving interests'.

Eve: Animal Heart Valve Refused in Advance of Memory Loss

Since her brain injury, Eve identifies as a woman, eats meat and exercises extensively. Before her brain injury, she was a sedentary man known as Evan. Evan had been diagnosed with a heart condition that would, at some future date, require a replacement heart valve. As a life-long vegan, he made an advance refusal of use of an animal valve in his treatment. The brain injury has caused apparently permanent memory loss. Eve's family say that she is now a different person to Evan. When informed that she needs a replacement heart valve, she opts for an animal valve because a mechanical valve would limit her physical activity and ability to exercise. Her doctors consider her competent to make this decision.

Irrespective of the personal identity objection, Evan's advance refusal lacks authority over Eve, because of her ability to make a contemporaneous decision. It does not matter whether Eve and Evan are the same or different individuals. Eve's will takes priority over her earlier will and, *a fortiori*, over the will of a different person who once inhabited her body. What is, however, interesting about this hypothetical patient is that Evan and Eve do not seem to share a personality or personality-related memories. It therefore seems to me that Dresser and Buchanan would consider Eve to lack sufficient psychological continuity with Evan to be regarded as the same individual.

The relationship between Evan and Eve is of relevance to matters outside the context of advance refusals. Yet, English law does not remove an individual's debts or property solely on account of a subsequent radical personality change or loss of competence. Evan is not, for any legal purposes, considered to be dead and

[22] Buchanan, n 4, 285.

replaced by another individual inhabiting or being his body. Eve is not, for example, freed from responsibility for Evan's crimes on account of her loss of memory or personality change. Evan is not regarded as having died, but is the same legal person as Eve.

III. The Mental Capacity Act and Court of Protection

This section will examine the response of English law to the three hypothetical patients outlined above. Our starting point must be the Mental Capacity Act 2005. The 2005 Act only applies where the patient is reasonably believed to lack capacity to make a particular decision. That is, where an impairment or disturbance in the functioning of the mind or brain (s 2(1)) has rendered the patient unable to understand the relevant information, retain it, use or weigh it, or communicate the resulting decision (s 3(1)). On this test, Eve will be regarded as able to make a legally valid contemporaneous decision. 'Evan's' advance refusal is therefore legally irrelevant. The law makes no inquiry as to whether or not Evan and Eve are the same person.

In contrast, Bob and Cuc now lack legal capacity. If their advance refusals lack legal validity, then they are to be treated in accordance with their 'best interests' under the 2005 Act (s 5). The decision-maker is to weigh all factors about which he or she is aware and 'it would be reasonable to regard as relevant' (s 4(2)/(11). This includes the patient's 'past and present wishes and feelings' and their relevant 'beliefs and values' (s 4(6)). Thus, whereas a 'valid' and 'applicable' advance refusal is binding, other past views and values are merely factors to be weighed by the decision-maker. The Act gives no guidance as to the weight to be given to any of these factors. Let us consider the application of the best interests test to Bob and Cuc, on the assumption that their advance refusals are not valid and applicable. Bob seems to have no experiences at all and English law would not regard his continued treatment to be in his best interests, but would, in practice, require referral to the Court of Protection to confirm his diagnosis and prognosis as one of a 'permanent vegetative state'.[23] Cuc has apparently positive experiences (such as reading and painting), so the best interest test operating (as it does) in accordance with a presumption in favour of life[24] would favour the administration of life-sustaining treatment, unless significant weight is given to her past views and values. Thus, a binding advance refusal would support a quicker rejection of life-sustaining treatment for Bob and would support removal of otherwise required life-sustaining treatment with regard to Cuc.

[23] See, eg, *Airedale NHS Trust v Bland* [1993] AC 789 and *Aintree University Hospitals NHS Foundation Trust v James* [2013] UKSC 67, [36] and [47].

[24] eg *Re T* [1993] Fam 95, 112 and *Aintree* [2013] UKSC 67, [35].

To be valid, an advance refusal must not have been directly or indirectly withdrawn. More specifically, it is rendered invalid where the patient has:

(a) withdrawn it when he/she has capacity to do so;
(b) subsequently conferred the authority to make the relevant decision on an attorney; or
(c) 'done anything else clearly inconsistent with the advance decision remaining his fixed decision' (s 25(2)).

Neither (a) nor (b) apply to Bob or Cuc. In my view (c), withdrawal by inconsistent conduct, should be interpreted as requiring that the inconsistent act take place while the patient has capacity.[25] That is because an alternative interpretation would render (a) superfluous and the restriction of (c) to the inconsistent behaviour of a patient *with capacity* is supported by the example given in the Code of Practice.[26] There is, however, a common law presumption in favour of prolonging life, which the European Court of Human Rights has opined (in a case concerning an advance *request*) 'accords with the spirit of the Convention'.[27] It is possible, though I believe unlikely, that this presumption could be used to support an interpretation of (c) that permits effect to be given to the desire of a patient lacking capacity for clinically indicated life-prolonging treatment refused in advance. Bob and Cuc cannot, however, be properly said to have 'done' anything 'clearly inconsistent' with the terms of their advance refusals. Losing the ability to interact or communicate (Bob) or being in a very happy demented state (Cuc) are not relevant actions.

To be applicable, the advance refusal must apply to the treatment and circumstances now faced by the patient (s 25(4)) and, in the case of life-sustaining treatment, must be explicit, in writing, signed and witnessed (s 25(5)/(6)). Section 25(4)(c) declares an advance refusal to be inapplicable where there are 'reasonable grounds for believing that circumstances exist which [the patient] … did not anticipate at the time of the advance decision and which would have affected his decision had he anticipated them' (s 25(4)(c)). This cannot be said to be the case with regard to Bob, whose advance refusal anticipates the very circumstances in which he now finds himself. Cuc clearly anticipated becoming more demented, but did she anticipate being in a very happy demented state and, if not, would that have changed her view? The sketch of her situation above does not specify why she made the advance refusal (there might, of course, be means of acquiring that information from others). But her blanket refusal of future treatment does not attempt to distinguish between situations where non-treatment would cause

[25] See SD Pattinson, *Medical Law and Ethics* 1st edn (Sweet & Maxwell, 2006) 483 and 4th edn (Sweet & Maxwell, 2014) 494.

[26] See Department for Constitutional Affairs, *Mental Capacity Act: Code of Practice* (The Stationery Office, 2007) para 9.40.

[27] *Burke v UK* (No 19807/06, 7 July 2006).

distress to her future self. This suggests that her concern was not to avoid any future suffering but being kept alive in a demented state.

Notice that neither validity nor applicability deny legal authority to an advance refusal on account of their drafter being a different person to the current patient. Rather, both are concerned with the first challenge identified in relation to Anna, namely, the challenge of ensuring that the advance refusal sufficiently represents her will on what should happen in the situation in which she now finds herself. On the face of it, the law's response to this first challenge makes it easy to disregard an advance refusal. Indeed, many commentators have pointed to the ease by which an advance refusal—previously under the common law and now under the Act—can be deprived of legal authority.[28]

The potential liability of doctors is, for example, loaded in favour of their disregarding an advance refusal, rather than following it. Under s 26(2), the doctor avoids liability for disregarding an advance refusal, unless 'he is satisfied' that it exists, is valid and is applicable. Under s 26(3), a doctor avoids liability when giving effect to an advance refusal where 'he reasonably believes' that it exists, is valid and is applicable. Thus, it appears to be harder to sue or convict a doctor for disregarding an advance refusal (it must be shown that he was satisfied that it had legal authority) than it is to sue/convict him for giving effect to it (it must be shown that either he did not believe it to have legal authority or any belief that it had legal authority was not reasonable).

Recent case law has, however, gone some way towards interpreting the provisions of the Act so as to ensure that effect is given to the will of the individual who made the advance refusal.

In *X Primary Care Trust v XB*, an advance refusal was interpreted so as to give effect to a patient's prior will, determined from oral evidence, despite the written document itself referring to his invasive ventilation device as 'non-invasive ventilation' and including the words 'valid until' followed by a date that had expired by the time of the hearing.[29] Thus, the terms of a written advance refusal are viewed as no more than evidence of the patient's previous will and thereby subject to interpretation in the light of other evidence.

In *Newcastle upon Tyne Hospitals Foundation Trust v LM*, the Court of Protection gave effect to the patient's prior wish not to be given a blood transfusion, despite her advance refusal apparently not having been written, signed and witnessed, as required for an advance refusal of life-sustaining treatment to be applicable under the 2005 Act.[30] Peter Jackson J held that in consequence of the refusal being clear and capacitated 'the doctors rightly considered [that it] must be respected' and 'in

[28] See, eg, S Michalowski, 'Advance Refusals of Life-Sustaining Medical Treatment: The Relativity of the Absolute Right' (2005) 68 *Modern Law Review* 958 and AR MacLean, 'Advance Directives and the Rocky Waters of Anticipatory Decision-Making' (2008) 16 *Medical Law Review* 1. For a comparative consideration see S Halliday, 'Legislating to Give Effect to Precedent Autonomy: Comparative Reflections on Legislative Incompetence' (2011) 11 *Medical Law International* 127.

[29] [2012] EWHC 1390, esp at [10] and [15].

[30] [2014] EWHC 454 (COP).

the alternative', giving 'determinate weight' to her long-standing beliefs and values when applying s 4(6), the blood transfusion was not in her best interests.[31] Thus, a refusal that technically does not satisfy the strict provisions of the 2005 Act for a binding advance refusal could still be given effect. In my view, his Lordship's 'alternative' is best understood as being no more than an alternative expression of the same point, rather than an alternative ground for the decision. This avoids his Lordship being interpreted as rejecting the clear words of the legislation.[32]

Giving considerable weight to the patient's previous views when applying the best interest test is the approach required by the Supreme Court in a case decided in the year before *LM*. In *Aintree University Hospitals NHS Foundation Trust v James*, Lady Hale (with whom the other Justices agreed) declared:

> insofar as Sir Alan Ward and Arden LJ were suggesting [in the court below] that the test of the patient's wishes and feelings was an objective one, what the reasonable patient would think, again I respectfully disagree. The purpose of the best interests test is to consider matters from the patient's point of view. That is not to say that his wishes must prevail, any more than those of a fully capable patient must prevail.[33]

This is a very significant judgment. As indicated earlier, on its face the 2005 Act appears to relegate previous views and values not satisfying the procedural requirements for a binding advance refusal to mere factors to be weighed against other potentially equally important factors. Indeed, operating in the context of a presumption in favour of life, the application of the best interests test seemed to give relatively little weight to the patient's prior views and values.[34] It is difficult to reconcile apparently binding force being given to advance refusals satisfying certain procedural requirements when advance refusals falling just short of satisfying those requirements are dealt with as mere factors in the application of the best interests test. The *best interests* test asks the decision-maker to determine what is in the patient's 'objective' interests, whereas a *substituted judgement* test seeks to ask the decision-maker to attempt to make the decision that the patient would have made by applying the patient's views and values.[35] Giving effect to advance refusals would seem, as a matter of normative consistency, to support adoption of the substituted judgement test over the best interests test in those cases where the patient had previous views and values that fall just short of the procedural clarity required for a binding advance refusal. *Aintree* and *LM*, however, go a long way towards removing any such normative inconsistency. They seem to take us as close to a 'substituted judgement' test as is possible without expressly adopting it over the 'best interests' test, which the courts cannot do within the terms of the 2005 Act.

[31] [2014] EWHC 454, [22] and [23].

[32] This would involve the replacement of the decision of a democratically elected body with those of a non-democratically elected judge without any weighty justification. See further below.

[33] [2013] UKSC 67, [45].

[34] See, eg, *Re T* [1993] Fam 95 and *HE v Hospital NHS Trust* [2003] EWHC 1017. See also the discussion in Michalowski, n 27.

[35] See further Pattinson, n 6, 148–50.

Lady Hale added, with regard to the patient in a minimally conscious state with whom she was concerned in *Aintree*, '[e]ven if it is possible to determine what his views were in the past, they might well have changed in the light of the stresses and strains of his current predicament'.[36] Notice that her concerns remain focused on the first challenge (that is, understanding what the patient would have actually wanted in the situation in which he now finds himself), rather than the second challenge (that is, the personal identity objection).

Hayden J in *Sheffield Teaching Hospitals NHS Foundation Trust v TH* has, however, interpreted Lady Hale's view on the best interests test to be further away from the substituted judgement test than I have suggested. His Lordship interprets Lady Hale as holding that best interests are to be considered 'in an holistic way'[37] and cautions that:

> 'Wishes' and 'best interests' should never be conflated, they are entirely separate matters which may ultimately weigh on different sides of the balance sheet.[38]

It may be that this is less of a retreat from the substituted judgement test than it first appears to be. In the sentences immediately before, Hayden J emphasised the importance of 'rigorous and scrupulous' attempts to seek out past views on the basis that 'the clarity, cogency and force that they are found to have will have a direct impact on the weight they are to be given'.[39] It is therefore possible to view Hayden J as emphasising caution when attributing determinate previous views to the patient. Indeed, as we shall see, moral precaution may legitimately require us to consider any ambiguities in the patient's past views in a way that is protective of their current positive experiences.

In summary, English law does not consider apparent memory loss or personality change as a basis for concluding that there has been a change of identity. Anna, Bob, Cuc and Eve would be considered to have retained their identities over time. An advance refusal may lack legal authority on the basis that it lacks sufficient compliance with procedural safeguards to be considered determinate of the patient's previous wishes, but those safeguards do not turn on a judgement concerned with loss of, or diminution in, psychological continuity.

IV. Advance Refusals and a Good Faith Attempt to Give Effect to the PGC

This section will first outline the moral theory under discussion in this book and then apply that moral theory to the personal identity objection to the authority of advance refusals.

[36] [2013] UKSC 67, [45].
[37] [2014] EWCOP 4, [36].
[38] [2014] EWCOP 4, [56].
[39] [2014] EWCOP 4, [56].

The Principle of Generic Consistency

In their book *Law as a Moral Judgment*, Beyleveld and Brownsword argue that legal validity consists in the exercise of morally legitimate power.[40] Their starting point for analysis is 'the enterprise of subjecting human conduct to the governance of rules'.[41] This enterprise, they argue, can only be understood in terms of the reasons that individuals have for complying with those rules, which is to say that the law must be viewed as an affair of practical reason. If practical reason can be shown to presuppose moral reason, it would follow that the legal enterprise is necessarily a moral enterprise. Gewirth's argument for the Principle of Generic Consistency (the PGC) seeks to show that practical reason does indeed presuppose moral reason. It uses a 'dialectically necessary' method, whereby the argument proceeds *dialectically* within the first-person perspective of an agent with all the steps of the argument following logically (that is, *necessarily*) from premises that cannot be coherently denied within this perspective (that is, *necessary* premises). In essence, Gewirth seeks to show that I (an agent) deny that I am an agent if I deny that all agents have rights to the generic conditions of agency (that is, the generic rights). This chapter will assume the soundness of Gewirth's dialectically necessary argument to the PGC. A summary of that argument can be found in the first and final chapters of this book.[42]

Gewirth distinguishes between the 'direct' and 'indirect' application of the PGC.[43] Direct applications involve substantive determinations as to whether or not actions are compatible with the generic rights of agents. For those matters that cannot be dealt with directly, the PGC requires certain procedural mechanisms in its application, which indirectly apply the PGC.

The generic rights established by Gewirth's dialectically necessary argument are claims-rights according to the will conception of rights.[44] That is to say, that they are to be understood as justifiable claims imposing correlative duties, the benefits of which are waivable by the rights-holder. Rights according to the will conception (will-rights) are to be contrasted with rights according to the interest conception (interest-rights), the benefits of which are not automatically waivable by the rights-holder.[45]

The generic rights are both negative (that is, rights of non-interference) and positive (that is, rights to assistance). They are rights to retain and obtain whatever

[40] D Beyleveld and R Brownsword, *Law as a Moral Judgment* (Sheffield Academic Press, 1994).

[41] See, eg, ibid, 120, citing L Fuller, *The Morality of Law* (Yale University Press, 1969).

[42] See P Capps and SD Pattinson, 'The Past, Present and Future of Ethical Rationalism' and D Beyleveld, 'What Is Gewirth and What is Beyleveld? A Retrospect with Comments on the Contributions'.

[43] See Gewirth, n 5, chs 4 and 5 respectively.

[44] On claim-rights see the seminal work of WN Hohfeld, *Fundamental Legal Conceptions: As Applied in Judicial Reasoning and Other Legal Essays* (WW Cook ed, Yale University Press, 1923).

[45] Compare, eg, HLA Hart, 'Are There Any Natural Rights?' (1955) 64 *Philosophical Review* 175 with N MacCormick, 'Rights in Legislation' in PMS Hacker and J Raz (eds), *Law, Morality and Society: Essays in Honour of HLA Hart* (Clarendon Press, 1977) 189.

an agent needs to act or act successfully, regardless of his specific purpose. These generic needs vary in degree. The generic needs and the corresponding generic rights can therefore be ranked according to the 'criterion of degrees of needfulness for action'.[46] Death may be an agent's purpose, or a consequence of it, but death itself is not a generic need. An agent who refuses life-sustaining treatment is therefore to be understood as exercising his or her generic rights, rather than claiming a generic right to die.

In addition to granting generic rights to agents, Gewirth considers the PGC to apply to non-agents who 'approach' being agents, and cites children and 'mentally deficient persons' as examples of beings with partial generic rights.[47] Unfortunately, Gewirth's argument to the PGC cannot establish that non-agents have any generic rights at all, no matter how close they approach being agents.[48] Gewirth has inferred that those others who act like agents (such as Cuc and Eve) are agents and those who display some but not all of the characteristics and behaviour expected of agents (such as Bob or a more demented Cuc) are non-agents who merely approach being agents. This inference is intuitive and seems perfectly reasonable, but it is not epistemologically secure. Agency involves a special kind of self-awareness (that is, reflective purposivity), which means that while I can know directly that I am an agent, I cannot know this directly of anyone other than myself. The inferences made by Gewirth about 'normal adults', children or 'mentally deficient persons'—which we all make on a day-to-day basis—depend on unverifiable metaphysical assumptions. I cannot eliminate the possibility that those others who behave like agents are very cleverly programmed robots without minds and that those others who do not behave like agents are actually locked-in agents unable to fully display their agency to me. Those possibilities are relevant to the application of the *categorical* requirement that I (any agent) act in accordance with the generic rights of agents.

I cannot strictly know whether or not Eve or Cuc are agents, but I can treat them as agents because they behave like agents. To mistakenly treat them as agents would involve unnecessarily restricting my freedom of action, but to mistakenly treat them as non-agents would be to fail to respect their generic rights, despite being able to do so. The PGC therefore requires me to treat Eva and Cuc (and anyone else who acts like an agent) as agents and act in accordance with their (presumed) generic rights. It follows that agency-like characteristics and behaviour must, under moral precaution, be considered evidence of agency.

Since Bob or a more demented Cuc do not behave like agents, I cannot coherently treat them as if they are able to exercise the generic rights. It is, however,

[46] See A Gewirth, *The Community of Rights* (Chicago University Press, 1996) 45–46. See also Gewirth, n 5, esp 53–58.

[47] See Gewirth, n 5, 120–24. The substance of the following argument, for the dialectical necessity of moral precaution, was seminally published in Beyleveld and Pattinson, n 5.

[48] See Beyleveld and Pattinson, n 5 and SD Pattinson, *Influencing Traits Before Birth* (Ashgate, 2002) ch 2.

possible and meaningful for me to guard against mistakenly treating them as non-agents by acting towards them in ways that would respect their generic rights should they (unknowably) happen to be agents. It is therefore dialectically necessary for me to grant Bob or any other being that displays some agency-like characteristics 'duties of protection' tracking their (presumed) generic interests. Thus, Eve and Cuc Now are to be treated as having will-rights to their presumed generic interests, whereas Bob and a more demented Cuc are to be treated as having interest-rights to their presumed generic interests.

What if I am faced with *a single-variable conflict* between respecting one of Eve's will-rights and respecting Bob's equivalent interest-right? *If no other variables arise*, my duties to Eve take precedence over my duties to Bob. This is an application of the 'criterion of avoidance of more probable harm'.[49] Moral precaution requires me to consider agency-like characteristics and behaviour to be evidence of agency, and Eve can be treated as an agent and therefore displays more of those characteristics than Bob, who cannot be treated as an agent. Thus, in a single-variable conflict of the type under consideration, an agent's duties to those others who can meaningfully be treated as having (presumed) generic interests will be proportionate to the degree to which those others approach being analogically agents. In single variable disputes, Eve and Cuc count for more than a very demented future Cuc, who in turn counts for more than Bob. There can, however, be differences not only between the agency-like behaviour displayed, but also the importance of the generic conditions affected[50] and the probability of any given action having effects on the generic conditions. Where, as here, the PGC-relevant values have not been rendered commensurable within an algorithm directly supported by the PGC, the best that we can do is rely on a procedural turn, operating to protect the unequivocally most important values of the PGC. The procedure must be one seeking, in good faith, to give effect to the PGC.

Beyleveld and Brownsword have considered the need for PGC-compliant procedures elsewhere.[51] Ultimately, they argue, the justification for proceduralism also requires that we avoid 'an infinite regress of one layer of proceduralism on another'.[52] In this light, they consider what a Gewirthian should make of the processes of representative government adopted by large modern democracies. It may well be the case that any given individual has not consented to the process by which delegated authority happens to be exercised by the State in which he or she lives and might not have voted for those who are elected at any given time. They argue that human agents, in recognising that their own judgement is not infallible, must consider a free, fair and transparent democratic process as simply the 'optimal compromise' by which committed Gewirthians can mutually co-exist in

[49] Beyleveld and Pattinson, n 5, 44.

[50] Measured by the criterion of degrees of needfulness for action.

[51] See, eg, D Beyleveld and R Brownsword, 'Principle, Proceduralism and Precaution in a Community of Rights' (2006) 19 *Ratio Juris* 141.

[52] ibid, 150.

a complex society governed by the PGC.[53] Gewirth refers to this as the 'method of consent'.[54] As an indirect application of the PGC, the democratic method only operates where there is 'rational and not unreasonable disagreement' over the direct application of the PGC for which there is no more optimal response.[55]

Applying the PGC to the Personal Identity Objection

The PGC only requires the personal identity objection to be dealt with indirectly where it cannot be dealt with directly. For the reasons below, any application of the PGC will place significant (and in some cases conclusive) restrictions on the permissibility of treating my past, present and future selves as distinct individuals and the past, present and future (presumed) selves of others as distinct individuals.

In *Human Dignity in Bioethics and Biolaw*, Beyleveld and Brownsword consider whether the PGC can be applied to give effect to the notion of duties to oneself by reference to a distinction between 'my future selves' and 'my present self'.[56] They argue that 'my future self' develops from, and is an extension of, 'my present self', and this makes the relationship between 'my present self' and 'future selves' different to my relations to others. It is for this reason, they argue, that 'my future selves' cannot call 'my present self' to account for harming them.

> If I could hold my 'past selves' to account, this would imply that I could never be held responsible in the future for my actions in the present. Therefore, in relation to a crucial aspect of rights-claims, I cannot properly be said to have past, present, and future selves. All there is, is me at different times.[57]

I agree. The PGC places significant limitations on how we must consider the relationship between a living body and a particular agent over time. To regard a person who has just awoken as a different person to the one who went to sleep last night is both to free the present person from responsibility for the actions of the person who went to sleep and to deprive the present person of the achievements, relationships and claims of the person who went to sleep. It deprives them of responsibility for infringing the rights of others and denies their claim to many specific rights for themselves. It follows that there are significant limits on the moral permissibility of treating a living human body as housing or being different agents over time. Continuity of identity over time cannot require an apparently unbroken continuity of consciousness.

But what does this mean in the context of an advance refusal made by Anna? The personal identity objection requires action contrary to any presumption of

[53] ibid, 152.
[54] See Gewirth, n 5, 304–12.
[55] Beyleveld and Brownsword, n 51, 147.
[56] D Beyleveld and R Brownsword, *Human Dignity in Bioethics and Biolaw* (OUP, 2001) 107.
[57] ibid, 107.

continuity of identity, as it requires a distinction between Anna Then and Anna Now. Anna's situation is not one where the costs of erring are all one way. We either mistakenly deny Anna's authority to exercise her will over her body in the future or mistakenly fail to attempt to extend the now incompetent Anna's biological life. But the conclusion that either is a morally significant risk is subject to a prior procedural assessment.

Before concluding that following an advance refusal presents a morally significant risk of failing to extend the patient's biological life, we must first conclude that, in the absence of the advance refusal, there is a duty to extend the patient's life. The PGC does not impose an absolute duty to provide life-sustaining treatment. For a start, positive generic rights are more limited than negative generic rights[58] and, when dealing with limited resources, relative moral status will be relevant (compare, for example, the status under moral precaution of Bob Now and Cuc Now). Determining whether there would otherwise be a duty to provide life-sustaining treatment involves a multiple variable calculation of the type requiring a PGC-compliant procedure.

Before concluding that failing to follow an advance refusal presents a morally significant risk of denying an agent's will over her body in the future, we must first conclude that the advance refusal captures what she would have wanted in the current situation. The PGC will again require a PGC-compliant response to this challenge. That response will need to take account of any procedural response to the question of whether there would otherwise be a duty to provide life-sustaining treatment to Anna. If it has been legitimately concluded that there would otherwise be such a duty, then moral precaution will need to be exercised when interpreting any ambiguities in her previously expressed views. Without examining this issue in depth, it is worth noting that the 2005 Act's requirements of 'validity' and 'applicability' are a response to this challenge by an elected body.

In short, the personal identity objection only arises for consideration as a challenge to the authority of Anna's advance refusal if we have already legitimately concluded that the refusal covers the current situation and there would otherwise be a duty to provide the life-sustaining treatment. Cuc's situation is one in which it is plausible that PGC-compatible procedures would support reaching these two conclusions. The demented Cuc currently behaves like an (incompetent) agent and administering the antibiotics poses no undue burden, she therefore has a very strong claim to a positive right to the antibiotics expected to save her life. If we assume that her refusal is witnessed, in writing, and expressly states that it applies even if she is in a happy demented state, it is difficult to see how it may be legitimately concluded that it did not represent her will with regard to the current situation. In these circumstances, is the case for accepting the personal

[58] See Gewirth, n 5, 217–30. See also the discussion of positive duties in SD Pattinson, 'Consent and Informational Responsibility' (2009) 35 *Journal of Medical Ethics* 176, 177, and the first chapter in this collection.

identity objection as plausible as the case for rejecting the objection? Two factors suggest not.

First, the criteria for identity and their application to Cuc must be compatible with the PGC, and this is questionable in relation to the personal identity objection. It vests identity in the retention of memories and personality traits above a certain threshold. But, it is not at all clear why an agent's identity must be defined and determined in this way. When Cuc makes an advance refusal that she intends to take effect even when her memory retention and personality traits fall below that threshold, why must she nonetheless accept that her future body will then house or be another agent? Why must others identify Cuc not in terms of her apparent retention of agency-like characteristics and behaviour over time, but in terms of a specific level of apparent retention of memory and personality traits?

Even if the PGC could support the Lockean-Parfitian theory of identity, it is unclear how we would identify the threshold point for apparent retention of memory and personality traits. At what point is it legitimate to conclude that Cuc's memories and personality traits are such that her body has ceased to be (or house) one presumed agent and is now (or now houses) another presumed agent? Wherever that point is, since Eve and Evan's memories and personality traits seem to be no more closely connected than those of Cuc Then and Cuc Now, they must also be regarded as having crossed that point. Any threshold of identity requiring Cuc Then to be regarded as a different agent to Cuc Now would have significant implications for when an individual is regarded as having ceased to exist. The psychological continuity criterion of identity implies that where an individual apparently loses and later regains their memories and personality traits, as in the case of some forms of mental illness, they are to be regarded as having lost one identity and then regained it; which seems to require that they be considered to have died and come back to life.

Secondly, the personal identity objection requires us to make more assumptions to accept it than it does to reject it. *To reject the personal identity objection*, I need to accept or assume that *either* Cuc has remained the same agent *or* consider Cuc Then's views on the treatment of Cuc Now to take priority over the views of other third parties. This second move is plausible because the two Cucs share a more intimate relationship than anyone else has with Cuc Now. *To accept the personal identity objection*, I need to accept or assume the converse of both of these points. Thus, I need to consider Cuc's body to be connected to, or be, a different agent to that to which it was connected when the advance refusal was made *and* consider her treatment decisions to be better made by someone other than Cuc Then.

If those factors do not, as I suggest, support rejection of the personal identity objection, they do at least justify the conclusion that a PGC-compliant procedure could in good faith reject the personal identity objection. That is to say that if the UK's democratic process is compatible with the PGC's requirements, then the approach of English law to the personal identity objection may at least be regarded as an indirect application of the PGC.

V. Conclusion

Assessing English law in terms of the requirements of an indirect application of the PGC, it need not be shown that the approach taken by English law is the only one capable of being supported by the PGC. Rather, it need only be shown that English law takes an approach compatible with a good faith attempt to give effect to the PGC. This I have done. I have argued that the personal identity objection requires more than the claim that life-sustaining treatment should not be removed at the whim of a third party. It requires the moral defensibility of three additional claims:

1. personal identity is to be determined according to 'psychological continuity', assessed by apparent retention of interpersonal memories and personality traits,
2. the threshold of psychological continuity is such that Anna Then is to be regarded as having a different identity to Anna Now, and
3. Anna Then has a weaker right to make decisions for Anna Now than another third party.

Since a good faith application of the PGC may legitimately reject these claims and assumptions, it is morally defensible for English law to reject the personal identity objection in relation to Anna, Bob and Cuc. These claims will similarly pose significant justificatory problems for other moral theories and their acceptance would require a radical reconsideration of when an individual is regarded as having died or otherwise freed from existing entitlements, obligations and relationships.

This chapter has examined the views of Dresser and Buchanan to demonstrate that the personal identity objection is no 'straw man' and there are, indeed, other supporters of this objection.[59] The position advanced by these theorists requires us to consider both Bob Now and Cuc Now to be different individuals to those who made the advance refusals. Dresser would seem to consider the personal identity objection to apply to Bob and Cuc, and Buchanan would consider it to apply to Cuc. It is morally and legally defensible for the Mental Capacity Act 2005 and the English Courts to reject these views.

[59] See, eg, N Gligorov and C Vitrano, 'The Impact of Personal Identity on Advance Directives' (2011) 45 *Journal of Value Inquiry* 147, esp 157–58.

7

Law as a Moral Judgment, the Domain of Jurisprudence, and Technological Management

ROGER BROWNSWORD*

I. Introduction

In the years immediately following the publication of *Law as a Moral Judgment*,[1] Deryck Beyleveld and I would sometimes reflect on the ways in which we might revise the book were we to rewrite it.[2] For the most part, our reflections focused on ways to make things simpler and clearer for readers—because there is no doubt that the difficulty that we had in articulating the key issues as we wrote the book converted into a challenging read. Thirty years on, I am sure that there are some respects in which we could make the book more accessible to readers. At the same time, however, unless readers are prepared to accept the validity of the Gewirthian[3] argument that, for agents, there is no coherent denial of the centrality of moral reason (and, indeed, a particular set of moral principles) within practical reason, then *Law as a Moral Judgment* needs to be read in conjunction with the major body of work that Deryck has subsequently undertaken in defending, elaborating, and extending the core Gewirthian themes.[4]

* Professor of Law, King's College London and honorary Professor of Law, University of Sheffield.

[1] D Beyleveld and R Brownsword, *Law as a Moral Judgment* (Sweet and Maxwell, 1986) (reprinted by Sheffield Academic Press, 1994).

[2] In the Preface to the reprinted edition of *Law as a Moral Judgment*, we give some indication of how our ideas had developed in the eight years that had intervened between the original and the reprinted edition of the book.

[3] A Gewirth, *Reason and Morality* (University of Chicago Press, 1978).

[4] Seminally, see D Beyleveld, *The Dialectical Necessity of Morality* (University of Chicago Press, 1991), followed by a stream of publications making the dialectically necessary argument his own as well as developing a series of dialectically contingent versions of the main argument.

For my own part, building on other collaborative projects with Deryck,[5] I developed an interest in the way in which new technologies have insinuated themselves into the regulatory enterprise[6]—indeed, so much so that, if we were rewriting *Law as a Moral Judgment*, I would certainly be seeking to persuade Deryck that we should say something about these regulatory developments. On one view, what we should say could be kept pretty short: quite simply, as ostensible components of the legal enterprise, the various uses of CCTV, or DNA databases, or tracking and profiling technologies, and so on, will pass muster only to the extent that they meet the relevant Gewirthian moral requirements; and, whatever background legislation supports the use of these technologies (particularly in the criminal justice system) will need to be compatible with these constitutive moral requirements.[7] However, in this chapter, I want to put the spotlight on a particular regulatory strategy that I will term 'technological management'. Distinctively, technological management—typically involving the design of products or places, or the automation of processes—seeks to exclude (i) the possibility of certain actions which, in the absence of this strategy, might be subject only to rule regulation or (ii) human agents who otherwise would be implicated in the regulated activities.

A well-known example of technological management in relation to products is so-called digital rights management, this being employed with a view to the protection, or possibly extension, of intellectual property (IP) rights.[8] While IP proprietors might try to protect their interests by imposing contractual restrictions on use as well as by enlisting the assistance of governments or internet service providers (ISPs) and so on, they might also try to achieve their purposes by designing their products in ways that 'code' against infringement.[9] Faced with this range of measures, the enduser of the product is constrained by various IP-protecting rules but, more importantly, by the technical limitations embedded in the product itself. Similarly, where technological management is incorporated in the design of places—for instance, in the architecture of transport systems such as the Metro—acts that were previously possible but prohibited (such as riding on the train without a ticket) are rendered impossible (or, at any rate, for all practical purposes, impossible). For agents who wish to ride the trains, it remains the case that the rules require a ticket to be purchased but the 'ought' of this rule is overtaken by the measures of technological management that ensure that, without a valid ticket, there will be no access to the trains and no ride.

[5] Principally, D Beyleveld and R Brownsword, *Mice, Morality and Patents* (Common Law Institute of Intellectual Property, 1993), *Human Dignity in Bioethics and Biolaw* (OUP, 2001), and *Consent in the Law* (Hart, 2007).

[6] See R Brownsword, 'What the World Needs Now: Techno-Regulation, Human Rights and Human Dignity' in R Brownsword (ed), *Human Rights* (Hart, 2004) 203; and 'Code, Control, and Choice: Why East is East and West is West' (2005) 25 *Legal Studies* 1.

[7] For compatibility with human rights, see B Bowling, A Marks and C Murphy, 'Crime Control Technologies: Towards an Analytical Framework and Research Agenda' in R Brownsword and K Yeung (eds), *Regulating Technologies* (Hart, 2008) 51.

[8] Compare, eg, Case C-355/12, *Nintendo v PC Box.*

[9] Seminally, see L Lessig, *Code and Other Laws of Cyberspace* (Basic Books, 1999).

Is the use of technological management a topic that fits within the compass of *Law as a Moral Judgment*? Arguably, it is not. *Law as a Moral Judgment* engages in one of the traditional debates about the concept of law, a debate that is anchored to the assumption that law is a rule-orientated activity. Granted, technological management is regulatory in the sense that it seeks to channel behaviour, but it does not seek to do this in the characteristic law-like way by (as Lon Fuller put it) subjecting human conduct to the governance of rules.[10] Even if we treat *Law as a Moral Judgment* as a general essay in 'jurisprudence', we might still see technological management as falling beyond the scope of law-centred juristic inquiry. Nevertheless, while I do not think that technological management in any way impacts on the *theoretical* argument for a legal idealist concept of law, I suggest that it would be a mistake for jurists to ignore this regulatory development. Why so? Well, in some of our earliest conversations about law, back in 1980, I recall that Deryck regularly highlighted the difference between places where there is law and places that are lawless, between places where a systematic attempt is made to subject human conduct to the governance of rules and places where no such attempt is made. In those places that are lawless—running from the proverbial 'Wild West' to Stalin's Russia—power simply rules.[11] Bearing in mind this distinction, it seems to me that much of what makes law—together with the Rule of Law and jurisprudence—of interest is that it stands against lawlessness and the world of unconstrained power. It follows that if, nestled within the legal enterprise, we find a shift in regulatory strategy such that regulatory power is exercised by unconstrained technological management, then jurists need to take a critical interest in this development. Moreover, for jurists who are guided by Gewirthian moral principles, the development of technological management raises important questions about *how* the generic conditions of agency may be legitimately secured (by rules and principles and/or by a technological fix), as well as about the limits that a community of rights might set on regulatory compulsion (agents being compelled by a technological intervention to do what they judge to be right or, equally, being forced by the technological matrix to do what they judge to be wrong).

In what follows, I will start by contrasting (non-normative) technological management with normative rules of law, drawing initially on a well-known passage in HLA Hart's *The Concept of Law*[12] and then on a less well-publicised story about golf carts. This leads to questions about the price that we might have to pay for effective technological management. Even if technological management works, even if it prevents the infringement of IP rights or free-riding on the Metro, even if it contributes to human health and safety, does it compromise the conditions for moral community and for agent autonomy? I will then consider how these reflections

[10] LL Fuller, *The Morality of Law* (Yale University Press, 1969).

[11] For a sustained and insightful focus on this aspect of legality, see JN Shklar, *Legalism* (Harvard University Press, 1964).

[12] HLA Hart, *The Concept of Law* (Clarendon Press, 1961) (2nd edn, 1994).

about technological management might impact on the concept of law and the domain of jurisprudence before setting out a new agenda for jurisprudence.

II. Law as a Normative Enterprise and Technological Management as a Non-normative Enterprise

We can start in a place that is well known to jurists, namely, the road intersection that HLA Hart invites us to imagine in order to draw his evocative contrast between the external and the internal point of view in relation to rules (whether these are rules of law or rules of a game). According to Hart, although an observer, whose viewpoint is external, can detect some regularities and patterns in the conduct of those who are observed, such an (external) account misses out the distinctively (internal) rule-guided dimension of social life. Famously, Hart underlines the seriousness of this limitation of the external account in the following terms:

> If … the observer really keeps austerely to this extreme external point of view and does not give any account of the manner in which members of the group who accept the rules view their own regular behaviour, his description of their life cannot be in terms of rules at all, and so not in the terms of the rule-dependent notions of obligation or duty. Instead, it will be in terms of observable regularities of conduct, predictions, probabilities, and signs … His view will be like the view of one who, having observed the working of a traffic signal in a busy street for some time, limits himself to saying that when the light turns red there is a high probability that the traffic will stop … In so doing he will miss out a whole dimension of the social life of those whom he is watching, since for them the red light is not merely a sign that others will stop: they look upon it as a *signal for* them to stop, and so a reason for stopping in conformity to rules which make stopping when the light is red a standard of behaviour and an obligation.[13]

While technological management does not invalidate the Hartian distinction between such an external and an internal account, any such account will continue to hold good *only where it relates to a rule-governed activity*. To the extent that rule-governed activities are overtaken by technological management, the distinction loses its relevance; for, where activities are so managed, the appropriate description will no longer be in terms of rules and rule-dependent notions.

Consider Hart's own example of the regulation of road traffic. In Hart's time, the idea that driverless cars might be developed was the stuff of futurology. However, today, with vehicles such as Google's driverless car[14] at an advanced stage of development—and, apparently, perfectly capable of transporting passengers safely

[13] ibid, 89–90.

[14] See E Schmidt and J Cohen, *The New Digital Age* (Alfred A Knopf, 2013) 25: 'Google's fleet of driverless cars, built by a team of Google and Stanford University engineers, has logged hundreds of thousands of miles without incident.'

along Californian freeways[15]—things look somewhat different. In the 'ubiquitous cities'[16] of the future, if the movement of vehicles is controlled by anything resembling traffic lights, the external account will be the only account; the practical reason and actions of the humans inside the cars will no longer be material. Rather, it will be each vehicle's on-board technologies that control the movement of the traffic—on the roads of the future, traffic control will have overtaken both traffic commands and traffic rules.[17]

Consider another example of technological management superseding rules and laws. At the Warwickshire Golf and Country Club, there are two championship 18-hole golf courses, together with many other facilities, all standing (as the club's website puts it) in '456 flowing acres of rolling Warwickshire countryside'.[18] The club also has a large fleet of golf carts. However, in 2011, the club experienced some problems with local 'joy-riders' who, in violation of the law, took the carts off the course. In response, the club used GPS technology so that 'a virtual geo-fence [was created] around the whole of the property, meaning that tagged carts [could not] be taken off the property'.[19] With this technological fix, anyone who tries to drive a cart beyond the geo-fence will find that it is simply immobilised. Problem solved. In the same way, the technology enables the club to restrict carts to paths in areas which have become wet or are under repair and to zone off greens, green approaches, water hazards, bunkers, and so on. Another problem solved. With these measures of technological management, the usual regulatory pressures and limitations are relieved; but the relief is supplied by the technology of GPS, not by the technique of rules.

The significance of the shift from normative rule-based regulation (which might or might not be supported by various technological instruments such as CCTV surveillance and DNA profiling) to non-normative technological management should not be under-estimated. Rule-based regulation speaks to the prudential and moral reason of regulatees. Agents who drive cars are given a combination of prudential and moral reasons to observe 'the rules of the road' and prospective joy-riders are given similar reasons to respect the property of others. By contrast, where technological management is employed, the signals change into a completely different mode: once cars or golf carts are redesigned, they can be used in a way that is safe and responsible but they are no longer used in a way for which users are responsible. What technological management signifies is that regulators are now restricting the range of possibilities that are open to their regulatees rather than prescribing a code of conduct that is superimposed on a given range of possibilities. Assuming that technological management works, the question is whether

[15] See E Brynjolfsson and A McAfee, *The Second Machine Age* (WW Norton and Co, 2014) ch 2.

[16] See, eg, J Wakefield, 'Building cities of the future now' BBC News Technology, 21 February 2013: available at www.bbc.co.uk/news/technology-20957953.

[17] Compare P O'Malley, 'The Politics of Mass Preventive Justice' in A Ashworth, L Zedner and P Tomlin (eds), *Prevention and the Limits of the Criminal Law* (OUP, 2013) 273.

[18] www.thewarwickshire.com.

[19] See www.hiseman.com/media/releases/dsg/dsg200412.htm.

it comes at any relevant cost to the community (and, particularly, in relation to a community of rights).

III. The Price of Technological Management

If we assume that technological management will be more effective than rules of law in protecting persons and their property, in making transport systems safer, in conserving energy and so on, why should anyone be concerned about its adoption?

In fact, the rise of technological management in place of traditional legal rules might give rise to several concerns. For example, some might fear that, in our quest for greater safety and well-being, we will develop and embed ever more intelligent devices to the point that there is a risk of the extinction of humans—or, if not that, then a risk of humanity surviving 'in some highly suboptimal state or in which a large portion of our potential for desirable development is irreversibly squandered'.[20] Even if we discount various kinds of catastrophe scenarios, and even if technological management is reliable and effective, I suggest that, as jurists, we should question the fate of the (seemingly now redundant) law, its practitioners, its institutions, its culture and its values. Moreover, for all agents, we should ask whether technological management, with its reduction of options, signifies a diminution of our legitimate interest in autonomy; and, to repeat a question that I have posed on many occasions, we should ask whether there is a risk that technological management—which compels or excludes actions regardless of the moral judgement of the acting agent—might compromise the conditions for *any kind of* moral community.[21] Let me say something more about each of these last two concerns.

Compromising the Conditions for Moral Community

I take it that the aspiration of any moral community is that regulators and regulatees alike should try to do the right thing. However, this presupposes a process of moral reflection and then action that accords with one's moral judgement. In this way, agents exercise judgement in trying to do the right thing and they do what they do for the right reason in the sense that they act in accordance with their moral judgement. Of course, this does not imply that each agent will make the same moral judgement or apply the same reasons. A utilitarian community is very different to a Kantian or a Gewirthian community; but, in each of these cases, we

[20] See N Bostrom, *Superintelligence* (OUP, 2014) 281 (note 1).

[21] See, eg, R Brownsword, 'Regulating Patient Safety: Is it Time for a Technological Response?' (2014) 6 *Law, Innovation and Technology* 1.

have an instantiation of a moral community; and it is their shared aspiration to do the right thing that is the lowest common denominator.[22]

There is more than one way in which the context for moral action can be compromised by the use of technological regulatory strategies. In the case of measures that fall short of technological management—for example, where CCTV surveillance or DNA profiling are used in support of the rules of the criminal law—prudential signals are amplified and moral reason might be crowded out.[23] However, where full-scale technological management takes over, what the agent actually does might be the only act that is available. In such a context, even if an act accords with the agent's own sense of the right thing, it is not a paradigmatic moral performance: moral virtue, as Ian Kerr has argued, is not to be automated.[24] Quite what the pathology is here is a matter for debate. Arguably, the problem with a complete technological fix is that it fails to leave open the possibility of 'doing wrong' (thereby disabling the agent from confirming to him or herself, as well as to others, their moral identity); or it is the implicit denial that the agent is any longer the author of the act in question; or, possibly the same point stated in other words, it is the denial of the agent's responsibility for the act.[25] At all events, it will be for each community with moral aspirations to engage with this question and to determine to what extent, and why, the possibility of moral agency is compromised in such circumstances.

If technological management that compels an agent to do x (or that prevents an agent from doing y) is morally problematic even where the agent judges that doing x (or not doing y) is the right thing to do, it is (at least) equally problematic where the agent judges that doing x (or not doing y) is either straightforwardly morally wrong or an option that should not be taken. To spell out more fully what is involved here, it is that a particular use of technological management compels an agent to do x, where the agent judges that doing x is either morally prohibited or that it is morally optional (and the agent who is so compelled would not opt to do x); or, it is that a particular use of technological management prevents an agent from doing y, where the agent judges that doing y is either morally required or that it is morally optional (and the agent who is so prevented would opt to do y). We can argue about whether these examples of compulsion are all equally

[22] See R Brownsword, 'Human Dignity, Human Rights, and Simply Trying to Do the Right Thing' in Christopher McCrudden (ed), *Understanding Human Dignity* (Proceedings of the British Academy 192) (The British Academy and OUP, 2013) 345.

[23] For an interesting study, see U Gneezy and A Rustichini, 'A Fine is a Price' (2009) 29 *Journal of Legal Studies* 1; and, for relevant insights about the use of CCTV, see B von Silva-Tarouca Larsen, *Setting the Watch: Privacy and the Ethics of CCTV Surveillance* (Hart, 2011).

[24] See I Kerr, 'Digital Locks and the Automation of Virtue' in Michael Geist (ed), *From 'Radical Extremism' to 'Balanced Copyright': Canadian Copyright and the Digital Agenda* (Irwin Law, 2010) 247.

[25] I am grateful for this point to Marcus Düwell and others who participated in a symposium on 'Human Dignity: A Major Concept in Ethics?' held at the University of Tübingen on 24 October 2014. I am also grateful to Patrick Capps for drawing my attention to F Neuhouser, *Rousseau's Theodicy of Self-Love: Evil, Rationality, and the Drive for Self-Recognition* (OUP, 2008), the precise bearing of which on my concerns about technological management is a topic for another paper.

morally problematic but, in the paradigmatic case of technological management being used to compel an agent to do an act that he or she judges to be morally prohibited, this is surely an extremely serious compromising of moral community. At least, in a normative order, there is a 'gap' between the rule and the agent's act of compliance or non-compliance; agents might have rule-based obligations but they are not obliged or compelled to follow the rule; typically, there is an opportunity for an agent to decline to act in a way that offends their conscience. This is a matter to which we will return in Section IV.

Let us suppose that, in any aspirant moral community, there must remain ample opportunities for agents to engage in moral reflection and then to do the right thing. Let us also suppose that it is an open question how far such a community can tolerate regulation by technological management. Given these suppositions, the cumulative effect of introducing various kinds of surveillance technologies as well as adopting hard technological fixes needs to be a standing item on the regulatory agenda.[26] If we knew just how much space a moral community needs to safeguard against the automation of virtue as well as to allow for conscientious objection, and if we had some kind of barometer to measure for this, we might be able to draw some regulatory red lines. It might well be that the technological measures that are adopted by the golf club neither make a significant difference to the general culture of the community nor materially reduce the opportunities that are presented for (authentic) moral action. On the other hand, if the community is at a 'tipping point', these regulatory interventions might be critical.[27] Accordingly, taking a precautionary approach, we might reason that, as regulators discover, and then increasingly adopt, measures of technological management, a generous margin for the development of moral virtue, for moral reflection, and for moral action needs to be maintained.

Compromising Autonomy

If technological management means that prospective joy-riders are unable to take away cars or carts, this does entail some restriction on their options; but, so long as we are sympathetic to property-protecting regulatory objectives, it is unclear why this use of technological management gives cause for concern. If, on the other hand, technological management is applied to eliminate options that we think should be available to agents (most strongly, options that are covered by protective rights), then this loss of agent autonomy would be a more plausible cause for concern.

[26] See R Brownsword, 'Lost in Translation: Legality, Regulatory Margins, and Technological Management' (2011) 26 *Berkeley Technology Law Journal* 1321.

[27] See generally K Yeung, 'Towards an Understanding of Regulation by Design' in Brownsword and Yeung (eds), n 7, 79; and, especially see K Yeung, 'Can We Employ Design-Based Regulation While Avoiding Brave New World?' (2011) 3 *Law, Innovation and Technology* 1.

To begin to test this out, consider the use of technological management in hospitals where the regulatory purpose is to improve the conditions for patient safety.[28] Suppose, for example, that we could staff our hospitals in all sections, from the kitchens to the front reception, from the wards to the intensive care unit, from accident and emergency to the operating theatre, with robots. Moreover, suppose that all hospital robot operatives were entirely reliable and were programmed (in the spirit of Asimov's laws) to make patient safety their top priority.[29] Why should we be concerned about autonomy?

First, the adoption of nursebots or the like might impact on patients who prefer to be cared for by human nurses. To be sure, by the time that nursebots are commonplace, humans will probably be surrounded by robot functionaries and they will be perfectly comfortable in the company of robots. However, in the still early days of the development of robotic technologies, many humans will not feel comfortable. Even if the technologies are reliable, many humans might prefer to be treated in hospitals that are staffed by humans—just as some Japanese apparently prefer human to robot carers.[30] Where human carers do their job well, it is entirely understandable that many will prefer the human touch. However, in a perceptive commentary, Sherry Turkle, having remarked on her own positive experience with the orderlies who looked after her following a fall on icy steps in Harvard Square,[31] goes on to showcase the views of one of her interviewees, 'Richard', who was left severely disabled by an automobile accident.[32] Despite being badly treated by his human carers, Richard seems to prefer such carers against more caring robots. Strikingly, as Turkle reports it, although Richard 'would not want his life endangered, he prefers the sadist to the robot'.[33]

While Richard's faith in humans might seem a bit surprising, his preferences are surely legitimate; and their accommodation does not necessarily present a serious regulatory problem. In principle, patients can be given appropriate choices: some may elect to be treated in a traditional robot-free hospital (with the usual warts and waiting lists), others in 24/7 facilities that involve various degrees of robotics (and, in all likelihood, rapid admission and treatment). Accordingly, so long as regulators are responsive to the legitimate different preferences of agents, autonomy is not challenged and might even be enhanced.

Secondly, we should be mindful that it is not just a matter of accommodating patients who prefer human carers to Nursebots. What about accommodating

[28] For discussion see Brownsword, n 22.

[29] According to the first of Asimov's three laws, 'A robot may not injure a human being or, through inaction, allow a human being to come to harm.' See http://en.wikipedia.org/wiki/Three_Laws_of_Robotics.

[30] See Michael Fitzpatrick, 'No, robot: Japan's elderly fail to welcome their robot overlords' BBC News, 4 February 2011: available at www.bbc.co.uk/news/business-12347219.

[31] S Turkle, *Alone Together* (Basic Books, 2011) 121–22.

[32] ibid, 281–82.

[33] ibid.

humans who would like to be nurses or other health care professionals?[34] Already, for example, there are a number of hospitals that utilise pharmacy dispensing robots—including a robot named 'Phred' (Pharmacy Robot-Efficient Dispensing) at the new Queen Elizabeth Hospital Birmingham[35]—which are claimed to be faster than human operatives and totally reliable. If robots can make the provision of pharmacy services safer—even to the point of detecting cases where doctors have mis-prescribed the drugs—then why, we might wonder, should we not generalise this good practice? Indeed, why not—but only so long as regulators are responsive to the legitimate preferences of would-be pharmacists, nurses and other hospital workers (for example, by ring-fencing so many jobs of this kind). Otherwise, the replacement of human operatives by robots is a threat to individual autonomy.

Without doubt, safety is extremely important. Nevertheless, there might remain a concern that our direction of travel is dangerous. What is happening with technological management is that we are moving from designing products so that they can be used more safely by humans (whether these are surgical instruments or motor cars) to making the product even more safe by altogether eliminating *human* control and use. So, whether it is driverless cars or Metro trains,[36] or robotic surgeons, or Nursebots, humans are being displaced. Where these technological developments, designed for safety, are simply viewed as further options, this enhances human autonomy; but, where they are viewed as de rigueur, there is a diminution in the conditions for autonomous living. In this way, Nursebots and robots such as Phred are emblematic of a further disruptive effect of technology.[37]

So, what price technological management? Possibly, GPS-enabled golf carts, Google cars, Nursebots and the like can be adopted in the best democratic fashion and without any significant cost, either to a context that aligns with the preferences of agents or the options available to them, or to the community's moral aspirations. Nevertheless, it would be reckless to proceed with technological management as if no such risk could possibly exist. It is at this point, and with this thought, that we should return, first, to the concept of law and, then, to the domain of jurisprudence.

[34] In some caring professions, the rate of reduction might be quite slow because the experience of robotics experts is that it is easier to program computers to play chess than to fold towels or to pick up glasses of water. So as Brynjolfsson and McAfee, n 15, conclude at 241: '[P]eople have skills and abilities that are not yet automated. They may be automatable at some point but this hasn't started in any serious way thus far, which leads us to believe that it will take a while. We think we'll have human data scientists, conference organizers, divisional managers, nurses, and busboys for some time to come.'

[35] See www.uhb.nhs.uk/news/new-pharmacy-robot-named.htm.

[36] For a short discussion, see W Wallach and C Allen, *Moral Machines* (OUP, 2009) 14. In addition to the safety considerations, robot-controlled trains are more flexible in dealing with situations where timetables need to be changed.

[37] For what is now an urgent debate about the disruptive impact of automation on the prospects for workers and the patterns of employment, see: M Ford, *The Rise of the Robots* (Oneworld Publications, 2015); G Colvin, *Humans are Underrated* (Nicholas Brealey Publishing, 2015); A Keen, *The Internet is Not the Answer* (Atlantic Books, 2015); J Lanier, *Who Owns the Future?* (Allen Lane, 2013). For those who are interested in a personal prognosis, see BBC News, 'Will a robot take your job?' (11 September 2015): available at www.bbc.co.uk/news/technology-34066941.

IV. Revisiting the Concept of Law

In my introductory remarks, I said that I do not believe that the use of technological management impacts on the arguments for the *theoretical* superiority of a particular concept of law, whether legal idealist or legal positivist in nature. The bearing of technological management, as I see it, is more on the scope of jurisprudence and the kinds of questions in which lawyers and legal theorists should take an interest. Nevertheless, the use of technological management does change the context in which law operates and it does have a potential impact on the argument that Hartians typically make for the *practical* superiority of a legal positivist concept of law.[38]

The gist of the Hartian argument is that, if we view the world through a legal positivist lens, then we will recognise laws where they are made in the 'officially' recognised and accepted way by the relevant institutions. So, there will be no denial of 'reality'. However, where particular laws require us to act in ways that seriously offend our conscience, then we have the option of expressing our objection to those laws by engaging in acts of disobedience. In this way, we do not disrupt social order by problematising what is and is not law (we are not 'revolutionaries') but we rightly subject the law to moral examination and, (probably) in the last resort, we can act on our moral judgement by refusing to comply with the law (we are not uncritically submissive reactionaries). However, in a world of technological management, the context changes in a way that challenges some of the assumptions made by this practical argument.

The key change is pinpointed by Evgeny Morozov[39] when he considers how technological management might impact on precisely the kind of responsible moral citizenship that is valued by (and not only by) Hartians. Recalling the famous case of Rosa Parks, who refused to move from the 'white-only' section of the bus, Morozov points out that this important act of civil disobedience was possible only because 'the bus and the sociotechnological system in which it operated were terribly inefficient. The bus driver asked Parks to move only because he couldn't anticipate how many people would need to be seated in the white-only section at the front; as the bus got full, the driver had to adjust the sections in real time, and Parks happened to be sitting in an area that suddenly became "white-only".'[40] However, if the bus and the bus-stops had been technologically enabled, this situation simply would not have arisen—Parks would either have been denied entry to the bus or she would have been sitting in the allocated section for black people. Morozov continues:

> Will this new transportation system be convenient? Sure. Will it give us Rosa Parks? Probably not, because she would never have gotten to the front of the bus to begin with. The odds are that a perfectly efficient seat-distribution system—abetted by ubiquitous

[38] See D Beyleveld and R Brownsword, 'The Practical Difference Between Natural-Law Theory and Legal Positivism' (1985) 5 *OJLS* 1; and *Law as a Moral Judgment*, n 1, ch 2.

[39] E Morozov, *To Save Everything, Click Here* (Allen Lane, 2013).

[40] ibid, 204.

> technology, sensors, and facial recognition—would have robbed us of one of the proudest moments in American history. Laws that are enforced by appealing to our moral or prudential registers leave just enough space for friction; friction breeds tension, tension creates conflict, and conflict produces change. In contrast, when laws are enforced through the technological register, there's little space for friction and tension—and quite likely for change.[41]

In short, technological management disrupts the setting in which Hart and others reckon on acts of direct civil disobedience being available as an expression of responsible moral citizenship. How, then, does this play in relation to the supposed practical superiority of a legal positivist view of law?

Legal positivists might try to nip the objection in the bud by insisting that technological management, because it is not a rule (or does not present in a normative way), is simply not a candidate for recognition as a law; whatever we make of technological management as a regulatory strategy, it falls beyond the scope of the debate about which rules we treat as candidate 'laws'. However, suppose that the use of technological management is authorised by legislation; indeed, suppose that legislation specifically authorises the use of a suite of smart technologies on and around buses in order to maintain a system of racial segregation on public transport. Is the authorising provision 'law'? There is no dodging this question on the ground that it does not concern a rule or norm; the authorising rule is clearly eligible as a 'law' provided that it meets the particular qualifying conditions. If the authorising rule is made by the legislature in the standard way—if, as Ronald Dworkin expressed it, the rule has the right 'pedigree'[42]—then legal positivists will want to recognise it as legally valid. For legal positivists, the fact that the rule is designed to make a policy of racial segregation more effective is not in itself disqualifying. Granted, many will consider this rule and its regulatory purpose deeply morally objectionable; but, for legal positivists, there is no conceptual necessity in there being a place for this debate to be conducted within (internal to) the law-making and law-reviewing processes and for it to have a bearing on the legality of the rule. That said, Hartians insist that responsible moral citizens can and should voice their criticisms of the law in whatever ways the polity permits. But, as Morozov points out, one way in which these criticisms might have been articulated has been closed off: it is not just the morally objectionable particular purpose of this provision that is at issue but its mandate for technological management, a mandate that is potentially corrosive of active and responsible moral citizenship.

While this looks like a point against the legal positivist claim to practical superiority, it needs more work to see just how damaging it really is. In some cases, it might be possible to 'circumvent' the technology; and this might allow for some acts of protest before patches are applied to the technology to make it more resilient. Regulators might also tackle circumvention by creating new criminal offences that are targeted at those who try to design round technological management—indeed,

[41] ibid, 205.

[42] R Dworkin, *Taking Rights Seriously*, rev edn (Duckworth, 1978).

in the context of copyright, Article 6 of Directive 2001/29/EC already requires Member States to provide adequate legal protection against the circumvention of technological measures (such as DRM).[43] In other words, technological management might not always be counter-technology proof. Moreover, there might remain opportunities for civil disobedients to express their opposition to the background regulatory purposes indirectly by old-fashioned 'occupations' and 'sit-ins', or by breaking anti-circumvention laws, or by initiating well-publicised 'hacks', or 'denial-of-service' attacks or their analogues.

Nevertheless, if the general effect of technological management is to squeeze the opportunities for acts of *direct* civil disobedience, legal positivists need to find ways of compensating for this potential diminution in responsible moral citizenship. By the time that technological management is in place, it is too late; for most citizens, non-compliance is no longer an option; and legal positivism looks in danger of tipping towards reaction. This suggests that the compensating adjustment needs to be ex ante: that is to say, it suggests that responsible moral citizens need to be able to air their objections before technological management has been authorised for a particular purpose; and, what is more, the opportunity needs to be there to challenge both an immoral regulatory purpose and the use of (morality-corroding) technological management. It looks, in other words, as if legal positivists need to embed in their conceptual scheme of law some measures that ensure that citizens are able to articulate their moral concerns as well as procedures that check for the compatibility of the use of technological management with the community's general moral aspirations. If this is correct, then in this particular context the clear water that legal positivists insist as separating law from morals looks considerably less clear.[44]

Finally, let me repeat that these remarks bear only on the argument for the practical superiority of a legal positivist conceptualisation of law. In *Law as a Moral Judgment*, we assessed these various practical considerations as contingent, context-specific, and inconclusive. To my mind, that remains the case: even if the technological trajectory of regulatory thinking creates potential challenges for legal positivists, it is in relation to the theoretical credentials of the rival conceptual schemes that the issue must ultimately be settled.

V. The Domain of Jurisprudence

For jurists, it is the 'law' that is the object of their inquiry; and the standard assumption is that, however one fine-tunes one's conception of law, the aim of the

[43] Directive 2001/29/EC on the harmonisation of certain aspects of copyright and related rights in the information society, OJ L 167, 22.06.2001, 0010–0019.

[44] Compare D Dyzenhaus, 'Preventive Justice and the Rule-of-Law Project' in Ashworth, Zedner and Tomlin, n 17, 91.

legal enterprise is to subject human conduct to the governance of *rules*. It follows that, whether one argues for a legal positivist or a legal idealist conception of law, whether one's conception of law is narrowly restricted to the operations of the high institutions of nation states (as in the 'Westphalian' view of law) or ranges more broadly and pluralistically across the ordering of social life, it is agreed that law is about rules, about prescription, about normativity; in all conceptions, law is a normative enterprise, the rules prescribing what ought and ought not to be done.

From the fact that law is conceived of as a normative phenomenon, it does not follow that the ambit of jurisprudence should be limited to legal norms (however conceived). Nevertheless, once law is conceived of in this way, and given that law is the object of jurisprudential inquiry, it is understandable that the domain of jurisprudence should be drawn in a way that stays pretty close to legal norms and normative legal orders. However, while this might seem to facilitate an efficient and clear division of labour between, on the one hand, jurists and, on the other, philosophers, sociologists, political theorists, economists, and so on, and while this specification of the domain of jurisprudence gives inquirers a clear and apparently coherent focus, it suffers from two major limiting tendencies. First, there is a (Westphalian) tendency to isolate a limited set of norms from a larger context of (non-legal) normative regulation; and, secondly, non-normative channelling strategies tend to be treated as beyond the field of juristic inquiry. While these tendencies to isolate and exclude do not altogether preclude broader lines of juristic inquiry, they hardly encourage them.[45] We can say a little more about these limiting tendencies, each of which creates a barrier to seeing the bigger regulatory picture.

The First Limitation: The Isolation of Legal Norms

Hart's conceptualisation of law invites jurists to focus their inquiries on high-level national rules of the kind that we find in legislation, codes, and the case-law. To be sure, this licenses a broad range of juristic inquiries; but, the fact of the matter is that 'law' in this sense is by no means the only kind of normative order that we find in societies. Religious and (secular) moral codes are normative as are the relatively formal codes of conduct that guide the practice of professional people (including lawyers themselves) and the less formal codes that are observed in a myriad of social settings. From Eugen Ehrlich's 'living law'[46] found in the customs and practices of provincial Bukowina (then part of the Austro-Hungarian

[45] Compare R Brownsword, 'Comparatively Speaking: "Law in its Regulatory Environment"' in M Adams and D Heirbaut (eds), *The Method and Culture of Comparative Law* (Festschrift for Mark van Hoecke) (Hart, 2014) 189.

[46] Eugen Ehrlich, *Fundamental Principles of the Sociology of Law* (Transaction Publishers, 2001 [1913]). For a useful introductory overview, see Neil O Littlefield, 'Eugen Ehrlich's Fundamental Principles of the Sociology of Law' (1967) 19 *Maine Law Review* 1.

empire) to Robert Ellickson's study of the informal norms of 'neighbourliness' and 'live and let live' recognised by the close-knit group of ranchers and farmers of Shasta County, California,[47] there is a literature that charts the extent of the norms that actually guide human conduct. Yet, in this ocean of normativity, Hartian-inspired jurisprudence invites inquiry directed at just one island of norms (the island that it characterises as 'law'). Where the domain of inquiry is restricted in this way, jurisprudence has nothing to say about the functioning of those many other islands of normativity that might sustain a particular kind of social order nor about the way in which they might interact with or disrupt the operation of (Westphalian) legal norms.[48]

If it were the case that non-legal norms were of marginal significance, this might not be too serious a restriction. However, if (as there is ample reason to believe) these other norms are at least as important as legal norms in the daily lives of people, then this is a serious limitation on our ability to understand not only what makes things tick in the social world but, more particularly, how legal norms fit into the full array of normative signals. To understand our legal and social world, we need a wide-lens approach.[49] In this context, we can recall the frequent references that are made in public life to the importance of getting the 'regulatory environment' right—right for banking and financial services, right for innovation, right for health care and patient safety, right for the European single market, right for small businesses, right for privacy and press freedom, and so on. Typically, these references are a common starting point for a public 'post mortem' following a crisis, collapse or catastrophe of some kind. While this might be a good place to start, the remarks made above indicate that we will go badly wrong if we try to reduce the regulatory environment to just *one* area of law, or indeed to several areas of (Hartian) *law*. The regulatory environment is more complex than that and it is layered. Accordingly, if we think that the regulatory environment is 'broken', our attempts at repair and renewal are unlikely to come to much if they are limited to replacing one set of legal norms with another. Or, to put this another way, it is one thing to grasp that the law is relatively ineffective in channelling

[47] RC Ellickson, *Order Without Law* (Harvard University Press, 1991). Although the rural group is close-knit, there are significant sub-groups—for example, there is a contrast between the 'traditionalists' who let their cattle roam, and the 'modernists' who 'keep their livestock behind fences at all times in order to increase their control over their herds' (at 24).

[48] But note the caveat in Simon Roberts, 'After Government? On Representing Law Without the State' (2005) 68 *Modern Law Review* 1, 12:

> We can probably all now go along with some general tenets of the legal pluralists. First, their insistence on the heterogeneity of the normative domain seems entirely uncontroversial. Practically any social field can be fairly represented as consisting of plural, interpenetrating normative orders/systems/discourses. Nor would many today wish to endorse fully the enormous claims to systemic qualities that state law has made for itself and that both lawyers and social scientists have in the past too often uncritically accepted. Beyond that, consensus is more difficult ... Will all the normative orders that the legal pluralists wish to embrace necessarily be comfortable with their rescue as 'legal' orders?

[49] For a good example of such an approach, see O Lobel, *Talent Wants to Be Free* (Yale University Press, 2013).

conduct but unless we open our inquiry to the full range of norms in play, we will not understand why law suffers from this shortcoming.[50]

The Second Limitation: The Exclusivity of the Normative

Even if the domain of jurisprudence is expanded to include the full set of norms, it is still limited so long as it treats norms, *and only norms*, as within its field of inquiry. So limited, while jurists are able to interrogate those technological instruments that are deployed in support of rules, they are disabled from assessing the significance of non-normative instruments such as technological management. At the time of *The Concept of Law*, and even of *Law as a Moral Judgment*, this did not seem to be a significant limitation. However, once regulators adopt strategies of technological management, the ocean of normativity contains potentially significant new currents.[51] To restrict the field of inquiry to the exclusively normative is to miss a sea-change in social ordering. To give ourselves the chance of understanding and assessing a radical transformation in the way that the State channels human conduct, we need to work with a notion of 'regulation' and of 'the regulatory environment' that includes both normative and non-normative instruments.

There is no denying that, by including non-normative instruments in the domain of jurisprudence, we are locating legal inquiry in a much larger and very different ball-park. To advocate a shift in focus from 'law' to 'regulation' might meet with resistance; but, at least, mainstream regulatory theorists conceive of regulation as starting with the setting of standards and, thus, as normative.[52] If the 'regulatory environment' adopted this conception of regulation, it would still be limited to normative signals; and many jurists might be comfortable with this. However, the comfort of jurists is not our concern. Our cognitive interest is in a perceived shift to technological management and, with that, the development of a pervasive risk management mentality. This is quite different to the traditional legal approach and legal mentality but the function of channelling human conduct (one of the principal 'law jobs', as Karl Llewellyn put it)[53] is the thread of connection. To understand what is happening with regard to the channelling of conduct within their own narrowly circumscribed domain, jurists have to broaden their horizons. When, at the Warwickshire, technological management is used to respond to a failure of normative governance, the lesson is not simply one to be

[50] It is also important, of course, to be aware of the full range of strategies available to regulators in trying to tweak the 'choice architecture' within which agents act: see, eg, CR Sunstein, *Simpler: The Future of Government* (Simon and Schuster, 2013) 38–39 for an indicative list of possible 'nudges'.

[51] Compare L Tien, 'Architectural Regulation and the Evolution of Social Norms' (2004) 9 *International Journal of Communications Law and Policy* 1.

[52] See, eg, J Black, 'What is Regulatory Innovation?' in J Black, M Lodge and M Thatcher (eds), *Regulatory Innovation* (Edward Elgar, 2005), 1, 11.

[53] See KN Llewellyn, 'The Normative, the Legal, and the Law-Jobs: The Problem of Juristic Method' (1940) 49 *Yale Law Journal* 1355.

taken by golf clubs; the lesson is a general one: namely, that law is not the only way of managing risks and, in some cases, a technological fix will be far more effective.

If my underlying prognosis is on the right lines then, in future, normative regulatory environments will co-exist and co-evolve with technologically managed environments—but not in a tidy, transparent, or necessarily accountable and legitimate way.[54] For jurists to turn away from the use of technological instruments for regulatory purposes is to diminish the significance of their inquiries and to ignore important questions about the way that power is exercised and social order maintained.

VI. A New Agenda for Jurisprudence

If we adopt the idea of 'the regulatory environment' as setting the field of jurisprudential inquiry, and if we embrace the notion that, in this environment, there will be both normative and non-normative dimensions, we facilitate an understanding of how legal norms relate to technological management. However, this is just the beginning: with this new domain for juristic inquiry, new questions abound as we reflect on the significance of technological management in the regulatory environment.

First, there are the organising ideas themselves: the regulatory environment and the idea of the 'complexion' of the regulatory signals that constitute that environment. With regard to the former, there is still much work to be done. For example, there are questions about the scope of the regulatory environment, about the significance of the source of the regulatory intervention, about the relevance of the intent that accompanies technological management, and about the conflict between competing regulatory interventions.[55] With regard to the latter—the still unfamiliar idea of the 'complexion' of the regulatory environment[56]—we need to be clear about why this matters. Why does it matter, for example, that agents might comply with the law, or other norms, for prudential rather than moral reasons? Or, why does it matter whether regulatees comply freely or only because, with technological management, they have no other choice?

Secondly, there are various 'ideals' that we assume to be, if not intrinsic to the legal enterprise, at least associated with best practice. At the head of this list is the Rule of Law; but also we need to examine the ideal of coherence (which

[54] See, eg, R Leenes and F Lucivero, 'Laws on Robots, Laws by Robots, Laws in Robots: Regulating Robots' Behaviour by Design' (2014) 6 *Law, Innovation and Technology* 194; and on (US) State regulation of automated cars, see JF Weaver, *Robots Are People Too* (Praeger, 2014) 55–60.

[55] The seeds of these questions can be found in R Brownsword, *Rights, Regulation and the Technological Revolution* (OUP, 2008); R Brownsword and M Goodwin, *Law and the Technologies of the Twenty-First Century* (CUP, 2012), ch 2.

[56] Compare Brownsword, 'Lost in Translation', n 26.

is highly valued by private lawyers)[57] and the Millian harm principle (which is regularly relied on to test the legitimacy of particular uses of the criminal law).[58] In each case, the adoption of technological management seems to be disruptive of these ideals and the question is whether we can re-engineer them for a regulatory environment that employs both normative and non-normative signals.

To illustrate one of the issues, consider the well-known Fullerian principles of legality and, concomitantly, the notion of the Rule of Law as the publication (promulgation) of rules and then the congruent administration of those rules. Can these principles be stretched across to non-normative strategies or do they again presuppose rules (and a normative dimension)? On the face of it, the Fullerian principles do presuppose rules (that the rules should be published, that the rules should be prospective, that the rules should be clear and relatively constant, that the rules should not be contradictory, and so on) and, indeed, they seem to be particularly focused on the rules of the criminal law (or other duty-imposing rules). That said, the underlying Fullerian idea that regulators should not set traps for their regulatees or resort to tricking them surely applies equally strongly to the use of technological management. So, for example, if the technological signals in a managed environment are confusing or unclear, or if regulatees in good faith interpret an action that is possible as implying permission ('can' being read as implying 'may'), they should not be penalised. If this is correct, the ideal of legality persists in requiring fair dealing by regulators. Nevertheless, once technological management takes hold one senses that the focus of legality shifts to (i) the processual public law values of transparency, accountability, inclusive participation, reason-giving, and the like together with (ii) the controls exerted by background fundamental values (such as compatibility with respect for human rights and human dignity—or, of course, for Gewirthians, compatibility with the PGC).[59] In this way, while the zone regulated *directly* by legal norms might shrink, the significance of law and legality (as a check on technological management) remains.

Thirdly, if we assume that there will be a major technological impingement on the way in which we transact and interact in the future, attention switches to the fate of those bodies of law—contract law, tort law, and criminal law in particular—that have hitherto regulated such activities. For example, if smart cars make much of road traffic laws redundant, if technological management in hospitals and workplaces ensures that patients and employees are safe, how much of both the criminal law and the law of negligence is sidelined? Where we are relying

[57] For a discussion of this ideal in the context of patenting new technologies, see R Brownsword, 'Regulatory Coherence—A European Challenge' in K Purnhagen and P Rott (eds), *Varieties of European Economic Law and Regulation: Essays in Honour of Hans Micklitz* (Springer, 2014) 235.

[58] See JS Mill, 'On Liberty', in JS Mill, *Utilitarianism*, M Warnock, ed (Collins/Fontana, 1962) (first published 1859); and, for a sketch of the necessary re-working of Millian liberalism, see R Brownsword, 'Criminal Law, Regulatory Frameworks and Public Health' in AM Viens, J Coggon and A Kessel (eds), *Criminal Law, Regulatory Frameworks and Public Health* (CUP, 2013) 19.

[59] Requiring respect for the generic conditions of agency: see Gewirth, n 3.

on technological management for health and safety purposes, it will be largely 'regulatory' criminal law that is displaced; and, given that this is a body of law that features strict and absolute liability offences, and about which we do not feel entirely comfortable, perhaps this is no bad thing.[60] Arguably, our moral concerns are heightened where it is the classical crimes of intent that are disrupted. Certainly, there is little or no enthusiasm for the adoption of absolute liability in relation to core (or, as some would have it, 'real' or 'true') crimes; but if the rules that specify such central criminal offences could be rendered redundant by preventive technological measures, should this be supported or opposed by ethical rationalists? Should Gewirthians perhaps support the use of technological management where it is more effective than the rules of the criminal law in securing the generic conditions for agency, but oppose its use where the questions to be settled by regulators are morally contested (and where there is a risk that agents might be compelled to act against their conscience)?

Again, if the technological infrastructure for transactions manages much of the process, what does this mean for the leading principles of contract law and a jurisprudence that is heavy with case-law from earlier centuries?[61] Rather than being an occasion for the celebration of new forms of contract, does this signify 'the end of contracts'?[62] Does contract law have a future when trading is automated;[63] when transactions are initiated and completed by avatars, vReps, digital buddies, and various kinds of shopping bots (removing humans from at least one side of the negotiation and performance of the 'deal');[64] and when, thanks to 'RFID tags and smart payment cards, together with a reader able to link the information together and some biometric security, [customers can] merrily wheel [their] trolley[s] out of the supermarket without either queuing or being arrested'?[65] Does contract have a future when potential breaches (most obviously, failure to pay for goods or services) are forestalled by technological interventions? Similarly, when so many

[60] Seminally, see FB Sayre, 'Public Welfare Offences' (1933) 33 *Columbia Law Review* 55; and see too P Ramsay, 'The Responsible Subject as Citizen: Criminal Law, Democracy, and the Welfare State' (2006) 69 *Modern Law Review* 29. However, the strictness of regulatory offences may be mitigated in practice by enforcement policies that restrict prosecutions to those cases where the offender is actually morally culpable. Classically, see W Carson, 'White Collar Crime and the Enforcement of Factory Legislation' (1970) 10 *British Journal of Criminology* 383.

[61] See further R Brownsword, 'Post-Technique: *The New Social Contract* Today' in D Campbell, L Mulcahy and S Wheeler (eds), *Changing Concepts of Contract* (Palgrave Macmillan, 2013) 14.

[62] S Zuboff, 'Big Other: Surveillance Capitalism and the Prospects of an Information Civilization' (2015) 30 *Journal of Information Technology* 75, 86 (and, for elaboration of such important matters as the compromising of conditions for making promises and for trusting others in transactions, see ibid, 81–83).

[63] Compare C Steiner, *Automate This: How Algorithms Came to Rule Our World* (Portfolio/Penguin, 2012).

[64] See, eg, EM Weitzenboeck, 'Electronic Agents and the Formation of Contracts' (2001) 9 *International Journal of Law and Information Technology* 204; IR Kerr, 'Bots, Babes and the Californication of Commerce' (2004) 1 *University of Ottawa Law and Technology Journal* 284.

[65] K O'Hara and N Shadbolt, *The Spy in the Coffee Machine* (Oneworld Publications, 2008) 193.

of our future transactions and interactions will take place in environments that are both data-gathering and data-giving, what does this signify for the laws of privacy, confidentiality, and data protection? Is privacy really dead? Must data flow? Are our informational interests to be reduced to a balance of acceptable risk and desired benefits?[66] Should Gewirthians support the use of 'privacy by design'?

Fourthly, if there is some possibility of effective bio-management of human conduct, there are yet more questions. Thus far, although advances in biotechnologies have received at least as much attention as developments in information and communication technologies, their penetration into daily life has been much more modest and their utility as regulatory instruments much less obvious. Genetics and genomics are extremely complex. To be sure, there is a considerable investment in big biobanking projects that seek to unravel these complexities in a way that improves health care;[67] but, even if major strides are made in biobanking and in genetic research, the chances are that for some time *behavioural* genetics will be extremely primitive.[68] However, given another one hundred years of research and development, it might be a different story. If so, and if bio-management operates through internal signalling mechanisms which we (humans) know to be operative but of which we are individually not conscious, there is a new internal dimension to the regulatory environment. In such a regulatory environment, there will be signals that are 'external' to regulatees and to which regulatees respond but there will also be signals that are 'internal' to regulatees. To engage with such a world, we will need to frame our inquiries by reference to a regulatory environment that has not only normative and non-normative dimensions but also external and internal dimensions.[69]

Finally, before we pursue these lines of inquiry, let me post one further question. Is technological management really so different to 'old-fashioned' measures (for example, the architecture of the pyramids, or the introduction of locks) that have been taken to protect our interests in person and property? I am not sure how best to respond to this question. However, the density, sophistication, and variety of today's (and tomorrow's) instruments of technological management distinguishes our circumstances, quantitatively and qualitatively, from those of both pre-industrial and early industrial societies. Whether or not this amounts to a difference of kind or degree scarcely seems important; we live in different times, with

[66] For a distinctive contribution to this debate, see JE Cohen, *Configuring the Networked Self* (Yale University Press, 2012); and, for a helpful review, see JM Balkin, 'Room for Maneuver: Julie Cohen's Theory of Freedom in the Information State' (2012) 6 *Jerusalem Review of Legal Studies* 79.

[67] For an overview, see J Kaye, SMC Gibbons, C Heeney, M Parker and A Smart, *Governing Biobanks* (Hart, 2012).

[68] See, eg, Nuffield Council on Bioethics, *Genetics and Human Behaviour: The Ethical Context* (2002).

[69] In fact, we might already need to revise the idea of the regulatory environment as an external signalling setting. With the development of the so-called 'Internet of Things', in which smart external technologies communicate with internally embedded technologies, and vice versa, the line between the internal and the external is already problematic.

significantly different regulatory technologies. In particular, there is much more to technological management than traditional target-hardening: the management involved might—by designing products and places, or by coding products and people—disable or exclude potential wrongdoers as much as harden targets or immunise potential victims; and, crucially, there is now the prospect of widespread automation that takes humans altogether out of the regulatory equation.[70]

To follow up the last point, with the industrialisation of societies and the development of transport systems, new machines and technologies presented many dangers which regulators tried to manage by introducing health and safety rules and the like.[71] In the twenty-first century, we have the technological capability to replace humans with robots in some dangerous places and to create safer environments where humans continue to operate. However, the technological management that we employ in this way can also be employed (pervasively so in on-line environments) to prevent acts that those with the relevant regulatory power regard as being contrary to their interests or to the interests of those for whom they have regulatory responsibility.

It is also the case that in modern societies, characterised by a good deal of anonymity and high mobility, modern surveillance, locating and identifying technologies take on the policing and compliance functions that were once carried out by the human members of smaller closed communities. These technologies, operating in support of criminal laws, do not replace the rules; technologically enabled legal orders of this kind remain normative but they anticipate a progression to non-normative technological management in the strict sense. Technologies are always disruptive; and technological management represents a serious disruption to the regulatory order. We need to be aware that technological management is happening; we need to try to understand why it is happening; and, above all, we need to debate (and respond to) the prudential and moral risks that it presents.

VII. Conclusion

In the Acknowledgements to *Law as a Moral Judgment*, Deryck Beyleveld and I expressed a special debt of gratitude to 'Annie Lutwama who patiently converted our drafts and re-drafts of at least half the book onto the word-processor'.[72] Note that we talk about '*the* word-processor'—and we do so for the very good reason that, at that time, there was just one so-called 'word-processor' in the Law

[70] For just such an example of 'taking humans out of the equation', see 'Norway hospital's "cure" for human error', BBC News, 9 May 2015: available at www.bbc.co.uk/news/health-32671111.

[71] Compare, eg, SW Brenner, *Law in an Era of 'Smart' Technology* (OUP, 2007) (for the early US regulation of bicycles); and M Martin-Casals (ed), *The Development of Liability in Relation to Technological Change* (CUP, 2010).

[72] *Law as a Moral Judgment*, n 1, ix.

Department at the University of Sheffield. Today, I doubt that we would dignify the primitive piece of equipment in question with the term 'word-processor'; but, as I recall, we thought that we were extremely fortunate to have access to this particular prototypical technology. We concluded our thanks to Annie by saying that, with her help, 'we all became a little wiser, about both the concept of law as well as the power of the word-processor'.[73] Little did we realise—or, at any rate, little did I realise—how powerful modern information and communication technologies would become and in what a short time they would transform our daily working practices. Little did we realise, either, that the acceleration in the development and application of this suite of technologies would place such power in the hands of those who appreciated its new regulatory potential.

My point in this chapter is that, in order to be a little wiser, jurists need to engage with the use of technological management (whether with driverless cars, the Internet of Things, or bio-management) that is surely set to join law, morals and religion as one of the principal instruments of social control. To a considerable extent, technological infrastructures that support our various transactions and interactions will structure social order. The domain of law is set to shrink. And this all has huge implications for a jurisprudence that is predicated on the use of rules and standards as regulatory tools or instruments. In particular, it has implications for the way that we understand the virtue of legality and the Rule of Law; it bears on the way that we understand (and value) regulatory coherence; and it calls for some re-focusing of those critiques of law that assume that power is exercised primarily through coercive rules. To bring these issues onto the jurisprudential agenda, I have argued that we must enlarge the field of interest; and I suggest that we should do this by developing a concept of the regulatory environment that accommodates both rules and technological management—that is to say, that facilitates inquiry into both the normative and the non-normative dimensions of the environment. With the field so drawn, we can begin to assess the changing complexion of the regulatory environment and its significance for traditional legal values as well as the communities who live through these transformative times.

[73] ibid.

8

Beyond Reason: The Legal Importance of Emotions

THOM BROOKS* AND DIANA SANKEY**

I. Introduction

Deryck Beyleveld has forged a theory of ethical rationalism that has made an important impact on legal and moral philosophy—which this collection of essays makes clear. He has not only refined and improved the original account developed by Alan Gewirth, but provides us with ethical rationalism's most prolific defender today. One area of particular insight is Beyleveld's many applications of ethical rationalism to practice and, most especially, to medical law and ethics, which has been especially influential.[1] This work has set the bar for all proponents and critics alike.

We focus narrowly on a specific concern that we have with ethical rationalism: its primacy of rationality over other characteristics, such as our emotions. This is not to deny the importance of reason in our thinking about law and ethical concerns. But we have concerns with any view that holds that reason is the only key to how any tensions should be resolved. Such a position claims for reason a privileged status it does not have or merit. One problem for us is that, in our view, ethical rationalism does not appear to adequately consider the importance

* Head of Durham Law School and Professor of Law and Government, Durham University.

** Lecturer in Law at Liverpool John Moores University. Our sincere thanks to Deryck Beyleveld, Roger Brownsword, Stuart Toddington and most especially Shaun Pattinson for their comments on earlier drafts. While we may remain in some disagreement, our chapter has benefited enormously through their feedback, for which we are grateful.

[1] See, eg, D Beyleveld, *The Dialectical Necessity of Morality: An Analysis and Defence of Alan Gewirth's Argument to the Principle of Generic Consistency* (University of Chicago Press, 1991); D Beyleveld, 'A Reply to Marcus G Singer on "Gewirth, Beyleveld and Dialectical Necessity"' (2002) 15 *Ratio Juris* 458; and D Beyleveld and R Brownsword, *Consent in the Law* (Hart, 2007).

of emotions and so it does not provide a satisfactory account of law and morality as a result. We examine this concern in section II.

Section III raises concerns with the application of ethical rationalism as a model for understanding sexual offences. We highlight both the need to foreground emotion in order to understand the current law, as well as the dangers from a normative perspective of appearing to marginalise the role of emotion in sexual offences. Not only would a prioritisation of rationality fail to reflect the role emotion can play in current rape law, but, we would argue, it is particularly problematic in this area of law in terms of promoting justice. In summary, Beyleveld's ethical rationalism exercises an important impact on legal theory and legal practices; nonetheless, we raise some reservations about its connection to these impacts that lead us to support revisions to this approach.

II. Law and Ethical Rationalism

This section spells out a key concern we have about ethical rationalism. This is as a kind of rationalism that prioritises rationality over sensibility and the emotions. We outline how ethical rationalism is committed to this view in its defence of the Principle of Generic Consistency (PGC). We argue that this position should be revised so that it more clearly accounts for human beings as having both reason and emotions—and build on the importance of emotions for the law in section III.

Rationalism or Reasonableness?

Our first concern is that ethical rationalism prioritises one feature—rationalism—above others, including sensibility. To this end, our emotions do not appear to play any important role on a par with rationality with little, if any, substantive effect on ethical rationalism. This is a concern because it is unclear that rationalism can provide the solid foundation its proponents claim with consequences for the suitability of such an approach for thinking about the law.

Developed from original work by Alan Gewirth, Deryck Beyleveld's ethical rationalism develops Gewirth's conception of the PGC. Beyleveld's argument is dialectical and it has three stages.[2] The first stage begins with the position that agents claim—as agents—that they do (or intend to do) some act voluntarily for some purpose. This claim necessarily accepts that my purpose for acting is good, that my 'freedom and well-being are generically necessary conditions' of my having agency and that my freedom and well-being are 'necessary goods'.

[2] Beyleveld, *The Dialectical Necessity of Morality*, 13–46.

At this stage of the argument, it does not matter what the purposes for acting might be.[3] We consider agency only from 'the internal viewpoint' of an agent.[4] Beyleveld claims the 'key question' here is to ask what an agent may do.[5] But this question is to be answered only from a specific perspective: agents 'must be able to ask the question, "What is it rational or permissible for me to do?"'.[6] Some purposes—namely, 'rational' purposes—count to the exclusion of others.

Stage two of the argument states that it is 'dialectically necessary' for an agent to consider 'that he has rights to the generic conditions of agency'.[7] It is not enough that an agent can do some action for a chosen purpose. These generic conditions of voluntarily choosing an agent's actions are rights held by this agent. This appears to be explained by the fact that if an agent did not have rights to the generic conditions for her agency then her ability to exist as an agent might become compromised.[8]

Stage three of the argument for the PGC holds that it follows 'purely logically' that any agent must consider that all other agents have the same 'generic rights' in equal measure.[9] Beyleveld states this view as 'It is merely because I am an agent that I have the generic rights'.[10] Agents must necessarily possess generic conditions of their agency as rights—that are recognised by any other agent. But these logical manoeuvres consider agents in general, in terms of what is rational for any agent *in general* to do.

It is then unsurprising to find that Beyleveld defends the PGC as a principle that 'is the supreme rational reference point for judging the permissibility of all actions'.[11] The PGC is '[l]ike Kant's argument for "the moral law"' and attempts to establish the PGC in a 'completely a priori' way.[12] This is 'not empirical' as an exercise—it is explicitly rationalist. Beyleveld claims that we are to ask: 'What is it *rational* or permissible for me to do?'[13] Only 'reason' is identified as being what 'may require' an agent 'to do something only to the extent that he can do it'—not our emotional or other responses to circumstances.[14] Not unlike the universalism of Kant's moral law, Beyleveld argues that 'since all agents must accept parallel reasoning, it follows that the PGC is dialectically necessary for all agents'.[15] A particular view of rationality dominates to the exclusion of rival possibilities.

[3] See D Beyleveld, 'The Principle of Generic Consistency as the Supreme Principle of Human Rights' (2012) 13 *Human Rights Review* 1, 2 ('ie in order to pursue or achieve his own purposes, *regardless of what these might be*') (italics given).

[4] ibid, 3.

[5] ibid, 4.

[6] ibid, 4.

[7] ibid, 3.

[8] See ibid, 5 ('generic damage to my capacity to act').

[9] ibid, 3.

[10] ibid, 5.

[11] See ibid, 2.

[12] ibid, 3.

[13] ibid, 3 (emphasis added).

[14] ibid, 5.

[15] ibid, 6.

This brief sketch of the argument for the PGC usefully highlights the clear rationalist nature of this project—and the relative absence of emotions. What counts for the argument is that it should 'follow purely logically' from one stage to the next in a manner that relates to every individual the same.[16] This logical path is the freeway of reason absent any clear influence of more twisting trails of emotions, sentimentality or inclination.

In *The Dialectical Necessity of Morality*, little mention is made of emotions beyond two short passages:

> Gewirth does not deny feelings or emotions legitimacy. On the contrary, it could be said that the theory provides a specification of what constitutes rational emotions and feelings … Gewirth does deny the irrational … has legitimacy.[17]

> It is true that particular occurrent emotions (or attitudes) are not employed as criteria for what is permissible. To do so would, however, beg the question against those with different attitudes.[18]

These brief passages express a clear view that feelings or emotions are not entirely irrelevant. It depends on whether they are 'rational' or not. So it is unimportant if an agent is motivated by any occurring emotional response because others might respond differently and, more specifically, in a non-rational way. It is our being 'rational' and thinking 'logically' that sets the terms for what is permissible under the PGC.

Emotions can factor into the argument only if they are consistent with rationality. Their relationship appears analogous to the relation between the rational and the reasonable in John Rawls's political liberalism.[19] For Rawls, the rational is defined by two principles of justice that any individual might accept under the specified conditions of a hypothetical original position. He recognises that the rational can set the boundaries for political decision-making, but not help us specify its content beyond constitutional essentials. This middle ground is the reasonable that exists within the bounds of rationality and cast as the use of public reasons that can connect more directly with the fact of reasonable pluralism—that any community will be composed of individuals with different conceptions of the good. So long as all are bound by the rational constraints discerned through the original position, free and equal citizens develop political liberalism through the use of public reason.

Similarly, Beyleveld's understanding of the PGC is that rationality sets the boundaries for what is permissible. Within these constraints, our emotions can have some role to play—although how this might work is underdeveloped and

[16] See ibid, 6.

[17] Beyleveld, *The Dialectical Necessity of Morality*, n 1, 159.

[18] ibid, 444.

[19] See J Rawls, *Political Liberalism* (Columbia University Press, 1996) 48–53; and T Brooks, 'The Capabilities Approach and Political Liberalism' in T Brooks and MC Nussbaum (eds), *Rawls's Political Liberalism* (Columbia University Press, 2015), 138 and S Freman, *Rawls* (Routledge, 2007), 324.

not specified. But what is clear is that emotions do not play a leading role and are not 'employed as criteria for what is permissible'. This is left only to rationality—which appears to be understood as a commitment to the law of non-contradiction and general consistency across all agents although there is more than one understanding of what 'rationality' consists in as an essentially contested concept that is not neutral.[20]

In sum, what counts for Beyleveld's ethical rationalism is to a large degree free from empirical attitudinal relations that people possess. Beyleveld's aim is to offer an account that is suitably universalistic to encompass any agent in principle, but we are unclear how well it accounts for agents in their concrete, everyday lives.

We believe Beyleveld's ethical rationalism can and should take greater account of our emotions. In the *Phaedrus*, Plato's allegory of the charioteer is used to help us imagine a charioteer steering two horses as they fly across the Earth.[21] One horse is white and pulls the chariot towards the sky; the other is black and pulls the chariot down towards the ground. Plato argues that we each face these tensions between our ethereal rationality and grounded sentiment. We should not choose one or the other because we'll either rise so high we will burn in the sun like Icarus or come crashing back to Earth like a lead zeppelin. Instead, we should forge a middle path between them both through moderation. Humans are rational agents, but they are also emotional beings—and both of these aspects must be considered to grasp the human condition. To accept one and deny the other is to reject or ignore an important feature of who we are and so is incomplete and unsatisfactory. Our concern with ethical rationalism is that it runs this risk in prioritising rationality over emotions.

One model for this kind of moderation can be found in Martha Nussbaum's capabilities approach.[22] She defends capabilities as our essential freedoms to do or be. They cover a wide range of individual capabilities from practical reason to the uses of our imagination. Nussbaum's argument is that any minimally decent human life must be guaranteed above some minimum threshold of capabilities across these different areas.[23] Capabilities are non-competitive: we cannot satisfy the threshold condition by having large capabilities in some areas but not others. Nussbaum rejects such trade-offs between capabilities on the grounds that each is a capability insofar as each is an essential freedom constitutive of a minimally decent life.[24] The satisfaction of the capabilities threshold need not require

[20] See DP Green and I Shapiro, *Pathologies of Rational Choice Theory: A Critique of Applications in Political Science* (Yale University Press, 1994); D Kahneman, *Thinking, Fast and Slow* (Penguin, 2011) and A Hindmoor, *Rational Choice* (Palgrave Macmillan, 2006).

[21] Plato, 'The Phaedrus' in *Complete Works* (JM Cooper ed, Hackett, 1991) 246a–54e.

[22] See M Nussbaum, *Women and Human Development* (CUP, 2000).

[23] ibid, 6.

[24] This raises questions about whether any individual should be free to reject enjoying several or all capabilities—as Nussbaum argues we can—where securing a minimal threshold of capability enjoyment across all capabilities is also argued to secure a minimally decent life. See T Brooks, 'A New Problem with the Capabilities Approach' (2014) 20 *Harvard Review of Philosophy* 100.

state intervention, but it does require that the state ensure individuals can pursue capabilities above a threshold—even if they can choose not to do so.[25]

The essential point here is that capabilities like our reasoning and imagination overlap. These are not entirely separate dimensions of human lives, but an integrated part of it—we require both for even a minimally decent life. This spills over into our understanding of reasonableness in law. Nussbaum argues that the reasonable person is not a rational automaton, but a thinking and feeling individual.[26] Take the case of a police officer who is called to a dark alley where gunshots have been heard. She sees a figure in the dark that looks like he might be holding a weapon and asks him to stop. He refuses so shoots him fatally only to discover he was unarmed. Nussbaum argues that however tragic, the police officer is innocent and this is because what he means to be a reasonable person is a person with anxieties, fears, aspirations and so on.[27] Yes, reason is important, but we aim for not rationality but reasonableness—and our emotions are a crucial component of that fundamental aspect of the human condition.

The upshot is that ethical rationalism denies an important part of who we are in conceiving human beings as essentially rationalist. This is because it downplays other important characteristics of human experience. As the neurologist Anthony Damasio argues, the human mind does not operate separately from a body.[28] None of us are a brain in a vat. Our emotions and feelings are essential to our reasoning and decision-making—at least from a neurological perspective. To deny it is to reject a part of our physiology. In sum, human beings—and human thinking—are more than pure rationalism. Our emotions matter for our humanity and for how we understand the world. This is because they colour and inform our experiences. Any view about human agency must take into account more than our capacity for rational thinking alone if it is to capture how human beings are agents.

In response, Beyleveld might reject this realist picture—he could deny the claim that our emotions matter in this way and that his account of ethical rationalism insufficiently accounts for them.[29] He might claim that rational agents give importance to hope and fear—powerful emotions that are afforded a central place in his account. Their place is in providing motivation for agents to think and act. If not for our having hopes and fears—so Beyleveld's argument goes—we might remain dormant and motionless. Human agents are rational, but it is our hope and fear that spurs agents to act. Agents act and their chosen purposes require motivation. Some rationally restricted view of emotions might play some part here.

[25] Nussbaum n 22, 51–53.

[26] M Nussbaum, *Hiding from Humanity: Shame, Disgust and the Law* (Princeton University Press, 2004) 12.

[27] ibid, 12–13.

[28] See A Damasio, *Descartes' Error: Emotion, Reason and the Human Brain* (Penguin, 2005).

[29] See D Beyleveld, 'Williams' False Dilemma: How to Give Categorically Binding Impartial Reasons to Real Agents' (2013) 10 *Journal of Moral Philosophy* 204.

We believe this account of the emotions is too weak. Agents—even rational agents—are human beings with emotions and these will include far more sentiments than only our being hopeful or fearful. There is no clear rationale offered for why these two emotions alone should enjoy the special position they are given, or why other emotions could not be included on similar grounds. Individuals are inspired to think or act for more reasons than their having hope or fear. We might be moved by joy or melancholy, for example. But if only two should count, we need to know why these two instead of others. We believe there is no such convincing account offered to clarify this distinction.

Nor is it clear that even the stated importance of our having hope and fear is a sufficient warrant for concluding they have importance for Beyleveld's account. This is because they count for little. Our having hope is largely an attitude about the future—that there will be a future. Acting like there will be a tomorrow is not clearly an emotional attitude, although it could be in cases of living like there is no tomorrow. It could be an assumption or postulate of moral reasoning. Indeed, Beyleveld's view of hope is described as 'not cognitive' and only 'conceptual'—a universal possibility for any agent. This understanding of emotions fails to acknowledge the cognitive states that emotions exist within and the ways in which they can affect our cognitive appreciation of ourselves in relation to others. Thus the ethical rationalist view of hope is it only gives us 'reason to think', but does not inform what or how we do or should think.[30]

So emotions—like hope and fear—might be stipulated as important, but they do not play an important role for shaping the way we choose or think. They do not add to the content of what is thought. To say we might posit other agents as motivated by hope and fear is only to claim they are motivated to think and act like us. This says little about the emotions we have and our emotional relation to others—even through our individual hopes and fears. There is nothing about an agent's motivation through hope and fear *as such* that influences the discussion—and it would make no substantive difference for Beyleveld's account if we substituted other motivational emotions—given the limited, and perhaps trivial, role that emotions play.

III. Ethical Rationalism and Sexual Offences

We now show how these problems with the conception of the person raise additional problems for applying ethical rationalism to criminal law relating to sexual offences. In prioritising rationality over emotionality, ethical rationalism may not fully reflect the realities and complexities of human behaviour in relation to sex and provide a comprehensive understanding of why the law regulates sexual

[30] See the chapter in this book by Düring and Düwell.

behaviour in the way that it does. Indeed, as Beyleveld emphasises, the PGC relates directly to agents and not to human beings, meaning that there is no requirement that agents are humans or gendered beings.[31] While the PGC is intended to be abstract, the application of it to sexual offences would require explicit recognition of the human context underlying sexual behaviour and the criminal law, which may be difficult given the conception of agency inherent within it, outlined above. Although Beyleveld's (and Roger Brownsword's) more recent work on consent applies Gewirthian principles to the law of consent, this is still in many ways an abstract project that, in our view, does not fully engage with the actual nature of the law or with the nature of human conduct.[32]

We argue that the emotional complexity of human behaviour in relation to sexual offences means that application of the PGC to this area of law requires careful consideration. First, sex is often intrinsically emotional and thus sexual offences law raises issues regarding how the law conceptualises the harm. Second, sexual offences constitute an area of law where issues of gender are prominent and where emotional/rational, body/mind dualisms may play out, but equally where such dualisms have arguably been challenged in recent legal reforms, such that a focus on rationality fails to fully reflect the current legal framework. Third, sexual offences law highlights the problems of a focus on legal moralism in a morally pluralist society where the current legal framework represents a compromise between different moralistic and liberal concerns. We contend that understanding sexual offences requires recognition of the interrelationship between emotionality and rationality and the value of affect. Emotion should play an important role in the law, but in a way that avoids the dangers of legal moralism.[33]

Emotion and Criminal Law

The role of emotion in the criminal law has been subject to increasing scholarly debate. In particular, there are emerging interdisciplinary literatures that have sought to explore the relationship between law and the emotions. Law and the emotions literatures provide insights into the ways in which criminal law is laden with emotion, thus challenging the traditional rational and objective representations of law.[34] Such scholarship has highlighted the problems of describing and

[31] D Beyleveld, 'A Reply to Marcus G Singer on Gewirth, Beyleveld and Dialectical Necessity' (2002) 15(4) *Ratio Juris* 458.

[32] Beyleveld and Brownsword, n 1. Despite many examples, including of sexual situations, drawn on in the book, these are not fully fleshed out and the discussion of the application of the PGC to the law remains abstract.

[33] M Nussbaum and DM Kahan, 'Two Conceptions of Emotion in Criminal Law' (1996) *Columbia Law Review* 269.

[34] For discussion of the growth of literature in this area see K Abrams and H Keren, 'Who's Afraid of Law and the Emotions?' (2009) 94 *Minnesota Law Review* 1997.

understanding the current legal framework if the role of emotions is excluded or marginalised, as well as the ways in which understanding emotion and affective responses can enrich the law.

As Nussbaum and Dan Kahan have highlighted, understanding the role of emotion in criminal law depends on the way in which emotion is conceptualised.[35] The history of criminal law reflects wider societal and philosophical debates between a mechanistic view of emotion, which emphasises the demarcation between emotion and cognition and prioritises rationality, and a more evaluative and cognitive approach that recognises that 'emotion is integral to the process of reasoning'.[36] Like other areas of law, criminal law has been influenced by a mechanistic demarcation between rationality and emotion.[37] Indeed, individual criminal responsibility is to some extent founded on a model of a rational individual, who is generally in control of his or her emotions. Emotionality has sometimes been constituted in law as an exceptional state, rather than as an intrinsic feature of humanity.

As feminist scholars have critiqued, the influence of the mechanistic demarcation between rationality and emotionality has served to marginalise women in law, as well as having significant racial and cultural overtones. Traditionally the masculine has been associated with rationality and objectivity, whilst the feminine has been associated with emotionality and subjectivity.[38] Moreover, 'the rationalist model of the person … has been, and really remains, a model of humanity in which a developed capacity for reason is thought to be the most important thing about us (it is most humanising, most dignifying, most central to our persons) and therefore tends to be exclusive of many men'.[39] Stemming most notably from Cartesian thought, the interrelationship between the emotional/rational and the body/mind dualisms also associates women with the body and embodiment, in opposition to rationality.[40] 'There is a fundamental sense in which women are constituted as "outsiders" to rationality precisely by being identified with embodiment (and its related emotionality)'.[41] As the liberal legal person has traditionally been constructed in law as rational and autonomous, legal subjectivity has not always been attainable for women.[42]

[35] Nussbaum and Kahan, n 33.

[36] Damasio, n 28, 144.

[37] A Reilly, 'The Heart of the Matter: Emotion in Criminal Defences' (1997) *Ottawa Law Review* 117.

[38] R Hunter, 'Contesting the Dominant Paradigm: Feminist Critiques of Liberal Legalism', in M Davies and V Munro (eds), *The Ashgate Research Companion to Feminist Legal Theory* (Ashgate, 2013) 13, 14.

[39] N Naffine, 'Women and the Cast of Legal Persons' in J Jones, A Grear et al, *Gender, Sexualities and Law* (Routledge, 2011) 15, 18.

[40] We note that Beyleveld's thought might not be considered either dualist or materialist. Our thanks to Shaun Pattinson for raising this important point.

[41] A Grear, '"Sexing the Matrix": Embodiment, Disembodiment and the Law: Towards the Re-Gendering of Legal Personality?', in J Jones, A Grear et al, *Gender, Sexualities and Law* (Routledge, 2011) 42.

[42] Hunter, n 38, 14.

Nevertheless, a closer examination of the criminal law reveals the influence of a more evaluative conceptualisation of emotion and the pervasive presence of emotion, illustrating that law is capable of incorporating understandings of emotionality.[43] While criminal law may appear to be based on mechanistic underpinnings, it has also been influenced by philosophical and scientific trends that have recognised the interrelationship between thought-processes and emotion. It is impossible to understand certain legal doctrines without incorporating a more evaluative approach to emotions.[44] For example, the loss of control defence (previously provocation) is based both on the defendant's experience of overwhelming emotion and on an appraisal of the reasonable nature of the emotion.[45] While the defence may seem to adhere to mechanistic understandings of emotion, in concerning a temporary loss of rationality, it is also based on evaluative understandings that consider the reasonability of the emotional response of the defendant.[46]

The legal framework, including that relating to sexual offences, is based not only on recognition of the role that emotion plays in cognitive processes but also on evaluations of the reasonability of such processes and resultant behaviour. As Nussbaum and Kahan explain, the evaluative conception 'holds that emotions express cognitive appraisals, that these appraisals can themselves be morally evaluated, and that persons (individually and collectively) can and should shape their emotions through moral education'.[47] In prioritising rationality, ethical rationalism may not recognise the extent to which legal processes rely on evaluations of emotional responses and how such evaluations are themselves subject to shifting views of morality: 'Because emotions involve appraisal, the appraisal of those emotions will reflect a society's norms'.[48] Evaluations of the reasonability of emotional responses in relation to sexual behaviour are, due to their very nature, a product of shifting views of morality. Thus, ethical rationalism may not be able to fully reflect the reality and complexity of sexual offences law.

The Role of Emotion in Rape Law

The mind/body, rational/emotional demarcation has historically played out in legal conceptualisations of the harm of rape and the ways in which the law assesses the state of mind of the defendant and the complainant. Exploration of the conceptualisation of the harm of rape in the criminal law illustrates how emotional complexity and emotional harm have traditionally been elided and silenced.[49]

[43] Nussbaum and Kahan, n 33.
[44] ibid.
[45] Coroners and Justice Act 2009, s 54.
[46] Nussbaum, n 26, 38–39.
[47] Nussbaum and Kahan, n 33, 274.
[48] Nussbaum, n 26, 46.
[49] KK Baker, 'Gender and Emotion in the Criminal Law' (2005) 28 *Harvard Journal of Law & Gender* 448, 453.

Historically, rape was conceptualised as a crime against property, and indeed the very term 'rape' stems from the Latin, 'rapio' meaning to steal or 'carry off'. Rape was traditionally framed as a harm centred on male property ownership over the female body, as evident in the marital rape exception, which existed in English law until 1991.[50] The feminine association with embodiment and the masculine association with the rational mind therefore traditionally lay at the heart of rape law. However, the conception of rape shifted dramatically in the last century, with a move in the common law away from the focus on physical force to an emphasis on individual consent, illustrating how moral understandings of the wrong of rape have been subject to considerable change over time. The focus on consent in the conceptualisation of rape, as confirmed in the Sexual Offences Act 2003, constitutes an important legal development that foregrounds the notion of sexual autonomy. While the concepts of autonomy and consent continue to reflect elements of a mechanistic approach to emotion, in terms of the mind/body, rational/emotion dualisms, they can also be used to foreground emotional understandings. Much therefore depends on how concepts of autonomy and consent are conceived.

Autonomy lies at the heart of a rationalist model of legal personhood in terms of the sovereign, rational actor endowed with objectivity and self-possession.[51] In this view, sexual autonomy is 'the inherent right of the bounded legal person with sovereign control over their bodily property. The wrong of rape then is the invasion and appropriation of that property without consent.'[52] Such understandings of sexual autonomy tend to presume 'a particular conception of the subject and an abstract, rational and self-serving framework for the operation of agency'.[53] This demarcation between the body and the self focuses the harm of rape on the body and on the violation of sexual autonomy and bodily ownership, thus potentially obscuring the complex emotional harms involved.[54] Such an understanding of autonomy may result in a failure to reflect the nature of the harm of rape and the experiences of complainants. As Nicola Lacey highlighted in relation to rape law prior to the 2003 reforms, 'At the level of doctrinal construction of criminal wrongdoing, affective experience is, if not absent, more or less invisible behind the veil of rational and abstract legal subjectivity'.[55]

Nevertheless, the focus on consent and sexual autonomy can also enable recognition of the interrelationship between emotion and cognitive processes and can potentially foreground the importance of affective responses in the law. Consent and autonomy are concepts that can include a more contextual approach and

[50] This exception, whereby rape within marriage was not recognised as women were deemed to have irrevocably consented upon marriage, was finally addressed in the case of *R v R* [1992] 1 AC 599.

[51] Hunter, n 38.

[52] Y Russell, 'Thinking sexual difference through the law of rape' (2013) 24(3) *Law and Critique* 255, 263.

[53] V Munro, 'Constructing Consent: Legislating Freedom and Legitimating Constraint in the Expression of Sexual Autonomy' (2008) 41(4) *Akron Law Review* 923, 928.

[54] N Lacey, 'Unspeakable Subjects, Impossible Rights: Sexuality, Integrity and Criminal Law' (1997) 8(2) *Women: A Cultural Review* 143, 153.

[55] ibid, 154.

can recognise the ways in which emotions relate to and are influenced by social and interpersonal contexts. Emotions are not simply experienced individually but are socially situated. Emotional responses are coloured and shaped by relationships with others, by social experiences and cultural values.[56] Sexual encounters and decisions to engage in sexual intercourse are not made in detached, abstract settings, but are a product of desires, feelings, circumstances and social understandings of sexual behaviour. While autonomy can be conceived in terms of individual separation and boundedness, it can also be reconceived as a capacity that can be fostered through relationships with others.[57] Similarly, '[c]onsent is a concept which we can fill with either narrow liberal values, based on the idea of the subject as an individual atomistic rational choice maker, or with feminist values encompassing attention to mutuality, embodiment, relational choice and communication'.[58]

Beyleveld and Brownsword have provided us with a comprehensive account of how ethical rationalism and the PGC relates to consent in law. Although their work is not specific to consent in sexual offences, it does include references to rape and does not seem to perceive the need for a different understanding of consent in sexual offences law. While we agree with many aspects of their account, we argue that fuller inclusion of emotionality is necessary in order to reflect the nature of consent in human interactions, particularly in the context of sexual offences. The understanding of consent underlying their account continues to reflect a too narrow focus on individual autonomy—in our view—that prioritises rationality and does not sufficiently reflect the complex emotional elements of consent.

Indeed, their predominant focus on rationality is evident in their inclusion of Gewirth's requirement that 'the recipient must be in an emotionally calm state of mind'.[59] While we would agree that clear emotional distress or anxiety is obviously detrimental to the exercise of consent, we would wish to problematise the idea of emotionality employed here. The fact that emotions are largely absent, at least explicitly, from their discussion of consent and thus only appear in terms of the need for emotional calm, results in a failure to explicitly recognise the inherent relationship between emotions and decision-making. This suggests a general detachment from emotion, rather than recognition of the centrality of emotionality to human behaviour, cognition and experience. This is a problem because such factors count whenever considering the criminal law—and it is unclear how a more restricted view of rationally bounded emotions offers us a more attractive alternative.

The focus in their account on the need for consent to be both unforced and informed is significant in potentially reflecting a broad conception of consent

[56] Abrams and Keren, n 34, 2071.

[57] J Nedelsky, *Law's Relations: A relational theory of self, autonomy, and law* (OUP, 2011).

[58] S Cowan, 'Freedom and Capacity to make a choice: A feminist analysis of consent in the criminal law of rape' in V Munro and C Stychin (eds), *Sexuality and the Law: Feminist Engagements* (Routledge-Cavendish, 2007) 51, 53.

[59] Beyleveld and Brownsword, n 1, 128.

that examines surrounding context. However, despite the potential to include emotional aspects, this is not explicitly incorporated into the concept of consent that they develop. The understanding of agency and subjectivity at the heart of their account still seems to reflect a focus on human boundedness and an abstract view of human conduct. Indeed, while they obviously recognise that consent operates in relation to others, their account does not encompass an understanding of consent that recognises the socially situated nature of the self and of emotionality. In line with this view of autonomy there remains an emphasis on the responsibility of the (consenting) agent in relation to whether or not the consent is informed, if they act recklessly or carelessly 'in relation to their own informational field'.[60] While there are obviously merits to this approach we would urge caution in applying this to sexual offences. Given the prevalence of sexual stereotypes and rape myths, there is a danger that it may be overly burdensome on the complainant.

Similarly, there is a need for caution in relation to their approach to the forced/unforced nature of consent. Although it may be in many (or even most) circumstances that 'positive pressure does not invalidate consent', to hold that it never does so may be too stringent an approach.[61] The emotional nature of sexual relationships means that even positive external pressure (in the sense of some incentive or inducement) can be problematic to consent to sex. Such pressure may be exercised in emotional terms, through emotional blackmail and playing on the emotional vulnerability of the complainant. There are also clear gendered implications of not seeing positive external pressure as invalidating consent, given societal stereotypes of male sexual activity (in terms of initiating and pressuring for sex) and female passivity. In terms of negative external pressure (which they argue does invalidate consent), their model allows for recognition of various degrees of pressure, seen through the Gewirthian hierarchy of generic needs.[62] However, this hierarchy may not recognise the complexities of pressure exercised in relation to sexual offences and the ways in which gendered relations may influence the experience and impact of external pressure. Our point here is not that ethical rationalism is problematic because it has not been applied before to an understanding of sexual offences, but rather our uncertainty about whether it can provide a compelling alternative view of these crimes given the priority of rationality over emotions that it endorses.[63]

The recent reforms to the law of rape in the Sexual Offences Act 2003 illustrate that while a broader approach to consent that includes elements of the wider

[60] ibid, 145–54.

[61] ibid, 135.

[62] ibid, 139.

[63] Our view takes seriously a point expressed by Beyleveld that there is a difference between what is recognised and what 'ought to be recognised whether or not they are recognised'. We are not claiming that ethical rationalism cannot offer a view of sexual offences. Instead, our concern is that ethical rationalism does not appear to provide us with a compelling alternative understanding of these crimes if applied to them. See Beyleveld n 3, 15.

context is significant, much depends on how the law is interpreted and applied in practice. Indeed, feminist critiques of the law on sexual offences highlight that, despite reforms, the law is often interpreted and applied in ways that delimit recognition of gendered and emotional experiences. In remaining relatively abstract Beyleveld's and Brownsword's account does not reflect or address these complexities. The 2003 Act provides for the first time a statutory definition of consent, defined in terms of the concepts of 'choice, freedom and capacity', under s 74, which in some ways reflect elements of informed consent and an unforced choice. The definition was aimed at providing a more communicative model that encourages attention to agreement between parties and a focus on the choice, freedom and capacity of the complainant to consent.[64] Rather than focusing on a simple binary of a yes/no decision of whether or not to engage in sexual intercourse, divorced from wider circumstances and emotions, the s 74 definition allows some of the context and emotional complexity surrounding consent to be considered.

The framework of consent in the Sexual Offences Act 2003 is also based on evidential and conclusive presumptions relating to consent and reasonable belief in consent.[65] Included within the six circumstances that give rise to a rebuttable presumption of lack of consent (and lack of reasonable belief in consent by the defendant) under s 75 of the Sexual Offences Act, are fear of immediate violence and fear in situations where the complainant is unlawful detained. As such, understandings of consent have begun to be more explicitly related to emotional responses and behaviours, albeit that there remains a focus on simplistic emotions of fear, rather than more complex emotional states.

However, the broad nature of the concepts of choice, freedom and capacity in the s 74 definition means that while they could be interpreted broadly, they may also be interpreted narrowly, potentially suppressing the significance of the wider contexts surrounding sexual relations and how such contexts impact on the complainant's and defendant's emotional understandings and responses.[66] Societal attitudes and morality feed into legal processes in terms of juror interpretations of consent and evaluations of complainant and defendant behaviour. This again illustrates the importance of perceiving the social situatedness of emotion and the role of social attitudes, and indeed law itself, in shaping emotional responses and juror evaluations of such responses.[67] Thus, while the shift in the *mens rea* of rape from an honest belief in consent to a reasonable belief can be seen to be positive, evaluation of the reasonability of such a belief is inevitably subject to societal attitudes regarding sexual behaviour.[68] Although we support Beyleveld's

[64] Home Office, *Setting the Boundaries: Reforming the Law on Sex Offences* (Home Office, 2000).

[65] Sections 75 and 76 deal with the evidential and conclusive presumptions as to consent.

[66] J Temkin and A Ashworth, 'Rape, Sexual Assault and the Problems of Consent' (2004) *Criminal Law Review* 328.

[67] Abrams and Keren, n 34, 2071.

[68] Sexual Offences Act 2003, s 1.

and Brownsword's emphasis on an honest and reasonable belief, there is a need to recognise that reasonability can also be problematic in such contexts.

In addition, societal attitudes feed into appraisals of the reasonability of the complainant's emotional responses. Rape complainants may suffer particularly during rape trials due to the failure of legal procedure to directly address the relationship between rationality and emotionality. While the liberal notion of consent presumes a rational, autonomous individual with agency over their actions, the female complainant has historically been portrayed in society as an emotional woman who changes her mind: no means yes. On the other hand, jurors may expect a degree of emotion from complainants, and may be more inclined to doubt testimony when complainants present an image of rationality and a calm demeanour. Indeed, Ellison and Munro's research on mock jurors illustrates the degree to which a calm demeanour at trial, not reporting the offence immediately and lack of physical resistance during the rape by the complainant can negatively influence juror perceptions and render them less likely to believe the complainant.[69] Their research indicated that mock jurors who had received education on possible emotional reactions of victims in the aftermath of rape 'were more willing to accept that a "genuine" victim could exhibit few signs of visible distress whilst testifying in court'.[70] This illustrates the importance of foregrounding emotions in the legal treatment of rape, both substantively and procedurally.

Legal Moralism and the Danger of Certain Emotions

While arguing for the legal importance of emotions, we also contend that law needs to be very careful which types of emotion exert influence and to be alert to the shifting nature of moral values. Again, it is important that an evaluative understanding of emotion is employed in order that there is recognition of the role that emotion necessarily plays in the law and of the need for emotions to be evaluated as to their reasonability.[71] While sexual offences law has traditionally elided the role of emotions, it has also been subject to strong moralistic influences in which certain emotions, such as disgust, have played a significant role.[72] In eliding the role of emotions and projecting an image of rationality, law thus hides the moral judgements inherent in it and the ways in which such moralism is itself unstable and subject to shifts over time. It is important that emotions are not viewed as monolithic, as this may serve to perpetuate perceptions of a simple dichotomy between reason and emotion.[73] Rather, emotions need to be differentiated and

[69] L Ellison and VE Munro, 'Turning mirrors into windows? Assessing the impact of (mock) juror education in rape trials' (2009) *British Journal of Criminology* 363.

[70] ibid.

[71] Nussbaum, n 26.

[72] ibid

[73] Abrams and Keren, n 34, 2035.

evaluated. While some emotions have a positive role to play in law, other emotions are more problematic.[74]

The nature of sexual offences law means that it has inevitably been subject to legal moralism in terms of the criminalisation of certain behaviours. Indeed, the historic criminalisation of homosexuality is a poignant reminder of the influence of legal moralism in sexual offences law. Debates between legal moralism and liberalism have been a feature of this area of law, most notably in the responses to the Wolfenden Report of 1957 and the Hart/Devlin debates. The tensions between legal moralism and liberalism continue to play out in current sexual offences law. Indeed, despite the liberal claims evident within the Setting the Boundaries Review, which led to the Sexual Offences Act 2003, strong elements of legal moralism or 'quasi-moralism' are also present.[75] This is seen, for example, in the criminalisation of bestiality in the Sexual Offences Act, which is justified on the basis that bestiality reflects 'profoundly disturbed behaviour' and that 'society had a profound abhorrence for this behaviour'.[76]

In a culturally diverse society, such as the UK, moral consensus is unlikely, particularly in the area of sexual behaviour.[77] The obvious danger of legal moralism is its impact on minority groups (and historically on women), whose behaviour may be subject to legal intervention on the basis of the offence taken by a reasonable man. This is not to argue against the influence of moral considerations per se, nor is it to draw a clear demarcation between harm and offence. Indeed, as various commentators have argued, these concepts are far more fluid than is often presented.[78] Instead, it is to argue that if moral considerations are to play a role, there needs to be careful appraisal of their basis. In particular, the emotional responses inherent in moral judgements need to be opened up and evaluated.[79] The danger of legal moralism is that the emotional responses inherent in moral judgements are not acknowledged and thus are not subject to scrutiny as to their reasonableness. In relation to the Sexual Offences Act the critique is therefore 'not so much that it betrays its liberal pretensions by criminalising offensive conduct or by intervening into previously unregulated areas of life, but rather that it does so without any examination of the grounds on which underlying determinations of "right" and "wrong" have been made'.[80] In applying ethical rationalism to the

[74] Nussbaum, n 26.

[75] N Lacey, 'Beset by boundaries: The Home Office Review of sex offences' (2001) *Criminal Law Review* 3.

[76] Home Office, n 65, 126.

[77] V Munro, 'Dev'l-in disguise? Harm, privacy and the Sexual Offences Act 2003' in Munro and Carl Stychin (eds), *Sexuality and the law: feminist engagements* (Routledge, 2007) 1–18, 4.

[78] See A Duff and S Marshall, 'How offensive can you get? In Simester and von Hirsch (eds), *Incivilities: Regulating offensive behaviour* (Hart Publishing, 2006) 57–90.

[79] Nussbaum, n 26.

[80] Munro, n 77, 15.

area of sexual offences there is the danger not only that it may obscure the tensions between liberalism and legal moralism inherent in the current law, but also that in obfuscating the emotion underlying moralistic responses it may prevent appraisal of the value of the particular emotion as a basis for legal intervention.

Beyleveld has argued that

> Gewirth's theory is 'ahistorical' in the sense that he does not derive the PGC from an assumption of any cultural norms. He derives the PGC dialectically from features that belong to [agents] necessarily, hence universally. These features are 'transhistorical' rather than ahistorical (here meaning not attending to the diversity of features of historically existing [agents]), belonging to [agents] regardless of the historical diversity that they manifest. They exist within historical diversity, not outside of it.[81]

This passage suggests that the PGC provides us with an objective—or at least objectivist— standard by which to make judgements about permissibility concerning generic conditions for agency. It represents a one-size-fits-all that any permissible view about sexual offences should satisfy. To be fair, this does not require all legal communities to possess the same statutes or case law—diversity is permissible provided it is consistent with the PGC's rationalism. This is an important point. But it is no less significant that our cultural norms inform much of our criminal law today—and not least sexual offences. Nor is it clear that these norms that are born from contingencies—and so may depart from the permissible boundaries set by an objective view of rationality—are mistaken as exposed through the application of the PGC. We do not doubt that the PGC can be used to construct a view of sexual offences, but we are unconvinced that it can provide a compelling alternative to the existing positions we have set out given how sexual offences have developed historically.

IV. Conclusion

This chapter raises concerns about ethical rationalism's relation to both legal theory and legal practices. We argue that rationalism is an important, but not the only or even primary factor in understanding ethical decision-making. We then considered the application of ethical rationalism to sexual offences and highlighted the need for careful consideration in applying the PGC to this area of law. While recognising many of the merits of Beyleveld's and Brownsword's approach to consent, we argued for the importance of recognising an evaluative understanding of emotion that reflects the socially situated nature of autonomy and consent.

[81] Beyleveld, *The Dialectical Necessity of Morality*, n 1, 157.

In arguing for the importance of emotionality we also highlighted the dangers of legal moralism and the need to evaluate the merits of legal responses that are founded on emotions. Our conclusion is that ethical rationalism represents an important voice in current debates, but it remains unclear for us that this view can provide a compelling alternative to how we understand certain areas of law like sexual offences—and we welcome more work to help develop this case by taking emotions more seriously.

9

Public Goods in the Ethical Reconsideration of Research Innovation

BENJAMIN CAPPS*

I. Introduction

This chapter focuses on how research innovation is developed as a public good. Innovation is about progress, brought about by investment in systems, organisations and technologies targeted at social problems.[1] It is the composite of both science and business. Here, I have in mind the various organisations that support biotechnological progress in broad aspects of human well-being, and are therefore important engines of economic and social change. One of the most resolute ideas of the public good can be found in the university—traditionally understood as a place of equitable learning and impartial research—but one that has become far less a sanctuary from market priorities. More recently, the growth of biobanking[2] and various configurations of 'Big Data'[3] have become emblems of the pursuit of the public good.[4] These are behemoths of organisation and scope; the sheer weight of data they contain makes possible discoveries, insight and value not possible otherwise. Biobanking is a large-scale undertaking to collect and share data,

* Associate Professor, Department of Bioethics, Faculty of Medicine, Dalhousie University. My thanks to the editors of this volume, Patrick Capps and Shaun Pattinson, for their guidance during the writing of my contribution; and to the comments from attendees of the Ethical Rationalism and the Law conference held in Durham University where this paper was first presented (October 2015). I would also like to acknowledge Deryck Beyleveld, without whose teaching I would likely be far less well acquainted with the work of Alan Gewirth, and the morality that has inspired me ever since.

[1] J Schumpeter, *The Theory of Economic Development: An Inquiry into Profits, Capital, Credit, Interest, and the Business Cycle* (OUP, 1961), 65.

[2] B Capps, 'Defining Variables of Access to UK Biobank: The Public Interest and the Public Good' (2013) 5 *Law, Innovation and Technology* 113.

[3] V Mayer-Schönberger and K Cukier, *Big Data: A Revolution that will Transform How we Live, Work, and Think* (John Murray, 2013).

[4] I use 'the public good' and 'public goods' interchangeably.

medical records and biological samples, all voluntarily donated, for research purposes. These libraries of the human organism enable systematic studies across lifetimes and between generations of many people simultaneously, and provide research infrastructure for community (that is, a discrete patient group) or population-wide public health benefit.[5] This can be contrasted with Big Data, which is an emergent idea emanating from unstructured or unplanned opportunities: data is collected in largely uncontrolled, unsolicited ways (for example from internet search engines), often from unaware people, and mined in innovative strategies to inform crime control, public health surveillance, population monitoring and disease study. Why are such institutions about public goods? In promising innovation beyond many typical capabilities, they are seemingly categorical in the benefits to be had by all—advocates evoke sometimes conflated ideas of the public interests or the public good, often couched as both economic and social values. These creative ventures are dependent on the public—the originators of the data—who receive no direct, immediate benefits as individuals. Taking part often conveys little personal advantage to individuals (such as receiving personalised medical information), but they are recipients of the organisation's integration into services and policy, such as health care practice, that ultimately impacts on their well-being. Justifying the contributions people make, and risks these entail, needs to be explained somehow.

Innovation of this kind is expensive and technically complex, involving many stakeholders and publics. In terms of governance, this informs distinct architectures of 'private' and 'public', thus creating a fertile ground for conflict and co-operation.[6] In this respect, partnerships between private and public organisations have become a feature of commercialisation in many areas, and these can be correlated with a rise in private sector funding of, and shrinking of state interest in, areas of biotechnological research. This raises questions about the suitability or even mutuality of private and public as defining models of innovation; this enquiry is the focus of this chapter. Although the roles that public and private organisations play in research are disconnected visions of social capital,[7] the

[5] D Shaw, B Elger and F Colledge, 'What is a Biobank? Differing Definitions Among Biobank Stakeholders' (2014) 85 *Clinical Genetics* 223.

[6] It is my contention that these architectures create separate agendas: one, 'for profit', where ethical exclusively is defined by framing the public as autonomous 'customers'; and the second, 'for the public good', which is prescriptive in securing inclusive benefits. Each represents a particular perspective of *social capital*, defined in note 7. See generally J Marks, *What's the Big Deal: The Ethics of Public-Private Partnerships Related to Food and Health*, Edmond J Safra Working Papers, No 11 (Harvard University, 2013) 5.

[7] I use *social capital* 'simply as the existence of a certain set of informal values or norms shared among members of a group that permit cooperation among them': F Fukuyama, *Trust: The Social Virtues and the Creation of Prosperity* (Hamish Hamilton, 1995). In the public sphere, this capital might be produced by a group of like-minded participants who commit to an organisation, based on its purpose *for the public good*. In the private sphere, it might be competitors agreeing to 'fair play' within economic networks. Social capital goes beyond regulations that impact on systems of co-operation (defining, among other things, what agreements are valid, terms of compensation, fair contract, and so on), to social agents' propensity to develop reciprocal and trustworthy relationships with each other.

emergence and popularity of partnerships that blur public goods with a profit agenda become curiosities of regulatory legitimacy. Proponents point to the relative advantages of synergies for each: public-private partnerships have the purpose of aligning interests and therefore can be a strategy for effectively creating and sharing goods.[8] However, they also raise questions about the legitimacy of the market system and its effect on public systems. One criticism is that markets create conditions for inequality; but how this is conceptualised as 'the public interest', or its effects on 'the public good', is less well understood. For this present chapter, questions therefore emerge as to how to stabilise, if at all possible, the perennially challenging balance between corporate rights and individual rights.

I use Beyleveld's 'co-operative model' to analyse the compatibility of two rights-based models of innovation governance: the *commodity* model and *welfarist* model. Beyleveld pitted two sets of rights claims against one another—privacy and the right to do medical research—and showed that finding mutuality was likely to create an enhanced research agenda, and that was something like a public interest.[9] One might suppose, then, that the organisations that are *for profit* and those that are *for the public good* are similarly conflicting, and we might also find that challenges to them working together might be met through co-operation. The commodities model (which I ultimately reject) considers public goods to be non-rivalrous and non-excludable. This encourages commodification as a way of innovating value from public goods. The welfarist model, which is based on Gewirth's generic goods,[10] is quite different from that neoclassical economics definition so often used uncritically in public good discourse. It imposes moral limits on commodification, using a range of social actors that produce, foster and protect public goods and distribute them through welfare. Although both models have concerns for collective action problems—in the sense of the best way to provide goods/public goods—they represent different ideas about commodities: goods that have economic value and that can be bought and sold. In the final section, I return to the examples of the university and about data acquisition, to see how we conceive of the public good within organisations, and argue that partnerships risk capture—the conversion of socially valuable public goods to commodities—because of the pre-eminence of market ideologies.

Social capital therefore can create solidarity between members; it also can cause conformity, partisan derision, and division from within and between groups: see generally R Putnam, 'Bowling Alone: America's Declining Social Capital' (1995) 6 *Journal of Democracy* 65.

[8] J Richter, 'Public–Private Partnerships for Health: A Trend with No Alternatives?' (2004) 47 *Development* 43.

[9] D Beyleveld, 'Data Protection and Genetics: Medical Research and the Public Good' (2007) 18 *King's Law Journal* 275; D Beyleveld, 'Conceptualising Privacy in Relation to Medical Research Values' in S McLean (ed), *First Do No Harm: Law, Ethics and Healthcare* (Ashgate Publishing, 2006) 151. Cited henceforth as Beyleveld, 'Data Protection and Genetics: Medical Research and the Public Good', n 9 and Beyleveld, 'Conceptualising Privacy in Relation to Medical Research Values', n 9. See also D Beyleveld and R Brownsword, 'Ethics Committees: Public Interest, Private Interest and the Ethics of Partnership' in G Lebeer (ed), *Ethical Function in Hospital Ethics Committees* (IOS Press, 2002).

[10] A Gewirth, *Reason and Morality* (Chicago University Press, 1978).

It is clear that I am a friend of the welfare state, and therefore not content to let market triumphalism allow for capture without first contemplating how it gives rise to a plausible model of public goods, and then comparing that commodities version's impact on research innovation to that of a welfarist model. From the analysis of these two models I show how capture is possible and why that is ethically undesirable. Whilst not wishing to dismantle the capitalism that drives capture, my modest point is that public and private architectures more often do different things, and it is an error to assume that these roles are either interchangeable or mutual in respect to public goods. If I am right about this, then some initiatives set themselves apart as being for the public good, and if the intention is to secure public goods, these institutions are far better left to this task. Moreover, partnerships with any organisation that disrupts this purpose are imprudent.

II. Beyleveld's Co-operative Model and Research as a Public Good

Beyleveld asks: 'Is genetic research for medical purposes a public good?' The context of his question is the role of privacy in data protection law, and specifically, how sometimes it becomes an obstacle to reasonable research enquiries. He holds that:

> while there are many conceptions of the public good, the most relevant one is that which ties it to the 'public interest' … if the public interest is to be capable of overriding [a principle like] privacy, then it must be conceived of as itself protecting fundamental rights and values.[11]

Beyleveld lists the various possible normative alignments of the public interest, cutting to the chase by affirming its purpose of grounding privacy and confidentiality, and simultaneously balancing countervailing collective rights—in this case, the right to conduct worthwhile medical research. He explains that, on the one hand, the public interest *grounds* right *x*; but on the other hand, there is an interest emanating from a *real* public—a public good—that creates an exception, or countervailing public interest, to *x*.[12] He concludes that, although rights like privacy are indomitable to people's interests, research that also enhances their well-being should rightly be seen as a public good, and he warns that privacy, if 'sacrosanct', may impede that. Beyleveld's co-operative model is explained in the following way:

> we are led away from a picture of the interests of patients [representing the norms such as privacy] being in conflict with the interests of researchers [representing the public interest in doing certain kinds of research]—who, of course, represent the interests of society

[11] Beyleveld, 'Data Protection and Genetics: Medical Research and the Public Good', n 9, 276.
[12] ibid, 283.

> [the public good]. We are reminded that researchers also have privacy interests and can also be patients and that patients also have research interests.[13]

Beyleveld's co-operative model can be used to consider other public interest circumstances in which rights are in conflict, and so this might help us to comprehend the public–private discord I have described that takes place in research innovation. In his account, the solution is one in which the agent *affected* and the agent *researcher's* rights are aligned, in the sense that each has their generic conditions of agency—the goods that are the objects of any rights claim—satisfied to the extent that it is practicable and socially desirable. Rights claims will often be in conflict; not only in respect to agents facing challenges or competition to the possession of objects (goods that are necessary and not just idiosyncratic to wants or desires), but also in respect to the expression of that right and its correlative duties. Absolute privacy would, for example, be contra to optimal social conditions (hiding an intention to plant a bomb, for example; or, as in this case, resistance to unobtrusive epidemiology-based research), but intrusive snooping, or indiscreet, non-consensual research, would likewise be intolerable. Drawing on Gewirth's 'categorically obligatory requirements for action that are addressed at least in part to every actual agent',[14] Beyleveld attempts to balance these claims through the impartial Principle of Generic Consistency (PGC)—which says 'Every agent ought to act in accord with the generic rights of his recipients as well as of himself'[15]—and scoping the needfulness for fulfilling this condition in the case of medical research. What is important to grasp for now is that any significant conditions which are instrumental to life, well-being, or other measure of flourishing might be claimed as a right. Health is generally considered as an object of these conditions, and one might therefore say that there is a right to health. Medical research, therefore, might be a necessary condition of health. But Beyleveld also writes, elsewhere, that research participants ought not to be treated 'as information crops to be harvested for the common good or their own purposes, but as partners whose purposes are to be respected'.[16] This sets up the kinds of public interest or public good debate (Beyleveld sometimes conflates these) in respect to what might justify limiting rights claims, on the stipulation that doing so contributes to better conditions for rights in general. So, in this way, the public interest might allow medical research greater discretion in cases of prospective privacy breaches because it is expected to benefit agents in some way; that is, a well-planned protocol might be permitted to transgress a person's rights because doing so might actually be in their interests as well.

Beyleveld's analysis is intriguing in respect to the concept of public goods as well. It moves us away from the usual view (which dominates the economic literature) of public goods as things that require state action for them to exist at all,

[13] ibid, 288.
[14] Gewirth, n 10, 1.
[15] ibid, 152.
[16] Beyleveld, 'Conceptualising Privacy in Relation to Medical Research Values', n 9, 159.

to one that hints at their fundamental social worth. For example, research makes both social and economic contributions; often these are mutual, and moreover, neither should be discounted as having value. Instead, however, a profit agenda has undervalued research that is neither lucrative nor commercial. Often, that research is worthy, or even, as in basic sciences, forms essential 'shoulders' on which all scientific and medical progress is made. Moreover, non-commercial science (research that is done for no other reason than the public good) contributes to evidence in ways that can identify the disingenuous effects of phenomena such as profit seeking. Perpetrators who claim extravagant rights to prosperity presumably have no interest in revealing how markets allow for mischievous ways and means to achieving profit; thus it takes a 'disinterested' investigation to uncover these potentially toxic influences. In this example, therefore, to forsake the public good/public interest of research would be to lose sight of the integrity and conduct of doing good science. But Beyleveld's analysis is not finished here: there are feasibly many conditions that support or hinder broadly medical research—not just public well-being and the individual's privacy—that have the duality of collective benefits and personal impositions. For example, the necessity to curtail rights for experimental public health interventions to work at all[17] or policies that promote industry while investing in infrastructural, rather than social goods.[18] Creating space for these conditions can have significant implications for governance through the public interest, especially in terms of social attitudes to policies and whether or not agents buy in to the particulars of innovation creation.[19]

III. Scoping the Public Interest and the Public Good

Research innovation occurs in all kinds of institutions. Each has a corresponding architecture that qualifies the 'benefits [or not] of coordinated behaviour'.[20] They reflect views of a Eunomic kind: governance defined by the fusion of values of law and ethics, with empirical data and methods of the objective sciences.[21] In this respect, innovation is possible because of the buildings and the networks that enable it. Within these organisations, goods are defined in respect to what they are, how they are to be accrued, and how then to regulate their use, via, for instance, codification of rules. It is my contention that from private and public architectures

[17] ie exceptions to rights so as to allow actions that secure short and long term health benefits: Nuffield Council on Bioethics, *Public Health: The Ethical Issues* (NCB, 2007).

[18] J Goodman and G Lovemen, 'Does Privatization Serve The Public Interest?' (1991) 69 *Harvard Business Review* 26.

[19] See generally T Caulfield et al, 'A Review of the Key Issues Associated with the Commercialization of Biobanks' (2014) 1 *Journal of Law and the Biosciences* 94.

[20] J Heath, 'The Benefits of Cooperation' (2006) 34 *Philosophy & Public Affairs* 313, 315.

[21] H Olsen and S Toddington, *Architectures of Justice: Legal Theory and the Idea of Institutional Design* (Ashgate, 2008).

emerges the distinctive character of innovation: what it is for, and how it should be achieved. A governance framework—seated in the social capital of the community that prevails—may therefore reflect different theories of the public good and public interest. The evidence of how these architectures actually contribute to public goods, however, tends to be controversially defined by these capitals rather than proper study.[22]

While I am not proposing to undertake this empirical study here, instead, I will look at the normative grounding of public goods, and, in particular, various key protagonists' theories about innovation strategies, to understand what is at stake in different models of innovation. In the following, the assumption that co-operation will benefit any one concept of public goods is contested. This is a quite separate claim from disputes about *effective* innovation (in discovery, development and production) and corruption that potentially plagues it in practice.[23] Accordingly, two public goods models that feature rights are iterated. My aim is to better situate a general critique, often aimed at private innovators, of their perennial disdain for fostering public goods and their cheapening of the public infrastructure. In fact, public investment and acumen is not only responsible for a great deal of innovation, but also creates, sometimes through partnerships, frameworks and the means to ensure that essential services continue.[24] Chiefly, then, my goal is to show how scenarios are often reinforced by one's own moral certitude about a given social capital (basically, why one associates with the ideology of a favoured group). Later in the chapter, I will return to the issues of capture and commodification as concrete examples of this; but first, it is necessary to understand how each of the two models creates public goods, and, from this, a picture of public interest will also be revealed.

IV. Two Models of the Public Good

Goods as Commodities

Goods, within a neoclassical economic commodities model, are broadly defined from a mono-utility strategy as products created from primarily egoistical, self-interested or selfish motivations. (Or at least, it is a perspective that all agents desire

[22] See especially H Rainey, R Backoff and C Levine, 'Comparing Public and Private Organizations' (1976) 36 *Public Administration Review* 233. See also G Boyne, 'Public and Private Management: What's the Difference?' (2002) 39 *Journal of Management Studies* 97.

[23] See especially M Mazzucato, 'The Entrepreneurial State' (2011) 49 *Soundings* 131. See also F Michelman, 'Ethics, Economics, and the Law of Property' in J Pennock and J Chapman (eds), *Ethics, Economics, and the Law. NOMOS XXIV* (New York University Press, 1982).

[24] For an example of the placation of industry, see especially B Capps and T Lysaght, 'Challenging the Production of Vaccines for a Future Influenza Pandemic' (2013) 5 *Asian Bioethics Review* 110.

to maximise their own preferences and the gains from generating and consuming goods, rather than promoting 'sociality' or 'solidarity'.[25] In this brief summary, I will have nothing more to say about this.)[26] This might create a specific rights culture—one in which each has a liberty to maximise their prosperity—against a backdrop of libertarian critique of central planning and a presumption that welfarism[27] should be minimised. An axiom emerges that stresses that increased competition means increased innovation.[28] In these market conditions, all goods are commodities, and leadership and fidelity in private organisations are the most efficient system for their production. These commodities have a value that exceeds those that are *non-rival* and *non-excludable*: the *theoretical* public goods that cannot be produced by markets, or it is inefficient to do so[29] (although, in reality, it is likely that a narrow delineation is impractical, public goods might be said to have this 'character'). The narrative that follows from this explains what markets can and cannot do, and the roles of government spending and intervention. It also creates a 'fictitious' public—although one that in reality has social rules that create a degree of communality—to ensure that to each comes liberty and the right to produce and consume goods.[30] Captured public goods, therefore, become 'collective consumption goods': commodities that are used by many people, such as roads, that can be transferred to markets, as in this case, by use of tolls. Innovation, in this sense, can be explained by the drive to convert struggling or inefficient public good systems (some public roles, like national defence, might have value) to be better positioned within markets: successful innovation is about encouraging entrepreneurial wit—ingenuity, investment and risk taking—as a means to collective prosperity.

Economies which adapt to pure commodities and the science of 'efficiencies' are often described as 'amoral' by neoliberal thinkers because there is little scope for the woolliness of ethics.[31] Of course, these thinkers are taking a socio-ethical position, and in doing so do not have exceptional claim to scientific integrity and pristine knowledge.[32] In respect to the actions of agents (mischaracterised as '*homo economicus*'), even simple markets draw ideas from

[25] 'Bringing human and social values into economic decisions will lead ultimately to a shift from market mechanisms to political mechanisms'; and this happens to the detriment of 'private [business's] right to be profit orientated, to protect its investments, and to be compensated for innovation': K Leisinger and K Schmitt, *Corporate Ethics in a Time of Globalisation* (Vishva Lekha, 2003).

[26] See especially L Herzog, 'Economic Ethics for Real Humans: The Contribution of Behavioural Economics to Economic Ethics' (2008) 9 *Zeitschrift für Wirtschafts und Unternehmensethik* 12.

[27] For the definition I prefer, and discussed below, A Gewirth, *Community of Rights* (Chicago University Press, 1998), 134.

[28] See generally M Hollis, *Reason in Action* (CUP, 1997) ch 2.

[29] P Samuelson, 'The Pure Theory of Public Expenditure' (1954) 36 *Review of Economics and Statistics* 387.

[30] Joseph Heath calls this: 'catallactic bias, which result[s] from a tacit conceptual privileging of gains from trade as the primary mechanism of cooperative benefit', n 20, 315.

[31] J Schumpeter, *History of Economic Analysis* (Routledge, 2006) 804–06.

[32] M Lutz, *Economics for the Common Good: Two Centuries of Social Economic Thought in the Humanistic Tradition* (Routledge, 1999) 106.

coordinating principles, which, as 'rules of the game', define things like 'fairness', 'benevolence', 'trust' and 'deceit' that influence their opinions and decisions. In this sense, all agents are grounded in practical reason.[33] More complex market theories involve political philosophising about the meaning of economic and social systems and the agents' actions within them (the 'free rider', for example, can be explained by both economics and ethical concepts). Thus, Leisinger and Schmitt are prompted to make a case that 'economic success can be termed ethically imperative', and they do so by affirming a rights hierarchy within 'corporate morality'.[34] Leisinger calls the most important rights 'non-negotiable "must" norms—these demand compliance with relevant national laws and regulations in all cases as an ethical minimum', and are spelled out as to 'be profitable; be successful in R&D; [and] make profitable strategic decisions'.[35] Staying within the law reduces corporate means, but doing so also requires leadership to reflect on the purpose and legitimacy of these bounds. Beyond these are the second- and third-generation rights, developed for 'the enlightened self-interest of companies'.[36] They read like quasi-Kantian *imperfect* duties: fair competition, proportionate rewards, good faith in the negotiation and performance of contracts, and strategic integrity, all of which tend to bring about a better state of affairs in social and economic terms, across both private and public spheres. (In the normal use, a hierarchy of rights is relative to the weight given to each when they are in conflict.) There might be conformity to the public good (charity or philanthropy), but only when it conforms to primary 'musts'.[37] These musts, then, steer industry away from non-economic utilities and towards purely efficiency gains via a meticulous weighing of the costs to be incurred and the prize to be obtained. Brabeck-Letmathe implies as much: reflecting upon the corporate reality to make a rational case for making profit from conventional public goods, he recommended that we should 'privatize the normal water supply for the population'.[38] In response to those who 'bang on about declaring water a public right', he decries problems of unequal distribution and unsustainable management as symptoms of opportunity costs brought about by welfarist talk.

[33] A Sen, 'On the Foundations of Welfare Economics: Utility, Capability and Practical Reason' in F Hahn et al (eds), *Ethics, Rationality and Economic Behavior* (OUP, 1996) 61.

[34] 'Every endeavour to exert ethical influence on how the economy is structured and on the conduct of those active in it must pay regard to what is economically apposite. Anything diametrically opposed to this can never be ethically defensible': Arthur Rich quoted in Leisinger and Schmitt, n 25, 9–11.

[35] K Leisinger, *On Corporate Responsibility for Human Rights* (Business & Human Rights Resource Centre, 2006) 6–9.

[36] ibid, 7.

[37] eg 'It is obvious that legitimate efforts to achieve profit ... can, under certain circumstances, come into conflict with the "right to life" of someone living in dire poverty. And it is equally clear that it cannot be the duty of a company to give away valuable goods if those who need them cannot afford to buy them': Leisinger and Schmitt, n 25, 17.

[38] J Confino, 'Nestlé's Peter Brabeck: Our Attitude Towards Water Needs to Change' (2013) *The Guardian* 4 February.

In terms of public goods, value conversion of this sort is *in the public interest.* Measured by its utility, the public interest is ambiguous in respect to upholding either aggregate or distributive meanings, thus, research could be *in the public interest* because it maximises contentedness of consumers; or it could be that people—the Benthamite 'common good'—generally support research because of the equal prospect of securing advantage from it.

Goods and Welfare

A quite different welfare model of public goods can be made from Gewirth's specificity of the rights and duties owed to and required by moral agents. Under the PGC, welfarism means fostering personal productive abilities (freedom and well-being) and providing the resources to do so (the generic conditions of agency (GCA), which are otherwise known as generic goods). This occurs in the broadest understanding of areas such as health, education and social security, and as such, extends the state into areas like innovation.[39] He often mentions public goods,[40] but the concept remains somewhat untested despite its significant role in the resolution of conflicts between 'corporatist' and generic rights often arising in the indirect application of the PGC.[41] Gewirth explains that public goods are conceptually created by scaling up GCA in the circumstances of the Community of Rights. What distinguishes public goods from GCA is that the agent's 'control' is on a different 'footing from the [for example] property rights whose private ownership contributes to individual freedom and autonomy'.[42] Public goods are therefore 'beneficial commodities' that 'while helping all members of the society, serve to increase the opportunities [such as] productive employment'.[43] Or to put it differently, the public good is the 'distributive provision of necessary goods as prerequisites for productive agency'.[44]

Gewirth does not consider public goods as strictly commodities, and it would be mistaken to presume that calling them such has any semblance to the view just outlined in the previous section. Principally, a strict theory of commodities undervalues public infrastructure and that is clearly not Gewirth's intention. Instead, he directly allocates responsibility for public good provision to democratic social institutions (*qua* public bodies). These create distributive access 'insofar as its subjects or right holders are individuals each of whom the system is designed to benefit',[45] in

[39] Gewirth, n 27, 134. On the idea that welfarism has a universal function, see generally J Hills, *Good Times, Bad Times: The Welfare Myth of Them and Us* (Policy Press, 2014).

[40] Gewirth, earlier, used the *common good* to indicate a collective interest as having a specifiable and substantive content: see A Gewirth, 'Political Justice' in R Brandt (ed), *Social Justice* (Prentice Hall, 1962).

[41] Gewirth, n 10, §5.1.

[42] Gewirth, n 27, 173.

[43] Gewirth, n 10, 314.

[44] Capps, n 2, 128.

[45] Gewirth, n 27, 48.

addition to absorbing efficiency costs that individuals would otherwise be overburdened with. The economic environment Gewirth envisages is one governed by moral imperatives that increase opportunities and aid those dependent on their own limited resources, by instrumentally promoting egalitarian equality;[46] and this requires incentives and coercion on the part of the state, under the rule of law, to instigate (policies), uphold (laws) and promote institutions (via taxation). Together, these provide conditions for various public goods, which *might include* partnerships between private and public institutions. Thus, developing bonds and working with industry is possible, but any arrangements must be based on agreements that 'help to facilitate the general increase of wealth and productive capacity for the whole society'.[47] Of direct relevance to this present chapter, this singles out the state's role in 'encouraging' economic development but '*within the limits* posed by the requirements of public goods.'[48] This has two implications. Firstly, individuals *contribute to the public good* in various ways. For example, directly by public employment, through taxation to fund civil/public service, or by taking part in charity work or making donations, and indirectly by seeking productive employment and developing expertise and skills. Secondly, by creating dignified living conditions, such as appropriate compensation and social security, the community is committed to provide services and, when necessary, (re)distribution of goods *for the public good*.

Gewirth's public goods are most closely predicated upon the economic and social rights. For example, additive goods create equality of opportunity in the place of frustration; and nonsubtractive goods, the loss of which affects the agent's purposivity, and can be addressed by looking at, for example, causes of poverty, such as generally unfair work condition and squalid living conditions.[49] Thus, public goods are often the side restraints of purely wealth-generating initiatives because they are GCA, and that is fundamentally different from pure commodities whose content is just non-rivalry and non-excludability. Welfarism may articulate the value of public goods in any number of ways: indebtedness to public investment; drawing from their value as invested taxpayers; and obligations arising from their inheritance from previous generations, or responsibility for stewarding them for the next.

The proper function of the public interest, then, is to protect the social opportunities, creativity and self-worth that give these expressions credence, and

[46] See generally: 'as agents, we should treat ourselves as having both rights and responsibilities with regard to the protection, preservation and promotion of the generic context for agency (that is to say, the agency commons). We can argue about the details of this context (or commons) but it will include elements pertaining to our well-being (clean air and water, food, environmental integrity, and the like) and our freedom (security, an absence of fear and intimidation, and so on). Not to harm one another directly is fine but the setting for flourishing agency requires more than this minimal interactive restraint.' R Brownsword, 'Friends, Romans, and Countrymen: Is There a Universal Right to Identity?' (2009) 1 *Law, Innovation and Technology* 223.

[47] Gewirth, n 10, 318.

[48] ibid, my emphasis.

[49] ibid, 314. Gewirth's public goods include 'unpolluted air, public roads, courts for resolving civil disputes, and protection against fire that are "common" goods in the distributive sense': ibid, 318.

accordingly, it serves as a procedural tool for judicial (or formal) enquiry where there are collective repercussions in respect of the realisation of opportunities and where there are violations to human rights.[50] The public good/public interest tie Beyleveld recognises also plays out as the hierarchical ordering of rights. Privacy and confidentiality can be considered the objects of human rights: the ethical and legal barriers that are conditional upon the public interest. Thus, only when there is a tangible gain to the public good—a collective right claim to a collective good—might there be an exception to an individual's right. Beyleveld cites *W v Egdell*, in which a justified public interest resulted from 'a real risk of consequent danger to the public',[51] thus recalling the idea that governments may act substantively and proportionally to avert or resolve these situations. In English courts at least, a public interest is likely to be a defined response to a significant threat, or, perhaps sometimes less convincingly, when human rights appear obstructive or too burdensome to the state's policy ambitions. (One can therefore see that the commodities model of the public interest is also tacitly in play in political decision-making.) However, the public interest determination, according to Beyleveld, ought not to be a balance between alienated values, but ought to consider plainly the individuals' rights at stake as matters of social justice. Social justice therefore invokes conflicting or competing right-claims to goods, or public goods when considered in collective terms. What this means is that the public interest is only that which is compatible with respect to human rights.

It is this distinguishing role, to provide necessary public services as a function of equity, which underlies the welfarist understanding of social justice and capital. In this respect, public goods are likely to have a central role in progress, so much so that innovation depends upon a substantial public investment in things like education and infrastructure. *For the public good* includes organisations that promote the idea of true collective achievements, but which are defined outside of profit narratives.[52] The public interest expresses the idea of *for the public good*, which is always *directly* correlative and defined by its contribution to the GCA.

V. Capture and Commodification

The increasing fuzziness between private and public functions makes comparative studies of effective innovation essential; but, philosophically, these two models

[50] B Capps, 'The Public Interest, Public Goods, and Third Party Access to UK Biobank' (2012) 5 *Public Health Ethics* 240.

[51] [1990] Ch 359, 424. In which it was held that the public interest was the balance between a duty of confidence in the doctor–patient relationship and that of protecting the public. A psychiatrist disclosed concerns about his patient, in this case the plaintiff, who had been confined to a mental hospital for killing several people and was being considered for release.

[52] Lutz, n 32, 106.

differ in respect to public goods in an important way. The welfarist model can accommodate an understanding of commodities; the difference between that, and the one used in the commodity model, is that when goods are necessary for the GCA to be achieved they take on a special moral status (rather than in the flat conception of goods that the commodity model proposes). In the commodity model, all goods are commodities, and that goes for public ones as well.

A significant distinction, therefore, is how commercialisation is viewed from these different models. While commercialisation has become part of the 'rhetoric of national advantage in the "global struggle"' to create a society that is best served by 'economic strategy',[53] the welfarist model looks to preserve public goods and public bodies because of concerns about how markets depreciate them. This might translate into the ways in which public goods are sold off to private interests (privatisation), or how public bodies are reformed which leads to their prior role for the public good being discontinued or significantly changed. These might be described as symptoms of 'capture', in which actors in the regulatory process have narrow, self-interested goals, and gain influence through political systems.[54] Partly borrowing from this definition, capture is also plausible when this same special interest uses influence to move public goods from state apparatus to their own pools. This is often conceptualised as the 'enclosure' of the 'commons' that defines the causes of frustration, poverty or destitution,[55] but the socio-political use of 'captive' also lends well to the moral content of public goods.

Capture/enclosure might occur by assuming legitimate, more efficient roles in supplying goods that were previously public ones. However, most problematically, it also happens by influencing the regulatory process (most cited examples here are about lobbying, bribery and conflicts of interest). There are a number of troubling effects that markets have on public goods.[56] One of these is commodification—the process of turning an object into a commodity. Capture, therefore, has become a drive for commodification of 'the good things in life'.[57] Sandel argues that the root of commodification is 'unfairness'; the transformation of goods to luxuries is part of a 'faith' system in which opportunities are replaced by inequality, greed and corruption, and 'corrosive' conditions that 'leave a mark'.[58] But we might not think that such things as he has in mind are necessarily 'market-inalienable', in the sense that forfeiting or trading in them violates rights; and, in fact, a system that creates rules convened by opinions, beliefs or vicarious interests might actually do more damage in this respect. There are hints that societies in many ways are shifting

[53] S Collini, 'Who Are the Spongers Now?' (2016) 38 *London Review of Books* 33.

[54] M Levine and J Forrence, 'Regulatory Capture, Public Interest, and the Public Agenda: Toward a Synthesis' (1990) 6 *Journal of Law, Economics, and Organization* 167.

[55] D Bollier, *Silent Theft: The Private Plunder of Our Common Wealth* (Routledge, 2003).

[56] ibid.

[57] M Sandel, 'What Isn't for Sale?' 2012 *The Atlantic* 27 February.

[58] ibid.

towards markets in all things: for example, commercial surrogacy has become 'rent a womb', and the few emerging markets for 'comprehensive reimbursement' for human organs suggest that repugnance and unsavouriness have been replaced by possibilities and opportunities of alienability. It is likely that, more than ever, 'contested commodities' feature commonly in markets and are thus potentially capturable.[59] The contrast is this: under a commodity model, a summation of cost–benefit is possible that justifies value creation from goods and therefore capture; for the welfarist model, public goods are created by GCA, thus are not designated adequately by purely economic strategies, and, if they are true public goods, then capture potentially violates the PGC. The PGC, however, does not rule out markets, but presumes that exchanges ought to occur according to it. Thus, although fungibility might be negotiated between consenting agents, the conditions that make this voluntary or otherwise might be exploitative in the long view.[60]

This disparity becomes a distinct challenge for partnerships in innovation, especially where there is a presumed expectation that economic priorities complement 'public good culture' and vice versa.[61] For example, the universities' duty to 'seek the truth'[62] has been repurposed as 'engines of growth'; where 'interested enquiry', 'secret knowledge'[63] and, most damagingly, conflicts of interest are tolerated. The university is no longer

> a partly protected space in which the search for deeper and wider understanding takes precedence over all more immediate goals; the belief that, in addition to preparing the young for future employment, the aim of developing analytical and creative human capacities is a worthwhile social purpose; the conviction that the existence of centres of disinterested inquiry and the transmission of a cultural and intellectual inheritance are self-evident public goods.[64]

Those that walk its halls are no longer 'sceptics', equally bound to interrogating evidence through pure and systematic method.[65] They have become opportunities for (and tempted by) vested interests who buy opinion, authority or intellectual influence, and thereby public legitimacy. This has changed the face of universities in many ways; students have become consumers and their degrees 'products', where once their achievements and experiences were synonymous with public goods. In respect to research, as has been shown in respect to commercial influence of 'Big Pharma' in medicine, these conditions breed secrecy, bias

[59] M Radin, *Contested Commodities: The Trouble with Trade in Sex, Children, Body Parts, and Other Things* (Harvard University Press, 1996).

[60] D Beyleveld and R Brownsword, *Human Dignity in Bioethics and Biolaw* (OUP, 2001) 192.

[61] A Schafer, 'Biomedical Conflicts of Interest: A Defence of the Sequestration Thesis—Learning from the Cases of Nancy Olivieri and David Healy' (2004) 30 *Journal of Medical Ethics* 8.

[62] S Lewis et al, 'Dancing with the Porcupine: Rules for Governing the University/Industry Relationship' (2001) 165 *Canadian Medical Association Journal* 783.

[63] J Atkinson-Grosjean, *Public Science Private Interests: Culture and Commerce in Canada's Networks of Centres of Excellence* (University of Toronto Press, 2006) 200.

[64] Collini (n 53).

[65] R Merton, 'Science and the Social Order' (1938) 5 *Philosophy of Sciences* 321.

and misinformation.[66] Scholarly success is no longer measured by the unpartisan (but not unproblematic) measures of citations and peer acknowledgement, but by prestige from industry funding and its contribution to university prosperity.[67] Universities are entitled to be profitable, and that can be diverted into a better experience for students and conditions for faculty; but the encouragement is often not about this, or perchance economic survival, but for market positioning. There is little consolation for the scholar concerned about commercialisation's effects on their own research. Certain strategies erode academic freedom,[68] and scholarship influenced in this way risks contributing to the same kinds of distrust held towards privatisation of socially valuable public goods.[69]

Capture is also a potential assault on rights, made possible by reframing them as burdens on economic pansophy. The concern is that capture has already become coercive, but generally gone unnoticed because of its appeal to the public interest. University scholars are already aware of this sea change in respect to public goods, and that should be a warning for the public's loss as well. The proposed sale of English National Health Service (NHS) medical records to pharmaceutical companies, for example, has been framed by 'Business and government [who] are united in their belief in the potential of "Big Data" to drive economic growth, scientific innovation and service efficiency'.[70] Consider, then, our two models in respect to this potential *conversion* of medical records to commodities. First, there is the opportunity to secure *economic* gains from investment, job creation and commodities production.[71] The sell-off of NHS data could be claimed to be in the public interest[72]—an expression of the Benthamite 'common good' that is tempered by the innovator's right to do good. This need not be achieved with consent.[73] However, even under a commodity model, private data or a duty of confidence might be protected as a right (a liberty to control information about oneself, or to have contracts honoured). This transfer therefore requires 'value conversion' from a confidential and private record to research data. So, the public interest argument might go: if anomalous persons are allowed to assert this right—to object to their data being used for commercial purposes—then that might affect goods within more general economic interests. Value conversion creates a narrative in which dissenters are hushed by pejorative interests, and profitability is duly amplified by

[66] B Goldacre, *Bad Pharma* (Fourth Estate, 2012).

[67] Collini, n 53.

[68] On the importance of freedom, see: J Harris, 'Moral Enhancement and Freedom' (2011) 25 *Bioethics* 102.

[69] Caulfield et al, n 19.

[70] Sciencewise Expert Resource Centre, *Big Data: Public Views on the Collection, Sharing and Use of Personal Data by Government and Companies* (2014) Version 1, April.

[71] For a critique of this argument, B Capps, 'Models of Biobanks and Implications for Reproductive Health Innovation' (2015) 33 *Monash Bioethics Review* 238.

[72] eg Academy of Medical Sciences, *Personal Data for Public Good: Using Health Information in Medical Research* (Academy of Medical Sciences, 2006).

[73] P Carter, G Laurie and M Dixon Woods, 'The Social Licence for Research: Why *care.data* Ran into Trouble' (2015) 41 *Journal of Medical Ethics* 404.

the public interest.[74] This rhetoric is tolerated because 'the unbearable lightness of politics' has created 'fragmented individualism',[75] where public concerns 'are united by nothing more than the expression of emotion',[76] ever more exploited by those expounding the virtues of profitable innovation; the result is a loss of spirited commitment to the public good, and the triumphant march of the market.

Alternatively, on the welfarist model, there is also space for research—in the sense that 'people have a right to medical research being carried out'[77]—but within the limits imposed by the PGC.[78] It is under the PGC that the use of the NHS data might be challenged.[79] Assuming that the public interest justifies grounds for duress in cases that can be tested,[80] the connection between competing interests is one in which the significance of rights violations is measured in terms of freedom and well-being, and in both occurrent and dispositional senses of the relative control a person has over her faculties and choices.[81] These medical records, otherwise kept in state hands, might be considered a public good—albeit only ostensibly such because realising their social worth is limited by the conditions of consent when the records were created.[82] The public interest in protecting fundamental rights might be expected to keep these medical records within the bounds of confidentiality because no patient explicitly agreed to this sale of their personal records and thus the profiteers' goals might appear somewhat off from the original consent that was provided during the course of clinical care. The public interest might also be expressed as violating en masse the confidentiality of the physician–patient relationship, without which people might not turn to their physicians when in need thus affecting the health of the population overall and public health capabilities. The simple explanation here is that patients did not consent to the value conversion, and thus capture is to be resisted on these grounds alone.

One might go further: Kingwell uses 'prison' as a metaphor to find public spaces as a 'vanishing value' to locate the threat of control through surveillance.[83] This allegory can be applied to the university and the non-consensual use of medical

[74] J Gunn, 'Jeremy Bentham and the Public Interest' (1968) 1 *Canadian Journal of Political Science* 398.

[75] T Judt, *Ill Fares the Land: A Treatise on Our Present Discontents* (Penguin, 2010) ch 3.

[76] ibid.

[77] Beyleveld, 'Data Protection and Genetics: Medical Research and the Public Good', n 9, 287.

[78] Gewirth, n 10, 318.

[79] In the UK's consideration of the *care.data database*—involving the proposed sell-off of NHS medical records, the oral evidence repeatedly raised the spectre of for profit motives: Health Committee, *Oral evidence: Handling NHS Patient Data*, HC 484 Tuesday 1 July 2014.

[80] Capps, n 50.

[81] Gewirth, n 27, 271.

[82] A Wolf, 'Thanks to care.data, Your Secrets are no Longer Safe with Your GP' (2014) 14 February *Wired.co.uk*.

[83] M Kingwell, 'The Prison of "Public Space": Before we take to the Streets, this Pervasive Concept needs Rethinking' (2008) 16 *Literary Review of Canada* 18–21. See also 'Public space may, in the end, be the ultimate barometer of our civilization, the gauge against which we can measure whether we are a country or just a collection of individuals living in fear of one another.' T Fisher, 'Is Public Space a Public Good?' (2005) 17 *Places Design* 81.

records. It foretells the disappearance of academic freedom, or the 'death of privacy', not only anticipated by snooping charters, but also technologies that open up our genes, health data and personal lives to insurmountable ways of interrogation.[84] As we witness another park bulldozed to be replaced by a gated community or membership-only golf course, we ought to challenge the ideologies that capture public goods and be hesitant in becoming bedfellows in this. The parallels I am drawing with other public goods should be obvious. Public spaces, in this sense, are not only a complex metaphor about loss of social standing, but are intrinsic to freedom and well-being in that they are for everyone's use (freedom) and contribute to a physical (exercise, games) and psychological well-being (for example, social gatherings, even connecting people in protest), and, as such, are the proper objects of rights claims. To resist commodification, then, is to conceive of public goods as 'something larger and looser: the right to gather and discuss, to interact with and debate one's fellow citizens … Public space enables a political conversation that favours the unforced force of the better argument, the basis of just social order.'[85] Public spaces have an intrinsic *opportunistic* value, and this, Kingwell explains, is because 'the public is not a summing of private preferences or interests, nor even a wide non-rival availability of resources to those preferences or interests. It is, instead, their precondition … [public spaces are] not a public good so much as an existential one: one without which democratic politics is impossible'.[86] If it is possible to manoeuvre this reiteration of the capture of public goods as one of resistance to commodification, privatisation, and other tendencies of markets, then it signals how supporting practices of exclusivity creates mercantilist outcomes that are bad for the public good.

Finally, then, doing something *for the public good* is quite different from the idle processes of commodification. One of the clearest affirmations of supporting innovation *for the public good* comes from biobanks where, elsewhere, I have argued that they encapsulate features otherwise absent in the idea of Big Data. A commitment to the public good not only means requiring consent, standing by that as stewards of persons' interests, and encouraging participation, but also putting that socially valid data 'out there' for all those that share this mission.[87] For Big Data the opportunities of economic gains are a public interest, and this trumps rights such as those seen as steadfast in biobanking.[88] It is understood, however, that if this substitution is a cost to privacy, it would be only justified by a public interest that was an assessment of the objects—the GCA—of the public good. It is in this respect that the public good resists commodification, because it affirms rights that are necessarily connected to the person's most important interests.

[84] G Annas, P Roche and R Green, 'GINA, Genism, and Civil Rights' (2008) 22 *Bioethics* iv; J Lunshof et al, 'Science and Society: From Genetic Privacy to Open Consent' (2008) 9 *Nature Reviews Genetics* 406.

[85] Kingwell, n 83, 8.

[86] ibid, 22.

[87] ibid, and Capps, n 2.

[88] Capps, n 71.

VI. Reconsidering Ethical Partnerships

For all that partnerships between public and private innovators might do well (this is an empirical point that requires supplementing in each case), they are also sources of iniquitous privilege and leverage in political, economic and legal fora. It is in these conditions that public goods are often captured. For neoliberals, such partnerships are an opportunity for both prosperity and influence. But many might see these arrangements as nothing more than parasitic on state infrastructure. In the examples I gave above, it should be obvious what the risks are: for universities the culture of disinterested enquiry is at stake; in data acquisition, the right to privacy, and any other conditions assumed by confiders, are threatened. This is not just about industry's role in capture, however. Ideological, ineffectual and corrupt *public* oversight grants leverage, and often the government of the time is complicit in what is, after all, industry's tendency to absorb profitable resources especially when there is little resistance. The argument is that the 'cadres' of private and public, after the fact, 'typically perform functions which are meant to restore a degree of cohesion, technically and ideologically, to the fragmented social substratum of capital accumulation'.[89] But as van der Pijl continues,

> The imagined community which results from this constitutes, in the cadre perspective, a terrain of social engineering rather than an authentic 'commons' to be protected in its own right … the cadres effectively integrate the various moments of alienation into an integral world of rules and norms, so that people subject to the dislocating effects of commodification and exploitation are surrounded by functionaries and organisations 'taking care' of their drives, aspirations and fears. This helps to sustain the inverted world of society seeking to adjust to the requirement of the market and capital.[90]

In this respect, the Human Genome Organisation (HUGO) wrote of a specific example: 'Benefit is not identical with profit in the monetary or economic sense. Determining a benefit depends on needs, values, priorities and cultural expectations.'[91] This task ahead is to identify conditions in which innovation contributes to 'quality of life' in more ways than just prosperity.[92] HUGO was responding to the increased activity of biotech companies capturing biodiversity across the genomes of people, fauna and flora. The critique was aimed at their perceived lack of respect for culture, tradition and ecological sustainability; they were likened to 'biopirates' (rather than 'bioprospectors'): fraudulent benefactors of a

[89] K van der Pijl, *Transnational Classes and International Relations* (Routledge, 1998) 138.

[90] ibid, references omitted.

[91] HUGO Ethics Committee, *Statement on Benefit-Sharing* April 9 2000, www.hugo-international.org/img/benefit_sharing_2000.pdf.

[92] Beyleveld, 'Data Protection and Genetics: Medical Research and the Public Good', n 9, 287.

system designed to protect their narrow economic interests.[93] Commodification, here, was about proprietary interests, and sometimes less than worthy ambitions to make exclusive claims to what others saw as public goods.[94] The lists of felonies included exploitation, misconduct, grossly disproportional reward and too few examples of value creation.[95] Partnerships, therefore, can *create scope* for rights infringements and derisory grounds for co-operation.[96] So, recalling Beyleveld's co-operative model, we must look deeper for the reasons for forming such partnerships, and that, I suggest, is conditional upon justifying the public interest. For example, benefit sharing proposes that research must engage with communities to create mutual advantages, thus empowering communities to resist acrimonious and divisive influences upon their rights.[97] The balance sought by HUGO *is not to negate rewards to the artist of science*, but to bring limits on those who brazenly trawl and ring-fence public goods. In this respect, it is right to resist the liberties taken by sketchy economies.

The partnerships that signal collusion with shady profiteers are the most heinous, especially since, as I have shown here, they use starkly different terms of purpose to define 'cosseted' deliverables.[98] This is not to say that partnerships might be legitimate with more ethical industries, but only if it is shown that they contribute to the well-being of the individuals as members of a rights community.[99] Such research partnerships would then meet Beyleveld's conditions for being a public good.

[93] A Pottage, 'The Inscription of Life in Law: Genes, Patents, and Bio-Politics' (1998) 61 *Modern Law Review* 740.

[94] There are at least two concerns here. One, that duress under the public interest is often most acutely felt by those vulnerable either socially or economically or both, because they are less valued as 'non-consumers' (J Curtis, 'Low Income, Low Priority' (2000) 26 *Marketing* 36). Two, many interests go unnoticed in the application of the public interests, partly because it is assumed that people *will* agree when they can be ostensibly convinced of the benefits accrued, but also because one can rely on a majority interest who *willingly* obeys the terms of the transactions, to make the case for them. These kinds of subjugation were stressed by Rousseau as being in a condition of inequality, domination and exploitation. In respect to capture: 'From how many crimes, wars, and murders, from how many horrors and misfortunes might not any one have saved mankind, by pulling up the stakes, or filling up the ditch, and crying to his fellows: Beware of listening to this impostor; you are undone if you once forget that the fruits of the earth belong to us all, and the earth itself to nobody.' J Rousseau, 'A Dissertation on the Origin and Foundation of the Inequality of Mankind' *The Social Contract and Discourses* (JM Dent tr, Everyman, 1993) 84. Also see F Neuhouser, 'Rousseau's Critique of Economic Inequality' (2013) 41 *Philosophy and Public Affairs* 193.

[95] D Dickenson, 'Consent, Commodification and Benefit-Sharing In Genetic Research' (2007) 4 *Developing World Bioethics* 109.

[96] Beyleveld, 'Conceptualising Privacy in Relation to Medical Research Values', n 9, 3.

[97] B Capps and J Ch'ng, 'Conducting Malaria Research in Developing Countries: A Right to Claim Healthcare' (2013) 5 *Asian Bioethics Review* 296.

[98] I Kohane and R Altman, 'Health-Information Altruists—A Potentially Critical Resource' (2005) 353 *New England Journal of Medicine* 2074.

[99] Brownsword, n 46.

VII. Conclusion: Rejecting the Commodities Model

I have used Beyleveld's co-operative model to propose that partnerships can be justified if, in each case, the conflicting parties can first define their common interests in terms of the public interest, so that, in jointly pursuing a public goods agenda their endeavours remain worthy (as Beyleveld did in the case of medical research and patient privacy). Thus, although goods may be produced from both private and state architectures, *the public interest* properly binds both to appropriate scrutiny of the risks of capture of public goods. Privatisation (a distinct kind of commodification) is one example where capture spells out anti-social 'public interest' rhetoric, which has found a foothold in capitalistic social capital—it is, I believe, the cloak necessary to obtain vested advantage. Increasingly, the public interest is used to exclude effective governance, and encourage complicity in 'public bads'. Instead of furthering welfarist social capital and civic responsibility, the neoliberal agenda purposively makes no real contribution to sociality, and critically contributes commodities (for example arms, or goods with high pollution by-products) that blight communities. These communities then become dependent on the state's ability to deliver welfare and mitigate the harm done. The catch is that capture already undermines the state's capacity to do so, and sometimes its *willingness* to provide welfare, because 'public bads' depreciate social cohesion or contribute to state interests. The producers of public bads have little ethical regard for the consumers they serve. Although these are the worst kind, there are still vast economic gains to be made from innovation, and this can be an especially powerful motivation for some to attempt to couple legitimate private interests with public infrastructure. Even these partnerships sometimes devalue and undermine social networks that foster public goods.

It is often thought that capture can be qualified, at least, by procedures that create ethical governance; but it is easy to create the impression of trust, responsibility or transparency while still embroiled in misinformation and misconduct.[100] And this is the challenge facing ethical industry. As Onora O'Neill opined, for example, 'We need to think much less about trust … much more about being trustworthy, and how you give people adequate, useful and simple evidence that you're trustworthy'.[101] There continues to be suspicion about the activities of industry across the board: the worst being found in banking, tobacco industry, pharmaceutical industry and so on. This distrust spills over to all commercially oriented endeavours that are perceived to distort the public interests.[102] It has long been

[100] There are many ways that industry influences good science: the best documented is the role of 'Big Pharma' in 'systemic bias' in published data. See especially J Lexchin, L Bero, B Djulbegovi and O Clark, Pharmaceutical Industry Sponsorship and Research Outcome and Quality: A Systematic Review (2003) 326 *British Medical Journal* 1167.

[101] O O'Neill, 'What we don't understand about trust' (2013) *TED Talks* (www.ted.com) September.

[102] eg G Annas, 'Outrageous Fortune: Selling Other People's Cells' (1990) 20 *The Hastings Center Report* 36; Capps, n 71.

held that for these industries to gain trust they must take action in respect to their own corporate morality.[103] But this is where the rhetoric of the public interest comes undone: it allows perpetrators to make statements about their competency, reliability and honesty; but until they do more, we have, in the end, no reason to trust them.

There is much more to be said about *effective* partnerships, and even more about exploitative ones, as witnessed by the tragedies caused by all sorts of tactics, from patent ring-fencing to monopolies, aggressive takeovers and data distortion; and all are often underwritten by hand-tied, ineffectual or partisan (public) institutions.[104] However, by *appreciating the shared risks and benefits* as comparable and *jointly assumed by all agents*[105]—a test of the public interest in fostering public goods—there is a better way to ground ethical partnerships. *The* public good in and of itself tells us why public goods are worth protecting at all; and it is here where we also find a role for private ventures to secure other goods, because, in some cases, the risks can be better tolerated than by public policy.[106] Unlike these commodities, the conditions for public goods should not be decided by the consumer alone, but by a rational enquiry into the GCA. Any statement of the public interest is an analysis of the rights engaged, and therefore ought to expose industries' sometimes distorted picture that in fact creates de facto obstacles to, or unfairly captures, public goods for its *own* interests.

[103] See my 'Principle of Institutional Responsibility' in Capps, n 2, 129.

[104] J Love and T Hubbard, 'Paying for Public Goods' in R Ghosh (ed), *Code: Collaborative Ownership and the Digital Economy* (MIT Press, 2005); Schafer, n 62.

[105] See my 'Principle of Comparable Cost' in Capps, n 2, 129.

[106] All innovation faces the problem of securing long-term funding; therefore a degree of commercialisation is to be expected. The problem, as argued here, is that economic theory often does not provide an adequate explanation of the puzzles of the public good. Working out rights and duties under a good public framework, however, also needs to address questions of *effective* governance (eg, overregulation, corruption, benefits of compensated exchange), as well as the ways in which ideologies about this are given weight through democracy. For example, 'public concern' might be over- or underrepresented in policies leading to delays and prohibitions. Witness, for example, the prohibition on embryonic stem cell research in some jurisdictions and the international calls to prohibit human 'therapeutic' cloning, despite both having clear scientific rationale and plausibly ethical justifications. Institutions that are *for the public good* dissipate these kinds of tensions through architectures that tend to prioritise the conditions for well-being through promoting good research that is subject to effective oversight: B Capps, 'Bioethics, Procedural Ethics, and Misrepresentation in the Stem Cell Debate' in J Gunning and S Holm (eds), *Ethics, Law and Society* Volume 3 (Ashgate, 2007). Also see R Brownsword, 'Stem Cells and Cloning: Where the Regulatory Consensus Fails' (2005) 39 *New England Law Review* 535.

10

Privacy, Politeness and the Boundary Between Theory and Practice in Ethical Rationalism

DAVID TOWNEND*

In their article 'Principle, Proceduralism, and Precaution in a Community of Rights',[1] Beyleveld and Brownsword contribute to a collection of essays on Discourse Ethics by exploring the difficulties of applying Alan Gewirth's Principle of Generic Consistency (PGC) in practical situations. They ask how the citizens of 'Gewirthia', who 'are universally committed to the PGC as both the supreme principle of morality and the constitutional first principle of dispute resolution',[2] put that commitment into practice. In this chapter, the same problem is placed in a different context, that of biobanking and specifically privacy in biobanking, and the potential of the seventeenth- and eighteenth-century philosophy and practice of 'politeness' is advanced as a suitable vehicle for the resolution of the difficulties in moving from the pure theory of the PGC to practical outworking of the same.

First, I explore the construction of the 'right to privacy', to indicate the difficulty in creating objective 'indirect' or secondary rights that support agency; I show the contested nature of the idea of rights, and that in this case, the 'right' is not objective, but strongly 'subjective'. I then consider what might replace privacy as the compass for understanding how the law in this area should be shaped and, perhaps more importantly, applied, thinking particularly about the attitude that individuals must adopt towards the operation of the law. I ask whether and how the concept of 'politeness' that emerged in the 'long eighteenth century' in England might be a useful attitude to adopt in operating data protection law in relation to medical research using genetic information and biobanking.

* Professor of Law and Legal Philosophy in Health, Medicine and Life Sciences, Maastricht University.

[1] D Beyleveld and R Brownsword, 'Principle, Proceduralism, and Precaution in a Community of Rights' (2006) 19(2) *Ratio Juris* 141.

[2] ibid, 143.

I. The Context of Data Protection and Medical Research Using Biobanking and Genetic Information

There is an interesting trajectory in the recent regulation of personal medical data that has gained increasing momentum as the potential of studying and using large data sets has been realised since the 1970s. Two elements have increased that momentum: advances through the increased understanding of genomics, and increased computing power. Interest in governance and regulation has kept pace; the area continuously provides both practical and theoretical challenges for those concerned with the interaction and definition of the fundamental rights and freedoms of the individual, particularly rights relating to privacy and data protection. It also provided a number of knotty problems about the outworking of the conflicting demands of citizens as individuals and collectively in relation to their participation in and benefitting from medical research, knotty problems that one might hope would be solved with the application of ethical rationalism.

In particular, the problems concern competing duties. Privacy law has, at its heart, the relationship between the right to private and family life under Article 8(1) of the European Convention on Human Rights and the power of the State to derogate from that right in the defined situations of 8(2)—essentially, in the public interest. This is the practical balance running throughout the European Union Directive 95/46/EC on the processing of personal data, and the regulation of processing for research purposes.

The PGC is created through a consideration of the necessary preconditions that an agent must acknowledge, for fear of self-contradiction, as universally necessary. There is a temptation to see human rights, and in the object case of data protection and medical research, as equal to those necessary preconditions. In the case of privacy or the right to a private life, this is difficult to sustain. Human rights should be read through the necessary lens of the PGC, but they are secondary rights; human rights compete with each other under the umbrella of agency, impacting upon agency, but not, of themselves, amounting to agency.[3] Ethical rationalism in practice must effectively provide mechanisms to resolve competing rights, for example when two individuals claim rights to privacy that place them in conflict—my privacy right to decide whether or not to participate in medical research, with your privacy right to the benefits of medical research as a right to a continuing private life.

The question to be resolved in the practice of data protection and medical research, perhaps brought to a particular focus in medical research using genetic information and biobanking, is 'how can a conflict between rights, between rights

[3] D Beyleveld, 'The Principle of Generic Consistency as the Supreme Principle of Human Rights' (2011) 13(1) *Human Rights Review* 1.

holders, be resolved?' A response to this challenge is to consider what happens when an individual claims a privacy right.[4] Starting from a simple, practical understanding of ethical rationalism as the logical requirement to respect one's own and others' primacy agency rights (not to instrumentalise others), when one makes a claim relating to secondary rights (for example, to privacy) one has to ask what one is doing in claiming that right. A claim to a secondary right must, as a human act, conform to the requirements of the PGC. This requires one to examine one's actions to assess the impact of the act upon another as a universal duty. When I claim a human right, in competition with the claims of other human rights holders (differentiating human rights from fundamental agency claims), I must ask, considering the impact that my claim will make on the others involved, 'am I respecting the primary agency rights of another in themselves when claiming my (secondary) privacy rights claiming: is my rights-claiming instrumentalising others?'

This breaks the impasse of competing rights, but only to some extent. Individual claims-makers have to make an evaluation of the competing values to give to differing claims, to the different understandings available of how to treat someone. This is where ethical rationalism might reach the end of its usefulness; determining this practical ethical question is wrapped up in each individual's political and emotional beliefs, and cannot be unravelled by simple recourse to the theory.[5] How might rights like privacy or data protection, so central to the governance of modern informatics-rich medical research, be considered and respected, and what does it suggest about the way in which ethical rationalism might be conducted in governance practice?

There is a very detailed literature that distinguishes in theory the difference between direct and indirect rights in the PGC, and the relationship between rationality and other modes of thinking, for example, emotion in decision making. There is still some room, however, in this literature to explore how ethical rationalism might operate in practice, to further consider how life in 'Gewirthia' might be conducted. In this chapter, I suggest some practical difficulties of living with privacy, particularly in the modern problem of the governance of medical research using genetic information and biobanking, and offer a solution from the long-eighteenth-century concept of politeness.

[4] D Townend, 'Who Owns Genetic Information?' in J Sandor (ed), *Society and Genetic Information: Codes and Laws in the Genetic Era* (Central European University Press, 2003) 125; and D Townend, 'Overriding Data Subjects' Rights in the Public Interest' in D Beyleveld, D Townend, S Rouillé-Mirza and J Wright (eds), *The Data Protection Directive and Medical Research Across Europe* (Ashgate, 2004) 89.

[5] So when seeking to apply Beyleveld and Brownsword's concept of property in the *Moore* case, they favour a more market-oriented solution, whereas I am drawn to a more communal property solution, from the same starting point in ethical rationalism. *Moore v Regents of the University of California* (1990) 793 P 2d 479 and (1991) 111 S Ct 1388. D. Beyleveld and R. Brownsword, Human Dignity in Bioethics and Biolaw (OUP 2001).

II. The Problem of Privacy

In the *PRIVILEGED* project, we concluded that 'privacy' was a contested concept, but our consensus was that it was a valuable concept in discussing the regulation and governance of medical research using genetic information and biobanking. This is in line with much of the general view of the importance of the concept of privacy.[6] However, privacy as a concept for law and to a very large extent ethics is highly problematic. It is culturally and conceptually broad, and I will argue here that for a variety of reasons it is of very limited use as a binding concept for law either in the area of medical research using genetic information and biobanking, or even, perhaps, more generally.

On its face, 'privacy' seems to be a word like 'poverty'. Alcock, in his book *Understanding Poverty*, makes the claim that 'poverty' requires a response.[7] Although he does not say it directly, he is identifying that there are some words that are of a strong, prescriptive, social normative character; others are merely descriptive of personal norms. Whilst people disagree about the material level at which a human's socio-economic circumstances place him or her in 'poverty', and even more so about appropriate responses to that state, labelling something as a state of 'poverty' is more than a description, it is a description that requires action; it is a normative statement that goes beyond an identification of 'inequality', it identifies the unacceptable state of 'inequity'. 'Privacy' seems to hold such a strong prescriptive normative character. Indeed, its 'go-to' persistence in modern life science governance suggests that it must have such a character. However, this can be questioned; there is a strong argument that 'privacy' is merely a description of individual's personal social expectations. Consider the following example.

> Imagine that one morning, you receive a letter from your local council. Following advice from the police, they say, they have decided to install CCTV surveillance cameras in your street. Five cameras will be located such that each of the thirty houses in your neighbourhood can be observed at the local police station. How do you feel? Well, let's assume you react as follows: 'I can't believe it! That is such an invasion of my privacy. They will be able to see every time I go in or out. It will be like living in a goldfish bowl.' You are so enraged that you resolve to form a neighbourhood committee to fight this 'violation', and you put leaflets through your neighbours' letterboxes announcing a meeting that evening to discuss the issue.
>
> You hold the meeting, and first of all you are surprised that only half of your neighbours attend. In fact, those who do attend report that many of the missing people said they

6 PRIVILEGED was funded under an EC FP6 call concerned with the protection of privacy and other fundamental rights and freedoms in medical research using genetic information and biobanking. Two legal monographs on the area show the centrality of privacy in the area: G Laurie, *Genetic Privacy: A Challenge to Medico-Legal Norms* (CUP, 2002) and MJ Taylor, *Genetic Data and the Law: A Critical Perspective on Privacy Protection* (CUP, 2012).

7 P Alcock, *Understanding Poverty* 2nd edn (Palgrave Macmillan Press, 1997) 6.

weren't really bothered about the issue either way. Okay, you think, well if half of the people are here, that's still enough to stop this nonsense.

You begin the discussion, and you find that there is strongly divided opinion. There are a few people who agree with you, but not all. Huub from number 6 and Julia from number 9 are very enthusiastic about the cameras. In fact, as soon as you start the discussion, they interrupt you. 'We're sorry', they say, 'but we disagree with the leaflets that you put through our letterboxes'. Huub and Julia both had break-ins at their homes recently, and they really welcome the cameras. 'At least the police and council are doing something to stop the burglaries. It's about time they valued our privacy', Julia says. Maureen adds that she was mugged last year, and these cameras will help her to feel that her privacy is being respected as well. In fact, the majority of the people at the meeting feel that the cameras are a good thing for their individual privacy. They urge you not to complain.

The next day, you receive a letter from the Department of Health, informing you that your health records and genetic information (gathered from a recent blood test) have been forwarded to the national biobank for inclusion in medical research. You are beginning to rant about your privacy, and start writing another letter for your neighbours, when you catch sight of your neighbour Guus, walking past your kitchen window. You are pleased to see him out and about again. He has recently received a new medical therapy for his heart condition. You return to the letter, and begin to wonder if your first instinct to organise another public meeting is appropriate.

The range of legitimate interpretations of privacy can include diametrically opposite interpretations, and it can do so not only between cultures, but also within the same cultural group and within the range of acceptable sensitivities within that society. Because of this, 'privacy' cannot, and does not, require a particular response.[8] It is simply a description of an individual's perception of his or her particular state, namely each individual citizen's perception about the boundary between his or her private and public lives. Being a citizen requires rights and duties that relate both to being independent and being part of a community. Privacy is the individual's description of his or her perception of the boundary between autonomy and solidarity. Privacy is subjective rather than objective, and that is why is it problematic for the function that has been asked of it in law and ethics. But how can this claim be reconciled to the great weight of academic work on the concept of privacy?

There is a great deal of work on the typology of privacy rights. However, there is academic disagreement about what 'privacy' as a concept can and should be concerned with and what it contains. Many writers give excellent descriptions of

[8] This is not to suggest that there is no objective value in privacy. It is clearly a shared value in Human Rights based societies. However, the subjective nature of its definition makes the objective value only a matter that we must agree that respecting individuals' personal need for, and to some extent construction of, privacy is valuable. The Human Rights agenda, as will be argued in this section, however, itself admits that the right to privacy is not absolute, and it is limited by the superiority of the claims of others, expressed as the operation of 'the public interest' (see, eg, Art 8.2 of the European Convention on Human Rights—The Convention for the Protection of Human Rights and Fundamental Freedoms (1950, and subsequently amended).

the major competing discussions of privacy and its chronological development.[9] Privacy is discussed in many different disciplines, and many different constructions are, all cogently, justified from different starting points.[10] Privacy within the law tends to be relatively narrow.[11] Its roots are commonly identified in the 1890 article by Warren and Brandeis, which has the starting point of a contemporarily familiar question about privacy in a technologically advancing world and the prurient interest of the general public in the lives of others.[12] Other legal writers show the rather narrow focus of law on informational controls. Prosser shows four 'torts' (civil wrongs) that by the 1960s formed much of privacy law in the United States.[13] And in the mid-1960s, privacy also emerged as a constitutional issue in the US, particularly debated around abortion.[14] Privacy in the law, as DeCew shows in her account of the field, reflects the general difficulty shared across the disciplines in agreeing the limits of privacy.[15]

In the *PRIVILEGED* project, we discussed the work of Allen,[16] and in particular her fourfold classification of privacy rights. Allen suggests that the discussions about privacy, indeed, privacy rights themselves, can be classified as 'informational privacy', 'decisional privacy', 'physical privacy', and 'proprietary privacy'.[17] These

[9] J DeCew, 'Privacy', *The Stanford Encyclopaedia of Philosophy* (EN Zalta ed, Fall 2008 edn) http://plato.stanford.edu/archives/fall2008/entries/privacy; AF Westin, 'Social and Political Dimensions of Privacy' (2003) 59(2) *Journal of Social Issues* 431 (see also Westin's seminal work *Privacy and Freedom* (The Bodley Head, 1970); E Etziono, *The Limits of Privacy* (Basic Books, 1999); F Schoeman, 'Privacy: Philosophical Dimensions' (1984) 21(3) *American Philosophical Quarterly* 199; and the very critical JJ Thomson, 'The Right to Privacy' (1975) 4(4) *Philosophy and Public Affairs* 295.

[10] I had expected to find a discussion of privacy within the psychology literature about the construction of the self. However, I found no such literature, and being convinced that this could not be correct, I discussed the matter with a number of colleagues in psychology. They confirmed that privacy was not on psychology's agenda. The only writer that I have found who explores the necessity for privacy in the human condition, or the need to 'retreat to the inner citadel', is the philosopher Isaiah Berlin. See, eg, I Berlin, 'Two Concepts of Liberty' (1958) in *Four Essays on Liberty* (OUP, 1969).

[11] For an extensive discussion of privacy in the law and the limits thereof, see R Gavison, 'Privacy and the Limits of Law' (1980) 89(3) *Yale Law Journal* 421; DJ Solove, 'A Taxonomy of Privacy' (2006) 154(3) *University of Pennsylvania Law Review* 477.

[12] SD Warren and LD Brandeis, 'The Right to Privacy' (1890) 4 *Harvard Law Review* 193.

[13] These are arranged around rights concerning 'intrusion', 'public disclosure of private facts', 'false light in the public eye', and 'appropriation' (of likeness or identity). WL Prosser, 'Privacy' (1960) 48(3) *California Law Review* 383.

[14] AL Allen, *Uneasy Access: Privacy for Women in a Free Society* (Rowman & Littlefield, 1988) 89.

[15] DeCew, n 9; see also AD Moore, 'Intangible Property: Privacy, Power and Information Control' (1998) 35(4) *American Philosophical Quarterly* 365; DJ Solove, 'Conceptualizing Privacy' (2002) 90(4) *California Law Review* 1087.

[16] Allen has produced a tremendously impressive body of work exploring privacy in many different philosophical and conceptual contexts, and in relation to different emerging technologies. She has, for example, made an enormous contribution to the understanding of the feminist perspective on privacy: see Allen, n 14; 'Gender and Privacy in Cyberspace' (1999–2000) 52 *Stanford Law Review* 1175. See, more generally: AL Allen, 'Taking Liberties: Privacy, Private Choice, and Social Contract Theory' (1987) 56 *Cincinnati Law Review* 461; 'Genetic testing, Nature and Trust' (1997) 27 *Seton Hall Law Review* 887; 'Coercing Privacy' (1999) 40(3) *William and Mary Law Review* 723; 'Privacy-as-Data Control: Conceptual, Practical, and Moral Limits of the Paradigm' (2000) 32 *Connecticut Law Review* 861.

[17] AL Allen, 'Genetic Privacy: Emerging Concepts and Values' in Rothstein (ed), *Genetic Secrets: Protecting Privacy and Confidentiality in the Genetic Era* (Yale University Press, 1997) 31, 33.

classifications of different aspects of the debate work well. Some disagree that they all constitute privacy, but all the commonly argued elements of privacy seem to be classifiable in this framework. Thus, the American constitutional debate about abortion, or the rights to contraceptives, can be understood as 'decisional privacy' discussions; rules about trespass to an individual's land or the removal of his or her things can be seen as questions of 'proprietary privacy'; and rules about the definition of physical assault, or the right to physical space, can be seen as issues of 'physical privacy'. The dispute is whether each of these elements, or inclusions within the elements, is or are a necessary part of 'privacy'. 'Informational privacy' is the area that seems to be least controversial in the literature, and, arguably, many privacy issues appear as 'informational privacy' issues. When we consider the sorts of issues that are commonly raised as privacy concerns, they relate to the use of information about individuals. At the beginning of his book, *Privacy: a very short introduction*, Wacks says the following:

> You are being watched. The ubiquity of Big Brother no longer shocks. 'Low-tech' collection of transactional data in both the public and private sector has become commonplace. In addition to the routine surveillance by CCTV in public places, the monitoring of mobile telephones, the workplace, vehicles, electronic communications, and online activity has swiftly become widespread in most advanced societies.[18]

These activities are very much about informational privacy, and, indeed, medical research using genetic information and biobanking concerns very sensitive, basic information about individuals. However, the fact that these uses are about the processing of information concerning individuals does not necessarily make them, or the changes in our societies that facilitate or require them, inappropriate. To some people, the changes will be desirable and non-intrusive, not even matters of 'privacy'.

Further, questions about the same privacy issue, for example, the processing of a piece of medical data, are not the same in different circumstances. Taylor explains that the discussion about privacy varies according to the relationship between the individuals involved in particular situations.[19] There is information that relates to me that I consider private and wish to limit to particular individuals.[20] Some information I am happy to disclose to the whole world. For example, I am happy to disclose to the whole world that I like the music of Malcolm Arnold, Hubert Parry and Julian Joseph. There is a degree of embarrassment from certain quarters in the pleasure that I derive from 'Easy Listening' music. To most people, my love of the music of Burt Bacharach is okay, and my collecting the theme music of television programmes from the 1960s and 70s is a tolerable eccentricity. I am comfortable that people know about this obsession. But I have other obsessions

[18] R Wacks, *Privacy: A Very Short Introduction* (OUP, 2010) 1.
[19] Taylor, n 6.
[20] For a further discussion of this, see J Rachels, 'Why Privacy is Important' (1975) 4(4) *Philosophy and Public Affairs* 323.

that I am more uncomfortable about sharing. I know that I will be embarrassed if some things about me are known (but only embarrassed). For example, my daughter Alice helpfully informed someone we met for the first time that I have some difficulties with checking that I have not lost things. She said it in Dutch, and it took me a few moments to realise what she had said, and that meant that I lost the chance to control the disclosure of the information, or limit the damage caused (that is, my embarrassment). But, there are worse things that she could have disclosed, because, like everyone, I also have things that I would not wish to disclose to other people, or would only disclose to particular individuals (perhaps to my wife, or to those who owe a professional duty of confidentiality towards me).

The interesting thing about my 'checking' is that it is information about myself that I cannot really control. Anyone who observes me, or is forced to go to a meeting or other event with me, will soon become aware that I have issues with checking—often looking around where I have been sitting or walking. It starts off as something amusing, but after a day of it, it becomes irritating (for which, I apologise). I explain it here, because although I might want to limit the information flow about this (because it embarrasses me), my simple participation in society means that the information is disclosed. This is the same for quite a lot of information about me, and about each of us. When we walk about in society, what we have chosen to wear, how we appear, how we act, are all information that we might want to control, but are inevitably open to others. The very fact of participation in society places much of our lives on show to others; participation requires publication of much of our life, not as invasion of privacy, but as the inevitable boundary between our inside and outside lives.

The question becomes, what can others do with this information? And this is the same question that has to be answered when the conditions for the disclosure are more obviously constrained than my simply walking down the street. When I have given information to my wife, family, doctor, bank, a researcher, my friends, there is the part of the relationship that is explicitly defined, and there is the part that is implied. There is also the part that is a matter of the other individual's judgement. Is the information that is disclosed necessarily information that can and should be kept 'private', or can it be made 'public'?

We will all disagree, from our own privacy perspectives, which information falls into which category. As I indicated above, 'privacy' is not a sufficiently agreed concept within society that different types of information will be agreed to be 'private' by everyone *through the concept of privacy itself*. And between societies these differences will also be pronounced. Privacy is a concept that we define for ourselves, and it changes according to our experiences. It also has a valuable function to each of us as this subjective concept as it helps us to react to others in our world and gives us an internal dialogue to understand what happens to ourselves in the world. If I have had the misfortune to be mugged in the street, my privacy might focus on my physical privacy; if my car has recently been stolen, or my house burgled, then I might be more worried about my proprietary privacy; if I have been denied access to particular services, then I might be concerned with decisional privacy; and if my bank details have been stolen by someone else and my identity used for fraud, then informational privacy could be my main concern. My concerns could be a matrix of these different elements, operating dynamically, changing according to my relationships with the different people with whom I am brought into contact; my level of concern about different aspects of my privacy could rise or fall. Equally, I might think that none of the issues above are important, or that they are not privacy matters but are rather matters about property, or assault, or administration, or banking security. And any of these judgements could (and do) change over time.

For each of us, privacy is our own subjective construction and individually we need it to function in this way as a defence dialogue. There are no agreed, objective aspects to privacy[21] because, for each of us, privacy is simply a reflection of my perception of my well-being in my society at any given point; privacy is a barometer of my sense of well-being in society. It is in this subjective way that privacy (or the right to a private life) makes sense as a human right. The duty of others is to respect the way each of us constructs our world, and responds to our world. It is a duty to allow individuals the freedom to react to the community of rights holders in different ways without having to accept a uniform boundary between the private self and the public self. This barometer nature is why it is useful in society. In a democracy, the individually reactive nature of privacy as well-being enables us to understand and respond to the needs of others without stifling them. But equally, this is not useful for finding objective values upon which to base the law. Equally, it does not necessarily imply that individuals are free to do exactly what they please in society without duties towards the needs of others.

Privacy, from within its own resources, does not give us definitive answers to the difficult questions of how we should behave. Privacy does not define the objective, conceptual boundary between autonomy and solidarity, because it is a descriptive and dynamic idea. We have to look outside 'privacy' to find a way of defining the boundary. We need an argument that, regardless of the position that an individual takes in relation to his or her privacy in a particular situation, gives a reason for denying (or at least objectively challenging) that privacy claim. The concept of 'the public interest' performs this function as the opposite concept to privacy, and is therefore the counter-balance to it. It is opposite to privacy both in the sense that it is the 'external' to privacy's 'internal', but also because to make a legitimate claim on the individual it has to make that claim objectively rather than subjectively.

By the public interest, I mean the rights of other individuals in society. It is traditionally the rights of the collective, or the community. When the council and police decide to install CCTV cameras, although not often explicitly, they use this 'public' dimension to make the decision (the claim against the private lives of

[21] That is beyond the idea stated in the footnote above that there is a general sense within which mutual respect for our subjective constructions of privacy is respected when they do not (significantly) override the interests of others.

individual citizens). However, this is not well defined. It is the counter-balance to the realm of privacy claims, but it is not well organised in law, politics and administration. In part this is because many public authorities making the claim to 'invade' an individual's privacy do not give a reasoned, detailed account of the argument. Often it is a matter of political expediency or power. Indeed, the concept of the public interest is perhaps as vague (and operationally subjective) as the concept of privacy, and it is not seen as the justification for one institution or individual's demand upon another for information that the individual may consider to be private or to accept an action that might encroach upon the individual's sense of their privacy. However, using an appeal to the public interest as the balancing concept has a better chance of developing objectivity than privacy does, because whereas privacy has its greatest social value in its subjective, barometer character, the public interest can only legitimately be claimed when it has an objective justification. That objective claim to an intervention that legitimately overrides the subjective claim of the individual is the function of the public interest in society.

This public–private balance is at the heart of the expressions of 'privacy' in the international instruments. In the human rights canon,[22] the right to privacy or a private life is balanced with the public interest. Privacy is not an absolute right. And the balance of the public interest is the external concept that gives purchase on defining the boundary of necessary, legitimately required participation in one's society. However, the crucial issue is how the public interest is defined.

The public interest is itself a highly problematic concept. However, at its heart, it can be constructed very effectively by focusing on harm and benefits, and on the needs of 'others' (or rather other people considered individually rather than as a single mass) requiring an action from the individual. The public interest often takes the form of a utilitarian calculation, and there is a danger that the interests of the mass are quantified and balanced against the interests of the individual who stands to lose his or her benefits. In that case, the balance is very strongly weighted in favour of society (the mass of 'others'). The danger is that, whilst the loss to the target individual[23] is very often heavy, the benefit (be that a positive gain or an avoided loss of amenity) to the 'public' is often individually very small.

This effect can be avoided by measuring the foreseeable loss to the target individual against the foreseeable benefit (in positive gain or avoided lost amenity) to a foreseeable, notional individual (one separate, imaginary person who can be isolated from within the mass of 'others'). This has a much greater chance of ensuring proportionality in the operation of the concept, because the rights of one individual are considered in relation to the rights of only one other individual.

Essentially this is an attempt to address the problem of competing rights in rights-based theories. If we are all equal rights holders, how do we adjudicate who

[22] The Universal Declaration of Human Rights; and The European Convention on Human Rights, above n 8. *cf* the Charter of Fundamental Rights of the European Union (2000/C 364/01).

[23] 'Target individual' refers to the person who stands to lose his or her amenity in the public interest.

has a greater claim to his or her right in a given situation? I seek to avoid this in a three-step argument.[24] My first step, as I have just outlined, is to focus the argument in a calculation between individuals, rather than the abstract, agglomerated mass. This hangs on the idea that an individual cannot enjoy more than a personal benefit; there is no individual enhancement of benefit or avoided loss by being part of a group of people (unless that is specifically quantifiable, for example, as a fear for the well-being of other people). Of course, this method is still confronted by the problem of placing a value upon different emotions and perceptions of harm and benefit (a problem shared with consequentialism). However, it is a first stage in addressing the difficulty of adjudicating between rights holders as individuals within a community of rights holders.

My second step is to move beyond a refined consequentialism. This individual-to-individual adjudication is justifiable (necessary), even within the strictest rights-based argument, because the act of rights-claiming is itself a human activity. If it is a human activity, it is subject to questions of its morality. The underlying basis for the calculation is that it concerns harm or the needs of individuals. The calculation confronts the individual rights-claimer with the harm or need effect of his or her rights-claim on another person. Whoever's needs are outweighed by the needs of the other, particularly in relation to the harm that could be caused to that individual, arguably cannot make a successful moral claim to his or her rights in that situation; it would be immoral for me to maintain my rights-claim in the face of the level of harm that it will thereby cause to another person because it would instrumentalise him or her.[25]

My third step is to ask whether society can legislate to assume that its members will take the morally correct decision, or whether a moral choice is a matter for the individual alone. At this boundary between making claims to individuality or collectivity (autonomy or solidarity), it is arguably acceptable for the society to make the demand for moral action upon the individual. The individual who claims, for example, that the CCTV camera should not be erected outside his house, is making a claim not just within rights-making, but *about* rights-making. He or she is depending upon a realm of rights-claiming within which to make his or her claim. He or she is, effectively, agreeing that others will also make rights claims, and that there must be some way of adjudicating between those claims, and that the superiority of the claims must be found within the realm of rights-claiming itself if those rights are to remain respected in the transaction. This, I think, implies an acceptance by rights-claimers that sometimes their rights can be overridden by the supervening quality of another's claims, and that this is effected through argument. In other words, by accepting that he or she is a rights claimer, and that this

[24] D Townend, 'Overriding Data Subjects' Rights in the Public Interest', in D Beyleveld, D Townend, S Rouillé-Mirza and J Wright (eds), *The Data Protection Directive and Medical Research Across Europe* (Ashgate Publishing, 2004) 89.

[25] The basis for this argument is my reading of the PGC. A Gewirth, *Reason and Morality* (Chicago University Press, 1978).

is a function of his or her general ability to exist as an individual, he or she must be accepting that this is a universal claim to individuality, and that he or she must defend that function in him- or herself and in all other rights-claimers.[26]

In this situation, arguably, the law can expect an individual rights-claimer by virtue of that rights-claiming to expect that the law will provide a forum whereby such disputes can be resolved, and arrange the conduct of society as an expression of the morally acceptable path. Another way of expressing this is that where the law has to be constructed to regulate behaviour, it must do so, as it is itself an act of human decision making, morally (because of the general relationship between human action and morality). Therefore, for the law to prescribe conduct other than moral conduct is not acceptable.

III. The Attitude Gap

Privacy, then, is not so much a normative concept as it is a cultural, and highly personal, construction. It is at a normative interface in governance between law and culture, between the individual and society, and, arguably, between the individual as the purely rational agent and the human being (where agency is only one element of his or her character). Broadly, in terms of the operation of the law in relation to medical research using genetic information and biobanking, privacy's subjectivity makes both its contribution to framing the substance of the law and the operation of the law rather weak. In terms of the substance of the law, the Data Protection Directive now has its own logic that has, to a large extent, replaced the need for a highly defined and objective concept of privacy within which to interpret the Directive. Indeed, Article 8 of the Charter of Fundamental Freedoms of the European Union introduces personal data protection as a free-standing fundamental right in itself. It does not, however, help to define how one should apply the law; it does not go very far in informing the attitude that one should adopt in operating that law. As a fundamental freedom, the duty is 'to respect the rights of individuals in relation to the processing of their personal data'. This leaves open how one should interpret the balances that those rights necessarily entail. Equally, that subjective nature, and the inability of humans to act as pure rational agents, makes the interpretation of these claims to privacy and the negotiation of competing interests extremely difficult.

In 'Principle, Proceduralism, and Precaution in a Community of Rights', Beyleveld and Brownsword acknowledge this fallibility of human beings as agents, and point to the necessity for procedures to ensure that their decision making is in line with the values of the PGC:

> the citizens of Gewirthia respect the generic rights of all agents and understand that no agent is infallible, thus that they are not infallible. They also presume (unless presented

[26] Again, this is an interpretation (or application), essentially, of the PGC, above.

> with direct evidence to the contrary) that other agents are sincere in their beliefs and preferences when these differ from their own. They do, not, therefore, insist on their own views at all costs.[27]

Further, they indicate that

> [t]he reasons why Gewirthians are bound by their procedural turn is because they are not omniscient super-beings and this is their best practical strategy for defending and promoting the values of the PGC. Gewirthians are fortunate enough to have a good government; they are bound to respect it; but they are not bound because they have consented but because their basic scheme of governance is right.[28]

We do not live in Gewirthia, and we are not perfect Gewirthians, but issues such as the proper ordering of governance in relation to medical research using biobanks and medical research are real concerns in society. How then can we cope with the choices that are presented and discern between competing interests and competing interest holders? We could do this through the procedure of democratic government. In Gewirthia, with the assumption that all follow the PGC, or attempt to do so in good faith, a system of delegation to elected representatives is possible. However, is it sufficient outside Gewirthia, where our elected representatives have a variety of guiding motivations and are not necessarily wedded to the PGC, for a PGC-motivated voter to delegate his or her decision making about such a wide range of public (moral) choices to others? Arguably, this is not satisfactory. The PGC must oblige each citizen to take an active scrutiny of decisions made in his or her name and concerning his or her community. To do otherwise is to be careless of the choices made about others, and that must equate to an instrumentalisation; one has a responsibility to use one's power well. At the very least, the PGC compels agents to participate in the political life of his or her community and to hold his or her representatives fully accountable for their actions through every means at his or her disposal.

The problem is brought into sharp focus when one considers how to generate a governance or regulatory environment for, for example, medical research using biobanks and genetic information. The laws relating to privacy, as argued above, leave much to be desired. They only provide frameworks within which to negotiate interactions between the various stakeholders involved, from the participants to the biobank managers, to the researchers, to the developers of therapies from that research, to the patients who use those therapies (to take just one line through biobanking), and the attitude that should be adopted in interpreting the rules is crucial. There are clearly a number of mechanisms that have been developed to address this attitude gap. In English law, equity and the fiduciary duty have long been applied, although its extension to aspects of medical practice has been

[27] Beyleveld and Brownsword, n 1, 152.
[28] ibid, 154.

resisted in English equity.[29] In ethics, one could reach to Habermas's discourse theory, or to virtue ethics as measures for ensuring the refining of the subjective to a sharper practical duty. However, here I wish to point to an earlier movement and philosophy in England that addressed the refining of subjective belief and could provide an inclusive procedure within which human beings could discharge their duties under the PGC.

IV. Politeness[30]

In England, the seventeenth century was an extraordinary and turbulent time. There were three Civil Wars, the second of which culminated in the trial and execution of the monarch, King Charles I, in 1649. Thereafter, the 'Commonwealth', 'Protectorate', and then 'Restoration' continued the period of one of extraordinary social and political change with some continued violence. This revolutionary period was fuelled in part by religious radicalism, which also found expression in new political philosophies.[31] At the same time, English society was transformed by other 'revolutions': in international trade (through the East India Company, which gained its charter at the beginning of the seventeenth century); through the expansion of the population; through the emergence (and importance) of towns; and through the beginnings of what would now be called the 'consumer society'.[32]

This was the setting for change in society concerning its manners, etiquette and 'taste'. With so much social upheaval, the basic rules of interaction had been challenged and removed, and had to be reordered if the social revolution was to be effective and managed. Society had lost the 'courtly' hierarchical structure of manners of the ancient regime.[33] By the beginning of the eighteenth century, order had been regained in no small part through 'politeness', as advanced in theoretical writing by Shaftesbury,[34] and in the practical hot-bed of the daily published essays

[29] *Sidaway v Bethlem Royal Hospital Governors* [1985] AC 871; for a discussion of this, see P Bartlett, 'Doctors as Fiduciaries: Equitable Regulation of the Doctor–Patient Relationship' (1997) 5 *Medical Law Review* 193.

[30] For a particularly interesting introduction to the concept of 'Politeness', see BBC Radio 4, *In Our Time*, 30 September 2004, www.bbc.co.uk/programmes/p004y29m.

[31] See, eg, C Hill, *The World Turned Upside Down: Radical Ideas During the English Revolution* (Maurice Temple Smith, 1972); LE Klein, 'Sociability, Solitude, and Enthusiasm' (1997) 60 *Huntingdon Library Quarterly* 153.

[32] A Vickery, *Behind Closed Doors: At Home in Georgian England* (Yale University Press, 2009); H Berry, 'Polite Consumption: Shopping in Eighteenth Century England' (2002) 12 *Transactions of the Royal Historical Society (Sixth Series)* 375; RH Sweet, 'Topographies of Politeness' (2002) 12 *Transactions of the Royal Historical Society* 355.

[33] See N Elias, *The Civilising Process: Sociogenetic and Psychogenetic Investigations (1936)* (E Jephcott tr, Blackwell Publishing, 2000); and N Elias, *The Society of Individuals (1939)* (E Jephcott tr, Continuum International Publishing, 2001).

[34] LE Klein, 'Politeness and the Interpretation of the British Eighteenth Century' (2002) 45(4) *The Historical Journal* 869.

of Addisson and Steele, and the coffee houses.[35] Courtly manners rigidly dictated with whom one could converse in a strict social hierarchy. Once that had been overthrown, and with the increased uncertainty of social mobility and burgeoning towns, rules of social conversation moved to a practical code; rather than depending on one's birth or station, manners became a matter of negotiated appropriate behaviour through 'politeness'. And through that negotiation, that conversation, individuals and concepts of appropriate manners were, in Shaftesbury's word, 'polished'. Porter indicates that this politeness, with its emphasis on debate and social interaction, was at the heart of the English Enlightenment from the late seventeenth century. It was not the Church or the Universities that saw this development in thinking, but rather it was polite society where Enlightenment was sought and found; it was not the great philosophers who framed English Enlightenment, but it was polite society, and it was politeness in society that facilitated the emergence of the Enlightenment ideas through essays and public discussion of ideas.[36]

Politeness: More than Table Manners[37]

Shaftesbury's politeness is not simply about the ordering of conversation. Politeness reaches into the way that the fabric of society is ordered.[38] As new towns emerged, their ordering was developed through politeness. Likewise, the way that one responded to the emerging consumerism of the period was equally a matter of taste, certainly, but taste through politeness had an objective rather than subjective quality and was an outworking of the process of politeness; the way that one ordered one's home, in its public and private spaces, showed one's taste, and that reflected one's inner character and one's ability to 'polish' one's self.[39] The central politeness of taste, or refining one's taste, was to ensure that one should not offend others; politeness ensured that individuals could live together in the socially revolutionary society of the early eighteenth century. Individuals in society changed their circumstances and themselves, asking how best to live in community.

Klein shows the depth of the philosophy of Shaftesbury.[40] He shows that Shaftesbury makes a philosophical break from Hobbes' view that human beings were primarily individuals, solitary in their natural state; for Shaftesbury, humans

[35] For complete copies of Joseph Addisson and Sir Richard Steele's *The Spectator* of March 1711 to December 1712, and then from June to December of 1714, see www.gutenberg.org/ebooks/12030.

[36] R Porter, *Enlightenment: Britain and the Creation of the Modern World* (Penguin Books, 2001).

[37] For an explanation of the use of 'Politeness' in the interpretation of eighteenth-century Britain, see LE Klein, 'Politeness and the Interpretation of the British Eighteenth Century' (2002) 45(4) *The Historical Journal* 869.

[38] LE Klein, 'The Third Earl of Shaftesbury and the Progress of Politeness' (1984–85) 18(2) *Eighteenth-Century Studies* 186, 188.

[39] See RH Sweet, 'Topographies of Politeness' (2002) 12 *Transactions of the Royal Historical Society* 355, 356; R Scruton, *Beauty* (OUP, 2009).

[40] LE Klein, *Shaftesbury and the Culture of Politeness: Moral Discourse and Cultural Politics in Early Eighteenth-Century England* (CUP, 1994).

were social, interdependent beings.[41] Further, for Hobbes and Locke, humans were not capable in their natural state of behaving virtuously; again, this was anathema to Shaftesbury's thinking.[42] Equally, Klein shows that Shaftesbury saw his purpose as radically different from that of others of the time, notably Descartes, Locke and Hobbes; for Shaftesbury philosophy concerned 'self-knowing wisdom' and ethics.[43] Klein indicates that Shaftesbury, like Addison and Steele, saw philosophy itself as something that had to be tempered by politeness: 'Polite philosophy implied a new space of public discourse and culture, occupied by a literate gentlemanly audience receptive to philosophy and a literate gentlemanly authorship purveying it'. Klein further states that this was 'not as a mode of apprehending truths but as a mode of regulating expression'.[44]

Shaftesbury's politeness is an imperative to sociability as a requirement to consider others, balancing self with others. Klein, in discussing Shaftesbury's *An Inquiry Concerning Virtue*, draws this out: 'This scheme created a place for selflessness, securing the self against radical egoism', and that Shaftesbury saw 'human sociability was a reliable criterion of morality'.[45] According to Klein, for Shaftesbury, 'ethical sociability was constituted by a large measure of selflessness'.[46] For Shaftesbury, his reader 'might be expected to embrace virtue for its own sake rather than on the basis of superstition or prescription'.[47] Further, whilst there was an element of pleasing others in politeness,[48] in Klein's words, Shaftesbury seeks to avoid this as 'fundamentally misdirected since it fixed the self's course by reference to others' and morality was found in critical self-reflection.[49] One must remember that this is a philosophy that is a response to the excesses of individual enthusiasm and fanaticism.[50]

That self-reflection, whilst interacting with others (who are also charged with the same imperative to self-criticism) is the central message of Shaftesbury's politeness, and is somewhat at odds with twenty-first century individualism. Politeness resonates with the PGC that to make a claim to rights, one must acknowledge that first the act of claiming a right is an act of demanding a duty from others; and second, the act of rights-claiming places the individual claimant in the position of valuing rights-claiming. This cannot be something that he or she is able to claim only for him- or herself, rather, the appeal to the right is because of a condition that is external to the self, and that gives a transcendent power to the claim by the individual, that makes it a compelling claim against others. In this way,

[41] ibid, 31, 68 and 69.
[42] ibid, 66.
[43] ibid, 27.
[44] ibid, 41.
[45] ibid, 57
[46] ibid, 58.
[47] ibid, 59.
[48] Klein n38, 190; RH Sweet, n 39, 356.
[49] Klein, n 40, 78.
[50] ibid, 167 etc.

by making a claim, the individual necessarily compels him- or herself to respect rights-claiming, and therefore the rights-claiming of others. In that way, rights-claiming compels the individual to duty-granting, as the individual rights-claimer is implicitly requiring duty-granting by rights-claiming.

Shaftesbury's politeness expresses the other-centredness of social living. It is a philosophy of solidarity. It is a philosophy that requires individuals to find, through self-criticism and reflection, 'character' which, as Klein encapsulates, 'referred to the qualities of consistency, unity and autonomy, founded on well-developed interiority, that defined the philosophical being and moral actor'.[51] And the person of character had to learn to balance seriousness with sociability: as Klein says, '[s]eeking a style of sociability that was neither so sociable that it sacrificed integrity nor magisterial in a way that repelled others, Shaftesbury urged a middle position that would honour claims of both autonomy and sociability.'[52]

This was the struggle for polite conversation, the vehicle that would produce that 'polishing' of individuals, that would give them 'character' and produce the moral society.[53] Summing up Shaftesbury's philosophical writing, Klein says this: 'Shaftesbury was the ideologist for a culture that would be both philosophical and gentlemanly, moral and conversable—in a word, polite'.[54] The willingness in Whig post-revolutionary England to accept and develop this culture of politeness is striking. It was the re-invention of the society, and this is what makes it so very interesting for today. There are great similarities in this philosophy between, for example, value ethics and discourse ethics. However, I have considered politeness here because it has a very real social or cultural aspect: politeness was the basis of a cultural reorientation, one that arguably set English culture for the industrial revolution. Politeness, therefore, reminds us, particularly in an age where the possibility of conscious changes in public orientation is often denied, that the public has the possibility of re-orientating itself where it sees the necessity.

V. Practical Politeness for Biobanking

What relevance does this have to modern medical research using genetic information and biobanking? The challenges of modern biotechnology produce new relationships between citizens, and thereby, as in the late seventeenth and early eighteenth centuries, we have a new society to negotiate. The medical research community, the pharmaceutical industry, and the political elite could of course choose to see others simply as resources for research, and could justify

[51] ibid, 91.
[52] ibid, 96.
[53] LE Klein, 'Liberty, Manners, and Politeness in Early Eighteenth-Century England' (1989) 32(3) *The Historical Journal* 583.
[54] Klein, n 40, 119.

compulsory participation by individuals on the basis of the public interest. And in some cultures within Europe, particularly the Scandinavian health cultures, this is a sufficient argument and strategy for compulsory, population-wide inclusion (that is to a very large extent seen as part of citizenship by many in those societies). Arguably, however, this could be remarkably counter-productive in the vast majority of European cultures, as the effort needed to enforce participation would be very high, and if individuals felt coerced and abused the action would be contrary to the interests of society generally.

The whole of biobanking's success hangs on the continued participation of individual members of the public. This involves both that they are engaged with the scientific benefits of the research, and that they see the research as a good thing. Equally, citizens' fears need to be addressed. One of the conclusions that has repeatedly come out of the responses to medical and scientific scandals is the need for greater connectedness with the participants. This is increasingly the standard in healthcare, but it also needs to become the standard in medical research. Politeness replaces the lost sense of professionalism and fiduciary duty. Politeness addresses the attitude gap in the application of the law.

Politeness was a philosophy of exploring the basis of interaction between individuals. It was 'other-centric', as we have seen, but it was also a negotiated rather than learnt philosophy. In that way, politeness was devised by the members of the society through discussion and self-evaluation. When I say that politeness can assist in the development of medical research using genetic information and biobanking, I mean simply this: that the community of researchers, managers, technologists, of all the 'professionals' working in the field should adopt the other-centred, discursive outlook of politeness to consider how best to develop medical research using genetic information and biobanking taking into account not only its own interests but taking seriously the interests and sensitivities of all the participants: that the professionals in medical research using genetic information and biobanks should look to politeness as their guide in considering their work with and for society. To this end, I suggest a measure from politeness that will assist the greater realisation of biobanking in society: an international society of medical research using genetic information and biobanking, perhaps the 'International Association of Biobanking' as a short title.

VI. International Association of Biobanking

There are associations of biobank professionals.[55] Many of these bodies have a commercial, practical focus, with industry membership and sponsorship. What is

[55] International Society for Biological and Environmental Repositories (ISBER), www.isber.org and its regional group the European, Middle Eastern and African Society for Biopreservation and Biobanking, www.esbb.org.

missing is an association that is either specifically 'governance' oriented, or preferably, an association that is truly a 'professional' body in the style of the Royal Society, or the British Medical Association. By that, I mean a (self-)governing, professional association that would, as a central part of its core activity, debate openly the ethical and legal questions raised by the activities of medical research using genetic information and biobanking, discussing the difficulties in balancing different positions, and creating 'best practice' guidelines and codes of conduct.

Membership of such a society would be open not only to the technical, 'bench science' research specialists, but all the disciplines involved in the area (including, for example, ethics, law, medical history, and computer software development). In order to respond to the international dimension of the area, regional groups (always interdisciplinary) should be developed, working to a common agreed agenda, and using web-based discussion fora to ensure broad, international discussion. As a condition of membership, members would agree to participate in discussions, with a requirement to gain 'continuing education points' through such participation as is common in many professions (for example, in law or medicine). The aim of the groups would be to develop and continuously refine 'best practice' approaches and standards.

Discussions amongst these groups would add significantly to the way that the practice of medical research using genetic information and biobanking is perceived. This self-regulatory vehicle could become a place where individual professionals within the industry showed the general public a seriousness about the ethical and legal dimensions of their work, engaging with ethicists, lawyers, and other members of metamedica to form transparent working practices and also to take account of the views of other citizens, particularly to research, and to take account of the fears of potential participants.

If membership of this independent association became a standard for those working within biobanking and with material from biobanks, and acceptance and adherence to its codes of conduct became an industry standard (perhaps expected by research ethics committees and funding bodies), the impact could be considerable. By being seen to take the ethical and legal aspects of the work very seriously, and to take the concerns of participants seriously through the 'polishing' of open debate and other-centred self-reflection, rather than only focusing on the medical, scientific and technical aspects of biobanking, citizens could build confidence in the research community.

VII. Conclusion: Politeness and the Attitude Gap

I have argued that the law that regulates medical research using genetic information and biobanking, particularly privacy, is problematic as it requires subjective evaluations after an acceptance of duty through ethical rationalism. Indeed, I have suggested that it is not useful to consider privacy as a 'right', but to rely on appeals to the more objective public interest as a justification to intervene in individuals' private lives. Therefore, there is a gap in the governance structure that can be addressed by the creation of an appropriate attitude in which this subjectivity is approached; in which those who operate the law consider those who are regulated and protected by the law. How they consider the operation of discretion, and how they interpret the law is crucial to ensuring that the law brings public trust and confidence in the system.

In market consumerism, one cannot assume that 'professionals' today have the 'other-centric' attitude towards self-interests and the fundamental rights of others. I have rather assumed that such an other-centricity remains a valuable part of ensuring public trust and confidence in professionals, because of the public reactions to medical scandals and from the sensitivities expressed by some of the individuals in the surveys of citizens' attitudes. I have introduced the philosophy of politeness both because it is a philosophy of this other-centred attitude, and because it was a philosophy that took hold of the imaginations of individuals in a changing society and empowered individuals to change their social order and their social (and personal) attitudes. Because of this power in politeness, I have suggested that its principles of self-reflection and social discussion in public spaces can be a basis for developing an international professional association for medical research using genetic information and biobanking.

I have addressed the potential of politeness entirely towards the professionals involved in biobanking. Of course, this is only part of its potential. Politeness in the coffee houses and polite society of Shaftesbury's England provided the manners of individuals. In that way, it is not confined to professional attitudes towards negotiating the competition of rights. It offers a way in which all citizens can reflect, both individually and collectively, on the operation of the demands they make upon each other, and provide a manner within which to explore practical ethical rationalism.

11

Fidelity to International Law: On International Courts and Politics

HENRIK PALMER OLSEN*

I. Introduction: International Law as a Moral Judgement

In *Law as a Moral Judgment* (*LMJ*), Deryck Beyleveld and Roger Brownsword argued that law, understood as formally organised and enforceable social rules, relied for its validity on it being compatible with the most basic imperative in practical reason. This basic imperative was identified as the Principle of Generic Consistency (PGC)—a principle of agent morality that was first articulated by the American philosopher Alan Gewirth in *Reason and Morality* in 1978.[1] Consequently, they argue, legality is conceptually tied to morality—more precisely, the PGC, which requires that all agents have a right to freedom and well-being, and a corresponding duty to respect every other agent's equal right to freedom and well-being.

In *LMJ*, Beyleveld and Brownsword unfolded the consequences of this position for a number of basic legal concepts, such as right, constitution and adjudication. One area of law which was not covered in the book, however, was international law and international courts.[2] There could well have been good reasons for this: they might have considered it unnecessary to distinguish between domestic and international law/courts, they could have perceived international law to be not really law, or they could have considered international law and international courts

* Professor of Jurisprudence, Faculty of Law, University of Copenhagen. This research is funded by the Danish National Research Foundation Grant No DNRF105 and conducted under the auspices of iCourts, the Danish National Research Foundation's Centre of Excellence for International Courts.

[1] Gewirth's PGC has been compared to Kant's Categorical Imperative, see D Beyleveld, 'Gewirth and Kant on Justifying the Supreme Principle of Morality' in M Boylan (ed), *Gewirth: Critical Essays on Action, Rationality, and Community* (Rowmann and Littlefield Publishers, 1999) 97 and the contribution by P Capps in this collection.

[2] The book does contain one small section of less than one page on international law at p 210, but there is no elucidation of the many difficult jurisprudential problems that attach to international law.

as being of too little significance to offer it attention in a book that was already packed with complex and difficult jurisprudential problems. Perhaps more probable is that they set out to provide the most basic set of ideas for thinking of law, leaving it for themselves and others to subsequently work out the implications for the more specialised and less basic elements of law.[3]

Whatever the reason, the absence of discussion of international law is not unusual within natural law theory. Neither Lon Fuller, Ronald Dworkin nor John Finnis give special attention to international law in their main contributions to jurisprudence.[4] This is most likely because the concept of law is considered at the most basic conceptual level in these works, and thus it is not considered relevant by the authors to operationalise a distinction between international and domestic law.[5] Today, however, someone writing a basic theory of jurisprudence might have a different view on this.

When *LMJ* was published in 1986, probably not many considered international law as being particularly important. This was during the cold war when international relations were dominated by the power politics of the USA and the USSR. International relations were mostly governed by rules concerning diplomacy and territory, and the EU and the ECHR had only just begun to advance a new form of real supranational law. At the time Beyleveld and Brownsword were writing *LMJ*, no one could have known about the transformation of international law and politics that lay ahead: in 1989 the Berlin Wall fell and the cold war ended, which appeared to give rise to a whole new political climate, one which is characterised unequivocally by a surge in international courts and international judicial activity.[6] In fact, one of the most important transformational processes in law and society over the last 30 years has been the significantly increased importance

[3] See also the contribution by R Brownsword in this collection.

[4] J Brunee and S Toope in their *Legitimacy and Legality in International Law* (Cambridge University Press, 2010) sets out to develop a so-called 'interactional account' of international law based on Lon Fuller's theory of law as developed in his *The Morality of Law* (Yale University Press, 1969), yet they acknowledge that Fuller himself did not pay any systematic attention to international law (see Brunee and Toope, ibid, 33, note 60). R Dworkin's *Law's Empire* (Fontana, 1986) does not address international law in any way. A posthumously published article, which was never finalised by Dworkin before his death, remains his only systematic attempt to theorise about international law (see Ronald Dworkin, 'A New Philosophy for International Law' (2013) 41(1) *Philosophy and Public Affairs* 2. John Finnis uses international law as an example of how 'an authoritative rule can emerge … without being made by anyone with authority to make it …', J Finnis, *Natural Law and Natural Rights* (OUP, 1980) 238. This part of the book, however, is primarily concerned with the need for authority and Finnis does not in any systematic way theorise about international law.

[5] HLA Hart, on the other hand, included in his *The Concept of Law* (OUP, 2012, first published in 1961) a whole separate chapter—the book's final chapter—on international law (213–37). For a recent review of the content and significance of this, see M Payandeh informative critique of Hart's views on international law in 'The Concept of International Law in the Jurisprudence of HLA Hart' (2010) 21(4) *The European Journal of International Law* 967. Here Payandeh sets out to revisit Hart's analysis in the light of the recent developments and changes in the structure of international law at the beginning of the twenty-first century.

[6] For the most elaborate explanation of this, see K Alter, *The New Terrain of International Law: Courts, Politics, Rights* (Princeton University Press, 2014).

of international law in both international and domestic governance in the form of an intensified juridification of international relations, and a steadily growing population of increasingly active international courts.

In the light of this, it seems uncontroversial to claim that international courts constitute a part of the legal enterprise as defined by Lon Fuller, and thereby form a part of the initial definition that was adopted by Beyleveld and Brownsword in their argument for a moral conception of law. International law can very well be identified—to paraphrase Fuller—as the enterprise of subjecting human conduct to the governance of international rules, and international courts, when and where they exist, can indeed be said to constitute an integrated part of that enterprise.

The problem I wish to discuss in this chapter, and which I take to be a major issue of judicial morality relevant to international courts, is a problem related to the issue of what with a Fullerian twist may be called fidelity to international law. It is the problem of how international courts may deal with having to operate in a politically hostile environment. More specifically the issue I will examine is a situation that international courts meet in various forms and degrees of severity, namely one in which a morally (that is, PGC) optimal interpretation of what the law requires in a concrete case submitted to the court for decision is so politically controversial for one or a group of dominant domestic governments that issuing a decision which implements such interpretation will more generally undermine the political support for the court. In the following I will first argue that international courts are indeed in a political situation that makes them more sensitive to political pressure than domestic constitutional courts. Then, I will set out the basic parameters for legal interpretation as explained in *LMJ*, and 'translate' those to an international setting. Finally, I will revert to the issue of political pressure, and in relation to a concrete recent example, that of the Southern African Development Community (SADC) Tribunal and the events leading to its suspension, consider the dilemma of whether it would not be morally preferable (in the light of PGC requirements) to give in to pressure in the concrete situation in return for a continued support for the court, with the aim of achieving a longer-term moral improvement in the overall legal regime.

II. International and Constitutional Courts Between Law and Politics

In a domestic setting, constitutional courts (or supreme courts with competence to adjudicate and rule on constitutional issues) occupy a special position in domestic political systems in that such courts have the final say with regard to the legal meaning of the constitution and hence may decide that legislative or executive decisions (or decisions by lower courts) are unconstitutional and thereby invalid.[7] This means that constitutional law may trump political will, thereby possibly inciting strong legislators to attempt to curb constitutional courts that make unpopular rulings. Such curbing may take many different forms, ranging from leading politicians making comments in the press about the courts' past or upcoming decisions, through informal interference by way of personal contacts to judges, over budget slashing to various reform proposals and ultimately constitutional changes.[8]

While such political pressure may be significant, it is nevertheless difficult for a government *openly* to support criticism of a constitutional court unless it has acted obviously beyond its mandate. This is because it is integral to the purpose of a constitutional court to check legislators and executives, which in turn indicates that a government will easily stand out as wanting absolute power if it engages in criticising its constitutional watchdog. Furthermore, constitutional judges in most constitutional settings will be constitutionally protected from interference through removability clauses etc. Finally, the option of totally dismantling the constitutional court will only be open to the government through a procedure for constitutional change, and such a procedure usually requires a broader democratic mandate than ordinary legislation. Removing a constitutional court through an amendment of the constitution, however, will usually involve legislative procedures that are longer and involve more thorough debate and scrutiny. Such debates will probably tend to involve basic considerations of political organisation, which will move the debate away from dissatisfaction with the outcome of individual cases, and will hence make it more difficult for a government to succeed.

Domestic courts, then, are usually part of a larger political structure, in which there is an overarching constitutional order which simultaneously forms the basis of the political and judicial system and which thereby provides a platform for the judicial system that goes beyond immediate day-to-day politics.

International courts are in a somewhat different situation and may easily be more sensitive to political pressure. First and foremost this is because international courts are not part of a more general constitutional set-up which involves the distribution and separation of powers. International courts are established by international treaty—not by constitution—and as a general principle, any state

[7] Other domestic courts may also make decisions that affect the executive branch of government, but if such decisions are not based on constitutional law, the executive may simply seek to have the law changed through legislative action. The constitution, however, will more often than not be much more difficult to change.

[8] An example of a study of court curbing can be found in TS Clark, 'The Separation of Powers, Court Curbing, and Judicial Legitimacy' (2009) 53(4) *American Journal of Political Science* 971. Clark believes there is evidence which indicates that public discontent with the court, as mediated through congressional hostility, creates an incentive for the court to exercise self-restraint. When Congress is hostile, the court uses judicial review to invalidate Acts of Congress less frequently than when Congress is not hostile towards the court.

is free to withdraw from the jurisdiction of an international court whenever it so wishes.[9] Moreover, most international courts have subject-specific competences (human rights, trade, regulating the sea, etc.), and although each must apply general international law they are not part of a systematic, hierarchical and co-ordinated system of judicial institutions.[10] Furthermore, there is no centralised international enforcement system, which ensures that decisions by international courts will be complied with (although states can enforce judgments and are even on some occasions required to).[11]

So while domestic courts are part of an existing constitutional system in which there is a background expectation (and legal duty) on the executive to enforce decisions from the domestic court, international courts need to rely on states to accept their jurisdictional competence and to offer enforcement or voluntary implementation measures. Domestic courts, at least those in modern democratic states, one could say, are embedded in a political and legal context, which generally presupposes and assures a commitment to the rule of law.[12] International courts do not operate in the same context. International law surely is law, and international courts surely are an integrated part of the legal enterprise, but one should not automatically impose assumptions taken from well-known domestic systems of law and impose them on international courts generally or on any one specific international court.

International law is a young phenomenon compared to state legal orders, and only very recently have international courts emerged as an integrated part of the structure of international law. Today even the most established courts cannot expect full compliance from Member States, which shows that these courts depend on the political willingness of states to submit to their decisions. States do not automatically accept and implement the decisions in quite the same way they would for decisions of domestic courts.

As an illustration of this claim, one could point to the reception of decisions from the ECtHR, whose judgments are undoubtedly legally binding on Member States according to the Convention.[13] The UK—acting through its Supreme Court—nevertheless openly declares that ECtHR decisions may be challenged, when the Supreme Court finds that such decisions do not sufficiently appreciate

[9] This could be said to follow from the principle of state sovereignty: just as states are free to enter into treaties with other states, so too are they free to sign out of such agreements. Moreover, some courts are made operational only on a principle of voluntary jurisdiction, which means that courts will only have the competence to adjudicate a conflict between two states if both states accept that the court be granted competence to rule in the individual case at hand.

[10] This situation is often referred to as the fragmentation of international law, a phenomenon that has given rise to much concern; see, eg, the International Law Commission's report from 2006 on this: http://legal.un.org/ilc/documentation/english/a_cn4_l682.pdf.

[11] See Payandeh, n 5.

[12] The Rule of Law is of course a complex notion, but see T Bingham, *The Rule of Law* (Penguin, 2011), for an accessible, yet nuanced and serious account of what that notion entails.

[13] Art 46 of the Convention requires States to 'abide by the final judgment of the Court in any case where they are parties'.

or accommodate particular aspects of the UK's legal practices (*in casu* criminal procedure).[14]

What this means is that the highest judicial authority in the UK considers itself competent to 'decline to follow'[15] decisions by an international court (*in casu* ECtHR).[16] This is not unusual. In the EU, it has long been the case that both the CJEU and Member States' supreme courts have, each within their own jurisdiction and from their own point of view, declared themselves to be the highest judicial authority with respect to the applicability of EU law.[17] The relativity of international judicial authority, in other words, is well known.

The problem I will be focusing on in this chapter is not, however, that of individual compliance, but rather that of a collective initiative from a group of Member States which, having set up an international court and subjected itself to its competence, subsequently, perhaps because of dissatisfaction with the court's decisions, aims to curb the behaviour of that same court.

One perspective on such court curbing is to view it as being simply an engagement with the politics of treaty making. In other words, just as these states have set up the court in question, so they may close it down or alter its composition, its *modus operandi*, its substantive jurisdiction, or some other dimension of the court. On this view—because the court is not part of a constitutional context—states can do more or less as they wish *vis-à-vis* the court. Because there is no basis for the court's existence outside the will of states to have such a court, the court has nowhere to turn with a plea for support for its existence. On this perspective, states exercise a kind of *pouvoir constituant*[18] when they shape the court's competences. In the same way that one could say that a community of people can decide to constitutionally delimit the competence of its courts, so too could one say that a community of states can delimit the competence of *its* courts. In that sense, international courts, like constitutional courts (and other courts for that matter), must be responsive to their audiences in order to gain the necessary support for their continued legitimacy and ultimately their continued existence.[19] International

[14] See www.supremecourt.uk/about/the-supreme-court-and-europe.html.

[15] ibid.

[16] According to s 2(1) of the Human Rights Act passed in 1998 by the UK Parliament, UK courts are required to take account of any relevant Strasbourg judgments or opinions when determining a question in connection with the Convention rights, but decisions of the ECtHR are not binding in the strict sense of the word. For a discussion of the extent to which lower UK courts may depart from precedent set by higher UK courts when such precedent is clearly at odds with ECtHR practice, see SD Pattinson, 'The Human Rights Act and the doctrine of precedent' (2015) 35(1) *Legal Studies* 142.

[17] See the *Costa v Enel* and *Simmenthal* decisions by the CJEU (formerly ECJ) and, eg, decisions by the German Constitutional Court in the so-called *Solange* cases, must recently the *Brunner* case (also referred to as *Solange III*).

[18] For a review of this concept and its relation to Public Law, see M Loughlin, *The Idea of Public Law* (OUP, 2003).

[19] Y Lupu, 'International Judicial Legitimacy: Lessons from National Courts' (2013) 14 *Theoretical Inquiries in Law* 437.

courts, then, *seem* to be confronted with the same political constraints as those of domestic courts: the law is never stronger than those who are charged with the task of creating it and promulgating it. Yet there are important differences that make international courts more vulnerable to political curbing. Most importantly, international courts operate in an international space, where there is no clearly definable demos/*Öffentlichkeit* which can be said to play the role of a *pouvoir constituant* for the court. Although international courts increasingly stand in a direct relationship to individual citizens (individual citizens may complain to the ECtHR and the International Criminal Court can charge individuals and hear testimony from individuals), they generally operate in a context where there is a much weaker democratic process surrounding the relationship between international courts and its founding Member States than the processes that surround the relationship between a constitutional court and *its* founder, which is the constitutional legislator.[20]

In the light of this, an international court is politically situated in such a way that it must, more than domestic constitutional courts, adjust its legal reasoning to the political preferences of the states whose support it depends on for its continued existence. In this situation, and assuming that international judges attempt in good faith to reason and act in accordance with the PGC, thereby attempting to uphold a legitimate international institution, a special dilemma emerges: when international judges are attempting to run a PGC-compatible international court, but are faced with the threat of having their entire institution suspended (or significantly weakened) by powerful states removing their support for the institution, these judges are forced to respond to a political challenge that cannot be fully circumscribed by either legal or moral reason. That is, these judges must somehow decide whether they should attempt to rule in a PGC-optimal way in each individual case before it, or whether it should issue rulings that are less demanding on states, thereby compromising PGC compatibility or PGC optimality in the individual case in return for the pursuit of long-term gains in PGC compatibility/optimality.

These judges therefore have to choose between applying the law to the best of their abilities and making the best judgments they can or adapting legal judgments to suit those Member States that are threatening to undermine the entire institution. Both solutions will undermine the rule of law and none of the solutions seem *prima facie* compatible with the requirements of the PGC. This dilemma raises the question of how one might attain rationality in legal interpretation. In the following I shall first introduce a general framework for such rationality and subsequently, through a case study of the rise and fall of the SADC tribunal, argue in favour of a model of incremental implementation of PGC optimality.

[20] As above, I presuppose the context of modern democratic states.

III. Courts and the Rationality of Legal Interpretation

In *LMJ*, Beyleveld and Brownsword are primarily occupied with analysing the defining features of law and of law-related phenomena, such as legal order, legal obligation and adjudication. In their analysis, the *legal* is necessarily connected to the moral in that the entertainment of practical reason (which is an integrated part of the social practice of subjecting human behaviour to the governance of rules) necessarily entails a commitment to a specific ethical principle—the PGC. To attempt to construe legal authority in a way that violates this principle is to engage in activity that cannot be lawful. To be legal, it must be moral in the sense of respecting the PGC (being at least a good faith attempt to uphold the PGC). This, according to Beyleveld and Brownsword, also implies that courts must attempt to uphold posited legislation as far as possible (in ways and as long as such posited legislation does not violate a good faith attempt to respect the PGC) by making decisions that resonate with an aspiration to implement and uphold the PGC. Legislation that is supportive of or at least not in violation of the PGC must be upheld by courts. Following Lon Fuller's demand for fidelity to law,[21] Beyleveld and Brownsword say:[22]

> the PGC encourages the development of a supportive context for action. It is essential, therefore, that official action be congruent with the public framework of rules if citizens are to be able to plan on a rational basis. Reliance upon the rules must be protected, and expectations engendered by the rules must not be frustrated by perverse official administration.

There is nothing unusual about this; in fact it might seem trivial. However, in the context that I will explore here—that of international courts operating under a regime of international law—I shall try to explain how it might make *moral* sense for courts to give in to political pressure and yield decisions that are perhaps not optimally 'congruent with the public framework of rules' (as construed under a PGC compatible interpretation) in return for (in extreme cases) its continued existence or (in less extreme cases) a continued general support for and compliance with its decisions. Far from being uncontroversial, this is a question of how international courts deal with the fragility of their institutional existence in situations where they may be threatened by those who are subject to their rulings—a

[21] Fuller, in *The Morality of Law* (Yale University Press, 1969) 209–10 says: 'Surely the very essence of the Rule of Law is that in acting upon the citizen … a government will faithfully apply rules previously declared as those to be followed by the citizen as being determinative of his rights and duties … law is not, like management, a matter of directing other persons how to accomplish tasks set by a superior, but is basically a matter of providing the citizenry with a sound and stable framework for their interactions with one another, the role of government being that of standing as a guardian of the integrity of the system'.

[22] *LMJ*, 322–23. See also Beyleveld and Brownsword, 'Principle, Procedure and Precaution in a Community of Rights' (2006) 18(2) *Ratio Juris* 141.

question that takes on a moral dimension once it is accepted that it is morally preferable to have international courts to adjudicate legal conflicts in international law, rather than having a regime of international law with no stable institutional setting in which to solve legal disputes under international law.[23] In other words, international courts may be safeguarding law and morality by giving in to political pressure, when doing so is necessary in order to avoid severe backlash or even suspension of the court's activity. The case of the SADC Tribunal will serve as a real example of this and I shall return to it in the section below. Before getting to that it is, however, necessary to give a more general outline of what is involved in judicial decision making and more specifically in legal interpretation as carried out by courts.

In rendering decisions, courts interpret what the law (which may be anything from very precise rules to very broadly formulated principles) says and apply these rules and principles to specific circumstances, with a view to judging the legality of a specific event or sequence of events involving conduct performed by the parties to the case at hand. What does this mean more precisely? Beyleveld and Brownsword characterise adjudication as an activity that 'involves the attempt to identify and *interpret correctly* the legal-moral materials',[24] but no further details about what this entails ensue.[25] It seems of quite crucial importance, though, to be able to determine in some further detail how one establishes whether the materials (sources of law) have been correctly interpreted. Indeed, what establishes correctness in this regard? Since Beyleveld and Brownsword generally endorse Fuller's notion of congruence as 'the nerve of the rule of law',[26] it would not seem out of place to suggest that they might agree that correct interpretation is one that aspires to achieve *congruity* between rule and action pursued by officials. It should be noted, however, that this notion of congruity is somewhat imprecise, for the measurement of congruity between rule and action will always be someone's measurement. In order to avoid bias towards the ruler's own perception of congruity between rule and action, it is therefore closer to the ideal of the rule of law to formulate this as a requirement of congruity between ruler's and subjects' understanding of what action is required by the enacted rules.[27] Consequently, interpretive correctness is better defined by the extent to which it is accepted by other agents (that is, other than the judge who is doing the interpretation for the purposes of handing down a ruling), so that the criterion of correctness is that other agents who are involved in establishing and maintaining the legal order of which the court is a part accept the decision as correct (valid). On this view, the

[23] See Bingham, n 12, 110–29 for a basic argument for this.

[24] *LMJ*, 395.

[25] It follows from the transcendental argument linking the concept of law to the PGC that correct interpretation is interpretation in accordance with the PGC, but other than that no criteria seem to be supplied.

[26] *LMJ*, 322 with a reference to Fuller, n 5, 209–10.

[27] See also the quote above from *LMJ*, 322–23.

court's interpretation and ensuing ruling are correct or incorrect depending on whether they are accepted or rejected as a valid judgment by other agents within the same legal order.

Validity, then, is relative to acceptance and hence to the social processes that generate acceptance. This also means that legal interpretation is linked more broadly to the establishment of semantic authority over the community.[28] Judges, then, although they formally have the role of final arbiters on legal questions in the community, must respond to and gauge the credibility of their interpretation against what will be accepted in the legal community as a whole. Ultimately this connects to general social acceptability. Congruence should be understood in this light, that is as the broader social acceptance of the meaning attributed to the sources of law.[29] The individual legal decision is part of a larger process of continuous interaction between equal agents constituted by the PGC.[30] This is a process in which courts are tasked with sustaining a supportive context for action, or, as Fuller says, of 'providing the citizenry with a sound and stable framework for their interactions with one another',[31] and, one may add, for interactions between citizens and their government and interactions between governments (states). Fuller's argument about congruity (endorsed by Beyleveld and Brownsword) is basically an argument that courts should interpret the law in a way that blends in with social and linguistic custom. This is true both for domestic and international communities. Jutta Brunnee and Stephen J Toope[32] draw on Gerald Postema to explain this point in their Fullerian exploration of international legal theory:

> Law guides human action by addressing *reasons for action* to agents, but these reasons are of a general nature, and agents must reason further with the norms to apply them in specific contexts, characteristically relying upon analogy to argue a point. It is therefore

[28] In *The Concept of Law*, Hart makes a distinction between 'a normal game' and a game called 'scorer's discretion' (a game in which 'the score is what the scorer says it is'). Hart likens law to 'a normal game' because legal rules, like rules in normal games, has 'a core of settled meaning'. Presumably this core is what makes law immune to politics and thereby what makes legal decisions different from decisions in the 'scorer's discretion' game. While this may be true in some (easy) cases, 'settled meaning' is not as fixed as Hart supposes, but depends more broadly on social processes through which meaning is assigned to text. As shown by Ingo Venzke in his *How Interpretation Makes International Law: On Semantic Change and Normative Twists* (OUP, 2012), interpretation can shift the meaning of texts and in the practice of interpretation, actors debate the meaning of legal texts. In such cases it is the actor's semantic authority that is key to what is perceived as the right meaning of the text. There is, then, no 'settled meaning' that exists independently and beyond the meaning that can be established through semantic authority, and thereby through the power to establish such authority.

[29] There is an obvious circularity here in that judges themselves possess semantic authority. Their community is therefore likely to accept their interpretations as the true meaning of the law.

[30] But it's important to note that equal moral status does not entail equal semantic authority. The distribution of semantic authority among agents can only be established empirically. See also note 29 above.

[31] Fuller, n 4, 209.

[32] J Brunnee and SJ Toope, *Legitimacy and Legality in International Law: An interactional Account* (CUP, 2010).

> essential that relatively stable patterns of expectation emerge amongst the governed and between the governed and the governing. But relatively stable expectations or, to adopt constructivist language, shared understandings, are only likely to arise from repeated social practice. Postema refers to this idea as the 'congruence thesis', emphasizing that 'legal norms and authoritative directives can guide self-directed social interaction only if they are broadly congruent with the practices and patterns of interaction extant in the society generally.[33]

In international law, of course, the notion of 'society' is extremely difficult to grasp, and identifying 'practices and patterns of interaction' is even more difficult. Nevertheless, this is the task that international judges face and which they must attempt in good faith to achieve. 'Correct interpretation' is an interpretation that resonates with the common understanding of what it means to act in accordance with a particular rule. Correct (or rational) interpretation, then, becomes a matter of being in touch with and understanding the social practices that the rules in question address.[34]

On a traditional/historical view, 'society' and 'social practices' in relation to international law would translate into notions of sovereign equality, *pacta sunt servanda*, with states as the individual units that when viewed together would constitute 'international society'. Hence, in international law, there has been a tradition for perceiving 'the law of nations' as a wholly separate kind of law with its own special logic. Increasingly, however, and especially with the increased number of increasingly active international courts, such as the European Court of Human Rights, Court of Justice of the European Union and World Trade Organisation Appellate Body, international law cannot be perceived as a body of law that is complementary to domestic law. Increasingly, international law is integrated into domestic law and has become an element of domestic legal systems.[35] In the following section I shall try to explain this development.

IV. Courts, International Relations and International Law

In international relations theory, it is customary to model the relationship between states and international agencies along the lines of a principal–agent model. On this model states are principals that decide to delegate some of their powers to

[33] Brunee and Toope, n 29, 24, citing GJ Postema, 'Implicit Law' in W Witteveen and W van der Burg (eds), *Rediscovering Fuller* (Amsterdam University Press, 1999).

[34] It might be useful to think of this in terms of HLA Hart's notion of 'internal aspect of rules'. The common understanding of what it means to act in accordance with a particular rule can hence be said to refer to the 'critical reflective attitude to certain patterns of behavior as a common standard' (HLA Hart, note 28 above).

[35] See also A Nollkaemper, *National Courts and the International Rule of Law* (OUP, 2011).

international agencies, which are then perceived as agents of the states. Agents carry out the will of their principals and they do so because their principals (the states) will disempower them if they act in contravention of their principals' (the states') interests. This model has been used numerous times to explain the behaviour of international agencies, including international courts.[36] In line with both positivistic conceptions of law and rational choice theory, this invites an image of international law as one contractual interaction among states. Accordingly, states will pursue their own interests *vis-à-vis* other states and sometimes they will do so through the means of agreements with other states. International law on this view then consists of contracts between states, and the role of international courts is to adjudicate conflicts on the basis of the common contractual will of states, as set out in international treaties.[37] Decisions that involve customary international law amount to more or less the same thing, except in this case the treaty is unwritten: it emerges from common state practice and a common subjective attitude towards this practice.

This simple image of international law takes state action as the primary source of law and adjudication. Such an image corresponds well with the emergence of international law as portrayed by Koskenniemi in *The Gentle Civilizer of Nations* from the politics of diplomatic relations.[38] It does not, however, correspond particularly well with more contemporary practices and understandings of international law,[39] and especially not with the new regime of international law, where international courts, and the adjudicative activity surrounding these, have built

[36] See, eg, C Carruba et al, 'Judicial Behavior under Political Constraints: Evidence from the European Court of Justice' (2008) 102(4) *American Political Science Review* 435.

[37] See also, eg, Art 31 of the Vienna Convention on the Law of Treaties.

[38] See, eg, Koskiennemi's description of Lauterpacht's reaction to his predecessors' perception of doctrine in international law, which Lauterpacht sees as partly responsible for the international development that led to the First World War. Koskiennemi writes: 'Lauterpacht's early work is written in the form of a doctrinal polemic against a voluntarist and state-centered "positivism", castigated as the main obstacle on the way to universal legal organization … In order to constrain politics one had to develop better doctrines. The problem, Lauterpacht held, was the low level of ambition in pre-war doctrine; its readiness to compromise with aggressive nationalism and to leave a large field of activity—such as the right to wage war—outside legal regulation. Lauterpacht's constructive work was directly aimed at such self-amputation.' M Koskenniemi, *The Gentle Civilizer of Nations* (CUP, 2001) 363. The 'low level of ambition' identified by Lauterpacht in the work of his predecessors should be assessed, however, in the light of tradition. As D Armitage explains in *Foundations of Modern International Thought* (CUP, 2013), law, since Hobbes, has been so closely identified with the state that legal thinking has required a de-coupling of the state from law in order to sustain the proposition that international relations can have the character of law (international law). Consequently it has been difficult to straightforwardly argue that a theory of law is also a theory of international law. 'The Self-Amputation' Lauterpacht refers to is therefore not an accurate metaphor—those early writers did not have a body from which they could amputate anything. Instead they were involved in attempting to build one.

[39] For a contemporary view on how non-state actors are participating in international law practices, see, eg, J d'Aspremont (ed), *Participants in the International Legal System: Multiple Perspectives on Non-State Actors in International Law* (Routledge, 2012). For a contemporary view on the relationship between international law and domestic law and politics see Alter, n 6.

rather dense legal practices in some areas of law.[40] This development has resulted in a situation where the identification of the social practices addressed by international legal regulation can no longer be narrowly identified with the expressions of governing elites in official documents.[41] What this means more concretely is that the meaning content of international law cannot be reduced to or controlled by domestic governments. International institutions such as international courts are participating in an interpretive process whereby those institutions provide an autonomous input to the definition of what meaning a particular rule of international law has at a given time in a given context.[42] Furthermore, from the point of view of a PGC-compatible interpretation of international law, those legal offices that constitute the state for the purposes of international collaboration should be understood as serving particular kinds of values associated with the enterprise of subjecting human conduct to the governance of international rules, that is, ultimately with the PGC. This means that state interests cannot be reduced to the sectional interests of a governing elite that represents a given state. State interests must instead be associated with the broader interests of all rational agents in organising society in ways that promote individual freedom and well-being for all.[43]

In the context of adjudicating international law and in relation to the requirement of aiming for congruence in the above-mentioned sense, this would entail that those social practices which judicial rulings should resonate with should not be limited to the interests of governments in protection of their sovereignty and hence in protection of governing elites to rule unhindered, but should be broadened out to include social practices of those parts of civil society that are affected by the rules and principles in question.

The background reason for such an approach is, in my view, prescribed by a basic principle of equality that can also be found in the PGC. Ultimately, international

[40] As Benedict Kingsbury observes, there is an uneven judicialisation of international law; see B Kingsbury, 'International Courts: Uneven Judicialization in Global Order' in J Crawford and M Koskenniemi (eds), *Cambridge Companion to International Law* (CUP, 2011). As a response to Kingsbury it is worth noting that, despite this unevenness, some legal fields, which have been the object of intense judicialisation, have legal as well as political consequences beyond the immediate scope of that field. Hence human rights jurisprudence has become important for many issues in criminal law, administrative law, and even welfare law. Furthermore case law from regional human rights courts, eg the European Court of Human Rights, seems to become increasingly important at other human rights courts around the world.

[41] See Brunnee and Toope, n 29, 56.

[42] See J Merrills, 'International Adjudication and Autonomy' in R Collins and ND White (eds), *International Organizations and the Idea of Autonomy: Institutional Independence in the International Legal Order* (Routledge, 2011). But see also section III above on interpretation and congruence.

[43] See also C Möllers, *The Three Branches* (OUP, 2015) who observes that the legitimacy of international law is tied to its capacity for enhancing broader equality. He writes that the tendency to favour domestic democratic governance over international law 'underestimate[s] the propensity of spatially or politically "close" structures of regulation to engage in discriminatory practices. Such proximity tends to favour historically evolved relations over abstract arguments for freedom. It is no coincidence that in federal systems the struggle against all forms of discrimination has often been led by the upper level. This is true not only for the fight against economic discrimination against women and minorities. The regulatory distance facilitates the application of abstract standards of equality' (Möllers at 152).

law is not only a matter for states. International law seeks to regulate state behaviour, not only for the purposes of facilitating diplomatic comity among ruling elites, but also (and increasingly) for the purposes of enhancing the explicit and implicit values that attach to the legal regulation in question for the benefit of civil society. Some of the most recent research on international courts—more specifically on the most prolific international courts in the world—confirms that these courts do in fact operate successfully on this premise about broader inclusion.[44] Alec Stone Sweet and Thomas L Brunell, in their study of majoritarian activism[45] in three international courts, conclude, among other things, that decisions in these courts (which they call Trustee Courts)[46] are based not only on state preferences, but also on 'relevant social beliefs and practices as they evolve' and that these courts manage to base their decisions on such broader basis because they engage in dialogue with the regime's beneficiaries.[47]

The ability of Trustee Courts to escape submission to government interests and to instead engage more broadly with the values of the regime of values they are set up to protect and to relate those values to the underlying interests of citizens' social beliefs and practices are made possible because these courts are tasked with the job of applying and interpreting legal norms. It is precisely in their exercise of this capacity that courts get involved in the politics identified by Shapiro.[48]

[44] See especially Alter, n 6.

[45] Majoritarian activism is a term that has been coined by M Maduro, former Advocate General at the Court of Justice of the European Union and presently professor at the European University Institute. See MP Maduro, *We, the Court: The European Court of Justice and the European Economic Constitution* (Hart, 1998). The term refers to the disposition of judges to produce rulings that reflect outcomes that states might adopt under majoritarian, but not unanimity, decision rules. According to Stone Sweet and Brunell, 'The strategy helps these courts manage judicialization, mitigate the legitimacy problems associated with judicial lawmaking under supremacy, and render efforts at curbing the growth of their authority improbable or ineffective': A Stone Sweet and TL Brunell, 'Trustee Courts and the Judicialization of International Regimes: The Politics of Majoritarian Activism in the ECHR, the EU, and the WTO' (2013) 1(1) *Journal of Law and Courts* 64.

[46] Trustee Courts are defined as courts that operate 'in an unusually permissive zone of discretion', which 'is determined by the sum of competences explicitly delegated to a court and possessed as a result of its own lawmaking, minus the sum of control instruments available for use by the principals [in a principal–agent relationship] to override the court or to curb it in other ways' (Stone Sweet and Brunell, ibid, 65). In line with what I suggested above, Stone Sweet and Brunel explain that many constitutional courts have an exceptional position within political polities that allows them to legitimately overturn legislative acts, thereby creating a difficult obstacle for governments who will find themselves in a position to have to carry out constitutional revisions in order to be able to pass the legislative act in question.

[47] ie those who benefit from human rights protection (ECHR), free movement (EU) and trade liberalisation (WTO). Dialogue is made possible through adjudicative processes in which the parties and the court collaborate in collecting information about relevant social and legal practices in the Member States.

[48] See above. It is very possible that judges themselves will object to a description of their decision-making practices as one that involves politics. They might, under the motto: *Da mihi factum, dabo tibi ius*, insist that they merely apply the law to the facts that have been presented to them. This, however, is a necessary part of the judicial ideology, and should, from a more scholarly point of view, be understood as such.

Stone Sweet and Brunell explain that a Trustee Court can only emerge if states accept that legal meaning is (at least partly) constructed through adjudication. This entails that states must be willing to accept that the legal meaning of terms and distinctions in international law may evolve over time and that this evolution may be determined by international courts. Furthermore, if this is accepted it also entails that states must be willing to use prior decisions from the courts in their legal reasoning in present cases.[49] For this situation to occur, the court must build a relationship of trust with state governments. Only if states trust that international courts will responsibly and in good faith apply the law will these courts be able to develop the trust and authority necessary to become trustee courts.

Building such trust and authority cannot be done in an instant or be established by a single decision. Instead, an international court must build authority and acceptance over time, by gradually making decisions that give them increased influence. The usual pattern for doing so is this:[50]

(1) The court confirms and clarifies its jurisdictional competence, but makes decisions in favour of Member States' ruling elites. It will do so in a number of cases, thereby establishing its own competence while simultaneously gaining the trust of governments, that its decisions are reasonable.
(2) The court uses the powers (that have been repeatedly confirmed in previous cases (see 1 above)) to hand down decisions that, to some extent, go against Member States' ruling elites on issues that are politically of minor significance.
(3) The court uses its established jurisprudence to gradually interfere on more and more issues that will have more and more significance.
(4) A proper balance of powers will develop in which courts will take on the role as Trustee Courts, operating a politic of majoritarian activism as outlined by Stone Sweet and Brunell.

Trustee Courts are in some sense an ideal type of court in the sense that they meet the aspirations of congruence and legal rationality in the broadest sense, as outlined in this and the previous section. On this background, and with the aim of exploring the dilemma outlined at the end of section 3, I shall finish by outlining a concrete example of how the development towards the establishment of a Trustee Court can be halted by decisions that are too far reaching in interfering

[49] K Pelc, 'The Politics of Precedent in International Law: A Social Network Application' (2013) (available at SSRN: http://ssrn.com/abstract=2299638 (accessed 4 May 2015)).

[50] The following sequence is just one way of describing the incremental building of judicial authority. For an overview of the research that I rely on for this, see S Dothan, *Reputation and Judicial Tactics* (CUP, 2015). In ch 4 of his book, Dothan sets out to explain the most important judicial tactics utilised by courts to enhance their reputation (essentially similar to authority and trust) and hence to enhance their ability to issue judgments that are costly to states who are subject to the court's jurisdiction. Some of the elements in this are tactics that relate to the need to gradually build reputation and are explained by Dothan at 128–40. In relying on this, I have attempted to identify stages in the building of judicial reputation and have arrived at the four stages mentioned.

with political preferences of governing elites at a too early stage, an outline that will show how international law is intimately intertwined with politics and how this mesh constitutes a moral dilemma.

V. International Law and Politics: The Case of the SADC Tribunal

The Southern African Development Community (SADC) is an international organisation established in 1992 for the purpose of developing a regional economic community that should support economic development and integration in the region, and should do so inter alia through the promotion of democracy and human rights (see SADC Treaty Articles 4–6). The Community is composed of 14 Member States and has set up a tribunal, which became operative in 2005. The tribunal was given jurisdiction over disputes between states and between states and natural/legal persons in the substantive legal areas covered by the Treaty and subsequent Protocols.

While the tribunal was seen, upon its reception, as 'the beginning of a new era in which Southern African States were willing to accept a limitation on their sovereignty through international judicial supervision',[51] it was in fact suspended immediately after attempting to implement precisely such a limitation of state sovereignty. Hence, in the autumn of 2010, the tribunal was *de facto* emasculated by the Summit (the highest political level within the SADC), which decided to carry out a review of the role and function of the Tribunal and simultaneously to refuse renewal of the term of judges eligible for reappointment.[52]

The background for this suspension of the Tribunal's powers is closely linked to its decisions in a number of cases which related to the expropriation of farmland in Zimbabwe. Although the tribunal was not primarily envisaged as a human rights court, it involuntarily became involved in the politically highly inflammatory issue of a land reform which, although not explicitly racist, sought to redistribute land ownership through a constitutional amendment. As the reform was carried through as a constitutional amendment, it was possible for the Zimbabwean government to circumvent ordinary legislation which prescribed

[51] E De Wet, 'The Rise and Fall of the Tribunal of the Southern African Development Community: Implications for Dispute Settlement in Southern Africa' (2013) *International Centre for Settlement of Investment Disputes Review* 1. For an account of the SADC Tribunal's history, see also M Hulse and A van der Vleuten, 'Agent Run Amuck: The SADC Tribunal and Governance Transfer Roll-back' in T Börzel and V van Hüllen (eds), *Governance Transfer by Regional Organizations* (Palgrave Macmillan, 2015).

[52] The current situation for the SADC Tribunal is such that SADC Member States are currently negotiating a new tribunal with a very limited role and limited powers compared to the now suspended tribunal, see www.sadc.int/about-sadc/sadc-institutions/tribun/ (accessed 4 May 2015).

normal compensation and access to judicial review. The affected farm owners were therefore left without domestic avenues through which they could challenge the legality of the expropriation, and this was probably what led to the case being brought to the SADC tribunal. The case *Campbell and others v Zimbabwe* (Case No SADC (T) 2/2007) (28 November 2008) in effect became the only legal remedy that the approximately 4,000 overwhelmingly white farm owners could rely on in their attempt to secure some compensation or alleviation from the consequences of the constitutional amendment which led to forced removal from their lands.

Apart from the procedural issues related to the question of whether or not the tribunal had jurisdiction to decide the case on its merits, the central doctrinal issue at stake in the case revolved around the obligation of Member States to generally respect human rights, democracy and the rule of law (SADC Treaty Article 4(c)) and to respect the principle of non-discrimination (SADC Treaty Article 6(2)). Since the SADC Treaty does not guarantee a right to property, the case was litigated on the issue of exclusion of judicial review for the affected parties and on the discriminatory manner in which the expropriation had been undertaken.

In its ruling on the matter, the tribunal decided that it had jurisdiction and it therefore proceeded to decide the case on its merits. In this decision, the Tribunal concluded that Zimbabwe had acted in contravention of Article 4(c) (unanimous vote) and Article 6(2) (4 to 1 vote) of the SADC Treaty. In support of its conclusion it relied to some extent on other international tribunals and case law from other international courts. It also, in deciding the case with regard to Article 6(2), took into account the Zimbabwean government's claim that the constitutional amendment sought to address historical advantages that had previously accrued to white farmers as a consequence of the country's colonial history and the systematic patterns of racial segregation that previously almost entirely prevented the black population's access to ownership of farm land.

Now, it is not the purpose of this outline to discuss whether or not the SADC Tribunal's decision in the *Campbell* case was correct or not. The point is instead to raise the question of how, as a judge in the SADC Tribunal, one might best implement and uphold one's institutional duties in the light of both a moral requirement to act in accordance with the PGC and in the light of relevant socio-political knowledge about how governments will most likely react to international institutions which act in ways that are not compatible with, or perhaps even in direct contradistinction to, domestic policies that are considered to be of vital importance to those governments.

In this particular case, there can be no doubt that the land reform initiated by the Mugabe government was a crucial and important element in the political programme of the government. While one may dispute, as the SADC Tribunal indeed did, whether the land reforms were truly aimed at redressing historical wrongs (the tribunal claimed that expropriated property was to a large extent turned over to supporters, including leading supporters, of the governing party (ZANU-PF)), there can be no doubt that the policy had wide support in the actual government, and that it did aim to uproot an economic structure, tied up in land ownership, that had been established and consolidated during the country's colonial history. A recent study of the consequences of the reform also gives a more nuanced picture of the consequences of the reform programme than was portrayed in European and American media coverage during the initial stages of the reform.[53] That the land reform programme was politically very important to the Zimbabwean government is hardly disputable. That it would have been unable to execute a reform programme of this scope if it had to offer full compensation to all affected land-owners is most probably also true.

It seems likely that the judges on the SADC Tribunal were aware of the political significance of the land reform programme, which is an important issue in the region as a whole. Nevertheless, the tribunal did not shy away from engaging the human rights issues head on. Nor did it elaborate any specific regional approach to these, but proceeded instead by drawing not only on the Convention text itself, but also relevant case law from other international courts. The tribunal, in its reasoning, also took into account various other international instruments that Zimbabwe had ratified, and could generally be said to base its conclusion on a broad view of what human rights standards in the field require of governmental conduct.[54]

What the decision does not show is to what extent the judges on the tribunal had thought strategically about the possible impact of their decision. There is, as far as I know, no evidence of any possible out-of-court informal discussions among judges over the astuteness of ruling in such a robust way on the issue. It is nevertheless worth raising the issue here, since it is precisely this problematic that judges need to consider. In the light of what has been said above, the exercise of judicial office must be sensitive to political context and social practices more generally. It will not do to succumb to juristic isolation. As the reactions to the *Campbell* ruling clearly show, there is an important and fundamental connection between international law and international politics. This also means that the moral fidelity to law cannot simply be described as a requirement to carry out pristine legal reasoning in the technical sense (which, by the way, easily turns into sterile legalism). If one takes seriously the moral obligation to uphold the law, one must go beyond an assessment of the individual decision and include an analysis of how an individual decision should be decided and written in the light of possible political reactions to it. This is necessary to avoid backlash: a rolling back of the rule of law. In the concrete circumstances discussed here, this translates into the following question: should the SADC Tribunal have prioritised its continual existence over the attempt to sanction Zimbabwe in the *Campbell* case? Asking this question assumes that the court not only has to consider what is legally right in the individual case. It also has to make an assessment of the possible political

[53] See I Scones et al, *Zimbabwe's Land Reform: Myths and Realities (African Issues)* (James Currey, 2010).

[54] M Hulse and A van der Vleuten observe that: 'The judges opted for a strictly legal, apolitical outlook. They felt that it was neither necessary nor desirable for the Tribunal to take political considerations into account' (Börzel and van Hüllen, n 51, 94).

impact of different decision scenarios on its own existence and ability to operate, and make that assessment part of the process of deciding how to rule in the case at hand.

Referring back to section IV above and the four phases of development towards trustee courtship, what happened in the *Campbell* case was that the SADC Tribunal handed down a stage 4 decision at a time when it was operating under stage 1 conditions. The tribunal was opened in 2005, handed down the *Campbell* decision in 2008 and was suspended in 2010. Compare this to the Court of Justice of the European Union, which was established in 1952/1957, and handed down the landmark decisions in 1963 (*Van Gend en Loos*, concerning direct effect) and 1964 (*Costa*, concerning supremacy), but it was not until the 1970s that the impact of these decisions started to take off in a serious way. Similarly, the European Court of Human Rights was established in 1959, but it was not until the 1970s that the Court started issuing decisions that affected important political issues.

Assuming that the judges in the SADC Tribunal had considered the need for building up its authority as a court before issuing the *Campbell* decision, which it must have known would be met with resistance from the Zimbabwean court, and assuming in addition that it could have foreseen that other Member States would not be willing to isolate Zimbabwe on its stand against the court, it is possible to articulate the court's real moral dilemma. Should it (a) apply streamlined pure legal reasoning to the case and ignore the political context? Doing so would entail that the court should indeed have issued the decision that it did in fact issue despite the political consequences following from this. As will be remembered, the plaintiffs (Campbell and others) won the case in the court, but they did not win the case on the ground. Instead, the tribunal got suspended and the overall support for human rights and international judicial protection of individual rights diminished in the region as a whole. Or should it (b) use the opportunity to cement its jurisdictional competence in human rights and its ability to hear complaints from individuals, while deferring on the substantial issue, mostly but not entirely to the discretion of Zimbabwean authorities, for instance by recognising the legitimacy of addressing historical inequality?[55] The SADC Tribunal could have created a margin of appreciation design similar to the one is used by the European Court of Human Rights to evade the politically explosive conclusions while still giving some directions for future handling of similar cases. As Moyo points out,[56] the land reform had clearly legitimate elements, and the overall complexity and political sensitivity of the issue allowed ample opportunity for the court to avoid the ruling in favour of Campbell.

An answer to this question may be found indirectly in Beyleveld and Brownsword's Theory of Restraint. In *LMJ*, Beyleveld and Brownsword develop

[55] See A Moyo, 'Defending human rights and the rule of law by the SADC Tribunal: Campbell and beyond' (2009) 9 *African Human Rights Law Journal* 590.

[56] ibid.

both a Theory of Accountability and a Theory of Restraint. The Theory of Accountability is developed as part of an elucidation of what is entailed in the notion of constitution. Beyleveld and Brownsword argue that a constitution should be seen as contract between officials and citizens which both establishes and limits the reach of public authority.[57] The limits of official freedom are basically established by a bill of rights, principles of self-governance (democracy), and the separation of powers (rule of law). The other side of this coin is established by the Theory of Restraint, which imposes an obligation on all citizens to accept and endure prima facie rational exercises of power within this framework. Just like the Theory of Accountability sets the bounds for legitimate use of public authority, so does the Theory of Restraint establish the obligation of citizens to obey.

Considering, on this background, whether the SADC Tribunal (or in principle any international court) should relax its standards of rights protection in the light of pressure from national governments must depend on whether it is possible for it to relax its standards and still make a ruling that is sufficiently rational to avoid the justification of civil disobedience. In deciding on this question, one must weigh the moral advantages of having and sustaining a functioning international legal order against the demand for such an order to be minimally morally justifiable. With regard to the question of when disobedience becomes permissible (and hence when the demand for minimum moral defensibility begins to outweigh the need for a functioning legal order) Beyleveld and Brownsword (after acknowledging, with Finnis, that any answer will depend much on social, political and cultural variables)[58] say:[59]

> the legitimacy of particular acts of non-compliance must be determined in the light of the hierarchy of values that comprise the PGC and in the light of the particular circumstances. The legitimate action will be the action which has the best consequences as measured by the PGC … what matters is how a particular action will impact on the interests protected under the PGC. It is the consequential effect of one's action on PGC protected rights and duties that is relevant.

The *Campbell* decision led to a major backlash for international human rights protection in the SADC region—a region where, according to several commentators, states 'have a poor domestic record in relation to human rights and judicial independence'.[60] Had the SADC Tribunal shown more deference to Zimbabwean law in the *Campbell* case with a view to a slower but steadier development of human rights protection in the region by following the pattern described above, it could, I would suggest, have contributed to a more efficient enhancement of rights

[57] *LMJ*, 295–304.

[58] *LMJ*, 374 with reference to Finnis, n 5, 362.

[59] *LMJ*, 374.

[60] De Wet, n 46, 18, with reference to OC Ruppel and FX Bangwamwabo, 'The SADC Tribunal: A Legal Analysis of Its Mandate and Role in Regional Integration' (2007) 8 *Monitoring Regional Integration in Southern Africa Yearbook* 187.

protection in the region. By using a margin of appreciation approach or a similar kind of principle, in combination with a more explicit and detailed account of the legitimacy of addressing historical wrongs, it could have been possible for the Tribunal to both criticise the Zimbabwean government for not sufficiently addressing the issues of discrimination and just compensation without ruling outright against the government. And doing so could well have benefited both *Campbell* and the citizens of the SADC region as a whole.

What the *Campbell* case shows, therefore, is that law and legal reasoning, even when perceived from a strong natural law perspective like that laid out by Beyleveld and Brownsword, is closely related to politics. Consequently, legal analysis must connect to political analysis. Just as there can be no sharp separation between law and morality, so too can there be no sharp separation of law from politics.

Ultimately jurisprudence can only be analytically separated from political prudence. In social practice, jurisprudence and political prudence are closely interwoven.

12

Legal Idealism and Global Law

PATRICK CAPPS*

I. Introduction

The public international legal order regulates the relations between the 200 or so sovereign states in the world. It is an interstate system, in which states themselves have discretion to create public international laws through their direct or indirect consent. Public international laws, in the form of multilateral treaties, constitute the powers of suprastate organisations, such as the United Nations. This is how classical international legal positivism[1] explains the legal authority of international organisations. Public international law and state legal orders can be said to be interlocking and mutually supportive components of a system of *global law*.[2] What is noticeable about the positivist conception of global law just described is that the sovereign state is the *locus* of legal authority.

It is well established that over the last few decades a complex system of global administration has emerged. The positivist struggles to explain how a significant proportion of global administration may have authority because its exercise of power cannot be traced back to state consent. Contrary to the positivist position, I argue in this chapter that state consent should be understood as one way in which political and economic power may be *mobilised* to create global administration, but it should not be mistaken as being *constitutive* of the authority of global administration. In order to develop this claim, I make use of the very similar conceptions of authority set out in *Law and Moral Judgment* (*LMJ*)[3] by Deryck Beyleveld and Roger Brownsword and the *Doctrine of Right* (*Rechtslehre*, *RL*) by

* Professor of International Law, University of Bristol. Thanks to Deryck Beyleveld, Henrik Palmer Olsen and Shaun Pattinson for comments on an earlier draft of this chapter. The ideas in this chapter have been presented at the University of Cambridge, Durham University and Utrecht University.

[1] See J Kammerhofer and J d'Aspremont, *International Legal Positivism in a Postmodern World* (CUP, 2014) ch 1.

[2] See H Kelsen, 'Sovereignty' in SL Paulson and BL Paulson (eds), *Normativity and Norms* (Clarendon Press, 1998) ch 28.

[3] D Beyleveld and R Brownsword, *Law as a Moral Judgment* (Sweet and Maxwell, 1986, reprinted by Sheffield University Press, 1994).

Immanuel Kant.[4] To begin with, though, it is useful to situate my argument by outlining what is meant by global administration.

II. Global Administration

Global administration refers to a set of non-state administrative bodies that have a reach that is not jurisdictionally restricted to the territory or nationals of one state, and which have specific and specialised regulatory mandates to, for example, regulate human rights, peace and security or markets. Richard Stewart claims that global administrative bodies have a public or private nature, or they can be a public/private hybrid.[5] Public administrative bodies are created by treaties between effective states (for example the United Nations) or through intergovernmental networks of domestic regulators (for example the European Systemic Risk Board (ESRB)). Private administrative bodies are created by non-state actors such as a group of companies in a particular sector of the economy (for example GLOBALG.A.P., which is a private sector body, whose membership is dominated by European producers and retailers of agricultural produce, and which sets ostensibly voluntary standards for the safety certification of agricultural production processes).[6]

Stewart's distinction between public and private forms of global administration should not be misunderstood as either replicating or implying the positivist conception of authority, or describing two different methods of governance by various global administrative bodies. Rather, it is my view that his distinction is best understood as referring to the manner in which political and economic power is mobilised to create global administration. Sometimes it is mobilised through the combined will of states, and sometimes through economic or other actors. This point can be expanded in at least four ways.

First, many bodies that are classified as public will have deep interconnections with private industry and private forms of global administration, and *vice versa*.[7] Also, academics have tracked the relatively fluid movement of

[4] *RL* forms the first part of I Kant, *The Metaphysics of Morals*. I refer to Kant's works as found in the Academy edition of the *Gesammmelte Schriften*, and cite the volume and page number in square brackets. Translations are to I Kant, *Groundwork of the Metaphysics of Morals* (HJ Paton tr, published as *The Moral Law*, Hutchinson, 1972) (vol 4 in Academy edition); I Kant, *The Metaphysics of Morals* (M Gregor tr, CUP, 1996) (vol 6 in Academy edition). My claims presented here about the model of authority in *RL* are defended in 'Authority and the Omnilateral Will' (2017, unpublished *MS*).

[5] R Stewart, 'Remedying Disregard in Global Regulatory Governance: Accountability, Participation, and Responsiveness' (2014) 108 *American Journal of International Law* 211.

[6] See N Hachez and J Wouters, 'A Glimpse at the Democratic Legitimacy of Private Standards: Assessing the Public Accountability of GLOBALG.A.P.' (2011) 14 *Journal of International Economic Law* 677, 682.

[7] M Goldmann, 'Inside Relative Normativity: From Sources to Standard Instruments for the Exercise of International Public Authority' (2008) 9 *German Law Journal* 1865, 1866.

administrative functions from treaty-based bodies to private business via the privatisation of forms of global administration. The most notorious example of this is the use of private companies to perform military and security functions on behalf of the state.[8] Another is the listing of those suspected of funding terrorism by the Security Council's 1267 Committee, which is now replicated by equivalent listings produced by private agencies, such as World Check (which is owned by Thompson Reuters).[9] Second, there is no substantial and principled difference in the form of administrative structures associated with private and public bodies.[10] Third, both public and private forms of global administration, on Stewart's classification, purport to resolve co-ordination problems, make judgements on the distribution of rights, or order coercively. For example, on the one hand, the ESRB (a public body established by the European Commission) claims to have a supervisory, and not a regulatory, role. On the other hand, it is well accepted that refusal to embrace GLOBALG.A.P.'s certification programme will result in suppliers of agricultural produce being *de facto* frozen out of major economic markets. Fourth, both public and private bodies are keen to establish their authoritative credentials to engage in coercive ordering. Both forms of global administration appeal to, for example, semantic authority,[11] epistemic authority or domestic administrative law concepts, although it is only some public forms of global administration that can look to state consent to ground their authority.

III. Coercion and Authority

Some may disagree with one of the arguments just made. They argue that to deprive a farmer of access to markets is simply not an act of coercive ordering. Rather, so the argument goes, this is simply the deprivation of a private benefit that GLOBALG.A.P. can distribute on whatever terms it likes. Its regulatory code is, then, voluntary and private, and there is no coercion involved. It is administered through a limited liability company incorporated in Germany and we tend not to think of companies as being forms of coercive ordering. Why is GLOBALG.A.P. any different? Surely, following this line of argument, the issue of whether GLOBALG.A.P.'s system of certification is authoritative is otiose?

[8] E Krahmann, *States, Citizens and the Privatization of Security* (CUP, 2010).

[9] See M de Goede and G Sullivan, 'The Politics of Security Listing' (2015) *Environment and Planning D: Society and Space* 1.

[10] S Cassese, 'Administrative Law without the State? The Challenge of Global Regulation' (2005) 37 *New York University Journal of International Law and Politics* 663.

[11] Semantic authority is 'an actor's capacity to influence and shape means as well as the ability to establish communications as authoritative reference points in legal discourse. Not only does an actor with authority influence the meaning of given norm texts, but its communications structure the space of contestation … To have authority is distinct from having power in that it implies a certain degree of deferred judgement on the part of others': I Venzke, *How Interpretation Makes International Law: On Semantic Change and Normative Twists* (OUP, 2012) 63.

While those advocating 'freedom of contract' might endorse this sort of argument, it has been regarded with scepticism for a long time. During the proliferation of state administration connected to the 'New Deal', Justice Owen Roberts considered whether agricultural subsidies—given to farmers on the condition that they restricted their agricultural output—were simply inducements that could be voluntarily accepted or rejected, or were rather an attempt at coercive ordering. Although ultimately striking down the subsidy legislation on the grounds that it violated commercial freedom, in *United States v Butler* he said:

> [t]he regulation is not in fact voluntary. The farmer, of course, may refuse to comply, but the price of such refusal is the loss of benefits. The amount offered is intended to be sufficient to exert pressure on him to agree to the proposed regulation. The power to confer or withhold unlimited benefits is the power to coerce or destroy. If the cotton grower elects not to accept the benefits, he will receive less for his crops; those who receive payments will be able to undersell him. The result may well be financial ruin ... This is coercion by economic pressure. The asserted power of choice is illusory.[12]

Likewise compliance to GLOBALG.A.P.'s regulatory scheme reaps benefits to, for example, western consumers, but the refusal to comply will restrict suppliers' access to key markets, and may put some of them out of business. So, what may appear to be simple market pressure becomes what Karl Llewellyn called the 'exercise of unofficial government of some by others'[13] given power inequities in this area of global economic activity.

Global administration, as a form of coercive ordering, may have authority or it may not. The implications of the coercive acts of global administration being authoritative is that the agent cannot rationally complain when subjected to that coercion. But that same agent can rationally object to the attempt by unauthorised global administration to order coercively, by seeking to *block* (for example by seeking judicial review) or *reform* (by mobilising political or economic power) the exercise of coercion.[14]

Here are two familiar ways by which we might begin to answer questions about when global administration may be authorised. As mentioned in the introduction, the classical international legal positivist holds that global administration has authority to the extent that it is constituted by the exercise of state consent. That is, consent is sufficient, on this model, to afford a pre-emptive reason why those subject to a global administrative body should act in accordance with its directives, and not act on other reasons. Strictly, assuming the listing of individuals by the Security Council is *intra vires* against the UN Charter, it has authority, and those subject to listing have no rational reason to complain about the

[12] *United States v Butler*, 297 US 1 (1936). Cited in R Hale, 'Our Equivocal Constitutional Guarantees' (1939) 39 *Columbia Law Review* 563, 578–79.

[13] K Llewellyn, 'What Price Contract? An Essay in Perspective' (1931) 40 *Yale Law Journal* 704, 731.

[14] On 'blocking' and 'reform' see 229–231, below.

exercise of coercion *given* the validity of the positivist model.[15] However, global administrative bodies that are not developed through the exercise of state consent (such as GLOBALG.A.P.) do not have authority. On the positivist account, while GLOBALG.A.P.'s internal procedures may be intended to give it an air of administrative rigour, it is better understood as a sort of cartel which uses the economic clout of its members to push around economically and organisationally weak farmers in developing states.

A different view is offered by Lon Fuller. In Chapter 3 of *The Morality of Law* he adopts a position close to pluralism or realism.[16] He explains that law—the enterprise of subjecting human conduct to the governance of rules—is an enterprise which stretches far beyond traditional state boundaries to clubs, churches, universities and beyond. And these bodies have authority to subject human conduct to the governance of rules to the extent that they comply with the inner morality of law. The same reasoning would undoubtedly apply to global administration. In principle, a body such as GLOBALG.A.P. could have authority to the extent that its rules are clear, promulgated, and so on.

Both *RL* and *LMJ* adopt an approach that is similar to Fuller's on this point. It is my view that both would accept that global administration, to the extent that it is a successful attempt at ordering through the exercise of power, ought to be authoritative.[17] To explain, in *RL*, Kant argues that successful agency alters the external world and, specifically, it restricts the capacity of others to act on their purposes. Coercion in a narrow and technical sense describes, then, simply a feature of successful action. Coercion, then, may be justified—authorised—or not: thus, 'Right and the authorization to use coercion mean one and the same thing'.[18] There must be an authorisation for coercive acts undertaken by individual agents, as well as for systematic, organised and institutionalised attempts to order human conduct through rules. If institutions do not coerce authoritatively, they should be reorganised so that they do. This is why, for Kant, the social contract should be understood as a successful attempt to reorganise the *unilateral* coercive structures which characterise the state of nature, so that they become authoritative *omnilateral* coercive structures. Authoritative omnilateral coercive structures need not take the form of the state. Omnilateral structures can, in international relations, be established by a *non-coercive confederation of republican states* which is administered by a congress modelled on those associated with Ancient Greek Amphictyonic Leagues and the

[15] On other models of authority that prioritise the rule of law and due process there is considerable reason for complaint. See also S Talmon, 'The Security Council as World Legislature' (2005) 99 *American Journal of International Law* 175.

[16] L Fuller, *The Morality of Law* (Yale University Press, 1963, revised edition, 1969) 124–29.

[17] On this point, see Roger Brownsword's contribution to this volume.

[18] [6: 232].

States-General in The Hague in the eighteenth century. Both were little more than a 'neutral space for competitive interaction'.[19]

Similarly, in *LMJ* Beyleveld and Brownsword write:

> the processes of Legal Ordering are not confined to those formal and institutionalized activities which involve a legislature and courts. They extend to executive and administrative decisions, to the activities of public inquiries, and other 'quasi-Legal' bodies, but most importantly, they extend to wholly informal, sometimes only tacit, processes of negotiation and social intercourse at all levels of social life. None of these processes or levels is inherently or centrally more Legal than the others.[20]

Authority arises when any attempt to order through the exercise of power by any agent or institution is consistent with Alan Gewirth's Principle of Generic Consistency (PGC).

For both Kant and Beyleveld and Brownsword it can be safely assumed, then, that those forms of social ordering that we call global administration may be authoritative. But I believe their actual position to be that *because forms of global administration order*, they ought to be authoritative. This, then, begs a justification of the conditions in which authority arises.

IV. The Model of Authority in *RL* and *LMJ*

There are three circumstances in which authority arises in *RL* and *LMJ*.

Ethical Laws

In general, and for the same reason as with any individual act, the directives of a system of coercive ordering have moral authority if those directives impose duties to uphold, or prohibit conduct that violates, the supreme principle of morality. For, Kant this principle is the Categorical Imperative. Kant argues that *ethical laws* are positive, but the authority for their imposition is drawn directly from the perfect moral *duties* that follow logically from the Categorical Imperative. They are 'obligatory *a priori* by reason even without external law-giving.'[21] Likewise, in *LMJ*, one of the ways by which an official has sufficient authority to impose legal norms is if the content of those legal norms follows directly from the PGC.[22] These laws are

[19] J Hall, 'International Relations' in P Sabin, H van Wees and M Whitby (eds) (2007) 1 *The Cambridge History of Free and Roman Warfare* 85, 100. This summary is based upon P Capps and J Rivers, 'Kant's Concept of International Law' (2010) 16 *Legal Theory* 229.

[20] *LMJ*, 163.

[21] [6: 224].

[22] *LMJ*, 292.

equivalent in form to Kant's ethical laws.[23] When ethical laws are imposed, the act of legislation adds no new reasons for agents: they have a categorical obligation to act morally, and rationally cannot complain if they are coerced (using proportionate force)[24] to do so. Although as a matter of fact there will be some who disagree with the content of ethical laws within a morally diverse society, the supreme principle of morality is capable of settling these disputes and directing the content of ethical laws. By way of example, murder, violence and fraud should be prohibited by ethical laws according to both the categorical imperative and the PGC.

In matters of empirical complexity, experts can engage in a detailed analysis of the relevant perfect moral rights and duties in light of the best empirical knowledge. In such circumstances, the expert official claims epistemic authority in her own person, but no new reasons for compliance are added. The expert official has merely clarified what is required by the perfect moral rights and duties possessed by each agent.

Ethical laws raise difficulties for a complete theory of the authority of law for two reasons. First, for both the Categorical Imperative and the PGC, there are either correlative perfect moral rights and duties, or there is moral discretion.[25] One might think that so long as agents do not violate the perfect right and duties they are under, they can pursue their life plans and otherwise act as they choose. However, to enforce legislation on matters of moral discretion or choice would seem to deny those agents, who choose to act in ways inconsistent with that legislation, their choice. Second, ethical laws presuppose that there is one relevant moral duty that is given expression in an act of legislation. Even the simplest moral prohibitions, when raised to the level of generality of legislation, require the balancing of competing perfect moral rights and duties.[26] And, furthermore, while a Herculean judge[27] may be able to rationally optimise competing moral rights and duties, in many circumstances there may be disagreement. Strictly, Kant regards such disagreement about the validity or weight or perfect duties as 'inconceivable' simply because 'the stronger *ground of obligation* prevails'.[28] But as a matter of fact,

[23] Like Kant, Gewirth accepts that there are categorical moral obligations, but his claim is that each agent has generic rights, whereas Kant's focus is on establishing moral duties. That said, given a correlativity between rights and duties, it does not do a disservice to either Kant or Gewirth to treat their arguments to be formally similar and their conclusions about the moral obligations agents owe to each other to be substantively similar. Both argue for *perfect* moral rights and duties. On the analytical relationship between the PGC and the Categorical Imperative, see D Beyleveld, 'Gewirth and Kant on Justifying the Supreme Principle of Morality' in M Boylan (ed), *Gewirth. Critical Essays on Action, Rationality, and Community* (Rowman and Littlefield, 1999) 97–117.

[24] See M Willaschek, 'Which Imperatives for Right? On the Non-Prescriptive Character of Juridical Law in Kant's Metaphysics of Morals', in M Timmons (ed), *Kant's Metaphysics of Morals: Interpretative Essays* (OUP, 2002) ch 3.

[25] This is the case even though moral discretion is structured by imperfect duties for Kant (so to not pursue these duties is evidence of moral deficiency rather than moral culpability).

[26] See R Alexy, *A Theory of Constitutional Rights* (OUP, 2009).

[27] R Dworkin, *Taking Rights Seriously* (Duckworth, 1977) 105–23.

[28] [6: 225]. For discussion of this point, see L MacInnis, 'The Kantian Core of Law as Integrity' (2015) 6 *Jurisprudence* 45, 56–57.

the officials and judges we know of are not Herculean, but still a decision has to be made in a way that is authoritative. Therefore, in matters of moral optionality and disagreement, a theory of authority is required that does not rely upon an appeal to consistency with perfect moral rights and duties as its justificatory basis.

Moral Optionality and Juridical Laws

Kant's view is that the structuring of moral optionality at the level of the political community is the function of juridical laws. Juridical laws establish, for example, whether charity is to be left to individual personal beneficence or systematically organised through welfare, or whether the development and self-improvement of the young is to be facilitated through a public or private system of education. Those areas of social life that are a matter of discretion are more limited for Gewirth given his endorsement of perfect *positive* rights. Agents have perfect rights to educational provision and welfare for Gewirth, and these rights should be given effect by institutions of government. In this sub-section, I will focus mainly on Kant's treatment of moral optionality given the limited treatment of the subject in *Reason and Morality* and *LMJ*.

Why should matters of moral optionality and discretion be organised at the level of the political community through juridical laws? One argument is that the exercise of individual discretion gives rise to co-ordination problems. A familiar example is choice in relation to the side of the road someone drives on. As is argued in *LMJ*,[29] this co-ordination problem results from the exercise of freedom in a way that would reliably lead to the violation of the moral right to well-being. Rules that resolve the co-ordination problem justify a minor infringement of freedom to drive where one wishes, so as to prevent the violation of a more fundamental right.[30] By itself, this reasoning invokes a very sparse category of juridical laws: (i) juridical laws should not violate weighty perfect moral rights and duties (where 'the stronger ground of obligation prevails'), but otherwise they may have any content and be made by any procedure; and (ii) the authority of juridical laws emerges from the same source as ethical laws as both enforce against violations of perfect moral duties. Kant rejects both (i) and (ii). Rejecting (i), he argues that the authority of juridical laws emerges from the procedural as well as substantive constraints placed on law making. Rejecting (ii), he argues that there are special reasons for the enforcement of juridical laws, which, I believe, give rise to his theory of *political* authority.

To explain his full position, it is helpful to consider a political community governed by an aristocracy in which a privileged few legislate juridical laws for the

[29] *LMJ*, 178–79 and *Consent and the Law* (Hart, 2007) 316–17.

[30] On the distinction between 'fulfilment', 'infringement' and 'violation' of rights (which is an unjustified infringement of a right) see A Gewirth, 'Are There Any Absolute Rights?' (1981) 31 *The Philosophical Quarterly* 1, 2.

whole of the community. Juridical laws legislated for by this aristocracy would be consistent with (i) and (ii) so long as those laws do not violate ethical laws. However, by definition, there are differential political rights in that society, and juridical laws only take direct account of choices of some members. Certain agents' choices about matters of moral optionality are subordinated to those with political participation rights, even if those other agents' perfect rights and duties are taken into account by those with political rights. This aristocracy is a form of government that fails to respect the 'mutual recognition of free and responsible agents' as Bielefeldt puts it in his discussion of Kant's moral philosophy.[31] And this failure to recognise fellow community members as free and responsible agents capable of exercising choice violates the categorical imperative (specifically, the 'formula of autonomy').[32]

To avoid this conclusion, law creation must conform to four constraints. The first constraint, which has already been discussed, is that juridical laws cannot be inconsistent with perfect moral duties.[33] The second constraint is 'lawful consent' to juridical law. Third, each citizen must have '[c]ivil equality': juridical law making should not recognise 'among the *people* any superior with the moral capacity to bind him as a matter of right in a way that he could not in turn bind the other'.[34] Jointly lawful consent and civil equality are the basis for political rights that allow each citizen to have an equal chance to influence the content of juridical laws, and by implication requires the rejection of all forms of government based upon unequal allocation of these political rights (such as aristocratic government). Fourth, 'the attribute of civil independence, of owning his existence and preservation to his own rights and powers as a member of the commonwealth, not to the choice of another among the people'[35] requires that each citizen must be able to participate as a moral, motivated, purposive agent without suffering unjustified hindrances from other members.[36] Citizens should have legally enforceable rights that express the four constraints just set out, against the institutions that govern their conduct such as the state. The four constraints just mentioned can be said to *constitute* freedom within a political community. Officials have *political* authority[37] to impose juridical laws if they respect these constraints. On this argument, political authority arises because each citizen recognises that they have a moral duty under the categorical imperative not to subordinate the will of others to their own will (by insisting that they have their way, that their views on the application

[31] H Bielefeldt, *Symbolic Representation in Kant's Practical Philosophy* (CUP, 2003) 99.

[32] HJ Paton, *The Moral Law* (Hutchinson, 1972, trans of Kant's *Groundwork of the Metaphysic of Morals*) [4: 430–31].

[33] Kant writes: 'these laws must still not be contrary to the natural laws of freedom and of the equality of everyone in the people corresponding to this freedom' [6: 315].

[34] [6: 314].

[35] [6: 313–14].

[36] How this cashes out within Kant's republican framework is unclear. It is unlikely that Kant envisaged that it required substantial economic reordering in the way it would for Rousseau, Marx, or, indeed, Beyleveld and Brownsword.

[37] See J Raz, *The Morality of Freedom* (Oxford, Clarendon Press, 1986) ch 4.

of morality are superior to others, or that they are infallible) and so they have a moral obligation to act on properly constituted juridical laws, and not on their own subjective or unilateral moral judgements.

Juridical Laws and Moral Disagreement

As mentioned, Beyleveld and Brownsword afford little space to considering the relationship between law and moral optionality in *LMJ*, although where it is discussed, their arguments appear similar to those offered by Kant.[38] Instead, they focus more on legal strategies for dealing with moral *disagreement*. Within highly complex and morally diverse societies such as ours, this position is understandable. Before exploring the position that is set out in *LMJ*, it is worth noting a difference between moral optionality and moral disagreement. There is no sense in which there is a correct moral answer in matters of optionality, although certain combinations of optional action may lead to infringements of perfect rights and duties as we have seen. By constrast, disagreement over perfect moral rights and duties concerns competing views on the application, or balancing, of those rights and duties in complex social situations. Potentially, these views may reflect better or correct moral answers. There may also be disagreement as to whether the issue to be legislated on is a matter in which perfect moral duties apply, or whether the matter is one of optionality.[39]

With these differences in mind, let us turn to Beyleveld and Brownsword's treatment of moral disagreement in *LMJ*. Their starting position is that legal officials should make a 'sincere, serious, and commensurate attempt to apply the PGC (that is, a good faith attempt)'.[40] If they do so, they have authority of some kind. Taken out of context it is unclear what their constraint implies given the distinction between optionality and disagreement just made. I raise this because there are at least two possibilities upon which a claim to authority could be generated in accordance with 'a good faith attempt'.

First, it could be that the official claims authority because she, in her role as official, is better able to get the right, better, or optimal moral answer when attempting to apply the PGC. Implicit here is that this attempt must *succeed*, when legislating or adjudicating, in establishing an optimum, or at least rationally defensible outcome against the PGC, if that attempt is to be authoritative. Particular forms of legal institution are authoritative, then, to the extent that they are part of an *instrumentally* 'rational strategy for handling moral controversy'.[41] Specifically, this means that a particular set of institutions is more likely to achieve a rationally defensible

[38] See *Consent and the Law*, n 29, 322–23.
[39] ibid, 317–18.
[40] *LMJ*, 293.
[41] *LMJ*, 282.

legal outcome against the PGC, relative to other configurations of institutions. Democratic institutions, and judicial review, are to be considered justified procedures to the extent that they are instrumentally rational in this sense. This, however, leaves open the possibility that the reverse could be the case: perhaps, 'government by experts' could be instrumentally rational when compared to democratic institutions.[42] Either way, officials, whether expert or democratically elected, may claim *epistemic* authority. However, those institutions add no new reasons to those that citizens already have. For this reason, the authority of law is ethical.

Second, in a way that is similar to Kant's juridical laws, the political authority of an official arises to the extent that she imposes legal directives within a community within which each member has equal legal rights to participate in the formation, and challenge the imposition, of the official's directives.

At places *LMJ* seems to offer an instrumental account of authority in that Beyleveld and Brownsword justifiably take the view that the content of law should conform as far as possible to PGC.[43] But in the end they adopt a 'Theory of Restraint' which is close to Kant's argument for the political authority of juridical laws. The theory is based upon two central ideas. The first is an account of the 'human social condition', which is that 'we are not morally omniscient, we are prepared to fight for our agental interests (whether or not conceived as moral interests), and resources are limited'.[44] The second is that citizens should both accept that they have moral duties to others, but are also rationally aware that they, like all other human agents, are morally fallible. For citizens to reject this second idea implies moral idealism, which is 'the danger of individuals settling for no version of the moral truth than their own'.[45] This is because 'the enterprise of constructing a legal order can only stand so much of citizens following their own moral lights … It is imperative, therefore, that citizens exercise some degree of restraint.'[46] I think that this point can be supported by Kant's argument for juridical law. That is, moral idealism implies a claim to epistemic superiority over the judgements of others, and to claim this implies a failure to respect others as equal members of a community. Conversely, it is the rational recognition of one's fallibility in light of one's moral duties to others which justifies why one should exercise restraint, and why a citizen should reserve judgement on the quality of law. But while citizens should not refuse to comply with laws, the content of which runs against their own moral judgements, they may have a point, and coercive institutions must afford each citizen an equal and meaningful opportunity to challenge the con-

[42] On this possibility see N Kolodny, 'Rules Over None I: What Justifies Democracy?' (2014) 42 *Philosophy and Public Affairs* 195, eg 202–03.

[43] *LMJ*, 368–69. See also D Beyleveld and R Brownsword, 'Principle, Proceduralism, and Precaution in a Community of Rights' (2006) 19 *Ratio Juris* 141, 149.

[44] *LMJ*, 369.

[45] ibid.

[46] ibid.

tent of their directives against the PGC.[47] In their major follow-up paper on this matter, Beyleveld and Brownsword make it clear that this is their view:

> What matters … is that [citizens] have the opportunity to participate and that the process of appointment of government and legislature … be a reviewable one that is itself transparent, fair, and so on. The reason why this is enough is because the citizens … respect the generic rights [justified by the PGC] of all agents and understand that no agent is infallible, thus that they are not infallible … They do not, therefore, insist on their own views at all costs. To do so is to place the most basic values that the PGC protects under threat both at the level of likely effects and the level of respect for the autonomy of other agents.[48]

But more than this, directives are not authoritative because they are morally optimal against the PGC in matters of disagreement, although moral optimality is an important *aspiration* of rational law making. It is the duty each agent has to respect others as agents, and exercise restraint, that explains why laws have political authority and why legal directives pre-empt individual moral judgements. Law is not authoritative because it aspires to, or achieves, moral perfection.

V. Authority and Global Administration

We can now return to the issue of the authority of global administration. Coercive ordering by global administration should be authoritative, and hence should take the form of ethical or juridical law.

Ethical Global Administrative Law

Stewart explains, in his discussion of 'disregard' in global administration, that the content of its directives often substantively coincides with the interests of powerful and organised economic and political groupings.[49] Furthermore, disregard by global administration is a cause of substantive harms to the objective 'interests and concerns'[50] of weaker and poorly organised political and economic groups. GLOBALG.A.P.'s attempts at regulation are a possible example of this issue. Poor farmers on small farms in less economically developed areas of the world have

[47] *LMJ*, 372.

[48] Beyleveld and Brownsword, 'Principle, Proceduralism and Precaution in a Community of Rights', n 43, 152.

[49] Stewart, n 5.

[50] Stewart defines 'interests' as 'grounded in the material conditions of human welfare, including sustenance, health, security, housing, and education, that can be more or less objectively determined'. 'Concerns' reflect 'values like individual dignity, justice and equity, integrity of institutions and community, and cultural, religious, social, and ecological ideals' (ibid, 212). 'Interests' overlap substantially with Gewirth's generic goods, although 'concerns' do so less.

suffered significant harms as a result of a failure to be accredited by GLOBALG.A.P. Simply, GLOBALG.A.P.'s certification procedure favours large-scale agribusiness that can operate on economies of scale. Farmers with small farms are either unable to afford to instigate safety measures to gain certification, or are frozen out of large markets. Either way, a putative right to well-being of poor farmers with small farms is infringed by GLOBALG.A.P.'s regulatory scheme. The directives of GLOBALG.A.P appear to not be morally authorised.

That said, we should not lose sight of the fact that GLOBALG.A.P. attempts to regulate to secure food safety for consumers. So, one might hypothesise that a relaxation of food standards may give effect to, or at least not infringe, the rights of some farmers, but it may result in the failure to give effect to, or an infringement of, the rights to well-being of consumers in the West.[51] It may be that small farms are simply less safe than large-scale agribusiness, and surely this is a morally relevant consideration. The point is that when GLOBALG.A.P. successfully orders through coercion, it will often infringe the rights of someone in its attempt to fulfil the rights of others, and its authority claim to do so must be justified. If its authority claim is justified, those subject to that coercion should not rationally object to its imposition, but they should rationally object if its authority claim is not justified. And this is a restatement of what these farmers are doing: they claim that GLOBALG.A.P.'s authority claim to infringe their rights is unjustified. But if this is remedied by GLOBALG.A.P., it may lead to infringements of the rights to well-being of consumers who are now subject to unsafe food. And then this infringement must be grounded on a justified authority claim. That is, there is disagreement how the effects of coercion to groups of agents' well-being should be distributed. How can disagreement be resolved in a way that is authoritative?

Epistemic Authority and Global Administration

Before we turn to what I believe to be the answer to this question, we should pause to consider epistemic authority. To explain, GLOBALG.A.P.'s claim to authority may be justified to the extent that it establishes a regulatory accreditation scheme that addresses problems of the global public good of food safety. For suppliers, adhering to the accreditation scheme allows them to provide safer food and thus reduce the probability, or severity, of a violation of the right to well-being of consumers. It could, then, be said that a farmer is better able to comply with the reasons that apply to him if he follows GLOBALG.A.P.'s accreditation scheme. But global food safety is not the only morally relevant concern. As we have seen, the obligation to provide safe food has to be balanced against the right to well-being of farmers.

To consider this issue, it is useful to turn to the ESRB, which is another body that claims epistemic authority. The ESRB's aims are to co-ordinate the policies

[51] See Hachez and Wouters, n 6.

of various bodies (for example, EU states and their central banks) so as to help ameliorate the risks of another global banking crisis. The ESRB is not considered a directly binding regulatory body, but instead asks that states act in accordance with its recommendations (on, for example, banks holding minimum capital requirements), or explain the reasons why they choose not to do so. States are rated by the ESRB according to the extent to which they comply. The governments of states, which have a plurality of other issues to balance alongside the riskiness of their banking system, can decide whether to act in accordance with these recommendations or not.

Having a stable banking system is a morally justified aim, and achievement of this aim by banking systems within the European Union is purported to be facilitated by the ESRB. The authority claim of the ESRB seems to be epistemic because it must, at least implicitly, claim that the risk of a future banking crisis is reduced if its recommendations are followed.

If the authority claim of the ESRB is best interpreted as being epistemic it may come as a surprise how much attention has been devoted to issues relating to its internal decision-making structures, as they resemble those that would be important if it were to claim political authority. Its internal structure comprises 65 members, 37 with voting rights, among whom are the governors of the 27 EU state central banks, President and Vice-President of the ECB, a member of the European Commission and the Chairpersons of three other European Supervisory Authorities. In its annual reports, the ESRB takes care to explain how it is to be accountable and transparent.

Commentators have worried that the ESRB is not accountable in the right way because its decision-making bodies do not represent those whom its recommendations affect. For example, Willem Buiter writes:

> Macro-prudential regulation and supervision inevitably involves guiding and [directing] the actions of, and even determining the fate of, large systemically important individual financial institutions. Such institutional life-or-death decisions involve property rights and other important distributional and wider political dimensions, as well as technical issues. They are inherently political, even party-political.[52]

But if the ESRB only claims epistemic authority on matters of banking risk, one may wonder why Buiter, and the ESRB itself, is so concerned about its procedural fairness. If it makes the right decisions, why should we care how it is procedurally constituted?

Here is a suggestion as to why this concern arises. At first blush the ESRB simply diagnoses the economic health of a state's banking system, and prescribes measures which can improve a banking system's health or limit the harm that may be caused by the way it functions. But as Ferran and Alexander suggest, there appear

[52] See the Treasury Committee's Opinion on Proposals for European Financial Supervision (Sixteenth Report of Session 2008–09) Ev 25.

to be serious and unavoidable reputational and economic consequences for a state that does not follow the ESRB's recommendations, which can be seriously destabilising for state economies.[53] What was sound advice about how one relevant moral concern might be given effect in economic policy, which must be balanced by states against other moral concerns, turns into an overriding concern of state policy because of the consequences for a state of being deemed to have a risky banking system. These consequences give the ESRB considerable coercive power similar to that considered in section II of this chapter, and this exercise of power needs to be justified by a valid argument for authority. The ESRB seems to attempt to justify this claim through procedures. However, why could the ESRB not validly claim epistemic authority? My view is that it cannot claim authority in this way because the ESRB is not simply issuing technical advice on a matter of moral concern, but instead its recommendations are undergirded by certain disputable, and 'highly sensitive and politically-charged'[54] premises about what sort of economic principles should underpin the regulation of economic risk within the European Union, and how those principles should be weighed against others. That is, there is fundamental disagreement about what sort of principles should be at the heart of judgements about banking risk. The existence of this disagreement explains why those affected by the ESRB's activities, rather than just those with fiscal or political power, should have a say in which macro-economic principles should underpin the attempt at regulation. This not only possibly motivates the efforts of the ESRB to develop its procedures, but it is also the basis for Buiter's concern with those same procedures. It is, fundamentally, the right problem that any attempt to establish global juridical administrative law, such as GLOBALG.A.P., which claims to authoritatively resolve disagreement, must seek to resolve.

Global Juridical Administrative Law

As established in section III, political authority of coercive institutions arises because each agent subject to it has certain political rights to lawful consent, civil equality and civil independence and not because the answer is optimal against perfect moral rights and duties. Moral optimality is an instrumental aspiration, but not the authoritative basis, of a well-formed system of juridical law making. The authority of global juridical administrative law is based upon the provision of these same political rights. These, alongside the substantive constraints of direct moral duties and rights, are institutional *ex ante* constraints on the formation of law, which presumably should be challengeable and remedied *ex post* if not adhered to.

[53] E Ferran and K Alexander, 'Can Soft Law Bodies be Effective? Soft Systemic Risk Oversight Bodies and the Special Case of the European Systemic Risk Board' (2010) *European Law Review* 751.
[54] ibid.

But global administration, like its state counterpart, is not simply concerned with simple 'command and control'[55] regulation in which directives are created and enforced. Alongside this function, inter alia, global administrative bodies co-ordinate, they supervise, they incentivise, they monitor or measure, and they mediate, arbitrate or adjudicate, and they also hold *other* bodies to account. Thus, Kant's procedural and substantive constraints do not straightforwardly map onto global administrative bodies with these functions.

We need to step back to move forwards. What underpins the constraints that give rise to political authority in *RL* and *LMJ* is the need to ensure that relevant agents are placed in a legally structured relationship with global administration so that it authentically expresses those agents' combined will. But as Oliver Wendell Holmes points out: '[w]here a rule of conduct applies to more than a few people it is impractical that everyone should have a direct voice in its adoption … Their rights are protected in the only way that they can be in a complex society, by their power, immediate or remote, over those who make the rule.'[56] So the relationship between global administration, and those subject to its attempt at regulation, can be structured in different ways, so long as global administration can be effectively *held to account* by those subject to it.

Stewart points out that it is not that global administration fails for a *lack* of accountability. Rather, the problem is that it tends to be accountable to the most powerful states and economic actors, and 'disregards' weakly organised and less powerful states and political and economic groups.[57] Global administration manifestly and generally fails to establish juridical law because it fails to afford an equal say in its decisions and directives to all those affected by it. Put another way, global administration fails to establish authoritative governance for similar reasons to the aristocratic form of governance discussed in section III. Both fail to institutionalise respect for the free choice of those affected by these attempts at governance.

Stewart's remedy for this problem is to restructure accountability within global administration. He envisages five types of accountability ((i) electoral; (ii) hierarchical; (iii) supervisory; (iv) fiscal; and, (v) legal) and considers all possibly appropriate to establish accountability in the global administrative space depending upon the powers and character of the particular global administrative body. I remain open to all of these possibilities, while recognising that the expectation is not that there is *some* form of accountability, but rather that accountability establishes a particular relationship between global administration and those subject to it, secured by the ubiquity of Kant's criteria of lawful consent, civil equality and civil independence within global administration, which is undergirded by direct moral rights and duties.

[55] R Stewart, 'Administrative Law in the Twenty-First Century' (2003) 78 *New York University Law Review* 437.

[56] *Bi-Metallic Investment Co v State Bd of Equalization*, 239 US 411, 445 (1915) (cited from Stewart, n 35, 228).

[57] Stewart, n 5, 213.

As mentioned, GLOBALG.A.P.'s decision-making processes are dominated by large, western, retail chains and the ESRB is dominated by European banks. Thus both tend to disregard the free choice of many affected by their decisions. If this is the case, by what means should they reform?

Reform of Global Administration

The positivist model of authority has it that political authority is rooted on state consent. Coercive ordering is authorised for global administrative bodies to the extent that states have given consent. Those subject to the directives of a global administrative body have sufficient reason to act on those directives if states have consented to that body. If there is no consent, there is no authority to coerce by global administrative bodies, and those subject can rationally object if subject to coercion. This rational objection can be acted on in order to prevent the effects of the act of coercion taking place. Because GLOBALG.A.P. is not created through consent, it does not have authority on the positivist model of authority, and other authoritative global administrative bodies (such as the WTO) or state courts may be able to give effect to the rational objections of those subject to coercion. States exercising political and economic power through a multilateral treaty to reconstitute and hence reform the global system of food safety is another way a rational objection to its acts of coercion could be given effect. So, rational opposition to the unjustified authority-claim of GLOBALG.A.P. may be given effect by attempting to *block* its coercive effects, or by pressurising for *reform*.

The positivist model of authority is problematic because it affords moral respectability, and political authority, both internally and in international relations, to *effective* but manifestly undemocratic states that do not warrant it, and by implication unjustifiably grants political authority to global administration founded by treaties ratified by these states. That said, the ideas of reform and blocking are useful in relation to the model of authority developed in *LMJ* and *RL*.

As just mentioned, GLOBALG.A.P. regulates a morally relevant concern by applying an accreditation process that can directly or indirectly lead to limitations to market access. In this sense, we should see GLOBALG.A.P. as an *attempt* to institutionalise a form of coercive ordering in the area of global food safety, even if it is not done by the agreement and joint actions of states.[58] The reason we might be sceptical about its attempt to do this is *not* because of the absence of a treaty ratified by states constituting GLOBALG.A.P., but because it fails to govern in a way that can be clothed by political authority. That is, its system of governance takes insufficient account of the interests of some of those affected by its governing structures in matters of disagreement.[59] Now, the *reformation* of

[58] A Brudner, 'Private Law and Kantian Right' (2011) 61 *University of Toronto Law Journal* 279.

[59] This point is made more generally in P Zumbansen, 'Neither "Public" nor "Private", "National" nor "International": Transnational Governance from a Legal Pluralist Perspective' (2011) 38 *Journal of Law and Society* 50, 69.

this body into an authoritative form of global administration could rely upon it being re-constituted by states via a multi-lateral treaty so that rights to participate in decision making are afforded to all agents that are affected by its coercive activities. The treaty-making process should be seen as the mobilisation of the political power of states to create authoritative global administration and not constitutive of that authority. But it is not the only way to reform global administration so that it can regulate through law. Reformation by states is just one of a number of pragmatic methods by which the global system of food quality regulation can be rendered authoritative. For example, in response to concerns by NGOs about the considerable power exercised by GLOBALG.A.P. over poor farmers, it has recently appointed 'the ambassador of smallholders'.[60] That said, this ambassador has no voting power, and this is one reason why Hachez and Wouters argue that its provision 'does not place stakeholders from developing countries on an equal footing with their western counterparts and does not ensure inclusive and egalitarian participation meeting the (deliberative) democratic standard'.[61]

For Holmes, power over those who make the rule need not be direct. Likewise, rights to participate in, and challenge, global administration need not afford rights directly to individual agents, but to other bodies within global administration who are able to protect certain interests agents have. Political authority may arise to the extent that it is subject to appropriate oversight by other bodies. This is equally plausible given that outcomes are often the result of the interaction between a range of global administrative bodies and states, between which various patterns of inter-institutional oversight exist. Inter-institutional oversight may be a way by which unauthorised coercion can be *blocked*.

The most famous example of blocking are the review powers exercised by the UK's Supreme Court in *A v HM Treasury*,[62] the European Court of Justice in *Kadi*[63] and the European Court of Human Rights in *Nada*,[64] which block the effect of state implementation of freezing orders of the UN 1267 Sanctions Committee. We should also note that this blocking has put pressure on the Security Council to reform its internal procedures.[65] The 1267 Sanctions Committee has now appointed an Ombudsperson who can be petitioned by those whose assets have been frozen, and who can recommend de-listing. But the powers of the Ombudsperson to garner evidence by which to make recommendations are distant relations of the forms of judicial review we find in states with developed legal orders.

[60] Hachez and Wouters, n 6, 703.

[61] ibid.

[62] *HM Treasury v Ahmed* [2010] UKSC 2.

[63] 1 Case C-402/05 P and C-415/05, *P Kadi and Al Barakaat International Foundation v Council and Commission* [2008] ECR I-6351.

[64] *Case of Nada v Switzerland* (Application no 10593/08) (2012) European Court of Human Rights.

[65] G Sullivan and M de Goede, 'Between Law and the Exception: The UN 1267 Ombudsperson as a Hybrid Model of Legal Expertise (2013) 26 *Leiden Journal of International Law* 833.

The developments just described within the GLOBALG.A.P. and the Security Council could indicate what Alan Brudner has called a 'germ of reciprocity' between those who govern and those who are governed, and which, if developed, may serve to establish true legal authority within these bodies.[66] However, there are countervailing trends we ought to be rightly less optimistic about. For example, we see regulation of those suspected of financing terrorism moving from the Security Council to private bodies such as World Check. One might worry that the 'privatisation' of global administration is a way to avoid accountability. However, even private bodies that exercise public functions can now be sometimes be subject to review, and it is but a short step to extend such reasoning to global administration.[67] There is, then, a battle to ensure that the globalisation of administration is not simply the next way by which those with power are insulated from hard-won forms of legal constraint. We should ensure (to paraphrase Scrutton LJ's language) that there are no global Alsatias by allowing the development of forms of administrative control free from the right sort of constraints.[68] If this end can be avoided, agents will be subject to a system of global administration, not as those whose interests are 'disregarded', but truly as global citizens.

VI. Conclusion

In cynical moments, we might regard the development of global administration as the latest attempt to insulate power from legal control. By developing the theory of authority presented in this chapter, I hope that I have provided a vocabulary by which we can articulate these concerns, and outlined how global administration can exercise moral and political authority. If the development of global administration is an attempt to give effect to the duty to govern authoritatively, then it must establish a particular relationship bounded by rights, between it and those that it seeks to govern. To do otherwise is an imperfect, deformed or failed attempt to govern.

[66] A Brudner, *Constitutional Goods* (OUP, 2004) 41–42.

[67] The reasoning in *Datafin* (*R v Panel on Take-overs and Mergers, ex p Datafin plc* [1987] QB 815) opens the door for review of private forms of global administration.

[68] *Czarnikow v Roth Schmidt & Co* [1922] 2 KB 478, [1922] All ER Rep 45.

13

What Is Gewirth and What Is Beyleveld? A Retrospect with Comments on the Contributions

DERYCK BEYLEVELD*

I. Introduction

Thirty-three years ago I discovered Alan Gewirth's moral philosophy.[1] Since then, my central academic preoccupation has been with analysing and defending the argument for the Principle of Generic Consistency (PGC)[2] and applying my interpretation of it to legal theory and numerous normative issues and questions (particularly ones arising in bioethics and the regulation of the biosciences). I have focused increasingly on the relationship between Gewirth and Kant, aiming to reconstruct Kant's philosophical anthropology on the premise that the PGC is the Categorical Imperative.[3]

This chapter summarises how I have developed Gewirth's foundational argument, offers what I now see as the best way to present it, indicates how I intend to further develop Gewirthian theory,[4] and comments briefly on the other contributions in this volume.

* Professor of Law and Bioethics at Durham University and Professor of Moral Philosophy and Applied Ethics at the University of Utrecht.

[1] Specifically, A Gewirth, *Reason and Morality* (University of Chicago Press, 1978).

[2] The PGC requires all agents to act in accord with the generic rights (GRs) of all agents, which are rights to generic conditions of agency (GCAs), which are conditions the absence of which has at least some negative effect on the ability of an agent to act or act successfully regardless of the purposes being pursued.

[3] See D Beyleveld, 'Gewirth and Kant on Kant's Maxim of Reason: Towards a Gewirthian Philosophical Anthropology' in P Bauhn (ed), *Gewirthian Perspectives on Human Rights* (Routledge, 2016) 13.

[4] 'Gewirthian theory' refers to my interpretation, development and application of Gewirth's argument for the PGC.

II. What Have I Done with Gewirth?

Commentators on my Gewirthian work rarely differentiate between Gewirth's views and my own. A number of things have contributed to this.

1. I portrayed *The Dialectical Necessity of Morality* (*DNM*)[5] as 'an analysis and defence' of Gewirth's argument for the PGC.
2. Gewirth fully endorsed my construction.[6]
3. I have routinely referred to my interpretations as what Gewirth holds even when this is only true in substance but not in form.

How, then, do my views relate to Gewirth's own?

DNM

My immediate reaction to *Reason and Morality* was that it mainly needed a better presentation of the logical structure of the argument to reveal more clearly the sequence of its inferences and the methodology it employs. Insofar as it is accurate to say that *DNM* rationally reconstructs Gewirth's argument, which is Gewirth's own view,[7] this reconstruction is mainly elucidatory not revisionary.

I presented the argument in three stages, which Gewirth does not do explicitly, the conclusions of which are:

I It is dialectically necessary for an agent (call her 'Agnes') to accept that she ought to defend her GCAs from interference against her will.

II It is dialectically necessary for Agnes to consider that she has both positive and negative rights to the GCAs under the 'will conception' (meaning that, absent any dialectically necessary commitments Agnes has to the contrary, she has the authority to release others from the positive and negative duties she must think they have to protect her GCAs).

III It is dialectically necessary for Agnes (thus for all agents) to grant equal rights to the GCAs (GRs) to all agents, from which it follows that Agnes may not exercise the GRs only if exercising them compromises the possession of more important GCAs of others.[8]

As Michael Boylan says,[9] I presented the argument in a direct way (in which Agnes reasons from her claim to choose purposes voluntarily) and in an indirect way

[5] D Beyleveld, *The Dialectical Necessity of Morality: An Analysis and Defense of Alan Gewirth's Argument to the Principle of Generic Consistency* (University of Chicago Press, 1991).

[6] See Gewirth, 'Foreword' in *DNM* vii.

[7] See Gewirth, 'Foreword' in *DNM* vii, vii.

[8] Measured by Gewirth's criterion of 'necessity' (or 'needfulness') for action (see *Reason and Morality* 62–63; 343–49).

[9] M Boylan, 'Introduction' in M Boylan (ed), *Gewirth: Critical Essays on Action, Rationality, and Community* (Rowman and Littlefield, 1999) 1, 2.

(as a *reductio ad absurdum* of the idea that Agnes can coherently accept any maxim about permissible/impermissible action inconsistent with the PGC).[10] However, I also maintained that the argument may be presented in two stages, because the reasoning that is applied to II to yield III can be applied to I to yield III without first establishing II.[11]

Apart from this, I presented additional arguments for some of Gewirth's inferences, such as my 'Argument from Attitudinal Consistency' for II,[12] which I see as elaborating and refining Gewirth's own reasoning (according to which Agnes must consider that she has rights to the GCAs because she must be opposed to interference with her GCAs,[13] which some commentators[14] wrongly allege conflates 'must' in a non-normative sense with 'ought'). I also employed the device of placing dialectically necessary claims in face brackets, subscripted with a letter or letters to indicate for whom acceptance of the bracketed claim is dialectically necessary. So, for example, $\{\text{MyR}\}_{\text{I}}$ means 'It is dialectically necessary for me to accept that I have the GRs', and $\{\text{PPAOR}\}_{\text{I}}$ means 'It is dialectically necessary for me to accept that any other prospective purposive agent (or just, any other agent) has the GRs'.

And I devoted an entire chapter to the argument for positive rights[15] because *Reason and Morality* places this argument in a section dealing with application of the PGC, not its justification, which courts the misunderstanding that Gewirth tries to derive positive rights from negative rights,[16] and because some of Gewirth's 'defenders' think that the argument does not justify positive rights.[17]

I also replied to critics not addressed by Gewirth, and dealt with all critics from the perspective of my 'reconstruction'.

Shortcomings

DNM has weaknesses. The following are a few examples.

As Ken Westphal says in this volume, Gewirth claims that the argument proceeds in terms of deductive and inductive logic.[18] But more than this is involved, because dialectically necessary 'oughts' are not logical 'oughts' or conceptually necessary (analytic) ones, but prescriptions *the acceptance of which* is a strict

[10] *DNM* ch 3.

[11] For example, *DNM* 60; 263–64.

[12] *DNM* 95–101.

[13] Gewirth, *Reason and Morality* 79–80.

[14] Such as K Nielsen, 'Against Ethical Rationalism' in E Regis Jr (ed), *Gewirth's Ethical Rationalism* (University of Chicago Press 1984), 72.

[15] *DNM* ch 10.

[16] See, eg, J Narveson, 'Negative and Positive Rights in Gewirth's *Reason and Morality*' in E Regis Jr (ed), *Gewirth's Ethical Rationalism* (University of Chicago Press, 1984).

[17] Like R Pilon, 'Ordering Rights Consistently: Or What We Do and Do Not Have Rights To' (1979) 13 *Georgia Law Review* 1171.

[18] Gewirth, *Reason and Morality* 22.

requirement of agential self-understanding, prescriptions that Agnes must accept on pain of misunderstanding what it is for her to be an agent, so must accept or imply that she is not an agent[19] (which, I maintain, is what Kant means by 'synthetic a priori').[20] I expended a lot of effort on this in *DNM*,[21] but still used the terms 'logically required' in places where it might have been better not to do so.

The most persistent misunderstanding of the argument derives from the fact that Gewirth uses the term 'prudential' in two senses. In the first, calling a claim 'prudential' signifies that it is justified relative to Agnes' need for the GCAs. In the second, calling a claim 'prudential' signifies that it has not yet been shown that Agnes must treat another agent's, say Brian's, dialectically necessary commitments as though they were her own. I could have explained better how the prudential (in the first sense) and the dialectically necessary aspects of the argument relate to each other.

I also paid insufficient attention to Gewirth's contention that the argument rests on ascribing some sense of free-will to agents[22] (though this neglect does not affect the validity of the argument); but the issue is more complex than I suggested because it is not so much whether agents must consider that they have free-will, as against in just what sense they must eschew belief in universal determinism.[23]

Furthermore, I too easily accepted[24] what Gewirth has to say about 'marginal' agents, specifically his claim that nonagents have the GRs in proportion to how closely they approach being agents, which is a mistake.

A shortcoming identified by Jesse Kalin when reviewing the manuscript of *DNM* for the University of Chicago Press[25] is that *DNM* does not explain the relationship between Gewirth and Kant. This is, in part, because my knowledge of Kant was not great at the time. It is also because Gewirth read Kant entirely through the lens of the first two chapters of *Groundwork of the Metaphysics of Morals*[26] without any attention to the third chapter, with the result that he viewed Kant as a preference utilitarian like RM Hare.[27] However, to go into this would have necessitated a much longer book. I regard this as the most serious shortcoming of *DNM*.

[19] Nevertheless, I think Westphal exaggerates the differences in substance between Gewirth and me on this point, and I do not think that he is right to say that Gewirth operates from the standpoint of rational egoism.

[20] See D Beyleveld, 'Gewirth and Kant on Justifying the Supreme Principle of Morality' in M Boylan (ed), *Gewirth: Critical Essays on Action, Rationality, and Community* (Rowman and Littlefield, 1999) 97; D Beyleveld, 'Korsgaard v Gewirth on Universalization: Why Gewirthians are Kantians and Kantians Ought to be Gewirthians' (2015) 12 *Journal of Moral Philosophy* 573; and D Beyleveld, 'Gewirth and Kant on Kant's Maxim of Reason', n 3.

[21] See *DNM*, esp ch 5.

[22] See Gewirth, *Reason and Morality*, 36–37.

[23] See Beyleveld, 'Gewirth and Kant on Kant's Maxim of Reason', n 3.

[24] *DNM* 447.

[25] He requested to be identified.

[26] I Kant, *Groundwork of the Metaphysics of Morals* (M Gregor ed, CUP, 1997).

[27] RM Hare, *Moral Thinking* (OUP, 1984).

Post-DNM

After *DNM*, Shaun Pattinson and I formulated a precautionary argument for granting the GRs to apparent agents and for agents to accept some duties to apparent nonagents (Gewirth's 'marginal agents') to correct Gewirth's invalid reasoning on this issue.[28]

I also clarified further the relationship between 'prudential' and dialectically necessary aspects of the argument.[29]

But most of my attention has been on the relationship to Kant.[30] Put simply, I consider that Gewirthians and Kant both ground morality in dialectically necessary commitments. Most of the important differences between them stem from the Gewirthian claim that it is dialectically necessary for Agnes to accept the Principle of Hypothetical Imperatives (PHI),[31] which claim does not figure in Kant's argument for morality. It is for this reason that the PGC grants rights to agents under the will conception, under which Agnes can have no perfect duties to herself *under* the PGC, only a perfect duty to herself (and others) to obey the PGC (though Gewirth courted the idea of perfect duties to oneself under the PGC),[32] whereas perfect duties to oneself under the moral law are central to Kant's view. Agnes' dialectically necessary commitment to the PHI also requires her to recognise positive as well as negative GRs, whereas Kant recognises only negative perfect duties to others. Most radically, I now contend that dialectically necessary commitment to the PHI entails a philosophical anthropology in which agents are essentially hoping-fearing beings (who ought to suspend belief in free-will in any positive metaphysical sense as well as in determinism), in contrast to Kant's view, which is built on linkage of the moral law to a presupposition of metaphysical free-will as against determinism.[33]

[28] See D Beyleveld and SD Pattinson, 'Precautionary Reasoning as a Link to Moral Action' in M Boylan (ed), *Medical Ethics* (Prentice Hall, 2000) 39; and 'Defending Moral Precaution as a Solution to the Problem of Other Minds: A Reply to Holm and Coggon' (2010) 23 *Ratio Juris* 258; and D Beyleveld and R Brownsword, *Human Dignity in Bioethics and Biolaw* (OUP, 2001) 117–34.

[29] See D Beyleveld and G Bos, 'The Foundational Role of the Principle of Instrumental Reason in Gewirth's Argument for the Principle of Generic Consistency: A Response to Andrew Chitty' (2009) 20 *King's Law Journal* 1; D Beyleveld, 'Williams' False Dilemma: How to Give Categorically Binding Impartial Reasons to Real Agents' (2013) 10 *Journal of Moral Philosophy* 204; and 'Korsgaard v Gewirth', n 20.

[30] See Beyleveld, 'Gewirth and Kant on Justifying the Supreme Principle of Morality', n 20; *Morality and the God of Reason* (Utrecht University, 2009); 'Williams' False Dilemma', n 29; 'Korsgaard v Gewirth'; 'Gewirth and Kant on Kant's Maxim of Reason', n 3; and Beyleveld and Brownsword, *Human Dignity in Bioethics and Biolaw*, n 28, ch 5. D Beyleveld, 'Hope and Belief' in RJ Jenkins and E Sullivan (eds), *Philosophy of Mind* (Nova Science Publishers, 2012) 1, and D Beyleveld and P Ziche, 'Towards a Kantian Phenomenology of Hope' (2015) 18 *Ethical Theory and Moral Practice* 927 are also relevant.

[31] The PHI states that if Agnes wishes to pursue E, and having X (or doing Y) is necessary for her to achieve E, then she ought to pursue/defend having X (or doing Y), or give up pursuing E.

[32] See Gewirth, *Reason and Morality*, 334–37, criticised in Beyleveld and Brownsword, *Human Dignity in Bioethics and Biolaw*, n 28, 106–08.

[33] Beyleveld, 'Morality and the God of Reason', n 30 and 'Gewirth and Kant on Kant's Maxim of Reason', n 3.

I have also presented dialectically contingent arguments for the PGC,[34] which Gewirth avoided doing because they cannot establish the PGC as categorically binding, being directed mainly at those who accept (for whatever reason) that agents ought to be treated impartially.

Recently, I have presented the following new argument for II (which I will portray here as '$\{AoGa^A\}_{Agnes}$ entails $\{AGR\}_{Agnes}$'):[35] *If* Agnes were to adopt the impartiality assumption, according to which she must treat $\{BoGb^B\}_{Brian}$ as ruling her action in the same way that she is required to treat $\{AoGa^A\}_{Agnes}$, she would have to accept that it is dialectically necessary for her to defend Brian's GCAs from interference against *his* will, which means $\{BGR\}_{Agnes}$. However, this cannot be the effect of Agnes adopting the impartiality assumption unless $\{AoGa^A\}_{Agnes} \equiv \{AGR\}_{Agnes}$.[36]

Because Article 1 of the Universal Declaration on Human Rights 1948 states that all human beings (hence all human agents) are equal in dignity and rights, and a right cannot be granted sincerely without granting a right to the necessary means to exercise it, it follows that the PGC must be considered to be the governing normative principle of the international system of human rights on pain of denying either that acceptance of the PHI is dialectically necessary and there are GCAs *or* that all human *agents* are equal in dignity and rights.

Applications

Apart from cases already mentioned, I have applied the PGC widely: for example, to the concept of law;[37] numerous issues in bioethics and biolaw;[38] genetic screening for Huntington's disease;[39] equity in allocating advances in biotechnology;[40]

[34] D Beyleveld, 'Legal Theory and Dialectically Contingent Justifications for the Principle of Generic Consistency' (1996) 9 *Ratio Juris* 15; Beyleveld and Brownsword, *Human Dignity in Bioethics and Biolaw*, n 28, 77–86; D Beyleveld and R Brownsword, *Consent in the Law* (Hart, 2007) 44–51; and most recently D Beyleveld, 'The Principle of Generic Consistency as the Supreme Principle of Human Rights' (2011) 13 *Human Rights Review* 1.

[35] 'AoGa' = 'Agnes ought to defend her possession of the GCAs'. 'AoGa^{A}' = 'Agnes ought to defend her possession of the GCAs from interference against her will'. 'AGR' = 'Agnes has the GR'.

[36] See Beyleveld, 'The Principle of Generic Consistency as the Supreme Principle of Human Rights'.

[37] In, eg, D Beyleveld and R Brownsword, *Law as a Moral Judgment* (Sweet and Maxwell, 1986; reprinted Sheffield Academic Press, 1994).

[38] Most comprehensively in Beyleveld and Brownsword, *Human Dignity in Bioethics and Biolaw*, n 28, ch 8 of which presents a theory of property rights that modifies Gewirth's position in *The Community of Rights* (University of Chicago Press, 1996).

[39] D Beyleveld, O Quarrell, and S Toddington, 'Generic Consistency in the Reproductive Enterprise: Ethical and Legal Implications of Exclusion Testing for Huntington's Disease' (1998) 3 *Medical Law International* 135.

[40] D Beyleveld and SD Pattinson, 'Individual Rights, Social Justice, and the Allocation of Advances in Biotechnology' in M Boylan (ed), *Public Health Policy and Ethics* (Kluwer, 2004) 59.

the right to privacy;[41] the right to a minimum wage;[42] morality exclusions in patent law;[43] rights of future generations;[44] the role of consent in law;[45] and precautionary reasoning in law.[46]

III. The Foundational Argument in Essence

The PGC is dialectically necessary *iff*

(1) $\{PHI\}_{Agnes.}$
(2) There are GCAs.[47]
(3) Dialectically necessary commitments are necessarily collectively universal, not merely distributively universal.

(1) coupled with (2) yields $\{AoGa^A\}_{Agnes}$, and coupling $\{AoGa^A\}_{Agnes}$ ($\equiv \{AGR\}_{Agnes}$) with (3), which yields $\{BoGb^B\}_{Brian}$ ($\equiv \{BGR\}_{Brian}$) by distributive universalisation,

[41] D Beyleveld, 'Conceptualising Privacy in Relation to Research Values' in SAM McLean (ed), *First Do No Harm* (Ashgate, 2006), 151; D Beyleveld, 'Data Protection and Genetics: Medical Research and the Public Good' (2007) 18 *King's Law Journal* 275; and D Beyleveld and SD Pattinson, 'Moral Interests, Privacy and Medical Research' in M Boylan (ed), *International Public Health Policy and Ethics* (Springer, 2008) 45.

[42] D Beyleveld and C Villiers, 'A General Right to a Minimum Wage in English Law: An Argument from Generic Consistency' (1997) 17 *Legal Studies* 234.

[43] eg D Beyleveld, 'Regulating Morality through Patent Law. Critique of the EC Directive' (2000) 12 *Law and the Human Genome Review* 141.

[44] D Beyleveld, M Düwell and A Spahn, 'Why and How Should We Represent Future Generations in Policy Making?' (2015) 6 *Jurisprudence* 549; and D Beyleveld, 'Duties to Future Generations: A Gewirthian Approach', in G Bos and M Düwell (eds), *Human Rights and Sustainability: Moral Responsibilities for the Future* (Routledge, 2016) 137.

[45] Beyleveld and Brownsword, *Consent in the Law*, n 34.

[46] D Beyleveld and R Brownsword, 'Complex Technology, Complex Calculations: Uses and Abuses of Precautionary Reasoning in Law' in P Sollie and M Düwell (eds), *Evaluating New Technologies: Methodological Problems for the Ethical Assessment of Technological Developments* (Springer, 2009) 175–90; and 'Emerging Technologies, Extreme Uncertainty, and the Principle of Rational Precautionary Reasoning' (2012) 4 *Law, Innovation and Technology* 35.

[47] Gewirth divides the GCAs into those needed to act at all (basic GCAs) and those needed for successful action (divided into nonsubtractive and additive GCAs). He also classifies GCAs at all three levels as either substantive (needed for well-being) or procedural (needed for freedom of action). He gives a few examples, such as life, mental equilibrium, and the necessary means to these (basic), accurate information (nonsubtractive) and further education (additive) (see *Reason and Morality* 54–57). It is important *in the argument for* the PGC not to try to specify what constitutes the GCAs beyond this level of abstraction. This is because what will, in practice, constitute the necessary means to the GCAs abstractly specified can and will vary according to contingent factors, such as the biological constitution of an agent, and resources available to an agent. For example, air of a certain composition is a necessary means to the life of human agents, but it need not be for agents with a different biological makeup (if such exist). Also, some things, like peanuts, which can threaten the life of an agent allergic to them can be, and are, healthy foods for other agents. So, this kind of specification must be left to the applications of the PGC. The fact that what instantiates a GCA, or interference with its possession, can vary does not affect the universality of the PGC because the PGC grants the GRs, not to the instantiations *in themselves* of the GCAs, but to the instantiations *as instantiations of the GCAs*.

yields $\{BGR\}_{Agnes}$ by collective universalisation.[48] And this means that $\{PGC\}_{Agnes}$ (hence $\{PGC\}_{Brian}$ by distributive universalisation, thus $\{PGC\}_{All\ agents}$).

But this makes the PGC categorically binding on Agnes only if

(4) Being dialectically necessary for Agnes to accept a principle renders the principle categorically binding on her.

And, even if (4) is true, Agnes is only categorically bound to comply with the PGC *in her practical dealings* if

(5) Agnes is categorically bound to treat those who behave as though they are agents as agents.

(3) is true if

(6) It is dialectically necessary for Agnes to hold that she ought to have X or do Y and that Brian ought to support her to have X or do Y, entails that it is dialectically necessary for Agnes to hold '"Agnes is an agent" entails "Agnes ought to have X or do Y and that Brian ought to support her to have X or do Y"'[49]

where 'being an agent' means 'belonging to the class of beings who have the capacity to pursue their chosen purposes voluntarily'.

Although Agnes cannot know for certain that anyone other than herself is an agent, only that some other beings behave as though they are agents, this does not imply that Agnes is not categorically bound to treat anyone other than herself as an agent. (5) is true because if Agnes mistakenly treats an apparent agent (whom she can treat as an agent) as a nonagent she violates the PGC (because she is categorically bound to grant the GRs to all agents), whereas if she mistakenly treats an apparent agent as an agent she does not violate the PGC. This reasoning does not require her to grant apparent nonagents the GRs (even though she cannot know that they are not agents) because it is only possible for her to treat apparent agents as agents. It does, however, require Agnes to accept duties to apparent nonagents insofar as she can identify interests that they have that she would have to treat as GCAs of agents if they were apparent agents.

If the PGC is categorically binding on Agnes, then she cannot coherently assent to any rule or principle inconsistent with the PGC. Therefore, rules issued by sources that legal positivists consider to be the sources of legal obligations can-

[48] Agnes' commitment to BGR holds unless defending Brian's possession of the GCAs in accordance with his will threatens disproportionate damage to her (or a third agent's, Carol's) GCAs against her (or Carol's) will.

[49] Gewirth argues for (3) by his Argument from the Sufficiency of Agency (ASA) (see *Reason and Morality* 110), according to which $\{AGR\}_{Agnes}$ entails {'Agnes is an agent' entails 'AGR'$\}_{Agnes}$. He reasons that if Agnes denies '"Agnes is an agent" entails "AGR"' she must hold '"AGR" entails "Agnes has a property D that she does not necessarily have as an agent"'. But then she must accept that if she does/did not have D then she does not/would not have the GRs, which is contrary to $\{AGR\}_{Agnes}$. Therefore, it is dialectically necessary for her to accept '"Agnes is an agent" entails "AGR"'. If this is sound then (6) is true. But from this it follows that it is dialectically necessary for Agnes to accept '"Brian is an agent" entails "BGR"', which entails that (3) is true.

not have any normative validity, cannot constitute rationally justified obligations (prescriptions of required action that any agent can coherently consider ought to be applied and obeyed) if they are inconsistent with the PGC. Being prescribed by these sources, or assented to by those who accept these sources, cannot make them normatively binding. If moral obligations are conceived as categorically binding impartial ones, the PGC is a moral principle, which entails that no rules can be valid (rationally binding) if they are inconsistent with one's moral obligations as laid down by the *PGC.* This is the basis for the natural law view propounded in *Law as a Moral Judgment.*[50]

Even if (3) is false, if (1) and (2) are true, then

(7) Anyone who holds that all agents are to be treated with equal concern and respect must accept that it is dialectically necessary for them (as agents *who hold* that all agents must be treated with equal concern and respect) to accept the PGC.

From this it follows, as already mentioned, that the PGC is the supreme principle of human rights of agents in any legal system that accepts that there are human rights and morality generally (so that no one who holds that there are genuine moral principles can coherently assent to rules having any normative validity that are contrary to the PGC).

IV. Critical Reaction and Misunderstandings

Objections to the Gewirthian Foundational Thesis

Most critics accept that it is categorically instrumentally irrational for Agnes not to accept AoGa because she needs her GCAs to act/act successfully whatever her purposes.

They generally claim, however, that Gewirthians hold that Agnes must hold AGR in order to be consistent with holding AoGa, so that the justification given for AGR is Agnes' need for the GCAs. But they object that, on such a basis, Agnes is categorically required to accept BGR only on the false premise that *she necessarily* needs Brian to have the GCAs. For Agnes to be required to accept BGR, she must have reason to defend Brian's agency that is not given merely by *her need* for the GCAs.

This line of objection[51] *is sound on its major premise*, which is that Gewirthians try to derive BGR_{Agnes} from $AoGa_{Agnes}$.

[50] Beyleveld and Brownsword, n 37.

[51] Which is presented influentially by B Williams, *Ethics and the Limits of Philosophy* (Fontana, 1984) ch 4.

But Gewirthians do not try to derive BGR_{Agnes} from $AoGa_{Agnes}$ (nor from $AoGa^{A}{}_{Agnes}$). They derive $\{BGR\}_{Agnes}$ from $\{AoGa^{A}\}_{Agnes}$. The dialectically necessary method operates only on propositions that are dialectically necessary for Agnes to accept. It is not dialectically necessary for Agnes to accept AoGa, because her required acceptance of AoGa is conditional on her being unwilling to accept generic damage to her ability to act, and Gewirthians do not assume that agents necessarily want to continue to be agents/successful agents. It is, however, dialectically necessary for Agnes to accept $AoGa^{A}$ = 'Agnes ought to accept AoGa if she wishes to be an agent/successful agent'. The rest of the argument elicits the purely logical and conceptual entailments *of Agnes understanding* $\{AoGa^{A}\}_{Agnes}$, not the logical and conceptual entailments of $AoGa^{A}{}_{Agnes}$.

In other words, the Gewirthian argument is not a form of rational egoism that operates on a Humean internalism trying to justify a categorically binding impartial principle on the basis of prudential (that is, generically instrumental) considerations. That Agnes generically needs the GCAs determines the interests she may and must claim rights to, while the PHI determines the kind of rights she must claim (namely, rights under the will conception). But that she must claim rights to the GCAs at all is because it is dialectically necessary for her to accept the PHI; and that she must grant these rights equally to Brian is a requirement of her understanding what follows from it being dialectically necessary for her to claim that she has these rights.

Thus, in being an argument from agential self-understanding, the argument does not presuppose that agents have value, either individually or collectively, the PGC is not derived from the presumption or imputation of any normative standpoint, from any contingent choices made by agents, and also not just from understanding what constitutes *being* an agent, but from understanding what constitutes *understanding what it is to be* an agent.

Regarding II, there are essentially three arguments for '$\{AoGa^{A}\}_{Agnes}$ entails $\{AGR\}_{Agnes}$'. The first is that (by the concept of a GCA) Agnes needs the GCAs in order to act in accordance with $AoGa^{A}$, and will not have them if Brian interferes with her possession. Therefore, to be consistent with $\{AoGa^{A}\}_{Agnes}$, she must hold $\{AGR\}_{Agnes}$. The second is that $\{AGR\}_{Agnes}$ strictly requires Agnes to be opposed to interference with her GCAs against her will, which attitude is not required by her acceptance of any other propositions about interference with her GCAs (the essence of my Argument from Attitudinal Consistency). The third argument (already mentioned above) is that, given $\{AoGa^{A}\}_{Agnes}$, if Agnes were to hold that all agents should be treated impartially, she would have to accept $\{BGR\}_{Agnes}$, which cannot be true unless $\{AoGa^{A}\}_{Agnes} \equiv \{AGR\}_{Agnes}$.

The canonical argument for III is that (by the ASA)[52] $\{AGR\}_{Agnes}$ entails {'Agnes is an agent' entails 'AGR'$\}_{Agnes}$, and logically universalising '"Agnes is an agent" entails "AGR"' entails '"Brian is an agent" entails "BGR"', from which it follows that {'Brian is an agent' entails 'BGR'$\}_{Agnes}$.

[52] See n 49.

Most commentators overlook the ASA, despite the fact that Chapter 8 of *DNM* is devoted to it (and I highlighted it as the most important aspect of the collective universalisation procedure),[53] probably because they continue to be deluded that the justification Agnes has for AGR_{Agnes} is the fact that, in being an agent, she generically instrumentally needs the GCAs, rather than in her understanding the dialectical necessity for her to hold AGR_{Agnes}.

However, two objections to the ASA must be taken into account.

The first[54] alleges that 'Agnes is an agent' is referentially opaque between Agnes being a member of the class of agents (those who necessarily proactively value their own chosen purposes) (Agnes as a type of agent, a Ta) and Agnes being the particular unique member of this class who *necessarily* proactively values only Agnes' chosen purposes (Agnes as a token of an agent, a ta). The allegation is that Agnes necessarily reasons from her position as the ta she is, on the basis of which she is only required to accept that she ought to defend Brian's GCAs unless he is willing to suffer generic damage to his ability to act, if he necessarily proactively values her purposes, which is not the case. In short, claiming that universalisation of '"Agnes is an agent" entails "$AoGa^A$ (≡ AGR)"' entails '"Brian is an agent" entails "$BoGb^B$ (≡ BGR)"' equivocates between Agnes as a Ta and Agnes as a ta.

The second objection[55] claims that because AGR ≡ $AoGa^A$, even if the ASA shows that $\{$'Agnes is a Ta' entails '$AoGa^A$/AGR'$\}_{Agnes}$, the universalised conclusion is not $\{$'Brian is a Ta' entails '$BoGb^B$/BGR'$\}_{Agnes}$ but $\{$'Brian is a Ta' entails 'Brian ought to defend his GCAs and have them defended only as required by *Agnes'* willingness to act'$\}$ ≡ $\{BoGb^A/BGR^A\}_{Agnes}$.

My response to the first objection is that Agnes cannot be the ta that she is (defined in part by the choices she makes and the normative standpoints she adopts), without being a Ta, without having the *capacities for* sensing, conceptualising, imagining, desiring, feeling, valuing, believing, reasoning, understanding, and possessing needs (physical, psychological, social) as well as cognitive vulnerabilities that are presupposed by the very idea that Agnes may or ought to do anything. For Agnes to misunderstand what these are and how they relate, is for her to misunderstand what it is for her to be the ta that she is, which is for her to imply that she does not have the particular sense-experiences, concepts, images, desires, feelings (emotions), values, beliefs, reasonings, understandings, and needs that constitute her being Agnes rather than Brian. In fact, within Agnes' dialectically necessary matrix, there is a biconditional relationship between Agnes being a Ta and Agnes being a ta, because the Principle of Reflective Judgement (PRJ) applies (according to which *Agnes* cannot understand that she is a ta without understanding that she is a Ta, and can only understand that she is a Ta from her position as the

[53] *DNM* 392–93.

[54] I attributed this to J Scheuermann, 'Gewirth's Concept of Prudential Rights' (1987) 37 *Philosophical Quarterly* 291 (see *DNM* 288–300).

[55] This is how I understand A Chitty, 'Protagonist and Subject in Gewirth's Argument for Human Rights' (2008) 19 *King's Law Journal* 1.

ta that she is). So even though it is true that Agnes reasons from her position as the ta that she is, she cannot escape having to regard being a Ta as the *ratio essendi* for $AoGa^A$/AGR.

My response to the second objection[56] is that it is in being grounded in Agnes' understanding that she is a Ta that Agnes must think of herself as the supreme authority over the disposal of her GCAs (that she must hold that $AoGa^A$/AGR). So, it cannot follow, as Chitty claims, that Agnes must consider her will to be the supreme authority over the disposal of Brian's GCAs (BRO^A), because this can only follow if Agnes' reason for $AoGa^A$/AGR is that this is for the sake of Agnes' generic needs (herself as a ta) rather than being justified by Agnes' understanding that she is a Ta. So, if Agnes recognises that Brian is a Ta (which she must do if it is intelligible for her to claim the GRs against Brian), Agnes must grant (subject to any dialectically necessary countervailing commitments that she has) that Brian is the supreme authority over the disposal of his GCAs.

But there is yet another strategy for attacking the Gewirthian foundational thesis.[57] It is that establishing that it is dialectically necessary for Agnes to accept a principle (assuming that this can be done) does not show that it is categorically binding on her, because, unless there is a reason independent of dialectical necessity that requires Agnes to value being an agent, the fact that acceptance of the principle is constitutive *of being an agent* does not show that Agnes ought to act according to the principle.

This objection, however, rests on misconstruing the thesis that it is dialectically necessary for Agnes to accept a principle (such as $AoGa^A$) as the claim that $AoGa^A$ falls out of understanding *what constitutes being an agent*, implying that Agnes *is not an agent* unless she accepts $AoGa^A$. But this is not the Gewirthian thesis, which is that required acceptance of $AoGa^A$ is produced by what constitutes *understanding what it is to be an agent.* This proposition does not entail that Agnes is not an agent if she does not accept $AoGa^A$.

It might be thought that this merely raises the question why Agnes ought to care whether or not she acts in accord with agential self-understanding. But to ask such a question presupposes Humean internalism and also that Agnes can coherently ascribe action-motivating attitudes to herself while implying that she is not an agent. Since the latter presupposition is incoherent, the implication is that a categorical ought is sufficiently justified, or even that it is constituted, by being dialectically necessary for Agnes to accept.

This leaves only the objection that Agnes cannot know that Brian is an agent, so cannot be categorically bound to treat Brian as an agent, on which I have already commented.

[56] See Beyleveld and Bos, 'The Foundational Role of the Principle of Instrumental Reason', n 29.

[57] See D Enoch, 'Agency, Shmagency: Why Normativity Won't Come from What is Constitutive of Action' (2006) 115 *Philosophical Review* 169.

Objections to Gewirthian Legal Idealism

These fall into two types: objections based on rejecting the foundational argument; and objections that accuse Gewirthian Legal Idealism of permitting or even requiring various moral failings.

In my opinion, all of the latter rest on conceiving of law as rules promulgated by the powerful, and legal obligations as requirements for action laid down by such rules (corresponding to which they treat moral obligations as requirements of rules that derive their obligatory status from having a different source) and on imposing this way of conceiving things on Gewirthians. In so doing, they attempt to characterise obligations (whether legal or moral) in a purely detached way, as what is validated on the presumption of a basic norm or rule of recognition that, in the case of legal obligations, simply mirrors the fact of acceptance by those whose rules are generally applied and obeyed.

However, while it is not impermissible *linguistically* to characterise obligations in this way, and when this is done it is clearly the case that there can be legal obligations that are not consistent with the requirements of the PGC, it is impermissible to presume that Gewirthians characterise obligations (legal or otherwise) in this way.

According to Gewirthians, claims to obligations are claims that those who have the obligations ought to act in a particular way whether they want to or not. As such, a claim to an obligation is not valid or veridical if it is not true that those to whom it is directed ought to accept that they ought to act in this way whether they want to or not, and the fact that the rule prescribed by someone else requires the addressee to act in accordance with the rule whether the addressee wants to or not, does not render the rule binding on the addressee. To say that something is an obligation from someone's point of view, or relative to some norm or principle, does not bind *anyone* normatively. That Hitler held that the Jews ought to be exterminated does not show that *anyone, not even Hitler, ought to hold* that the Jews ought to be exterminated. To show that there really is an obligation to do something can, if the Gewirthian argument for the PGC is valid, only be shown by showing that it is validated (directly or indirectly) by the PGC, as itself a strict requirement of agential self-understanding.

Of course, it might be said that this does not mean that obligations lose their *legally* binding character if they contravene the PGC, merely that they are immoral obligations. But this misses the point. If the PGC is, as Gewirthians maintain, categorically binding, then there is no point in characterising statements of obligation as obligations (as against mere claims to obligations) if they are not consistent with the requirements of the PGC. Since even detached descriptions of 'obligation' are descriptions about what someone holds to be normatively valid, if it can be shown that agents categorically ought not to hold what they hold to be normatively valid to be normatively valid, then it is categorically irrational not to give priority to the conceptualisation consonant with what they ought to hold to be normatively valid.

Future Directions

As I have already said, it seems to me to be of primary importance to elucidate how the validity of the Gewirthian argument for the PGC impacts on Kant's philosophy as a whole.

Since, I consider that Kant's *theoretical* philosophy[58] is essentially sound, this leaves at least three important remaining tasks for Gewirthians: (i) to formulate a Gewirthian theory of punishment (upon which Roger Brownsword and I intend to write a monograph);[59] (ii) to develop a Gewirthian theory of Aesthetics (which Dascha During and Marcus Düwell have already embarked upon in this volume); and (iii) to integrate all of this into a Gewirthian philosophical anthropology.[60]

However, regarding (iii), not only does this require an integrating analysis of Gewirth's monograph on self-fulfilment,[61] it now seems to me that it requires detailed attention to the relationship between Gewirthian theory and the theories of post-Kantian idealists like Fichte, Schelling and Hegel (about which Stuart Toddington and Ken Westphal have things to say in this volume).

V. Comments on Contributions

My comments do not follow the order of contributions. Very roughly, the contributions can be divided into two categories: those that apply the PGC to a number of issues or cases that are significant for interpreting positive law or for legal theory generally; and those that reflect, either in application or critique, on central aspects of Gewirthian moral epistemology.

Reflections on Law

Shaun Pattinson presents an exemplary analysis of the validity and applicability of advance directives that is completely consistent with the PGC. I have nothing of substance to add to his analysis.

Roger Brownsword is worried that technological advances make possible crime prevention and other behavioural control strategies that are problematic ethically and in the way in which they can be incorporated into the rules of a legal sys-

58 Per W Waxman, *Kant's Anatomy of the Intelligent Mind* (OUP, 2014).

59 See also SP Brown, *The Moral Justification of Retributive Punishment by Reference to the Notion of Balance.* Unpublished PhD Thesis (University of Sheffield, 1998).

The relationship between Kantian and Gewirthian legal theory also needs further elaboration, which is something on which Patrick Capps has commented in this collection.

60 On which see Beyleveld, 'Gewirth and Kant on Kant's Maxim of Reason', n 3.

61 A Gewirth, *Self-Fulfillment* (Princeton University Press, 1998).

tem. I will not go into the details of his thought-provoking analysis. Instead, I will confine myself to a few schematic remarks.

The problem cannot be, and he does not suggest that it is, that making certain kinds of behaviour impossible or very difficult threatens to destroy the capacity of agents to act. More intriguing is the thought that if behaviour is comprehensively channelled by technologies, children might lose the capacity to think reflectively about their behaviour, and might lose the capacity to respond effectively to breakdowns in the system of control. However, it is difficult to predict at what point this might happen. What is most worrying about these technologies is that, almost by definition, they will be in the hands of an elite, and could be used to effect an unprecedented degree of control by such groups. The biggest question is how society and its legal system can and should go about securing democratic control of these technologies in accordance with the requirements of the PGC.

Henrik Palmer Olsen's chapter illustrates how what the PGC requires can vary according the circumstances. I only wish to emphasise that his claim that political factors can require compromising what the PGC ideally requires means only that in the real world it might not (indeed, will not) be possible to grant everyone all of the GRs, and to set up institutions that guarantee that everyone's possession of the GCAs will not be compromised. It does not and cannot mean that, in the context of international relations (or any other relations) the PGC does not remain the supreme principle of all practical reason. What the PGC requires, and always requires, is that the GRs of all agents must be respected as much as possible in the circumstances that prevail.

Patrick Capps, likewise, provides an analysis of the Gewirthian (and Kantian) approach to issues of global governance that I am happy to endorse in the main. I do, however, think that he underplays the extent to which the PGC permits and often requires procedural solutions in the enterprise of subjecting human conduct to the governance of rules.[62]

Ben Capps builds upon the 'co-operative model' of conflicts between privacy and medical research interests that I have developed[63] to show how appeals to the public good and public interest should be conceptualised to guard against unjustifiable misappropriation of these concepts. What he says is basically sound, though I think he could have made more of the fact (which he recognises) that, under the PGC, GRs and rights granted to serve GRs can only be overridden by conflicting GRs, so that 'the public interest' can never override human rights unless it serves the GRs grounded in at least equally important GCAs.

David Townend appeals to the value and importance of 'politeness' to describe how persons ought to regard others in relation to personal data interests. What he says about this is very interesting, and captures at least part of the idea that

[62] For analysis of which, see Beyleveld and Brownsword, *Consent in the Law* ch 10, n 34.

[63] In D Beyleveld, 'Conceptualising Privacy in Relation to Research Values' in SAM McLean (ed), *First Do No Harm* (Ashgate, 2006) 151 and 'Data Protection and Genetics: Medical Research and the Public Good' (2007) 18 *King's Law Journal* 275.

moral rights and duties describe the behaviour of those who treat others with equal concern and respect. He recognises that politeness is normally contrasted with rudeness, with behaviour that is boorish or uncultured, which puts it on a scale of worse to better behaviour, not on one of wrong versus right behaviour, and that so conceived (as a matter of etiquette), politeness does not and cannot capture fully the conduct imposed by rights in relation to personal data. It must be understood as a matter of morality.

While I consider the actual picture he paints to have considerable merit, I am puzzled by some of the terminology he uses to relate it to the PGC. For example, he says that privacy is a subjective right, because what persons consider to violate it varies according to their personal preferences. And he also portrays privacy as something to be weighed against the public interest. But if, as Gewirthians claim, the PGC is the supreme principle of practical reason, there can be no rights except those legitimated by the PGC, and under the PGC, rights are either generic (rights to the GCAs under the will-conception), or required to be granted to protect the generic rights, or conferred (consistent with the generic rights, but not required by them), and neither the GCAs, nor legitimate interpretation of their concrete instantiation, are subject to contingent preferences. Also, if anything to which someone wishes to attach the term 'privacy' is a right under the PGC then there is a public (that is, generic) interest in it (one that serves the universal needs of agency), which can only be overridden by more important public interests as assessed by the Gewirthian criterion of needfulness for agency. In terminology used in this chapter, public interests capable of overriding a right are grounded, directly or indirectly in Agnes as a Ta, not in Agnes as a ta. They must be rights under the PGC themselves. In addition, the criterion of needfulness for agency (the importance of which Townend underplays) is the ultimate Gewirthian criterion for adjudicating conflicts between rights. While not all potential conflicts between rights can be adjudicated directly by this criterion, so that procedural solutions are required, these (for which the institution of 'politeness' is a good candidate) are only legitimate if their operation is consistent with the direct applications of the PGC governed by the criterion of needfulness for agency.

Philosophical Reflections

Thom Brooks and Diane Sankey maintain that the problem with Gewirthian ethical rationalism is that it privileges reason over the emotions and sensibility, as a result of which it cannot give an adequate account of law and morality. They use the history and context of current sexual offences law to illustrate and justify their claims.[64]

[64] I comment on their contribution in this subsection because it is directed against the dialectically necessary method.

There are three overarching problems with their critique.

First, they do not correctly portray the criterion of rationality that the foundational Gewirthian argument employs, which is not that of logical consistency, nor that of instrumental rationality itself, but acceptance of the requirements of agential self-understanding (one of which is acceptance of the PHI) and what follows logically and conceptually from understanding these. In Kant's terms, agents act rationally when they act in accord with themselves, and in order to do this, they must render acting for themselves (acting on and in terms of the contingent particularities that differentiate them from other agents) consistent with acting from the universal viewpoint of all agents (with the idea that they are agents at all). They focus on agential self-understanding because only agents (those with the capacities and disposition to pursue means voluntarily to their chosen ends) are intelligible subjects and objects of practical discourse (normative or not). Now, to be an agent (so defined) requires the possession of many faculties or capabilities, which include those of understanding, conceptualisation, deliberation, judgement, feeling (having emotions), sensing, desiring, inferring, and imagining, and to be vulnerable in the sense of having ends that can be thwarted and need means to be secured for their pursuit and achievement. All agents, *to be agents*, have and must have these features, whether they are human or not; and they cannot think of themselves as sensing anything, having any emotions, desires, and so on, if they do not have these.[65] Because agents require *all* these features in at least some degree *to be agents*, it is false that Gewirthians prioritise what Brooks and Sankey call 'reason' over the emotions in their account of agency and rationality.

Second, they do not distinguish what must be appealed to in order to justify the PGC as the supreme principle of practical reasoning (not merely of morality) from what is required to apply the PGC to judge the rationality (the normative validity) of actions and institutions. *In arguing for* the PGC, agents may only accept what *is* dialectically necessary for them to accept; but *in acting* agents *may* accept anything *that does not conflict with* their dialectically necessary commitments. But this criterion for rational action rests on recognition that agents *can (as against may)* have all sorts of desires, feelings and physical characteristics, and can inhabit various social contexts. Only on this basis can agents be individuated and it make any sense to think that they may or ought to do anything. Now, in arguing for the PGC, the argument necessarily abstracts from all these contingencies, because only in this way and at this level can a categorical imperative be justified. One of the basic GCAs is mental (which includes emotional) equilibrium, which can be disturbed or lost by grief, pain, rage, panic, lack of self-esteem or self-confidence, and despair. In arguing for the PGC, Gewirthians do not attend to these *separately* because it is unnecessary and distracting to do so when the task is simply to show

[65] These capabilities must be distinguished from GCAs, which are conditions that those with agency capabilities need generically in order to act/act successfully (which does not preclude some capabilities also being GCAs).

that it is dialectically necessary for all agents to respect the GCAs of all agents. But, because agents can and do differ in their biological makeups, sensitivities and other contingent factors and circumstances, what will, for example, cause an agent grief so as to disturb the agent's emotional equilibrium can vary, and all of this contingency is and must be taken into account when applying the PGC to specific actions, rules and institutions.

Third, the way in which they use their case study to 'test' Gewirthian ethical rationalism presupposes that it is intended to be a strategy for explaining the history of positivistically viewed law and regulation, which is not the case. While Gewirthians consider that understanding and explaining what has produced particular regimes of regulation is important (even necessary) to judge what can (or cannot), may (and may not) be done practicably to ameliorate or change these in line with the PGC's normative requirements, it is not the task of Gewirthian ethical rationalism itself to provide such understanding or explanation.

There are many other ways in which Brooks and Sankey mischaracterise the Gewirthian position, and I cannot delineate them all in detail here. I will mention only the following: (i) their summary of the argument for the PGC does not attend to the argument's modalities; (ii) I have never said that pressure cannot invalidate a consent; (iii) the Gewirthian view does not restrict 'autonomy' to authority over what may be done with or to one's body (it grants self-autonomy over one's possession of all the GCAs); (iv) hope-fear is not the only emotion that Gewirthians recognise, but it does have a special place in characterising the phenomenology of agency; (v) Gewirthians do not subscribe to Cartesian dualism or any other metaphysical thesis about the relationship between body and mind.[66]

Michael Boylan argues that utilitarianism and contractualism are incapable of providing a basis for rights and duties, because they cannot be grounded in contingent preferences or choices. What he says is essentially in line with the Gewirthian position on consent. In outline, the Gewirthian position is that Agnes is permitted to do anything so long as this does not conflict with the possession of at least as important GCAs of other agents against their will. So, while (prima facie) Agnes' free and informed consent is required not to interfere with her possession of the GCAs, it is not necessary if obtaining it would threaten Brian's at least as important GCAs against his will. So it is a fallacy to think that consent is always sufficient or always necessary to justify actions. Conflicts, here, are to be adjudicated by application of Gewirth's criterion of needfulness for action in the circumstances in which it is to be applied. There are, however, circumstances in which what the PGC requires is not clear, and matters over which the PGC has nothing directly to say but requires choices to be made. To deal with these, the PGC requires authority to make decisions to be delegated to persons, bodies, or procedures with the general consent of all agents who will be affected by them, with the proviso that

66 The justification for points (iv) and (v) is given elsewhere. See Beyleveld, 'Hope and Belief', n 30; and 'Gewirth and Kant on Kant's Maxim of Reason', n 30; and Beyleveld and Ziche, 'Towards a Kantian Phenomenology of Hope', n 30.

the decisions (which can prescribe rights and duties) be made in good faith and do not clearly run contrary to the direct requirements of the PGC. Absent such underpinning, consent cannot ground rights or duties.

Dascha During and Marcus Düwell take up my contention that Gewirth's argument implies that human dignity resides in the capacity of human agents to hope and fear.[67] In an exceptionally penetrating paper they contribute significantly to the development of Gewirthian philosophical anthropology by reflecting on the centrality of hope for Gewirthian theory within the aesthetic frame to which they rightly say it belongs.

Stuart Toddington takes issue with the idea that the Gewirthian argument cannot show that Agnes must grant the GR to Brian because it is 'monological', and that such an ambition requires a 'dialogical' argument, which many take Hegel's critique of Kant to demonstrate. He maintains that Hegel's own argument for morality needs to operate in the 'monological' manner employed by Gewirth and Kant. Indeed, he suggests that Hegel gets close to arguing in just such a way.

I don't know enough about Hegel to pass judgement on this suggestion. But I agree unequivocally with Toddington's claim that the way in which the Gewirthian argument is generally characterised as 'monological' is specious. What he says about this is very much in line with my own thoughts on the matter, which are as follows.

The Gewirthian argument is monological in the sense that, being conducted from Agnes' internal viewpoint as an agent, it follows Kant's maxim of understanding 'Think for oneself',[68] which is to say that Agnes should (indeed, may) only accept reasons for belief or action that provide *her* with reasons. As I have explained above, to say this is not to espouse Humean internalism; nor is it to operate in a solipsistic matrix divorced from any recognition of the existence of other agents. Agnes tries to answer the question 'What may I do?' and the criterion that the Gewirthian dialectically necessary method imposes for answering it (driven by the PRJ) is that Agnes may only accept rules or principles that are consistent with what Agnes must accept by virtue of understanding what it is for her to be a member of the class of agents. In other words, in Kant's terms, the Gewirthian argument is driven by the claim that Agnes only 'thinks for' herself when she thinks 'in accord with' herself, which is to say, in a way that renders *her* thinking consistent with the universal viewpoint of agents as agents.[69] Consequently, the Gewirthian argument is, in a sense, 'dialogical' in the way in which it is 'monological', the 'dialogue' being between Agnes thought of as the ta that she is, and Agnes thought of as a Ta (in which terms Agnes and Brian are united).

[67] See Beyleveld,' Hope and Belief'; and Beyleveld and Ziche, 'Towards a Kantian Phenomenology of Hope', n 30.

[68] I Kant, *Critique of the Power of Judgment* (P Guyer ed, CUP, 2000) 174 (5: 294 in the Academy edition).

[69] ibid 174–75 (5: 294–95).

Ken Westphal has made a conscientious and engaged attempt to understand the Gewirthian argument. As I read him, he considers that my arguments for dialectically necessary acceptance of the PGC do render it dialectically necessary, but only because I impute inadequately justified moral force to dialectically necessary claims, because adequate justification for this requires recognition of a GCA that I do not recognise (Agnes' need for the co-operation of other agents to become a rational agent). Furthermore, he claims that this recognition coupled with the fact that rational nature is an end in itself enables moral principles to be justified assertorically, not merely dialectically.

Given space constraints, it is impossible for me to reply adequately to him, or to comment on every relevant aspect of his analysis. But I am not persuaded

(a) that my arguments rely on a moral imputation that I have not fully justified;
(b) that the 'GCA' recognition he presses can justify moral imputation within the Gewirthian dialectically necessary matrix;
(c) that an appeal to rational nature being an end in itself can yield assertorically valid moral principles.

Re (a), my argument for dialectically necessary mutual recognition[70] relies on it being dialectically necessary for Agnes to recognise that $\{BoGb^{B}\}_{Brian}$ ($\equiv \{BGR\}_{Brian}$). Westphal claims that this recourse involves an unjustified moral imputation in departing from my contention that the dialectically necessary argument must be and is conducted entirely first-person. If no moral imputation is involved, why (he asks) not elicit Agnes' required commitment to BGR directly from her required commitment to AGR?[71] His thought, perhaps, is that to reason from Agnes' taking account of Brian's internal point of view is to rely on her thinking morally.

Before I answer this question directly, note that Gewirth's argument using the ASA *does* elicit $\{BGR\}_{Agnes}$ *directly* from $\{AGR\}_{Agnes}$. $\{AGR\}_{Agnes}$ entails (purely first-person) {'Agnes is an agent' entails 'AGR'}$_{Agnes}$, which logically requires Agnes (if she recognises Brian as an agent, which she must do to claim AGR against him) to accept $\{BGR\}_{Agnes}$. This makes no reference to Brian's dialectically necessary commitments.

But returning to Westphal's question; rather than consider my argument for dialectically necessary mutual recognition, consider the following additional argument for $\{BGR\}_{Agnes}$, which also relies on the fact that it is dialectically necessary for Agnes to recognise that $\{BGR\}_{Brian}$.

$\{BGR\}_{Brian}$ follows by distributive universalisation from $\{AGR\}_{Agnes}$. Hence, $\{\{BGR\}_{Brian}\}_{Agnes}$. However, the intelligibility of $\{AGR\}_{Agnes}$ (while it neither requires that Brian actually accept AGR, nor that AGR be acceptable to Brian in terms of any contingent view on normativity he has), does require not only that

[70] Beyleveld, 'Williams' False Dilemma', n 29, 204, 218–19.
[71] See his questions at n 41 of his contribution to this volume.

Brian *could* act in compliance with AGR, but also that Agnes can coherently consider that Brian *may (that is could, without implying that he is not an agent)* accept that he ought to hold that he ought to act in compliance with AGR (≡ that he ought to act in compliance with $AoGa^A$). This is because, in prescribing anything to Brian, Agnes is purporting to give Brian a reason to act in a particular way, and because it is only as an agent that Brian is intelligibly an addressee of a practical prescription, it is incoherent for Agnes to think that Brian could coherently regard something prescribed by Agnes to him as a reason for him to act if his acceptance of this would involve him implying that he is not an agent. So, it is dialectically necessary for Agnes to accept that Brian may not choose to act in compliance with $AoGa^A$ if by so choosing he does not honour *his* dialectically necessary commitments, which is to say, if his acting in compliance with $AoGa^A$ is inconsistent with BGR. Consequently, it is intelligible for Agnes to prescribe AGR to Brian *only if*, in so doing, she does not prescribe that Brian act inconsistently with BGR. But *it is* dialectically necessary for Agnes to prescribe AGR to Brian. Thus, it is dialectically necessary for Agnes to regulate her practical reasoning on the basis of BGR as well as AGR, which means that $\{AGR\}_{Agnes}$ entails $\{BGR)_{Agnes}$.

Despite reference to $\{BGR\}_{Brian}$, this reasoning is entirely (Agnes) first person, because what constitutes being a first-person consideration in the Gewirthian foundational argument conducted from Agnes' viewpoint is whatever is dialectically necessary for her to accept (and only what is dialectically necessary for her to accept), which includes whatever follows purely logically or analytically from her understanding what is dialectically necessary for her to accept.[72] And it is dialectically necessary for Agnes to recognise that $\{BGR\}_{Brian}$. The point is this. The mere fact that it is dialectically necessary for Agnes to recognise that $\{BGR\}_{Brian}$ involves no moral imputation. Moral imputation only occurs in the argument at the point at which it is shown that $\{BGR\}_{Agnes}$, which acceptance is driven by Agnes' understanding the effect of combining the fact that $\{\{BGR\}_{Brian}\}_{Agnes}$ with Agnes' required recognition that only agents are intelligible addressees of practical prescriptions, neither of which involves moral imputation.

Related to this, it is misleading for Westphal to say that, in Stage II, $\{$I shall defend my GCAs$\}_I$ ≡ $\{$I prudentially ought to defend my GCAs$\}_I$ (or, as I prefer with reference to Agnes as the protagonist, $\{AoGa^A\}_{Agnes}$) is imputed to be biconditionally related to $\{$I (morally) ought to defend my GCAs$\}_{I.}$ The operative biconditional relationship I assert is between 'Agnes is a ta' and 'Agnes is a Ta' (per the PRJ) within Agnes' dialectically necessary matrix. In consequence of this, I maintain that it follows logically that $\{AoGa^A\}_{Agnes}$ is biconditionally related to $\{$Agnes ought (by virtue of being a Ta) to defend her GCAs from interference against her will$\}_{Agnes}$ (which is biconditionally related to $\{$Agnes ought (because Brian is a Ta) to defend Brian's GCAs from interference against his will'$\}_{Agnes}$. *In consequence of this*, to say that Agnes *morally ought* to defend her GCAs from

[72] This, I hope, answers Westphal's second question at n 41.

interference against her will is to say that *it is dialectically necessary for her to accept* that she prudentially (categorically instrumentally) ought to defend her GCAs. This is not simply imputed, it is argued for via the ASA/the other arguments that I have offered for the collective universalisation step.

This leads me to suspect that Westphal does not appreciate fully that Agnes' categorical instrumental need for the GCAs plays no part in the collective universalisation, which is effected solely by the PRJ operating within Agnes' dialectically necessary matrix.[73] Consequently, he mistakenly presents the Gewirthian 'dialectically necessary' argument as a dialectically contingent argument from moral imputation, not as the pure dialectically necessary argument from agential self-understanding that it is.

Re (b), I do not recognise conditions necessary to become an agent as GCAs, because GCAs are generically instrumental conditions required by agents to pursue/achieve their purposes. A GCA necessarily contributes to Agnes, *who is already an agent*, being able to act/act successfully. So, I do not see how recognising the existence of conditions for becoming an agent can figure within the Gewirthian dialectically necessary argument rather than outside of it.

Westphal might respond that the proper focus is on becoming an *effective rational* agent (one who possesses sound understanding), not on becoming an agent per se. If so, then he might reason as follows: Rational nature is an end in itself, meaning that to act in accord with a categorical imperative (with one's dialectically necessary commitments) is an end in itself. However, Agnes' appreciation of her dialectically necessary commitments is best achieved together with others (because Agnes develops the capacities for agential self-understanding from/with others[74] and her use of these capacities is better when checked by others in relations of equal concern and respect). Therefore, Agnes ought to respect Brian's agency needs equally with her own.

If this is what he has in mind, then why does this not merely require Agnes to have regard for the GCAs of those who have regard for her GCAs?

In any case, that Agnes needs Brian's co-operation to secure her GCAs, as required by $\{AoGa^A\}_{Agnes}$, is one reason Gewirthians give for $\{AGR\}_{Agnes}$. If this is the GCA that Westphal has in mind, then Gewirthians rely on it, but it is not enough to justify any moral imputation if the arguments I have given for collective universalisation are not sufficient.

Re (c), since the only sense in which I accept that rational nature is an end in itself is that it is an end in itself for Agnes to act in accord with her dialectically necessary commitments, I do not see how an argument from the claim that agents can only become rational agents by acting in accord with reason together,

[73] So, I agree with Westphal that Kant does not need to refer to the GCAs to justify a moral imperative. But such an imperative is underspecified without attention to the GCAs.

[74] Which she surely must already possess in at least some rudimentary form to be able to learn from and with others.

can constitute a nondialectical derivation of a moral 'ought'. So, I do not see how, without debating realism/idealism, it is possible to defend a nondialectical naturalism (the Gewirthian position being a dialectical naturalism, in maintaining, via the ASA, that it is dialectically necessary for Agnes to hold that being an agent is the *ratio essendi* for having the GR). Indeed, as I see it, the considerations that Westphal appeals to are highly relevant to the conditions for adequate application of the PGC but not to the justification of moral imputation.

I look forward to being enlightened on this highly truncated response.

VI. Finally

It remains only for me to express my heartfelt thanks to Shaun Pattinson and Patrick Capps for editing this volume, and for arranging the conference in Durham at which earlier versions of the contributions were presented. My thanks also to Marion Tate, who organised the conference, and, of course, to all the contributors and others who attended the conference and contributed to the discussions and debate.

INDEX

Abbreviations used in the index:

ASA (Argument from the Sufficiency of Agency)
CI (Categorical Imperative)
CJEU (Court of Justice of the European Union)
Consent in the Law (*Consent in the Law* by Beyleveld and Brownsword)
DNM (*The Dialectical Necessity of Morality* by Beyleveld)
ECtHR (European Court of Human Rights)
ESRB (European Systemic Risk Board)
GCA (generic conditions of agency/action)
HUGO (Human Genome Organisation)
ICC (International Criminal Court)
LMJ (*Law as a Moral Judgment* by Beyleveld and Brownsword))
PGC (Principle of Generic Consistency)
PHI (Principle of Hypothetical Imperatives)
PPA (prospective, purposive agent)
PRJ (Principle of Reflective Judgement)
RL (*Rechtslehre* (Doctrine of Right) by Kant))
SADC (Southern African Development Community)
UDHR (Universal Declaration of Human Rights)
WTO (World Trade Organisation)

www.ingramcontent.com/pod-product-compliance
Lightning Source LLC
LaVergne TN
LVHW052258200926
848481LV00002B/406